Crime in Context

CRIME IN CONTEXT

A Critical Criminology of Market Societies

IAN TAYLOR

Polity Press

First published in 1999 by Polity Press
in association with Blackwell Publishers Ltd.

Editorial office:
Polity Press
65 Bridge Street
Cambridge CB2 1UR, UK

Marketing and production:
Blackwell Publishers Ltd
108 Cowley Road
Oxford OX4 1JF, UK

ISBN 0–7456–0666–0
ISBN 0–7456–0667–9 (pbk)

A catalogue record for this book is available from the British Library.

Typeset in 10 on 12 pt Times
by York House Typographic Ltd
Printed in Great Britain by T. J. International, Padstow, Cornwall

This book is printed on acid-free paper.

CONTENTS

LIST OF FIGURES

LIST OF TABLES

Acknowledgements

We are grateful for permission to reproduce the following:

Figure 1: Reprinted by permission of the publisher, The University of Chicago Press, from E. Burgess, 'The Growth of the City' in R. E. Park, E. W. Burgess and R. D. Mackenzie (eds) *The City* 1967.
Figure 2: Reprinted by permission of Oxford University Press from Arnold Toynbee *Cities on the Move* (O.U.P., 1970).
Figure 3: Reprinted by permission of the publisher from Paul M. Hohenberg and Lynn Hollen Lees, *The Making of Urban Europe 1000–1950* (Cambridge, Mass.: Harvard University Press). Copyright © 1985, 1995 by the President and Fellows of Harvard College.

INTRODUCTION

At the end of the twentieth century, the bookstores are full of books on crime, though this title will certainly not find a place on the same shelves. In the massive Waterstones bookstore in the city of Manchester, England, where I lived through most of the 1990s, the ground floor display area was rearranged in 1995 so as to accommodate, right at the front of the store, several hundred new titles, on topics like Serial Murderers and Sexual Crimes of the Twentieth Century.[1] Several of these new books are companion volumes to movies on release in the city's cinemas or, in some instances, are simply the original text on which the movies are based. The movies in question – *Shallow Grave*, *Silence of the Lambs*, *Reservoir Dogs*, *Natural Born Killers* and others – focus heavily on interpersonal violence and murder and also place great emphasis – in the manner of many earlier cinematic genres – on the idea of the 'criminal mind' (not least, as a way of dramatizing the detection of the originating criminal act) but also – to a significant extent, these are movies which emphasize the idea and contemporary social presence of evil. Similar moral and psychologistic preoccupations are now also widely apparent on prime-time television – most notably, in Britain, in the extraordinarily powerful *Cracker* series, produced by Granada Television in 1994 and 1995, watched by over 15 million people, and featuring, *inter alia*, the forensic investigation of serial and sexual murders, some of them extremely graphically displayed (Crace 1994).[2] The prominence of 'Gothic' themes in movies about violent death is not new in itself: there is a long history of interest in the cinema in horror and, indeed, in 'transgression' and evil. What may be definitive about the present genre of movies as well as the range of fictional and non-fictional titles in the bookstores about crime is the overwhelming focus on murder and killing represented in very contemporary and mundane, ordinary and, indeed, 'respectable' settings, and the powerful suggestion that these movies are a representation of the risks and dangers involved in everyday life at the end of the twentieth century. The bookstore display in Waterstones is straightforwardly called the 'Real Crimes' section.

Other than this, however, the murder movies and the Real Crime literature are distinctive for their insistent representation of the criminal in terms of one or other individualistic account – that is, of the *individual criminal*. Lurking not very far below the surface of these different representations of crime as 'a form of behaviour' are two themes of enormously long vintage in the analysis of crime, both in industrial and pre-industrial society – on the one hand, some version or other of an individual as being under the influence of evil ('possessed' by 'the Devil' or some other malign influence from outside society as we know it), and, on the other, some explanation of that crime in terms of the individualistic analysis of pathology or species underdevelopment as mobilized within evolutionary biology. In this respect, the violent crime movies and the Real Crime books are an expression of a search that has also been being encouraged throughout the 1980s and 1990s in some parts of the academy, especially on the part of clinical psychiatrists and behavioural psychologists, in North America. In the mid-1980s, for example, as David Kelley observed, there was a sudden explosion of such texts of widely differing quality released in the United States, 'stalking the criminal mind' (Kelley 1985). Kelley paid particular attention to the massive tome by Samuel Yochelson and Stanton Samenow, *The Criminal Personality*, which somehow managed to construct psychopathy as a general paradigm for the analysis of all criminal violence, whilst also wanting to insist on such violence as a voluntary and freely willed act for which all perpetrators should be held personally responsible. In the same year, Yochelson and Samenow's text was to be superseded in many quarters by the publication of James Q. Wilson and Richard Herrnstein's *Crime and Human Nature*, and, in the 1990s, in North America and Britain, the analytically individualistic behavioural interpretation of crime has seen the development of 'offender-profiling' by forensic psychiatrists, specifically in its application to police detection (Cantor and Alison 1997), and also the attempt to use the framework of socio-biology to explain apparently social phenomena (like crime) in terms of measurable variations in the age, sex, intelligence and personality-formation of individuals (Gottfredson and Hirschi 1990).[3]

It is impossible to ignore the way in which these cinematic and televisual representations, and the accompanying forensic and socio-biological literature, are helping to construct and legitimize a form of commonsense and populist criminology, with a much more influential social presence in many societies (certainly in Britain – for example, in daily newspaper crime reports) than at any time since the 1950s. It is a form of commonsense criminology organized around 'the criminal' and, particularly, 'the criminal mind' as an 'object of analysis', and also complicit in the task of identification, prevention and containment of the individual criminal. It is closely associated, in what sociologists would call 'a discourse', with a new penological project that is concerned with the identification and incapacitation of the 'dangerous offender' as well as with new ways of surveillance – social insurance, the minimization of the personal risk arising from the sudden emergence of dangerous individuals in the broader society (Feeley and Simon 1992). It is also a kind of individualistic and 'commonsensical', practical criminological discourse which is winning the attention of vast cohorts of students enrolled on undergraduate and graduate programmes in criminal justice in North America, as well as, increasingly, in Britain, Australia and elsewhere.

The advance of these various forms of 'analytically individualist' criminology has occurred almost without comment or response, so far as many well-established figures in the criminological and social scientific academy based in Western universities are concerned.[4] In the United States, throughout much of the last twenty years, the social scientific study of crime has been conducted under the influence of the 'symbolic interactionist' and 'social constructionist' traditions, focusing, *not* on 'the crime' itself (whose reality is sometimes denied or ignored) so much as on the processes which construct certain behaviours as crime, and the social reactions which such behaviours and crimes provoke (Becker 1963; Lemert 1967). In other parts of the social science academy, influenced by more critical traditions (especially, in the early 1970s, by some form of Marxism) the concern was to locate such crimes as an expression of the contradictions (and especially the rank inequalities) inherent in a capitalist political economy, and to see any or all attempts to control such forms of primitive rebellion and resistance as confirming evidence of the real oppression at the heart of 'liberal' capitalist democracy (Center for Research on Criminal Justice 1975; Quinney 1969, 1970, 1973, 1974). The influence of North American labelling theory and symbolic interactionism, and, to a lesser extent, the particular versions of Marxism and conflict theory which were developed in North America, was high in the 1970s, both within North America and elsewhere in the Western academy – but, in the subsequent twenty-five years, this intellectual tradition has withered on the vine or, alternatively, merely been institutionalized within the academy as a part of the catechism of 'political correctness'.

Social, economic and cultural developments in Western societies since the late 1960s have been momentous, though it is fair to say that the direction of change has not been that which was emblazoned on the banners of '1968', other than for those for whom 'the cause' was simply that of enhancement of personal liberties (the free market society which is the subject of this book certainly advances a version of this 'libertarianism', no matter how much it withdraws the personal liberty of material security from large numbers of people). Inasmuch as the objectives of '1968' were anti-capitalist, then the developments since then have violently contradicted the aspirations of that generation. 'Socialism' itself as a utopian alternative to capitalism (in both its master definitions – the achievement of greater equality in the distribution of goods and of life-chances, and a planned economy dominated by the State acting for the general public interest) is dead, not least because of the collapse of the only existing experiment with that form of societal organization, the Soviet Union. In the last years of the twentieth century, no serious political or social commentator speaks of an alternative to living with 'a free market', which seems to be well entrenched as the only conceivable model of economic survival and/or development. In these 'new times' – dominated by what I will be calling a post-Fordist market society – the issue which is then posed for social commentators (including those in the academy who conceive of themselves as having a special position from which to advance some kind of critique) can be expressed in very familiar terms: 'What is to be done (or said)?'

One very popular option in the academy in recent years has been that of close description – particularly, I would argue, the close description of 'the discourses' – the cultural signs and languages of 'the texts' of the form of fast-changing society of consumption which has emerged in the wake of the demise of more long-established and (in retrospect) rather unchanging societies based on the priorities and demands of mass industrial production. For many academicians, it has been attractive to describe the changes that have so quickly occurred through the language of 'postmodernism'. There has been continuing ambiguity in much of the social scientific debate as to whether 'postmodernism', as a term, should be understood as a reference to the form of analysis of social science itself (that is, an epistemological argument, about what is said to be the impossibility of any kind of 'foundational' analysis, analysis constructed on what are seen to be redundant 'modernist' foundations, like class, gender and race) or whether postmodernism is simply a description of the condition of the culture (as in the work of Fredric Jameson or Zygmunt Bauman) for systematic analysis according to clear principles (which do not themselves simply 'melt into air').[5] As several commentators have observed, the pursuit of forms of social and cultural analysis in which there are no agreed foundations may be akin to the pursuit of a personal life within which there are no a-priori limits, or no clear moral basis from which to proceed. So, in the sphere of sexuality, for example – an explosive consumer item in the contemporary international market place – the postmodern analyst may choose simply to record and/or 'deconstruct' the fast-moving new images and enticements. But, of course, as Ian Hacking (1997) observes in a recently published lecture, this kind of postmodernist social (de)constructionism leaves the analyst with no position on child sexual abuse or other forms of sexual cruelty or coercion.

The concern in this text is to explore one of the most obvious areas of discontent in post-Fordist societies – those established, 'developed' societies which have been so fundamentally transformed by the demise of mass manufacturing industry over the last quarter-century – the ever-intrusive fear and reality of crime. I want, on the one hand, to advance an analysis that makes sense of, or explains, many of the varieties of actually occurring behaviours (burglaries, car theft, the use of guns, the sale of drugs) which certainly are very firmly defined by their victims (as well as by an anxious media) as crime. But I want to locate my analysis against the background of the rapidly transformed social and economic relations of the emergent post-Fordist society. I *will* be concerned to understand these new social relations, in significant measure, as a product of the competitive individualism that has been widely identified (on a broad canvas – from the problem of 'road rage', so pressing an area of popular concern in the late 1990s in Britain – through to the widely feared emergence of 'in-your-face' incivility in many other public encounters – in the United States as well as in other market societies) as an essential feature of 'market culture' itself. I will also want to register the way in which the advance of the logic of market competition insinuates new systems of social classification and evaluation into just about every workplace as well as into the biographies of just about every working citizen – namely, through the measurement of performance within particular markets, the classification of individuals as 'winners' and 'losers' – a process which, as Oliver James (1995) has shown in respect of the struggles of young people in Britain in the mid-1990s, is at the core of the defensive/aggressive individualism which many young people exhibit in a 'winner–loser culture'. Taken alongside Edward Luttwak's (1995) analyses of the constant turmoil and change that the liberalized markets (or 'turbo-charged capitalism', in Luttwak's own memorable phrase) impose on workplaces and workers alike, we begin to get closer to an understanding of the cultural conditions of violent crime and property crime alike. The theoretical argument I want to develop will take 'the post-Fordist market' as a vital and, indeed, hegemonic feature of modern-day experience, especially for young people confronting the challenge of transition into 'adulthood' and 'independence' – that is, as a *social fact* that is inescapable for young people. Given the fact of 'post-Fordism', indeed, those same young people constitute the first youthful generation of the entire post-Second World War period with a *declining* set of material expectations (in respect of employment and remuneration), by comparison with those of their own parents and the cohorts of young people who immediately preceded them in the crucial period of adolescence. It is in no sense my argument that this truth constitutes the rationale *per se* for the explosion in the rise of crime that is reported in societies like Britain, where an experiment in free market economics has been in full flow since 1979. The unfolding of the post-Fordist transformation in each of the hitherto Fordist societies has occurred alongside the development of a set of other 'crises' or fundamental transitions, moving at different speeds and with different priorities, along many other dimensions in these different social formations (for example, the relations of the sexes, and especially the gender-order in the home and in the workplace), and in respect of the broader cultural universe through which individuals in each society have interpreted the fundamental and deep transformation of the forms of organization (of those households, workplaces, and broader social relations) that occurred, in the 1980s and 1990s, in most Fordist societies.[6] I will begin the analysis, in chapters 1 and 2, with an extended summary account of nine discrete transitions in the forms of social life that were definitive under Fordist conditions in the earlier twentieth century – intending to show how these different transitions, though always interconnected in the personal experience of any one individual and the 'shared culture' of specific social groups, also have a definite autonomy, with their own logic of ongoing development and change.

I do *not* want to suggest that any one of these logics of development can be reduced, in a straightforward social scientific model, to 'the basic' facts of the economy itself: I do not think that 'unemployment' causes (*sic*) 'crime' in some mechanical and deterministic fashion. What I *do* want to argue, however, is that there has been an absolutely fundamental transformation in the organization of economic life in most Western societies over the last quarter-century (very often summarized as the move from economies organized around production to economies organized around consumption) and that this transformation has had absolutely fundamental effects on the forms and the substance of social life. The effects of this transformation on 'crime' itself – including, here, the actually occurring behaviours that the victims of such behaviours certainly define as real crime (burglary, theft, assaults, use of guns, trading in drugs, and many other behaviours which also find their way into the sets of criminal statistics produced every year by local and national police forces) will be one of the main areas of concern of this text. But I should add that it is in no sense my concern to advance the argument that the regulated mixed economies of the Fordist period (which I will discuss, in chapter 1, as a particular historic form of 'market society') were free of 'crime': what matters is *the kinds of crime* with which they were associated – in reality as well as in the popular imagination – and the *real probabilities* of criminal victimization in such societies. So I also will be concerned in this text to examine the ways in which the culture of the new post-Fordist societies (including, indeed, the 'postmodern' cultural market place itself), articulated around the sovereignty of the individual as a consumer of private goods, plays into the spiralling sense of anxiety and of danger that is a feature of everyday life in most newly marketized post-Fordist societies. Once again, it will not be my concern to argue, like some contemporary social scientists of great renown, that the facts of 'risk' and uncertainty about the future shape and direction of social order are entirely new – it makes good sense to see here the return of many aspects of life in late medieval Europe (like the widespread demands, in effect, for the reintroduction of the nightwatchman) – but it will be my concern to try and capture the specificity of the configuration of risks and uncertainties that are so central a feature of the culture of the new post-Fordist market societies. As a graphic illustration of this argument, I include a specific and detailed discussion in chapter 6 of the phenomenon of firearms crime, and the heightened anxieties which are produced amongst citizens of market society with respect to the perceived increase in prevalence of this form of violent crime in different market societies. Not least of my concerns is to encourage a way of thinking the issue of some forms of contemporary crime themselves as 'market phenomena': as being complicit (as firearms crime in the United States clearly is) with the more or less unregulated marketing of particular products (cheap handguns and a ready supply of willing salespeople) in particular market societies at particular times, but also with the kind of competitive individualism which the culture of market societies encourages.

I see this text as a contribution to the continuing debate amongst social scientists as to the character of the transformation that has so fundamentally unsettled the Grand Compromise that was the Keynesian welfare-state mixed economies in the mid-twentieth century. But I also hope the eight connected essays here will constitute a kind of textbook for any student of criminology who wants some kind of resource through which to make sense of the 'crimes' that are so staple a feature of the everyday news of post-

Fordist societies, without wanting to reduce all such media reports simply to 'a moral panic' or alternatively falling back on those moralistic and clinical populist criminologies of our time, contemplating, on the one hand, the unexplained explosion of pathologies or the Devil himself. At the end of one century and the beginning of another, we might all hope for a better and more sophisticated explanation of the specific relationship between the explosive development of market society and the problem of social order itself.

1

SOCIAL TRANSITIONS OF THE LATE TWENTIETH CENTURY: 'CRIME' AND 'FEAR' IN CONTEXT

The idea of 'social crisis' is uncomfortable territory for the professional field of criminology. It is also a messy area for those journalists, politicians and other contemporary 'soothsayers' who, in modern Western society, are given the responsibility of interpreting the outbreak of individual or collective instances of crime. The usual preference of these commentators, in most Western societies in the 1990s, is for the 'blaming' of individuals. In British crime reportage, there is very often also a resort to some kind of cultural nostalgia.[1] Professional criminologists often spend any time they have in the public sphere of television, radio or newspapers trying to deny the reality of people's fears or, alternatively, reduced into the recital of vulgar forms of nineteenth-century statistical positivism. Taking seriously the idea of a *social* crisis would involve engaging in some kind of analysis of historical processes and logics – the kind of analysis which, as Roland Barthes explained, is beyond the imagination (and the practical mandate) of journalists employed in the unending everyday production – against fast-approaching deadlines – of readable and immediate, newsworthy material for the next edition. Far easier to draw on that body of individualistic, largely psychologistic, but sometimes theological 'mythologies' (Barthes 1973) that is now constituted as 'criminology' in the popular mind. In most Western societies at the end of the twentieth century, the mass of audiences for newspapers, television and cinema are bombarded by the day with an essentially theological, medieval criminology, with a gallery of insane or evil individuals, devils and witches, and a range of theories of individual possession, through which they are asked to make sense of a fast-breaking story about 'crime'.

The notion of crisis *has* probably been overdone in most post-war Western societies. The analysis of capitalist crisis developed by Marxists and other oppositional voices in the turbulent – but relatively affluent – 'full-employment' 1960s now looks strained indeed. But in the last years of the twentieth century, a number of important commentators, of different persuasions, on the economic, cultural and social realities in North America, Europe or other late-capitalist societies are speaking in such terms. In his magisterial historical retrospect on 'the short twentieth century' Eric Hobsbawm identified three major logics of social transformation which, in these last decades, have begun to exhibit 'crisis tendencies'. I vary the order in which Hobsbawm identified these dimensions of change in order to highlight, first, what so many different authors refer to as the phenomenon of globalization:

> Between 1914 and the early 1990s, the globe has become far more of a single operational unit, as it was not, and could not have been, in 1914. In fact, for many purposes, notably in economic affairs, the globe is now the primary operational unit and older units such as the 'national economies', defined by the politics of territorial states, are reduced to complications of transnational activities. (Hobsbawm 1994: 15)

This particular engine of change, globalization, is accelerating so fast, Hobsbawm suggests, as to problematize the capacity of any existing set of 'public institutions' in any one nation – or, indeed, he adds, the 'collective behaviour' of human beings – 'to come to terms with it' (1994: 15).

Closely associated with this acceleration of economic transformation, according to Hobsbawm, is 'a disintegration of the old patterns of human social relations' and, in particular, 'the snapping of links between generations, that is to say, between past and present'. Hobsbawm sees this process of 'disintegration' of 'old patterns' as having a global, rather than merely Western, importance:

> [It] has been particularly evident in the most developed countries of the Western version of capitalism, in which the values of an absolute a-social individualism have been dominant, both in official and unofficial ideologies . . . Nevertheless, the tendencies [are] to be found elsewhere, reinforced by the erosion of traditional societies and religions, as well as by the destruction, or autodestruction, of the societies of 'real socialism'. (1994: 15)

Finally, by comparison with the early years of the century, the world is no longer 'Eurocentric':

> Europeans and their descendants were now reduced from perhaps one third of humanity to at most one sixth, a diminishing minority living in countries which barely, if at all, reproduced their populations, surrounding themselves by, and in most cases – with some shining exceptions such as the USA (until the 1960s) – barricading themselves against the pressures of immigration from the countries of the poor. The industries Europe had pioneered were migrating elsewhere. The countries which had once looked across the ocean to Europe were looking elsewhere. Australia, New Zealand, even the bi-oceanic USA, saw the future in the Pacific. (1994: 14)

There are, in truth, many other formulations available with which we can try and account for the kind of fundamental social and economic transformation currently occurring in Western 'late-capitalist societies' – not least, within sociology, the analysis offered by Scott Lash and John Urry of a transnational, 'disorganized', post-industrial capitalism, now committed to the non-stop, competitive search for new products for sale, and therefore new sources of profit and accumulation, within what they call the 'economies of signs and space', and endlessly competing across the globe for new markets and also for new ways of savings on human labour and investment (Lash and Urry 1987: 1994). In Britain, Stuart Hall and Martin Jacques follow the example of many scholars in political economy in wanting to identify the economic motor driving the transformation as the collapse of the 'Fordist' system of mass, factory-based, production resulting from the exhaustion of demand in the West for the kind of consumables these factories produced (Hall and Jacques 1990). Ash Amin (1994) has provided a useful summary account of these changes, especially in respect of their effects within the sphere of work, employment and productive activity, which is set out schematically in table 1.

This emergent post-Fordist market society is discussed in more detail in chapter 2; for the moment, the need is to situate the recurrent panics about crime that are so obvious a feature of contemporary experience in the context of this broader framework of fundamental social transition (rather than within some individualistic psychology or theology of individual amorality or depravation). The stances adopted by different social scientists and social commentators towards these changes vary – for example, as between, on the one hand, sympathetic enquiries by Anthony Giddens and Scott Lash into 'de-traditionalization' as a social and economic process which creates the conditions for 'reflexive' re-negotiation of personal identity (not least amongst enquiring social scientists in the academy themselves), and, on the other, the veritable dislocation of life of particular social groups (the homeless and the long-term unemployed) and communities (the 'sink estates', mining communities) offered by enquiring journalists (N. Davies 1994; Danziger 1997), as well as by people in the psychiatric and social work professions (James 1995). So there is significant variation in the analysis being attempted – as between Hobsbawm's generalizations about the 'disintegration' – simply – of 'old patterns', on the one hand, and Giddens's attentive hermeneutic interpretation of the different ways in which people are creatively making use of past understandings and immediate contingencies of everyday life in order to construct new personal languages and assumptions for practical, everyday purposes in the 'new times' of 'High Modernity'.

The purposes in this text on crime are not to adjudicate, abstractly, on the merits or limitations of these particular theoretical accounts. It surely is clear, however, to all but the most uncompromising moral conservative and behavioural psychologist, that the analysis of crime itself (the object of analysis of any serious 'criminological' project) must be located in relation to the fundamental transformation of social formation that is currently in progress (resulting from a deep crisis in the pre-existing configurations of social and economic organization). This text, in part informed by Eric Hobsbawm, tries to follow through the unfolding of a set of different crises – or fundamental

Table 1 Fordist and post-Fordist cultures of work

	Fordism	Post-Fordism
Social character of work	Masculinist domination, muscularity, male bonding	Increasingly feminine
Organized forms of work	'Production lines', workgroups, shifts	'Decentred' in shops, offices, small enterprises
Objectives of work	Production	Distribution and sale
Induction into work/ training/	Informal (exc. apprenticeship for craft positions)	Qualifications, accreditation
Regulation of the worker	Contractual and corporate through trade unions	Individual agreements, withdrawal of contractual guarantees
Working prospects, careers	Lifetime employment	Short-term 'full-time' contracts; part-time and temporary employments; return of 'sweatshops'
Domestic sphere	Sphere of social reproduction, dominated by matriarch	Families in work: increase in two-career households, 'family speed-up', and a range of ad-hoc arrangements for routine social reproduction (childcare, shopping etc.) Families out of work: imaginary re-invention of Fordist divisions of labour
'Leisure'	Male dominated: drinking, participant/ spectator sport/ Sunday family time	Increasingly individualist and consumerist, but also related to relief of stress and maintenance of physical and mental fitness and competivity in a competitive market

Source: developed from Amin 1994

transitions – occurring at the end of the twentieth century. However, where Hobsbawm speaks of three crises, I want to provide separate but focused discussion, of *nine* discrete and fundamental transitions – nearly all of which appear, but with uneven power and influence, in different Western capitalist societies at the end of 'the Fordist period'. My concern in recommending the separate treatment of these nine dimensions is not merely narrative convenience and clarity. In contrast to some of the generalizing cultural social commentaries of our time (for example, within the postmodernist canon), this device will enable us more clearly and carefully to *identify*, analytically, the discrete social strains which may be being experienced by any one individual. Against the apparently chaotic whole of contemporary change

glimpsed in postmodern theory (for example, 'chaos theory'), with its promise to extinguish sociology, I want to examine the analytic and social-political
purchase of a sociological analysis of different logics of social change running
in parallel, overdetermined by the economic crisis of Fordist society. These
nine different 'transitions' will each have real effects – sometimes in a
singular fashion but usually in combination with other elements – on the lived
biography of individual actors. In contrast to the metaphysicians of 'free
market' economics, I recognize and understand that people are born and are
raised into adulthood *from particular positions (of advantage and disadvantage) in an* 'imperatively coordinated' social order: that is, to recognize that
every human actor is socially, economically and culturally situated in historical time and place. In the Fordist period, only a proportion of any one new
cohort of youthful social actors can escape the 'destinies' which these situated
processes of social reproduction inscribe for them in adult life.[2] So this book
follows the example of a host of writers and scholars – from James Agee,
Daniel Bertaux, Albert Camus, Jean Paul Sartre, to the criminologist David
Matza – in recognizing that we all only live once. Today's youthful generations will have to live their lives, not with the certainties of the Fordist period
(including the near-certainties of High Modern Capitalism) but with the
manifold uncertainties of life in societies which are in constant process of
'restructuring' and change. Thinking forward from the work of Ulrich Beck,
in his analysis of the emergence of a set of different 'risk-positions' in risk
society, I suggest that the emergence of a post-Fordist world, or a set of
different 'market societies', carries with it the production of a new set of
'market-positions' within market societies themselves, with profound effects
on the life-chances and possibilities of individuals located in these specific
positions. It is becoming more and more clear by the year, especially to the
young, that the prospects for paid employment for life (and, with it, the
security, status and means to self-advancement taken for granted in earlier
periods) are in steep decline. The 1990s generation is one of the first
generations in the post-war period to confront the prospect of a reduction in
overall material prospects in the employment market, by comparison with
preceding generations. For a large proportion of these youthful cohorts,
therefore, the experience of 'post-Fordist society' will involve new and
different forms of inequality and subordination, on a temporary or long-term
basis – in the casual labour markets of fast-changing economies or in the
underclasses, the 'new poor', being left behind by the motor of change. The
factors which will inform young people's recruitment into these new positions
of opportunity within market society will be far more complex and variable
than the social processes which 'determined' the reproduction of the labour
force or the 'bourgeois class' in the era of mass manufacturing capitalism. The
relationship between the legitimate labour markets and the illegitimate,
alternative economies (including, in particular, the 'economies of crime')
seems likely to be far more contingent and uncertain than in earlier periods –
for example, as discussed in chapter 4, in the developing night-time economies of post-industrial cities. In developing discussion of the nine transitions
of the late twentieth century, it must be remembered, all the while, after the

example of Daniel Bertaux (1981), that these transitions are not only abstractions helping analysis, but also a part of the turmoil of any individual's biographical experience in a particular moment of historical change (a particular 'time'). Eight of these transitions are dealt with in this first chapter, leaving focused discussion of the definitive transition to a post-Fordist market society for separate discussion in chapter 2.

THE JOB CRISIS

In the course of the last fifteen years, during what Piore and Sabel refer to as 'the crisis of mass manufacturing', and Hall and Jacques call 'the crisis of Fordism', there has been a massive haemorrhaging of full-time employment in most Western societies, particularly in heavy or manufacturing industries. At the beginning of 1997, some 12 per cent of all people officially registering for work across the European Community (20 million people) were unable to find any employment – an increase of 2 million people on 1995 (*The Economist*, 14–20 June 1997: 50). This ongoing process of 'job loss' had gathered pace throughout the early 1990s – in 1981 EEC unemployment totalled just 9.1 million (Massey and Meegan, 1982: 3) – in a process described by a leading Gaullist politician in France, Philippe Séguin, as 'a social Munich', a million and half Europeans having just lost their job in the twelve months before November 1993.[3] In the mid-1990s the crisis appeared still more severe in statistical and political terms in Spain than in most other large European societies: unemployment in Spain was still being measured officially in February 1997 at 21.7 per cent, by comparison with official rates of 7.1 per cent in Britain and 6 per cent in the Netherlands.[4] But European anxieties focused, in particular, on France, where unemployment, on official measures, continued to creep upwards (reaching 12.5 per cent in 1997).[5] The presidential election campaign of 1995 had been fought between Jacques Chirac and Lionel Jospin around competing programmes for job-creation, and in 1997 Lionel Jospin's persistence was repaid with an election victory. In Germany, the survival of Helmut Kohl in the Presidency was clearly threatened by unemployment rates reaching 9.5 per cent in 1997, up 3.1 per cent from 1992.

The telling contrast was with the 1960s: the average unemployment rate in France, on the official measures then adopted, was less than 1.8 per cent throughout that decade. In Germany over the same period, unemployment averaged about 0.6 per cent; in Britain some 2.7 per cent (adjusted to US concepts) and in Italy 3.2 per cent (Sinfield 1981: 15). The changes in the official definitions used to measure unemployment since the 1960s make direct comparison precarious – and it *is* also important, as official spokespeople often insist, to recognize the increase in the absolute number of people in paid employment in the 1970s and 1980s. For these and other reasons, any direct and one-dimensional comparison between the 'mass unemployment' of the 1990s and that of the inter-war Depression is also potentially misleading. At the peak of this great 'Slump', in 1935, some 11.4

per cent of 'the civilian workforce' (i.e. of those, largely male, citizens registering for work) in the United Kingdom was unemployed, and some 17.5 per cent in the United States (Jordan 1982: 2). The highest levels of unemployment, as officially measured, in the year after the oil shocks of 1982 were 14.3 per cent in the United Kingdom and 9.5 per cent in the United States (Kemp 1990: 155). From another perspective, however, the comparison with the 1930s *is* illuminating. The total number of officially unemployed people in the United Kingdom in July 1936 was measured at 1,717,000 (Stevenson and Cook 1977: 56). About one-tenth of these had been unemployed for more than a year, and of these over two-thirds were aged between forty-five and sixty-five (1977: 60). In April 1997 the official unemployment total for the United Kingdom was 'only' 8 per cent of the workforce, but this amounted to an absolute number of 1,748,000 (on official measures[6]). Within this overall total, 887,400 men and 183,000 women had been unsuccessful in their search for employment for more than a year.[7] More than 60 per cent of those looking for work were under forty years of age. The unemployment of the 1980s and 1990s, in other words, in absolute terms involved significantly more people actively looking for work than the unemployment of the 1930s, and involved long periods of unemployment. It also was having significantly more impact on younger people, including many who had never worked.

In the early 1990s, in the meantime, across much of Western Europe and North America, there was increasing recognition that such new employment opportunities as were being created (whether by newly enterprising individuals or multinational companies) were largely part-time or short-term contract-based types of employment, and therefore essentially insecure forms of employment. In the early 1990s some commentators, especially those based in the United States – paying close attention to the logic of the much-vaunted 'economic recovery' in that society – had begun to speak of an economic recovery *without* serious new job-creation – a new phenomenon of 'jobless growth' – made possible by the labour-saving capacities of the new (computer and other) technologies ceaselessly being developed and improved in the new, competitive circumstances (Currie 1990, 1993a; Aronowitz and DiFazio 1994).[8] More classically Keynesian-minded social commentators, like Britain's Will Hutton and America's J. K. Galbraith, were anxious that these new forms of employment were so poorly paid that they undermined the possibility of a new surge of demand-led recovery within Western economies, and so guaranteed, once again, the famous 'crisis of over-production' that gave rise to the last Great Depression (Hutton 1995; Galbraith 1992). This was 'a recession' of a very new kind, in which the long-awaited 'recovery' constructed few long-awaited jobs, and in which the evidence of significant increases in personal poverty, homelessness and destitution was increasingly visible on the streets – a 'return of the repressed truth' about capitalism for an older generation which had believed that it had advanced to a higher stage (of post-unemployment, post-scarcity capitalism), but a taken-for-granted reality for young people who had had no personal experience of the 'high point' of post-war Fordism. In France, by the mid-1990s (and in many other 'advanced' European societies), many young people had begun to identify themselves, politically and culturally, as young people in Britain (the 'Punks') had done in the mid-1980s, as a generation with 'No Future'.

THE CRISIS OF MATERIAL POVERTY AND SOCIAL INEQUALITY

Closely linked to the increase in registered and unregistered unemployment that has occurred in many (though not all) Western societies, especially since the late 1970s, has been an unmistakable increase in poverty, whether measured in absolute or relative terms, and inequality. The two-volume report released by the Joseph Rowntree Foundation's Inquiry into Income and Wealth, released in 1995, outlined a steady shift in the distribution of wealth away from the poorest sections of the population towards the better-off in the United Kingdom, New Zealand, Sweden, the United States, Japan and West Germany, with a sharp 1 per cent shift per year in New Zealand, and 0.75 per cent in the UK. In the UK the bottom 10 per cent of the population, born after 1960, were actually earning wages that were in real terms significantly below those earned by their predecessors. Real incomes for the poorest 10 per cent of the population in the United Kingdom fell by some 17 per cent between 1979 and 1991–2.[9] A further 25 per cent, if in work, were struggling to earn anything more than their parents. It was only the middle and upper fractions of the working population who were earning more in absolute terms than earlier generations (Rowntree 1995). Looked at in relative terms, in terms of the distribution of wealth and income, the picture looks even more dramatic, especially in the United Kingdom, where there has been a faster increase in income inequality than in any comparable industrial country. In the period since 1977, the proportion of the population with less than half the national income has trebled.[10] The Commission on Social Justice, in its major report released in 1994, confirmed, firstly, that 'the bottom half of the population, who received a third of our national income in 1979, now receive only a quarter' (Commission on Social Justice, 1994: 29) and also that 'the gap between the earnings of the highest-paid and those of the lowest-paid workers is greater than at any time since records were first kept in 1886' (1994: 28).

Three features of this re-emergence of absolute and relative poverty need further emphasis here. First, as further statistical survey work has revealed, this 'new poverty' has been having a major impact on the lives of the very young and the youthful during the 1980s and 1990s – to an extent not experienced by the young in the earlier post-war period. In the United Kingdom, in particular, in 1991–2 some 32 per cent of all children under the age of eighteen (4.1 million young people) were living in households whose incomes placed them below the official poverty line, compared to only 10 per cent of under-eighteens in 1979.[11] At no time in the earlier post-war period was there any such statistically identifiable discrete population of the youthful poor: the visible evidence on the streets of Britain is no deceit.

Secondly, what little research has been conducted into this new poverty confirms a close link with the return of a cluster of other serious individual and social problems – thought previously to have been consigned to the past, notably the inter-war Depression. The most visible expression of these old problems, beginning in the 1980s, was the return of homelessness and public begging. These developments were not confined to Britain, being also very high in France and Germany – but, despite a number of emergency campaigns to deal with the problem of homelessness in Britain, over a third of a million households were still registered as homeless in 1992 (Commission on Social Justice 1994: 48). Very closely linked to the increase in poverty was a significant increase in different measures of poor health and early mortality. Richard Wilkinson's research, quoted in the Commission on Social Justice report, suggests a strong correlation between increases in mortality and increases in the levels of inequality across different European societies (Wilkinson 1994). Overall, in Britain, the picture with regard to the health of the poor is unambiguous:

> In some poorest parts of Britain, death rates are now as high as they were forty years ago ... The damage done by unemployment is [particularly] clear. Not only are unemployed people much more likely to suffer a chronic illness or disability, but a middle-aged man made redundant or taking early retirement is twice as likely to die within five years as a man who stays in work ... According to studies in Edinburgh and Oxford, unemployed men are between ten and fifteen times more likely to attempt suicide. Most horrifying is the fact that the suicide rate amongst young men doubled between 1983 and 1990. (Commission on Social Justice 1994: 45)

The evidence on health in Britain – deep in the thrall of a prolonged experiment in the application of a particularly pure version of free market theory – is particularly striking: the United Kingdom slipped from tenth to seventeenth position in the 'life-expectancy' league of OECD countries in the period between 1983 and 1990. So also, some commentators have argued, there is a compelling case for understanding the extraordinary increases in recorded crime in Britain, which were in the 1980s and early 1990s without parallel in any developed country, as being a dramatic and more or less direct expression of the return of poverty and the intensification of absolute and relative inequalities. Will Hutton puts the case in a characteristically succinct fashion:

> Britain in the 1980s had the most rapid crime growth in Europe and it was also a country where the top 20 per cent had six times the disposable incomes of the bottom 20 per cent, at the beginning of the decade. They ended it with nine times more. More telling still is that the growth of inequality is associated with the growth of crime. Britain topped the crime growth table of the European Big Four, with Italy second, France third and Germany fourth; and between 1980 and 1985 the rankings in income inequality growth were exactly the same ... The more inequality grows, the more crime grows.[12]

But the third feature of this return of poverty is perhaps the most important of all in sociological and cultural terms – namely, its *being unexpected*, a shock to generations of adults and young people attuned, in school and in popular media, to a Whiggish, uncritical conception of a constantly developing and 'improving' society. As recently as the 1960s, the political, academic and popular characterizations of the broader society were of a form of mature, planned, mixed-economy welfare capitalism which, under the tutelage of John Maynard Keynes and others, had learnt the lessons of the 1930s. Such problems as did exist had to do with what were seen as the negative aspects of the developing popular media and consumerism (the rise of a 'Mass Society') and the relatively slow pace of the post-war movement towards greater social equality.[13] By the mid-1980s, there was a growing awareness, especially among national elites, that 'the revolution of rising expectations' produced by the post-war Keynesian settlement in Europe and by the New Deal had run its course. What was in question economically were the choices available in underwriting the future of companies and corporations. What was at issue politically was the policy direction of national governments. And what was at issue *in a sociological sense* was the modification of that post-war culture of rising expectations, in the form that it assumed within each of the Western, developed industrial societies. A particular challenge was the continuing viability of the assumptions inherited within sociology from the work of Robert Merton, in his classic essay on 'Social Structure and Anomie' (1938) and in *Social Theory and Social Structure* (1957). Merton's analysis of modernist American capitalism in the middle of the twentieth century postulated a widespread majority acceptance both of the dominant goals of that society ('material success') and also of the (orderly pursuit) of 'the institutionalized means' for the attainment of such material success (progress at school, advancement to college, postponement of gratification, entry into a successful career etc.). In other European societies – for example, in social-democratic Sweden – the emphasis in discussions of the character of social order and of visions of the good society were decidedly less individualistic in form, but the concern with a high standard of living was equally prominent. In societies like Britain, still without experiencing the benefits of a thorough-going bourgeois revolution, and in process of recovery from the efforts of the Second World War, the desire for affluence was real enough but was antici-pated with rather less confidence than in the United States or in Scandinavia. It is vital to understand how the arrival of post-Fordist market society in the 1980s has carried with it a recognition that the unevenly distributed material attainments of the earlier Fordist period were now under threat, and to understand how this 'fear of failure' or 'fear of falling' were entering into other areas of social life, from questioning the legitimacy of 'traditional' forms of college education (which no longer carry the same social guarantees) to what some commentators call the crisis of civility in everyday life (Taylor and Jamieson 1998).

FEAR OF FALLING AND FEAR OF THE OTHER

There have been a range of different kinds of popular responses in different Western societies to the new economic realities. In the United States – a society in which the self-confident mid-twentieth-century belief in economic success (at both national and individual level) remains a powerful recent memory – an ever-increasing proportion of households consist of two adults in paid employment ('dual-career' households) struggling to stay in work in order to retain the standards of living available to such households on a single income some three decades ago. These accelerated and overworked households are burdened with a range of problems in respect of daily domestic management, particularly – if and when they have children – in respect of child-care, everyday domestic management, and stress. The consequences for the quality of 'family life' and local and neighbourhood institutions of this acceleration of work-life in North America – where in terms of the routine investment of time and emotion, the workplace has become for many millions the equivalent in earlier historical periods of 'the home' (Hochschild 1990) – are incalculable. This process has become an object of urgent concern in the writing and public arguments of Amitai Etzioni and the 'new communitarians' (Etzioni 1994). In the United States there has been a troubled, inchoate recognition from the late 1980s that these new conditions – of over-accelerated work and job-insecurity – are a serious challenge to previously taken-for-granted assumptions regarding the 'American way of life' ('Happy Families') and, in particular, to America's assumed destiny as an affluent and successful economy. In 1992, for example, one of the most popular movies on release in the United States, *Falling Down*, featured a panic-stricken and paranoid redundant executive called 'D-fens' (played by Michael Douglas) doing battle with a series of 'foreign Others' (most notably, Korean shopkeepers and Puerto Rican street-gang members) – on the one hand representing the threat of overseas competition and, on the other, personifying the incivility and parasitism attributed in populist media ideology to an ethnic underclass.

This movie gave voice to what was, at this time, a widespread concern within America as to the capacity of American industry and commerce to deal with international competition on the basis of its existing practices. The Secretary of Labour in the first Clinton administration, Robert Reich, was one of several well-placed US economists arguing that American industry was not well placed to respond to the demands of economies increasingly driven by demands for high-technology products, speedily and creatively produced to respond to ephemeral market demand (Reich 1991; Magaziner and Reich 1982; Tyson 1992; Krugman 1994). Other economists argued at the time that Western domination of the world economy itself was increasingly seriously threatened by the rise of the economies of South-East Asia. Following hard on the heels of Japan, the economies of Singapore, Hong Kong and South Korea were growing at a rate which had never been attained in most Western countries. The growth rate of these three countries over the last three decades was equivalent to the growth achieved in Britain and Germany *over a century* (Jacques 1995: 6). On the basis of a growth rate of 10 per cent in recent years, China (with over one-fifth of the world's population) was predicted at this time to become the largest economy in the world (in terms of gross purchasing power) by the year 2020, at some 40 per cent higher on this measure than the United States; the economies of India and Indonesia were also predicted to overtake the economies of France and Germany over the same period (1995: 7). The implications of this global shift for weaker national European economies (Spain, Greece and, increasingly, Britain), particularly for citizens looking for first employment within those societies, looked bleak indeed.[14]

Economists worried that in the face of such competitive global pressures, individual national governments, particularly of nations like the United States – threatened by a loss of global economic leadership – might be tempted into some form of defensive 'protectionism', attempting to save individual industries and workforces within that country by erecting heavy tariffs against cheaper overseas products. So also were many other commentators worrying that one of this increasing global interpenetration of national economies might be the reactive development of a defensive and nationalistic mind-set or tribalism. There is no question that the 1990s have seen a 'return of the tribes' in many different, but connected, senses – especially in Europe, but also elsewhere (Walzer 1992). One intriguing analytical issue is how this protectionist tribalism displays itself in the area defined by professional criminology as the 'fear of crime' (Taylor and Jamieson 1998). But there are a number of connected issues here (like the generalized fear that is provoked by the ever-increasing number of homeless people in free market societies, or the inchoate sets of fears that appear to be produced in the privatized suburban developments of North America by the sighting of any 'strangers' in the neighbourhood).[15]

The prevalence of this new 'fortress' or 'drawbridge' mentality in the suburbs – to be discussed in some detail in chapter 4 – can be understood in part as a metaphorical displacement of a wider set of fears – now very widespread throughout the 'middle class' of Western societies – over personal market position in market society (the possibility of personal redundancy or the redundancy of a partner or other family member, or even, however subconsciously, anxiety over a more precipitous loss of social position – the descent to homelessness and 'the street') (Ehrenreich 1989). There is a widespread perception that the 'quality of life' (especially the amount of material consumption) which was taken for granted by earlier generations of middle-class households) can now only be a realistic expectation for highly mobile, and flexibly skilled, elements of the citizenry. Will Hutton has argued that Britain has become a '30 : 30 : 40' society, in which only about 40 per cent of adults above the age of sixteen are in 'tenured' employment, allowing them to anticipate receiving their present income for the foreseeable future. However, even this 40 per cent are 'insecure', given the widespread perception that the numbers of full-time jobs 'for life' have been shrinking fast. There is a further 30 per cent of the population in forms of employment that are structurally insecure (having held their positions or been self-employed for two years or less or being specified as being in temporary or part-time work); and, finally, there is a further 30 per cent who are unemployed or economically marginalized. The development of this particular, very insecure and unequal, labour market has been particularly pronounced in Britain, by comparison with other European societies, but there is a general tendency, discussed in more detail in the final section of this chapter, towards the further casualization of labour markets in all competitive market societies. Hutton argues: 'By the year 2000, full-time tenured employment, around which stable family life has been constructed (with the capacity to service 25-year mortgages) will be a minority form of work.'[16]

THE CRISIS OF THE NATION-STATE

Nearly every traditional criminological text of the earlier post-war period, in both North America and Europe, is written against a set of 'statist assumptions'. That is to say that the discussions of crime prevention and/or correction which these texts inevitably contain involve assumptions, for example, about the capacity of individual nation-states, especially in the aftermath of the work of Keynes and his disciples, to manage their own economic policies – with a view, perhaps, to minimizing circumstances of poverty and destitution thought to be associated with 'crime'. Scholarly commentators focusing on the work of the police or other 'institutions of social control' have worked with a set of long-established wisdoms about the exclusive mandate of institutions of the State (like the police) to provide a sense of personal and community safety and security. Other commentators (for example, philosophers commenting on issues of personal conduct or the broader social and moral order) have worked with sets of assumptions about the capacity of 'the State' – in the form of its education systems, its public broadcasting media, or other socially accredited spokespersons (including, even, certain political leaders) to provide a sense of shared moral script, within which the different interests of individuals or different interest groups, can be subsumed in a grand compromise called the Public Interest.

In the last years of the twentieth century, however, there is a widespread feeling in most 'advanced' societies that these different institutions of the State (like those managing the national economy and guarding social peace, that is, the police and criminal justice system) are failing to deliver. The suspicion that the nation-state is in difficulties often coexists ironically, however, with a growing sense of nationalistic or tribal assertion within the boundaries of those same nation-states. This nationalistic sentiment arises as one response to the perception that the economic fulcrum has gone transnational, with the range of threats this might imply for the workforce employed within any one national boundary. The re-emergence of nationalism in the world in the 1990s is not simply a response to economic threat, and clearly also involves – as in Bosnia and other parts of Eastern Europe – a fundamental cultural response to political change, especially, in this instance, the collapse of the supra-national institutions of the Soviet Union and Yugoslavia. On one view, there is a reversion to a notion of 'blood and belonging' kind of nationalism, in which nationalistic leaders emerge to reinvent and celebrate the history and contemporary importance of nationally located ethnic groups and to lay claim to traditional rights or territories (Ignatieff

1994). It is this version of the nation-state which appears able to mobilize citizens as 'subjects' of the national power, and to go to war on its behalf, in defence of a national collective interest.

Two notions of nation are in flux in the 1990s. On the one hand, there is the primordialist concept of the nation (over which a civil war rages in the old Yugoslavia, and which also threatens to provoke hostilities in and around the old Soviet Union, on the continent of Africa and even – in the struggle of Quebec nationalism – in 'high modern' North America). Against this is a notion of the nation-state, above all, as a child of modernity – a product of the two centuries of struggle to create a modern industrial society, governed according to the tenets of the Enlightenment, and therefore organized around a social contract rationally entered into between rational and free-thinking individuals and the State (Gellner 1995; Hobsbawm 1994). Both the primordial and the modernist versions of the nation-state have the capacity to act on the popular imagination and to construct a sense of the nation as what Benedict Anderson calls 'an imagined community', uniting citizens in the imagination with other fellow citizens they have never met, and who never will meet (Anderson 1983: 15).

The nation-state achieves this task on many different levels. Not least, as Gramsci, Marx and many other writers have understood, the modern nation-state, like its medieval precursors, was a creature of colourful and evocative ceremonies and rituals (coronations, military and other pageants etc.). These helped construct *a culture* of the nation with enormous emotional appeal, which was continuously elaborated in heroic tales of military or imperial exploits and victories as well as sporting, artistic or technological accomplishment. Such national pride was often celebrated iconically in terms of individual national heroes, who then became cultural signifiers in their own right of 'national' achievement. This sense of nation was also constantly affirmed, throughout the calendar year, in a predictable timetable of national events with its own nation-specific historical significance (in England, the Opening of Parliament, the Cup Final, Wimbledon, Derby Day, Guy Fawkes Day and many others) – many of which were and are fixed and coded in the national-popular imagination in relation to particular buildings, architectural sites or simply 'places'. It is interesting, given the focus in this text, to note the significance, in terms of this ongoing process of cultural signification, within nations of national uniforms, particularly of the uniformed police – the symbolic guardians of social peace and order within individual countries – in Canada, the Mountie; in France, 'le flic' and in Britain 'the bobby'. There is a clue, here, to the truth which Gramsci and Weber, from different perspectives, both understood – namely, that the individual nation-state must constantly *struggle for* legitimacy, not least (at the ideological level) in ceremonies of national unification or also (at other times) in its provision of various economic or material support for the citizenry. The contract between the modern state and the citizen involves not simply the willingness of citizens to satisfy purely egoistic self-interest and a willingness to 'fight for the country': it also involves a constant struggle by national leaderships to make political and economic adjustments in the face of different political and social demands from different subordinate populations in different historical conjunctures. Over the last century, beginning in Germany and in Britain, that struggle for legitimacy saw the transformation of many bourgeois capitalist societies into 'welfare states', associated with the provision to all citizens (so entitled by virtue of their citizenship in the nation) of free health services and education, and a variety of state benefits for the ill, the elderly and the unemployed. In nearly every case, the provision of these 'public goods' was a responsibility assumed by the State in response to struggles by popular and political movements for such 'reform' and State provision. From the vantage point of the 1990s, the achievements of the movements, and the individual activists involved in these struggles for social reform and social welfare, is self-evident.

It is also important to register the importance for social reformers and activists of the State as a key arena for the advancement of what they saw as a 'universal' or a 'public interest'. In the first half of the twentieth century, certainly in Britain, the provision of compulsory education *by the State* was one objective amongst many others (including self-education through evening classes) of a Labour movement made aware, from experience, of its effective exclusion from education and, indirectly, therefore, from social and political power. 'Education' was also an instrument, in this vision – not just of democratization (enhancing popular access to power) – but also of *moral order*, in helping to inform the civic senses, of both the rights and the duties of an educated citizenry. The Education Act of 1944 in Britain, in this sense, was the affirmation of the State's acceptance of the role it should play in this larger project of education of all citizens. For all that this legislation is usually attributed to R. A. Butler (the Tory grandee and Education Secretary of the wartime government), it is more accurately understood in terms of the lengthy earlier history of individual social democrats and reformers, like R. H. Tawney, and also of organizations like the Workers' Educational Association, the Plebs League, the arts colleges, and many other sites of popular education that had first developed in the early years of the century. So also is it important to see the continuing influence of this vision of the State 'as an educator' in the expansion of universities in the 1960s and, under the driving influence of Jennie Lee, the creation of the Open University, given its Royal Charter in 1969. It is also important to retrieve, in this connection, a sense of the State's pivotal role in the other rapidly developing 'public sphere' of radio and television broadcasting. Some of the defining features of public broadcasting in Britain, especially of the BBC under Lord Reith, have been subject to scathing criticisms – for example, in the 1970s by the social scientific liberal-left (Kumar 1977) and, in the 1980s and 1990s, by the free market, populist Right (including Rupert Murdoch) specifically for the 'voice' and 'mode of address' adopted in news and current affairs programming – the voice of an inert, tradition-bound fraction of the ruling class, speaking in the clipped tones of 'BBC English'.

What these critiques may have underestimated, however, was the role which the public broadcast media may have played in endowing the broad society with a sense of shared knowledge and understanding – a sense of a society in conversation with itself, organized in part around the shared, if differently interpreted, programming of radio and television. There was surely an important sense in which public television and radio were a source of moral and social education, *providing information in the public realm to all citizens* about the direction of the broader society but also a sense in which 'a public' might be involved, directly in current affairs programmes, but also indirectly and at the level of the imagination – for example, in television and film. There is an important sense in which the existence of national public broadcasting contributed to a sense of a society 'under control': of national public institutions being accountable to a larger public, and certainly influenced by this 'national public'. The advance of satellite and cable television, video and other 'narrow-cast' private media in the 1990s – responding to fast-moving 'markets' for entertainment or specific private interests – is a serious challenge to this sphere of public education, public debate and public influence. Even the most vigorous, pluralistic and creative private market of media cannot reproduce a sense of a shared public sphere of debate and influence, routinely linked to centres of national, international, and public democratic power. It is in this sense that the decline of influence of national public broadcasting is one dimension in the fast-developing sense of crisis in a number of institutions of 'the modern State', the public sphere and public provision associated with it. Outside Europe, one of the best examples of this process is the marginalization of the Canadian Broadcasting Corporation both on television and within the broader culture of that enormous, multi-cultural but now very fractured, society.

Critically, of course, the 'crisis of the nation-state' in the 1990s is also widely understood to be a crisis of in respect of the effectivity of the State (and, specifically, the Keynesian mixed-economy and welfare state) in the management and encouragement of economic development and progress. In the aftermath of the disaster of the inter-war Depression and the shared experience and knowledge of the Second World War, the nation-state had, of course, been transformed into an instrument of planning and economic development: the mixed economy, characterized by a range of 'neo-corporate' partnerships between private industry and the State in the sphere of planning, in particular, and in research and development. We have already identified in earlier discussion one of the most immediate expressions of this crisis – the job-crisis of the 1980s and 1990s – as a definitive contemporary social transition. That is another way of identifying the failure of 'the State' (by comparison with the market) to generate a coherent strategy for responding to popular aspirations for 'the future'. The promise of the Keynesian mixed economy and welfare state no longer has purchase, at least in its individual national form, in most Western societies.

Critical analysis of the 'modern welfare state' in the 1960s and 1970s identified the legitimizing and social control function which the welfare state performed 'for capitalism', in providing a veneer of care and protection, on at least two levels, for citizens who continued to experience the boom and slump, and class inequalities, of industrial capitalism (O'Connor 1973; Gough 1979). The 'welfare state' as it began to develop in Britain in the aftermath of the Second World War, had been envisaged by its author, Lord Beveridge, in 1942 as a means of providing all citizens with 'security from the cradle to the grave'. State intervention was to take place into the working of the wider capitalist order in order to eliminate the five 'giant evils' of Want (poverty), Disease, Ignorance (lack of education), Squalor and Idleness (unemployment). Though proclaimed at the time as a revolutionary document, the Beveridge Report's vision of the post-war order was relatively unambitious – by comparison, for example, with the imperial scope of economic vision entertained by leaderships of the United States. The objective in Beveridge was that of returning, in the immediate post-war period, to the compromise between Capital and Labour, mediated through the State, which had begun to be institutionalized in the 'recovery' period of the 1930s prior to the outbreak of war (Dahrendorf 1985), in which the modest demands of the working people and the majority of other citizens (for health, education, welfare, jobs and social peace) were met within a slowly modernizing, low-wage but low-unemployment mixed economy. In the United States, during the middle years of this century, a much more ambitious economic project had been underwritten, by the Roosevelt administration's 'New Deal', in a series of federally funded measures in support of farmers, in the creation of a 300,000-strong civilian Conservation Corps working in forests and parks, and the Public Works Administration programme, involving over 26,500 employment-creation programmes at federal and state level, and a range of other measures.

One important ideological theme in the construction of the post-war settlements in Britain and America was the issue of ensuring social peace and providing a sense of protection for 'the person' (in Britain, the 'citizen' of the modest new post-war welfare state; in America, the new affluent individual and housing areas). I have argued elsewhere that the development of public policing within divided class societies like Britain should be understood, in part, as a response to 'popular demands for social peace' or, in other words, for the presence in local communities of an instrument of State power to guarantee social order in local communities (Taylor 1981).[17] The continuing appeal within Britain of the image of the constable in *Dixon of Dock Green* – the friendly, unarmed, and avuncular local policeman immersed in his local community – the signifying figure in one of the longest-running programmes ever shown on British television (a total of 434 episodes, screened between 1955 and 1976 (A. Clarke 1982: 42) – is the best-known expression in Britain of this notion of a 'public police' acting as a local agent (of the State) in the maintenance of social peace. Allan Clarke's close reading of the series is still instructive for our times:

> Not only was *Dixon of Dock Green* the prototype of the British police series, it was also the classic series of its period, drawing together the discourses of crime, legality, justice, community, family and national pride. In the period of post-war reconstruction, this articulation of the community as consisting of decent, friendly, upright folk united against the unruly element of minor criminals causing disruption by making quick and dishonest money instead of working

hard and saving, had a widespread appeal amongst people who had lived through the war. This definition was brought alive in the series with a working-class hero – in this respect the actor (Jack Warner) and the character (PC Dixon) shared the same parentage – from the East End of London, and it was an easy identification for hard working people to make with the hard-working, dedicated and diligent copper ... At the same time as depicting dedication, Dixon's home life demonstrated that it was possible both to work long, arduous hours and to maintain a successful and happy domestic life. This particular weighting of the discourse, its relative prominence in the narrative, says much about the nature of the social order being constructed in the series. The primacy of social responsibility, presented repeatedly as the necessity for parents to accept responsibility for their children, in terms of setting good examples for them, entails an order of strict morality, or rigidly defined rights and wrongs. How clear the moral order of the world was can be seen from Dixon's summaries of each episode, where the justice of the legal penalties was stressed and the position of the police stated unequivocally. (1982: 44)

To take note of the powerful ideological appeal of 'Dixon' in early post-war England is not argue that this form of policing faithfully corresponded with actually existing police practice. Nor is it to ignore the direct role which police have been called upon to play in major class conflicts (for example, during major strikes) or during political confrontations (most notoriously, in the 1930s and again in the 1960s, defending the 'freedoms' of fascists and racists, whilst vigorously curtailing the freedoms of the organized Left and ethnic minority populations. Nor should we ignore the important ideological influence which the image of the British police has had in the construction of a *mythological* sense of shared national community and identity, powerfully symbolized for many years in the notion of the unarmed bobby, identified by the wearing of that curious headpiece, the helmet, an icon derived from the British army in India.

What I do want to suggest, however, is that the notion of a public police in England, and in the wider Britain – for all that it has been a part of the apparatus of State at key moments of national crisis – has also been a key element in the construction of a publicly provided and accountable body (the 'police service') at the local level. Policing in England first emerged, in London, Manchester and other provincial cities, after all, *as a local (rather than national) peace-keeping force*, modelled, more or less consciously, after the fashion of the night watch, first promulgated in the Statute of Winchester in 1283, under the auspices of the local Justice of the Peace (Hibbert 1963: 26).

In Canada, the image of the Mountie is one of the most important and enduring sources of a sense of national identity (Walden 1982), and, despite being an armed frontier force with some history of violent confrontations with the native peoples of that country (Brown and Brown 1973), there is also a sense in which the later development of the Royal Canadian Mounted Police (RCMP) as a particular police force regime – forging a link between federal and provincial government authorities and also between several different language groups – is central to the imaginative construction of Canada as 'a secure and peaceable kingdom'.[18] Similar conceptions of the symbolic importance of the public police with respect to national identity are widespread across most developed societies.

In many Western societies, however, in the 1990s, this notion of public policing, working more or less effectively in the public interest, is in crisis. Most obviously, this has to do with a generalized sense that the police are 'losing the war' against crime – specifically, that the 'clear-up rates' of most of the commonly experienced crimes (burglaries, car-thefts or assaults) are low and declining (Kinsey, Lea and Young 1996). But also it has to do with a general turn towards a private or tribal form of self-protection, which is closely connected with the deepening accentuation of self-interest inherent in competitive free market societies. This marketization of social relations is discussed later in this chapter. For the moment, I simply want to emphasize this crisis of public policing – in societies which had such a tradition (alongside the other more nationally symbolic and repressive aspects of policing – as an integral aspect of the more general crisis of the 'nation-state'.

So one of the absolutely defining aspects of 'the culture' in the 1990s is a widespread disenchantment with this earlier, post-war reformist and utopian vision of the State. In the United States, this process has been in train for some considerable time, encouraged by a series of individual intellectuals whose initial commitments were to the New Deal and post-war reform, but whose subsequent disappointments have turned into reaction (Steinfels 1977). For James Q. Wilson (1975) the crippling contradiction was that the rise of affluence (and a continuing commitment to state support for welfare) *coexisted* with ever higher levels of crime, including violent and predatory crime, at levels far beyond those of the inter-war years (Wilson, 1975). Writing in the mid-1970s, Wilson could foresee only a continuing increase in reported crime, and the continuing failure of 'liberal' or 'social-democratic' state interventions. In one angry text of this period, several American intellectuals, moving relentlessly to the right, looked across the Atlantic to Britain and indicted the kind of mixed-economy Keynesian strategy apparently in place at national level as 'the future that doesn't work' (Tyrrell 1982). There were many ways in which this view could be challenged (arguments about 'the quality of community life' etc.) but economic dynamism was not one of them.

What was increasingly obvious in the later 1980s and early 1990s, as already indicated, was the intrusive new presence of homelessness and begging on the streets and the return of Beveridge's 'five evils' of Want, Disease, Ignorance, Squalor and Idleness (Seabrook 1985). The national press in Britain reported at several moments the discovery of rickets, polio and of other diseases associated either with poverty or with an unreformed pre-modern society. It also gave prominent treatment, almost every quarter during the late 1980s and early 1990s, to the release of the latest set of criminal statistics by the Home Office, appearing to register ineluctable continuing increases in levels of reported crime, as well as giving headline treatment to a series of individual criminal incidents (notably, the murders of Rachel Nickell, Jamie Bulger and Benji Stanley; the sequence of sexual murders committed by Dennis Nilsen and Fred and Rosemary West; and the 'massacre' of fifteen five-year-olds and a teacher in a school gymnasium in Dunblane, Scotland by the gun-wielding

Thomas Hamilton in March 1996) – all of which were without obvious parallel, at least in respect of popular memory and common sense.[19]

Similar developments were observable in particular baroque instances of crime in the United States, notably in respect of serial killing and in the spread of firearms use to school-age children.[20] Amongst opinion-forming social commentators, a consensus seemed to be emerging around the relative powerlessness of the 'Keynesian welfare-state' or any other national state structure to prevent random outbursts of violent crime, and, in some accounts, the play of 'Evil' itself. The Enlightenment's central idea of 'progress', guaranteed and symbolized by a strong and beneficent State in partnership with a rational and enlightened public, now had critics on all sides, including, it should be said, commentators on the left (Lasch 1991) as well as on the right (D. Anderson 1992). One of the continuing paradoxes of the times, as indicated earlier, is with the way that this disenchantment with the nation-state (taking the form, for example, in the United States, a populist revulsion against 'Washington' or 'big Government') sits alongside a growth of nationalist self-assertion, which, importantly, is in some way associated with a belief in the possibility of restoring a strong civil society – not through the State as a set of institutions – but through the State conceived of as the 'nation'.

CRISES OF INCLUSION AND EXCLUSION

The growth of the new nationalism and social and political 'particularism' – summarized by Michael Walzer in 1992 as 'the new tribalism' – is one of the most profound 'crises' in the familiar sphere of political culture at the end of the twentieth century. Opinion polls in France in 1996 suggested that fully 30 per cent of voters supported the policies of Le Pen's Front National, whilst in Austria there were echoes of the 1930s in the continuing rise of Jorge Haider's Freedom Party. Elsewhere within Europe, in Belgium, with its formally defined 'linguistic communities', in parts of Germany, in Spain (both inside and beyond the Basque country), in northern and southern Italy (the regional Leagues in the north and the neo-fascist MSI in the South) and even, in a small way, in social-democratic Norway and Sweden, there has been evidence of support for different forms of 'Blood or Belonging' politics – articulated, above all, around the defence (*against 'Others'*) of the interests of 'national peoples' or particularist, local 'communities'. American political life, at the end of the twentieth century, is dominated by a continuing and anxious attempt to control the growth in influence of a variety of fundamentalist movements of the populist Right (from religious fundamentalists to the armed militias) angrily attempting to insulate the American people from foreign competition and from 'Washington' itself. Throughout 1994 and 1995, the then most influential politician in America, Mr Newt Gingrich, actively pursued the task of unpacking the social provisions put in place by the New Deal in that country in the 1930s. Mass support was mobilized amongst an anxious middle class for 'a new Contract with America'. Further north, the unity of the Canadian nation itself (defined, from the first days of 'Confedera-tion', in terms of a compromise between French and English Canadian elites), was seriously threatened by the determination of the separatist bloc in Quebec to end such arrangements. In English Canada itself, in the meantime, the traditions of political liberalism – a specific product of the history of immigration into that country, particularly of refugees and asylum-seekers, were being undermined by the rise of a fundamentalist party of the Right, the Reform Party, which in the general election of 1996 became the official Opposition.

Some of these new 'particularist' and tribal political movements, like the Front National in France, have an explicitly racialist stance and agenda, whilst others (the Northern Leagues in Italy, the Canadian Reform Party) do not. Some movements claim, in effect, to be the carriers of new forms of personal, regional or cultural 'identity' which they see to have been unrecog-nized in 'traditional' or outdated form of modernist politics organized around the polarity of 'Left' and 'Right'. Other specifically 'primordialist' move-ments claim to be the benign representatives of national-popular traditions which had been repressed throughout the modernist twentieth century, now intent on returning 'a tribe' to its authentic national trajectory. This is particularly marked an emphasis, as Michael Ignatieff (1994) and Michael Walzer (1992) have shown, amongst the new nationalist movements of Middle and Eastern Europe. But what all these militant particularist move-ments have in common is an attempt to define, defend or advance the interests of a particular 'people' usually within a particular geographical space (northern Italy, the Flemish part of Belgium, Quebec etc.) against the intrusion or competition of others within that space, and the demands which they may make for equality and inclusion in that space. This is a very old question; Michael Walzer, for instance, suggests: 'Who is in and who is out? – these are the first questions that any political community asks about itself. Particular communities are constituted by the answers they give or, better, through the process through which it is decided whose answers count' (Walzer 1993: 55). In ancient Greece, debating its relationship with its 'guest workers' and other 'foreigners', the decision of the democratic assemblies was to establish an 'intermediate group' of 'resident aliens' who shared a large part of the rights and duties of full citizens. Over time, this intermediate group then proceeded to build up through its own initiatives what Walzer calls a 'complex equality' across the pre-existing boundaries of class and status (for example, slavery), and establish the foundations of the modern and inclusive *demos*, participating in all debates about 'justice' and 'sharing' in the developing spheres of economic activity and social life (Walzer, 1993). This particular and ancient conception of a complex and pluralist democratic community is the source of the 'modern' forms of democratic liberalism, which have been so influential, at least rhetorically, in the descriptions adopted of themselves by Western societies – for example, with its Jefferson-ian emphasis, of the American Constitution, or in the Charters of Rights defended in various European courts. In the late twentieth century, however, it is precisely that form of democratic liberalism which is under attack, in various different ways (in America, in the attacks on 'statecraft' itself). A defining feature of the contemporary attack on the democratic-liberal tradition is the attempt to curtail or restrict the numbers and the variety of minorities and 'aliens' which can be allowed the opportunity of being included in the developed 'democratic community'. Under the influence of the so-called Ad Hoc Convention on Immigration, for example, every single member-state of the European Community had tightened its rules on immigration, refugees and asylum-seekers,[21] whilst in the North American Free Trade Area considerable energy has gone into closing the borders between Mexico and the United States, on the one hand, and also into limiting illegal immigration into Canada, one of the most underpopulated landscapes on the face of the globe (Jamieson et al. 1997). There is also a powerful, but very problematic, underlying common sense economic theory at work here – not only to the effect that the declining resources of individual national communities cannot be extended to outsiders but also that 'economic downturns' or decline in the late twentieth century cannot be offset by the energy and innovation of new immigrant populations.[22]

I refer this broader economic 'realism', in part, in order to underline the naïveté of any discussion of issues of ethnic difference and citizenship in terms just of an abstract appeal to principles of democratic pluralism, a philosophy which is itself now under threat. In some parts of Eastern Europe the 'new freedom' produced by the collapse of the Soviet Union is accompanied by a form of nationalist assertion that is relatively unchallenged by two centuries of Enlightenment social and cultural thought: the result is the spread of what Eric Hobsbawm identifies in that part of Europe specifically, but potentially elsewhere as well, as 'the return of barbarism' (Hobsbawm 1994).

So my concern is also to underline an argument about any contemporary study of race and racialism as well – that is, to insist that the analysis of race and racialism is no longer effectively undertaken in terms of an anthropology or a psychology of 'difference' ('prejudice') – against which, as used to be argued in some liberal circles, could be ranged the multifold benefits of a minority group's economic advancement and 'assimilation'. In market societies there is no dominant economic and political logic which requires such an assimilationist project to be mobilized by a national government. So also, it might be argued, there is a challenge to studies of race relations that are framed only in terms of the colonial legacy, in which the approach to the analysis and understanding of citizenship in the host society is interpreted only through the prism of colonial responsibility and guilt, and all activities of racial minorities (including crime) interpreted in terms of an anti-colonialist 'struggle'. The study of racial or ethnic 'relations' in the late 1990s must surely be thought of in terms of the relations of refugees and new migrants, people of colour or different ethnic identities, to the ongoing processes of social reorganization (including the specific processes of social exclusion) which are characteristic of contemporary post-Fordist and marketized societies. That is to say, they have to be understood as part of the *changing social relations* occurring in societies in which the absolute number of *economic opportunities* is in decline by comparison with earlier moments in the post-war history of capitalism – and also the *relative decline* in the proportion of such opportunities that provide full-time and continuing personal and social security. In such circumstances, the struggles of 'ethnic minority groups' as a whole, but more particularly the struggles of different generational groups and individuals of different sexes within those minority groups are best thought of as a particular 'struggle for position' within transformed economies. Across Europe as a whole, there will be millions of ethnic minority peoples who had succeeded – often against the obstacles of institutionalized prejudice and racism – in obtaining some kind of employment position or career within the host society during the period of relatively high employment in the 1960s to early 1980s. There are likewise many millions of black Americans and other Americans 'of colour' who will have attained positions within that economy, especially in the aftermath of the Civil Rights Movement of the 1960s ('the black bourgeoisie' first discussed by Frazier). In the 1980s and 1990s, however, in the aftermath of the crisis of the mass manufacturing economy on both continents, millions of ethnic minority people have found themselves struggling, often alongside the 'poor white' population for secure employment within post-Fordist economies. Mike Davis's classic account (1990) of the 'deindustrialization' of Los Angeles during the 1980s describes a process not only of a 'haemorrhaging' of employment possibilities for blacks (and particularly for black males) in this massive conurbation during this period (exacerbated by an intensification of informal colour bars in the labour markets of the outer suburbs and 'edge cities'). It is also an account of the *restructuring* of a labour market to replace the loss of mass manufacturing capacity, and especially the new emphasis being placed on technological skill and skills in the service trades, rather than on the muscular power required of the labouring classes in the Fordist period. The networks of street gangs which emerged in this period, fuelled by the developing trade in cocaine and other illegal drugs, is understood by Davis in one sense as a rational response by unemployed (and unemployable) young black men: an alternative economy in which young men from that segment of the Los Angeles 'working class' could find 'employment'. But it is clear that the work was of a kind which enabled many of those young men, excluded from the labour market entered by their fathers, to reaffirm their muscular masculinity, but in a refashioned form (in an ostentatious commitment to the demands and risk of a criminal economy and to the culture, Gangsta Rap, which underlay it). The impact of these two different crises – the demise of mass manufacturing and the concomitant crisis of an industrialized masculinity – is obviously not felt exclusively within areas of black residence in the United States. But, as William Julius Wilson has so conclusively demonstrated, they are experienced in a particularly intense form in inner city and other neighbourhoods in which – for reasons to do with the post-war history of migration within America – the majority populations are black. In these areas in the 1990s, according to Wilson, large proportions of households exhibit a vast range of 'presenting' or 'behavioural' problems – which are far more complex and multifaceted than the problems of ghetto families only a couple of decades earlier. The multiplicity of problems in the black and poor white families should be understood as what Wilson refers to as a 'concentration effect' – a function not just of exclusion of many of the adults and young people from the formal labour market, or the general increase in inequality, but also the increasing sequestration and isolation of these areas of intense and multidimensional deprivation (W. J. Wilson 1987, ch. 2).[23] Loïc Wacquant's more recent analytical work (1994, 1996) suggests that we are witness to a distinctive new process of 'hyper-ghettoization' – the development of discrete urban territories where the mass of residents are permanently excluded from legitimate employment and where the writ of public authorities, like the police, does not run. The concentration of these effects results not simply from the racism of the surrounding society, but also from the dynamic interplay of the broader political economy (the collapse of mass industry) and the dominant cultures of 'the ghetto'.[24]

In America as a whole, the effects of these combined processes of racial discrimination, racialization of neighbourhoods ('hyper-ghettoization'), accelerating joblessness, poverty and inequality, and the masculinist culture of the black neighbourhood are unambiguous. Some 40 to 50 per cent of all serious crimes against the person (homicides, forcible rapes, armed robberies and aggravated assaults) in America in the early 1990s were committed by African-Americans. The vast majority of those African-Americans apprehended for these offences were young: amongst 15- to 19-year-old Americans, for example, firearms murders were ten times more common than amongst whites (Hagan and Peterson 1995: 19). African-Americans were also being arrested in this period for a smaller, but still vastly disproportionate, percentage of less serious property crimes – something in the order of a quarter to a third of all arsons, car-thefts, burglaries and larcenies in the late 1980s (Harriss 1991). There is no doubt, as studies of the unequal use of capital punishment have shown dramatically, that the responses of the American courts to 'black criminals' displayed deeply racist assumptions. But it is also clear that the response of the courts to 'black criminals' is a reflection of the concentrated participation of young black men in these different types of serious crime, and also that it is sometimes a response to the disproportionate level of criminal victimization experienced by the black population of particular neighbourhoods and cities in America – a 25 per cent higher level of victimization, for example, by rape, aggravated assault and robbery than that experienced by American whites (Hagan and Peterson 1995: 23). It is also important to note that the response of the local police and courts to 'black crime' results from demands made upon them by other ethnic minority populations, and not solely by the dominant white group. In cities like Los Angeles, the struggle between blacks and 'Latinos' is not only a struggle for position in the local labour markets or in local politics: it is also a struggle to encourage effective policing of one ethnic people in the name of effective defence against Others (Miles 1992). However these processes are understood, one widely reported study released in the early 1990s showed that approximately one-fifth of all 16- to 34-year-old black males in America were under criminal justice supervision; that three-quarters of 25- to 34-year-old

African-American school drop-outs were under justice system supervision; that three-quarters of all black prison inmates had under twelve years' schooling, and, also, that homicide had become the leading cause of death amongst African-American youth (Freeman 1991).

In Britain, where the presence of a significant black population is a product of recruitment of immigrant labour in the 1950s and 1960s – to offset a labour shortage in public transport and the health service – no new labour markets have emerged as the obvious alternative employment specifically demanding the service of young black men. By the late 1970s, unemployment amongst UK-born blacks as a whole was already four times higher (at over 20 per cent) than amongst whites born in Britain (Cross 1982: 47). There was also some evidence, as early as 1980, that the few craft apprenticeships on offer from private industry did not generally recruit young blacks, and that, regardless of aptitude or commitment, young blacks were being forced back onto the various training schemes created by Government – which have a low reputation amongst more demanding employers (Cross 1982: 46–50). Through the 1980s and 1990s, the exclusion of young black men took on new forms, as the demand for labour within the newly emergent service, high-technology and communications industries focused, increasingly, on the kinds of interpersonal skills and flexibilities more closely associated with relatively highly trained young men and women. In the meantime, young men and women in other minority populations (for example, the English Asian population, including those exiled from Uganda in the 1970s) were making use of a cultural capital and experience in commerce (the corner store) and trade (for example, in new textiles) – and following the rhetoric of the enterprise culture – to create their own employment possibilities, often as a base from which to build other professional careers. By the mid-1990s, this Darwinian competition for survival or personal position in a failing national economy was leaving the two discrete populations of young black men, on the one hand, and unskilled young poor white men struggling for 'the bottom rung' in the official labour markets, as well as in the local alternative hidden economies of crime and graft. At this level of the social formation, a specific and desperate form of tribalism was often in evidence, with young men of one ethnic group set against young men (or, sometimes, whole peoples) of other ethnic backgrounds or identities – conflicts which might be played out in ritualized confrontations in particular 'symbolic locations' (a football stadium, a public house, a playing field) at particular times of the weekend.[25] Evidence on the involvement of black English men and women in crime (and their victimization by crime) is far less extensive than for America. According to one Home Office study in 1989, about half of the 17–20-year-old 'Afro-Caribbeans' in Metropolitan London had been prosecuted for a criminal offence.[26] In July 1995, in a highly controversial speech, the Metropolitan Commissioner for Police, Paul Condon, claimed that 70 per cent of all street robberies in London were committed by black males. The response of the English courts to 'black crime' has been 'firm' and on the face of it discriminatory: according to one study, the chances of a black offender receiving a custodial sentence in broad terms are about 8 per cent higher, on average, than for whites (Hood 1992). Whatever the logic of this or other processes, the end result was a significant over-representation of black offenders in prison – some 16 per cent of the 45,490 people in jails in England and Wales on 30 June 1992 (as against only 14 per cent in 1985), and some 26 per cent of all women prisoners (Home Office Statistical Bulletin 7/93). In the meantime, the official figures released by the Home Office (widely criticized for their underestimation of this form of criminal violence[27]) reported a total of 12,199 racial incidents in 1996, up 10 per cent on 1994.[28] The British Crime Survey, based on interviews with victims, suggests that the 'true figure' in respect of annual totals of racially motivated incidents, should be something in the region of 130,000.[29]

Across Europe as a whole in the late 1990s, there was widespread evidence of increasing levels of racial tension, of increased involvement by racial minorities in crime and also of increased numbers of assaults (ranging from verbal harassment all the way through to murder) committed against ethnic minorities. In most European societies, the official statistics suggested some significant over-representation of immigrants, of both first and second generation, in the prison population (Killias 1989) and a series of different studies suggested that there was also a patterned over-representation of different migrant groups in specific forms of crime in particular countries – for example, of recently arrived North African and Eastern European women migrants in prostitution and prostitution-related crime in Italy (Pavarini 1995), or of Turkish migrants from particular regions in Turkey in the drugs trade in Germany. The Swedish criminologists Hanns von Hofer, Jerzy Sarnecki and Henrik Tham identify six distinct forms of explanations of this over-representation (Hofer et al. 1996). The more familiar explanations would include the institutionalized discrimination against minorities (particularly in the housing and labour markets) and, closely associated with this, a certain 'marginalization' in conditions of life (what others would call 'ghettoization'). They also want to recognize the *strain* between a migrant group's expectations vis-à-vis the 'host society' and the realities which that society presents to new migrants. But they think it important to recognize that there may be processes of 'selective migration' occurring, in which some proportion of migrants may come from chaotic or 'problematic' backgrounds; and they also want to recognize that the forced migrations that are now occurring across Europe (for example, from Middle or South-Eastern Europe) may be generating highly contradictory forms of cultural contact (as, for example, between Bosnian refugee families trying to adapt to the unitary welfare state social democracy of Sweden itself). These different approaches to an explanation of race-and-crime may have a different strength and importance in different locations across Europe. Hofer et al. place a particular emphasis on what they call the *ceteris paribus* argument – namely, the argument that immigrants and ethnic minorities are likely to have no different a rate of criminal involvement from that of other citizens of a society *in identical or similar structural positions* (assuming that analysts can agree on which 'structural variables' are of most consequence; cf. Lea and Young 1984: ch. 4). Hofer et al. acknowledge that the *ceteris paribus* argument is unlikely to be particularly influential during the course of agitated public debates or 'moral panics' about race-and-crime (they have no illusions about the convenience of having a 'visible minority' available as the 'obvious' scapegoat for ongoing public anxieties in respect of crime and social dislocation). What Hofer et al. do not discuss, however, is the future prospects for racial and social relations for societies in which the chances of mobility and escape from racialized enclaves of relative or absolute poverty (the existing sites of concentrated 'structural deprivation or inequality') are actually in decline, that is, when the 'zone of transition' becomes *a more or less permanent* zone of minority group residence – or what Mike Davis (1990) and Christian Parenti (1995) in the United States have called 'the new Bantustans'.

The crisis in question here is primarily a crisis for the ethnic minorities themselves – not least in terms of the future prospects of its youthful generations, even within the wider markets of the European Union. That crisis finds immediate expression in the violence committed against minority populations – for example, within the 'new Europe'. Nearly all member-states of the European Union have reported increases in the late 1980s and early 1990s in the number of incidents of violence committed against migrants, refugees and visible minorities, though the frequency and serious-ness of incidents seem to vary between different member-states and also over time. There is some evidence, for example, of an increase in the number of such incidents occurring in response to particular news items in the national press of a particular country (Bjorgo and Witte 1993: 3). Problems in the classification and measurement of these incidents have bedeviled the analysis of these perceived or reported increases in 'hate crime'. In his analysis of such hate crime in Germany and the US, Aronowitz (1994: 46) concluded that the most reliable measure of racial tension (and the likely extent of victimization) is the number of individuals identified by national police as active in 'extreme right-wing organizations' (42,100 in Germany in 1993, a slight increase on the previous year). A different diagnosis of the crisis confronting ethnic minor-ities across Europe, and especially new migrants, however, might involve a close examination of the different 'survival strategies' being adopted by these peoples in different parts of the European Union, especially in the absence of a strong and expanding official labour market. In Italy in the mid-1990s – to take one example – this would involve close scrutiny of the role of organized crime in the recruitment of women of North African and Eastern European origins ('extra-communitarians' without European Union citizenship and protection) into the mushrooming street economy of prostitution and drug trading. In a Europe in which over 20 million people on official measures are unemployed, we would expect to find immigrants in different European Union member-states pursuing many other *different survival strategies*.

CRISIS IN 'THE CULTURE'

Nearly all contemporary commentators on the condition of 'popular' and media culture speak of the existence of a condition of crisis and many of them do so using the language of postmodernist theory or via some kind of reference to 'postmodern conditions'. According to the Canadian cultural theorist Arthur Kroker, writing about the present condition of American popular television and magazines, art and political debate, the situation is not simply a crisis: it is best understood as a 'panic' situation, in which the empty space of North American culture 'naturally' calls forth violence and excess, particularly in the sphere of sexuality, as the only consumer pleasure which has not yet been finally satiated (Kroker and Cook 1986; Kroker et al. 1989). Living in America itself, another cultural theorist, Larry Grossberg, is also reduced to a desperate *cri de coeur*, 'We Gotta Get Out of this Place' (Grossberg 1994) whilst the critical criminologist-turned-critical cultural theorist Steven Pfohl, neatly turning postmodern theorists of pleasure on their head – in *Death at the Parasite Cafe* – admits to being personally terrified by a culture which appears unable to respond, for example, to the death of hundreds of thousands of feeling Iraqi young soldiers on the road to Baghdad (the infamous US Army helicopter gunners' 'turkey shoot') except as a video-game that happened to be screened on CNN television (Baudrillard 1991; Pfohl 1992).

A defining feature of this literature is its preoccupation with the cultural condition of America, and, in particular, the contradiction between the presentational hyper-modernity of the urban landscape in America and American commercial culture, on the one hand, and the 'shallowness' and ephemerality of its *lived culture*, on the other. Fredric Jameson's pioneering essay of 1984 on 'the cultural logic of late capitalism' focuses heavily on a single hotel in Los Angeles, the Bonaventura Hotel – a building in which, he argues, it is impossible 'for the individual human body to locate itself, to organize its immediate surroundings perceptually, and cognitively to map its position in a mappable external world' (Jameson 1984: 83). It is a building, we are told, which has destroyed all sense of 'the ground', or 'depth' or 'distance', and therefore the possibility of a person charting a route, as by a map, through the space it occupies. In addition, like so many other examples of hotel architecture in the United States, it is jam-packed full of statues and other artifacts (like player-pianos, which play music all day without a pianist in sight) which Jean Baudrillard would recognize as 'simulacra' – inauthentic replicas or copies of 'the real'. It is, in this sense, another piece of the hypermodernized America in which – as Baudrillard was later to say – '*nothing* is real' (Baudrillard 1988). I do not intend to advance a critique here of this particular analysis of the condition of America (cf. B. Turner and Rojek 1993). But it is important to say that the hypermodernization of the downtown core of certain American cities, as such, is a specifically American (Atlanta), Canadian (Toronto) and South-East Asian phenomenon (Singapore): it is not transparently accurate a description of the city centres of the old world (Europe). According to Arthur Vidich, it is only a partial description of America itself, substantially inattentive to the local cultures (as well as the street-scape) of small-town or rural America (Vidich 1991), which are by no means completely hegemonized by metropolitan urban culture. With respect to Los Angeles itself, Mike Davis emphasizes how unchecked commercial redevelopment has sucked up the life and soul of the old industrial city, including the city centre, leaving behind in many neighbourhoods, especially in the old industrial areas, 'junkyards of dreams' (Davis 1990), places where memory still operates in a myriad of different ways. It is also intriguing to recognize that whilst the aesthetics of commercial enterprise and innovation may have currently achieved some dominance amongst the new urban elites in North America, they are far from being so universally popular amongst the urban elites of Britain, France or Italy, for whom the exploration of the different possibilities of regeneration of old Europe remains an intriguing possibility.

These are merely empirical queries. At the core of Jameson's arguments, as well as the work of Jean Baudrillard, Zygmunt Bauman, Marshall Berman, Jean-François Lyotard and many others, is the insistence that modern society (the society of the Enlightenment) has undergone a fundamental and defining rupture, and that we live in 'postmodern' social conditions. The meaning of this 'postmodernism' varies between different commentators. For Lyotard, for example, the defining aspect of postmodernism is just the empirical fact of the demise of the 'grand narrative' – especially the Enlightenment argument that science and rationality can and will come to the aid of humankind in a progressive amelioration of the human condition (Lyotard 1984). According to Lyotard, the demise of the master narrative is, in part, an honest recognition of the horrors of the twentieth century – as witnessed, for example, in the victories of fascism. But there is also the development of *very different* modernist projects (not least, of socialism, environmentalism, feminism, and the free market): in the late twentieth century, indeed, Lyotard insists, we witness the advance of 'incommensurable teleologies'. For other postmodern critics, indeed, (like Derrida and Foucault) 'postmodernist' reality involves a collapse of all possible teleologies – the effacement, for example, of boundaries between high and low art, between television advertising and news, between any sense of standards or aesthetic codes in the adjudication of culture (Featherstone 1988). For more utopian theorists like Zygmunt Bauman (1988, 1993) postmodernism represents a new set of possibilities in social life – particularly in respect of forms of social organization, moral order or guiding regimes for individual conduct, that are respectful of 'differences' between peoples. For some feminist writers (like Carol Smart), postmodernity is to be celebrated for the defeat it has imposed on the 'master narratives' of masculinist Enlightenment thought:

> Modernity has now become associated with some of the most deep-seated intellectual problems of the end of the twentieth century. It is seen as synonymous with racism, sexism, Euro-centredness and the attempt to reduce cultural and sexual differences to one dominant set of values. Modernism is the intellectual mode of thought which has been identified as male or phallogocentric (for example, by Gilligan 1982 and Duchen 1986) and as white or Eurocentric (for example, by Dixon 1976 and Harding 1987). It is also seen as an exhausted mode, one which has failed to live up to its promise and which is losing credibility. (Smart 1990: 75)

The whole range of theoretical issues involved in the postmodern debate cannot be adjudicated here, except to insist that any jettisoning of the Enlightenment project – with its commitment, at least in rhetoric, to ideas of universalism and social justice ought really only to occur once a viable alternative programme has been identified. The idea that other objectives – the abolition of institutionalized sexism, for example – can be accomplished by individual or group action, in the absence of any guarantees (for example, in law) of formal democracy and justice and in the absence of some acceptance of notions of reasoned debate – strains credibility. It may be helpful to return to Fredric Jameson's classic paper of 1984 and his subsequent, lengthier text of the same title (Jameson, 1984, 1993). Jameson accepts that postmodernist sensibility and 'style' has taken on 'cultural dominance' – that this depthless and 'schizophrenic' cultural text is unquestionably the dominant framework or agenda, in particular in television, advertising and popular culture. But he is also very careful to note that the speedy embrace of postmodernist approaches to texts as a form of social analysis suppresses the possibility of advancing what he calls hermeneutic analysis of the content of these texts and also of the ways in which such texts may be interpreted in the broad society. He contrasts the preoccupation of postmodern theorists with *the surface* of 'the text' with what he calls the 'depth models' of social analysis which are intrinsic, first, to the hermeneutic tradition that had characterized modernist thinking about art, literature and architecture, the dialectical traditions of Marxism and critical theory, Freudian theories of all that is 'latent' or 'repressed' in manifest culture, the existential tradition and its interest in the search for individual 'authenticity' and, finally, the traditions of structuralism and semiotics, with their particular interest in the deconstruction of texts or images in terms of their underlying 'deep structures' of meanings and feeling (Jameson 1984: 62). It is in the dialectic between these flickering texts of a currently dominant postmodern sensibility, the traces of history and received culture, and human practice that the secrets of modern life are to be encountered. Even in the fast-accelerating world of cyberspace, according to Jameson – for all its obvious alienation of people from each other and its powerfully individualizing effects – we can find evidence of a 'postmodern sublime' – in which users of the personal computer and the World Wide Web are energetically pursuing some notion of an aesthetic life and some idea of communication with other distant individuals. Attention is drawn on the one hand to the new communities of friends and acquaintances apparently being created in cyberspace – but our attention is also alerted to the long-term implications of communities of citizens known primarily to each other by their log-in numbers, a new form of 'market in friendship and sociability' defined by the possession of a desk-top.

CRISES OF MASCULINITY AND THE GENDER ORDER

As a large number of criminological scholars in the academy have come to recognize and declare in recent years (e.g. Messerschmidt, 1986, 1993, 1997;

Newburn and Stanko 1994; Walklate 1995: ch. 6), the activities we come to know as 'crime' are heavily monopolized by men. In England and Wales in 1996, for example, 89.3 per cent of offenders found guilty of indictable offences in the courts were men – some 1,177,000 out of a total of 1,438,000 guilty findings.[30] In the case of some of the offences of violence which are of most serious concern to 'the population at large' and especially the potential victim population, the domination of men is even more pronounced.[31] None of this is news, for example, to that group of women journalists in Britain, like Beatrix Campbell (1993) and Suzanne Moore, who have been specializing for some years in a pointed and distinctive form of widely read social commentary on the issue of masculinity. It is arguable that it is this work of women journalists – working by preference outside the academy – that has been most influential in reorganizing thought in the broader society (and even – more slowly – within the academy itself) on the issue of gender and crime. Aided in part by a more general breakdown of the distinction between private issues and public culture, these women journalists have succeeded in the 1980s and 1990s in giving a *public voice* to those 'private understandings' of women which would previously have been unrepresented in what feminists for many years dismissed as 'the malestream' public media.

Within the body of analytical writing that has emerged within and outside the academy, however, there are several distinct if connected arguments. Most obvious is a preoccupation with *male power*. Twenty years ago, this was an argument, advanced by a large number of 'second-wave' feminist writers and activitists like Andrea Dworkin and Susan Griffin, about the silencing of gender issues, and specifically of gender inequality (but also women as victims), in forms of academic and other more-or-less public discourse that was presented in ostensibly gender-neutral terms. In general, the issue of women was 'a problem that knew no name'. In the literature of academic criminology, considerable attention was paid to the work of Carol Smart and others, powerfully arguing against the silences of hitherto-existing criminological work – notably, on the systematic, continuing, largely unrecognized and undiscussed victimization of women by different kinds of crime (Smart 1976). Subsequent work by Betsy Stanko, Rebecca and Russell Dobash and others gave expression to the fears of violence and assault which, it was argued, had been silently taken for granted within a gender order and for which there was no public recognition (Stanko 1985, 1990; Dobash and Dobash 1979).[32] In the meantime, also in the 1970s, Angela McRobbie prised open the gendered preoccupations of hitherto-existing 'subcultural theory' within criminology and the sociology of deviance, as an essentially male field of work, directing its gaze exclusively to the close examination (and, she might have added, the critical appreciation) of the activities of other (young) men, with very little interest being displayed analytically in the male-ness of such subcultures or the absence of women from the analytical picture (McRobbie and Garber 1975; McRobbie 1980). In the United States, this angry glimpsing by 'second-wave feminism' of the routine working of male power, as a set of practices marginalizing and silencing women, quickly gave rise to a forceful and extensive literature on other key aspects of this powerful masculinity – not least, it was argued, its ability to suppress, both in routine masculinist practice and in male-dominated disciplines like criminology, the importance of violence against women. In this perspective, subsequently identified by Sandra Harding with an epistemology that she called 'standpoint feminism', the objective was to expose the manifold and hitherto invisible workings of 'the patriarchy', and to lay out new and separate agendas for feminist action (Harding 1991). It is fair to comment that this second-wave approach to the understanding of 'male power' or 'the patriarchy' is now widely seen to be an essentially self-confirming and reductionist form of argument, in the sense of providing only a description of the violent totalitarianism of many of these men who eventually appear in criminal trials – but not yielding an explanatory account of the nature of masculinity *per se*.

One of the most promising developments in the project of theorizing the social and political articulation (coding and distribution) of masculinity is to be found in the work of the Australian feminist Bob Connell, now working in America (1987, 1995) (cf. also Carrigan, Connell and Lee 1985). In the first of his two major books, in particular, Connell advances the defining and organizing notion of what he calls 'hegemonic masculinity'. There is a structure – or *gender order* – which is 'society-wide' (and not confined to interpersonal relations or the individual psyche) and which also appears to have characterized Communist as well as capitalist societies, at least in the twentieth century. This is to say that there is a kind of preordained ordering or relationship of power enjoyed by men over women in most known twentieth-century societies, and also that this relationship of power has largely been taken for granted (and constructed almost as a form of common sense in most known societies). The forms assumed by masculinity have, in that sense, been 'hegemonic' in precisely the sense in which other forms of social and economic power were so described by Antonio Gramsci – they were reproduced in and through popular culture and common sense, rather than being, for example, in this instance the product of an organized male conspiracy. Connell sees this hegemony as 'a social ascendancy achieved in a play of social forces that extends beyond contests of brute power into the organization of private life and cultural processes' (Carrigan et al. 1985: 184). Or, as he immediately elaborates the point, in faithfully Gramscian a manner: 'Ascendancy of one group of men over another achieved at the point of a gun, or by the threat of unemployment, is not hegemony. Ascendancy which is embedded in religious doctrine and practice, mass media content, wage structures, the design of houses, welfare-taxation policies and so forth is.' This perspective conceives of male power, then, not in any direct sense as the exercise of physical force or coercion (though it can involve both) but rather as the routine *structure of practices* or within a given gendered division of social labour, 'naturally' associated, in particular societies at particular historical moments, with the differential allocation of men and boys or women and girls to particular and different social tasks, roles and responsibilities.

In his more recent work, Connell has developed this particular model of 'masculinity' in several important ways. He notes, for example, how the kinds of practices and values involved in a 'hegemonic masculinity' may be exhibited only by quite small numbers of men, but how, nonetheless, 'the majority of men gain from its hegemony, since they benefit from the patriarchal divided, the advantage men in general gain from the overall subordination of women' (Connell, 1995: 79). This routine 'complicity' of men as a whole in gender orders hegemonized by 'masculinist' values and practices is one key element in the ongoing reproduction of this form of masculinity, even though the men who reap 'the patriarchal dividend' may 'also respect their wives and mothers, and never be violent towards women, and do their accustomed share of the housework' (Connell 1995: 80). One of the chains which holds this complicity of men to the gender order in place is what Connell, following Freud, calls 'the structure of cathexis' involved in the gender order (Connell 1987: 111) – namely, that mix of emotional and psychic investments which are made by men with significant members of the opposite sex – for example, by male infants' emotional dependency on the mother, on the one hand, and the fixation by the pubescent male adolescent on 'woman' either a Madonna (the mother made sublime) or a Whore.

We shall return to some of Connell's themes, as initially outlined here, in the discussion of 'the crisis of families and parenting' in the next section. The point to emphasize is Connell's insistence on seeing gender relations, and the gender order, as 'a social pattern' (produced 'in history' and also productive of future history) rather than as some fixed division of labour naturally and one-dimensionally produced by biological difference, some set of more or less trans-historical normative patterns or what he calls 'fixed character types' (Connell 1995: 81). Connell's approach also identifies the potentiality of any particular formulation of masculinity, *to encounter crisis*, rather than assuming that there is always an effortless assimilation into hegemonic masculinity and the hegemonic gender order. He focuses, for example, in a series of life-history interviews, on the attempts of homosexually or bisexually active men, 'new men' involved in the radical environmentalist movement and newly affluent men of the professional middle class to construct new configurations or stances towards the dominant gender order, giving some form and expression to their own preferred and 'non-traditional' version of masculinity. But he also spends considerable space investigating the angry and violent form of masculinity he encountered in a group of unemployed young men encountered in the early 1990s in Sydney, Australia. Connell introduces his discussion of these young men's 'masculinity', very much in line with the observations at the opening of this first chapter, in noting how:

> In the wake of the economic downturn in the 1970s, it is estimated that thirty million people were out of work in the OECD countries. Unemployment or underemployment is chronic in less developed economies. Large numbers of youth are growing up without any expectation of the stable employment around which familiar models of working-class masculinity were organized. Instead, they face intermittent employment and economic marginality in the long term, and often severe deprivation in the short term. (Connell 1995: 93–4)

The daily life of these young men involved a predictable routine of 'school resistance, minor crime, heavy drug use/alcohol use, occasional manual labour, motorbikes or cars, short heterosexual liaisons (and violence)' (1995: 110), more or less enthusiastically defended by these young men in coarse and aggressive fashion, but constantly appearing to land them in various forms of trouble with the police, other young men and, indeed, with women. Connell sees this to be a caricature of the masculinity of the unskilled industrial worker from an earlier historical period (for example, 'the navvy' or the unskilled road worker), but a masculinity which – in the absence of any large number of industrial workplaces – is marginal to the mainstream, reconstructed gender order. Connell summarizes this set of gender practices as 'protest masculinity', which he defines as a 'marginalized masculinity, which picks up themes of masculinity in the society at large but reworks them in the context of poverty' (1995: 114).

Unlike the 'profane' masculinities of the navvy (as described for English young men in the 1970s by Paul Willis (1977, 1978), Connell's protesting young men are not located in any set of familiar social institutions (the workplace, a neighbourhood pub, or a football terrace) and they contribute little or nothing to the dominant economy. They are in these senses fundamentally disconnected from the wider civil society (they have no 'stake' in it) and they feel no sense of membership of that society. Their relationship to women has to be understood in that light: the possibility of marriage to a woman taking on the role of domestic servant and support has been more or less extinguished by the logic of recent social and economic change. Young men have increasingly had to 'find a place' (in both employment and cultural terms) and have had to adjust to local labour markets in which employment possibilities, albeit of an insecure and part-time character, are actually more widespread for women than for men. Borrowing from the ego-psychology of Alfred Adler, Connell suggests that there is an intensified need for unskilled young men in deindustrialized areas (in the interest of their own fragile 'egos') to reject the competition of more socially powerful women by any means possible – in order to try and keep women subordinate, and to insist on the continuing reality of 'feminine weakness'. This might indeed involve the use of muscle power. His argument is that this is at the core of much contemporary violence against women, as well as the threatening displays in which young men engage, in colonizing particular stretches of public space (bus stations, rail stations, high street corners and car parks). It is precisely this form of masculinity which is so vividly described by the journalist Beatrix Campbell in her best-selling narrative account of the riots of the early 1990s on British council estates (1993), with the one difference that Campbell takes the psychoanalytical argument further in her specifically Freudian reading of some aspects of the marauding of these angry and dislocated young men (for example, in their physical destruction of the local community centres, run by young mothers and other women of the local community) as exhibiting some aspects of the Death Wish.

There is no question but that 'the fear of crime' discussed throughout this book reduces for many people to a practical and empirical fear, precisely, of these angry young men – whether in the immediate neighbourhood of residence or in some other public places in the wider conurbation. In the study I completed, with Karen Evans and Penny Fraser, of the two North of England cities of Manchester and Sheffield in the early 1990s, this was probably the most widely expressed fear with respect to their routine use of the wider city, on the part of women of all different backgrounds, children and adolescents and also by other men (see Taylor, Evans and Fraser, 1996: chs 8, 9, 10). So 'fear of angry (protest) masculinity' in the form it assumes within public space, in a society like Britain's, has become a kind of *general fear* among many publics – analogous, perhaps, and also additional to the fears which many women have had (until very recently without recognition or support on the part of wider public institutions) of the violence of angry men in their private and domestic lives.

CRISES OF THE FAMILY AND PARENTING

There is nothing specifically contemporary about an anxious public debate over 'the condition of the family' or over the quality of parenting. In late nineteenth-century America, for example, anxiety over the widespread involvement of young people from the mushrooming urban centres in delinquency famously gave birth to the development, amongst women of the new commercial middle class, of the 'child-saving' movement, dedicated to rescuing children from the cultural depravations of 'the ghetto' and the slum, in this way contributing, it was hoped, to the social peace of industrial America (Platt 1969). Rather later, in the aftermath of the Second World War, in both North America and Europe, there was another outburst of social and political anxiety over the condition of youth and its contribution to delinquency and social disorder, focused, in particular, on the problems of young people who had been deprived of the 'normal' socialization of the two-parent family, because of the exigencies of war. In Britain the anxieties over this wartime generation found both theoretical expression in John Bowlby's theories of delinquency as a product of under-socialization and failure of attachment on the part of adolescent young men resulting from the absence of the 'exemplary' figure of the father (Bowlby 1946) and also, rather later, empirical form in a widely publicized Home Office study by Leslie Wilkins which purported to demonstrate statistically the existence and continuing activity of 'a delinquent generation' of disruptive orphans and/or other youthful casualties of wartime broken families (Wilkins 1960). The influence of these widespread anxieties over cohorts of delinquent young people, suffering from a deficit of socialization as a result of wartime separation, is seen by many scholars to have contributed definitively to the reforms in the juvenile justice system in England and Wales during the 1950s and 1960s, and, in particular, to the overwhelming emphasis on the delivery of 'care' for such young people, in the name of their social 'rehabilitation' (see e.g. J. Clarke 1980).[33]

From the 1960s onwards, however, a variety of new theories of youthful and familial disorder and pathology have emerged, most especially (though not exclusively) in the instantaneous forms of 'popular criminology' in television and newspaper responses to particular incidents of juvenile crime and wrongdoing. In Britain, indeed, many of these theoretical arguments about the failures of the family and of parents were powerfully distilled in the pained national debate that followed the murder in February 1993 of the two-year-old Jamie Bulger (as it turned out, by two ten-year-old boys). On other occasions, the problem of youthful crime was very specifically attributed to a very particular problem of 'parenting' – namely, the rise of the single-parent (specifically, the single-mother) 'family' – which, in the refrain of most of the popular press and much of the broadsheet press – was *by very definition* an inadequate vehicle for the socialization of young people as 'responsible' and conforming adults.

Underpinning this kind of popular criminology – for all that it was and is so often presented simply as 'common sense' – is a particular vision (indeed, theory) of the 'normal' family – a more or less nuclear family, comprising two adults, male and female, and an unspecified number of children, sharing with other agencies (notably local schools and, perhaps, churches) the responsibility of education and socialization of the next generation. In some Marxist criticisms of this popular theory of the family, indeed – drawing on Engels's pamphlet of the early nineteenth century – the argument is reformulated: the nuclear family *is* 'normal' in the sense that it is the preferred (or, indeed, 'functional') domestic arrangement for supporting the organization of productive labour in nineteenth-century industrial capitalism (Zaretsky 1976). Saying this, however, is not to say that 'the family' (at least in the form it assumed in the context of the development of mass manufacturing capitalism throughout the nineteenth century) – even when it was formally successful in its role in socializing children – was experienced as a source of personal reward and well-being for all its members, and particularly, of course, for women. In this respect, the widely quoted analysis of the family as an instrument of oppression on women offered in *The Second Sex* by Simone de Beauvoir (1974) and, in the field of social theory, by Michèle Barrett (1980) and then by Michèle Barrett and Mary McIntosh (1982) builds on a long tradition. There has been a persistent critique *throughout* the twentieth century of the inequalities of material reward and of esteem involved in the 'patriarchal' family of the industrial working class, finding expression in England, for example, in continuing polemical critiques in the lively socialist press of the period (see e.g. Pallister 1929; Horrabin 1935), but also in the account by Robert Roberts of the gender order of families living in the slums of Salford in the first quarter of the twentieth century (1971), as well as in a range of critical reflections on the working-class family in feminist novels published in the post-war period for example, in Pat Barker's *Union Street* (1982). In the 1960s, the accusation made by the 'anti-psychiatry' school of R. D. Laing that the domestic family was the originating source of 'schizophrenia', particularly amongst young women, because of the 'double-bind' that it places on children to become independent adults whilst simultaneously being grateful and dependent children (Bateson et al. 1956; Laing and

Esterson 1964), added to the range of criticism being made of the family as an oppressive form.

The critique of the family as an oppressive institution delivered by the women's movement and from anti-psychiatrists, especially when voiced on mass broadcast television in the late 1960s and 1970s, provoked an immediate and angry reaction, especially in America – most notably, in this period, in the sanctification of Motherhood (Anita Bryant's 'Real Women's movement', initiated as a response to emergence of the Gay Liberation movement) as a more or less religious vocation (Gordon and Hunter 1977–8). These arche-typically suburban American sentiments were given great support in this period, not only by television evangelists but also by the newly emerging popular movements of the 'New Right', not least because of the sentimental preference of the free-market Right for civil and familial life as an alternative to the lived, democratic idea of 'community' but in particular their active dislike of State-provided solutions to social problems. In the mid-1970s, however, these popular movements 'of the emotion' were given some philo-sophical support in the newly published writing of a number of intellectuals of the Right, many of whom had previously been associated, in one way or another, with the liberal-progressivism of the New Deal period, but who were now changing direction.[34] In 1975, one of the best-known of these intellec-tuals, James Q. Wilson, Professor of Political Science at Harvard, published a broadside attack on liberalism in criminology, *Thinking about Crime*, which quickly became a best-seller in American bookstores. *Thinking about Crime* identifies the central contradiction of the United States in the mid-1970s as the existence of massive levels of 'predatory crime' in a 'society of affluence', and argues that the source of this contradiction is to be found in the failure of the family to perform its required role as an agency of socialization. In Wilson's apparently benign account, this failure of the family was in part to be attributed to demographic change: the sheer numbers of children born during the early post-war period ('the baby-boomers' or what Wilson called 'the invading army') presented parents (the 'defending army') with 'a magnitude of socialization tasks' (especially in respect of the management of 'affluence') which they could not hope to fulfil. In other, rather less benign, accounts of the failure of the family which began to be produced (initially) outside the academy in the 1970s, however, the problems facing the family were seen without ambiguity as a pernicious consequence of the rise of the Women's Liberation and Gay movements. The righteous anger which these move-ments provoked, particularly in America outside the metropolitan centres, is a subject for analysis in and of itself (and such analysis would clearly help inform an understanding of the renaissance of a religious fundamentalism and right-wing populism in that country through the following twenty years). One of the persistent refrains in this reaction against the Women's Liberation movement in particular, however, was the effect which it was having (in its encouragement of the independence of women) on 'the family' and, not least, it was argued, on the effective nurturing and socialization of young children.[35] There were particularly angry responses from this broad, popular mass of working parents to speeches, pamphlets or academic texts from leading spokespeople for the women's movements which appeared to dis-value or to undermine the everyday responsibilities which these working parents felt they had assumed for their children.[36]

In the 1980s this particular refrain has been considerably elaborated, particularly in the United States, around two new themes: the rise of the 'dual-career' family and the issue of the single-parent (read, single-mother) family. In the United States, in particular, the phenomenon of the dual-career family became ever more widespread through the late 1970s and 1980s. In 1986 54 per cent of married women in the United States were working in the 'waged labour market', compared with only 23 per cent in 1950 (Hochschild 1990: 2). The entry of women into the labour market was clearly influenced by a change in the aspirations of women – most notably a desire for self-regard, independently of their partners – but also a desire for some freedom from dependence on the wage of the working man (the 'family wage' so celebrated by the male leaderships of the trade union movement, but so often resented by women for the unchallenged power it accorded men in the 'private sphere' of the family).

An additional factor driving the entry of women into the labour market in the 1970s and 1980s, however, was the increasing difficulty which a very large number of American families were facing in the struggle to avoid falling actually into poverty, as identified in official statistics. Within the enormous American middle class, at the same time, adults and parents were increasingly finding that a second income was essential, in the ongoing struggle to maintain an accustomed standard of living. Across America and Canada in the 1970s and 1980s, a major transformation took place in the social organiza-tion of domestic life, as the number of households involved in the production of two incomes, and the pursuit of two adult careers, increased exponentially, and a concomitant change took place in the organization of domestic time, the re-scheduling of the decision to have children, and the reorganization of parent–child relationships. One particular, practical aspect of the latter was the deployment of young children in various different kinds of 'pre-school' or child-minding arrangement, in an ongoing daily partnership with working parents. Another key aspect was a general 'acceleration' of everyday life, characterized by increasingly complicated personal and domestic timetables, a reduction in amount of personal leisure time, and, according to many medical surveys, significant increases in exhaustion, stress and illness (not least amongst working women themselves, engaged in the waged labour market and, very frequently, also responsible for the 'second shift' of domes-tic labour at home). Another key aspect of the rise of the dual-career household, as emphasized by Amitai Etzioni (1993) was the diminished presence of adults in local neighbourhoods during the day, with the con-sequences this might be having for the more general surveillance of youthful activity in the neighbourhood, and also for any chance of sustaining a community built around continuing social contact and exchange between generations or voluntarism (see Bellah et al. 1985; Putnam 1996). In some of the commentaries on the 'dual-career' phenomenon in America, indeed, the perception was dawning that the workplace itself was becoming the only source for most adults of a social or community life, and that the domestic sphere was increasingly viewed as an *obstacle* to full participation in social life (i.e. in the workplace) and, therefore, a danger to the career prospects of the working adult. There seems little doubt, for example, that this recognition (that 'domestic responsibilities' were seen as an obstacle to career advancement in a competitive labour market) was a key element in the rapid increases taking place in divorce and separation in the United States in the 1970s and 1980s. As is so often the case in the United States, these strains in the family were glimpsed and most dramatically portrayed in a Hollywood movie, *Home Alone*, released by Twentieth Century Fox in 1990; by the mid-1990s, the American courts were dealing with cases in which children were bringing their own parents to court – on the one hand, to sue for independence from parents, and, on the other, to try to enforce parental divorce.

The second familial issue to have provoked enormous levels of anxiety in the United States in the 1980s was the increase in the proportion of American families headed by single parents, but particularly by single women (see table 2).

Table 2 Percentage of female-headed households, no husband present, USA, 1950–1983

Year	% of total families
1950	9.4
1960	10.0
1970	10.8
1975	13.0
1980	14.6
1983	15.4

Source: US Bureau of the Census, presented in W. J. Wilson 1987: 65

This American debate of the 1980s on 'single parents', and especially the 'single-mother' family, is heavily focused on the disproportionate representation of inner-city black families within this overall social trend, and the disastrous consequences which the absence of the father was thought to be having on the socialization of new generations of young black men (W. J. Wilson 1987).[37] In 1980, 57 per cent of all black births in the United States occurred 'outside marriage' and 43 per cent of all black households were headed by women (1987: 21). In Wilson's account, the rise of the single-mother family in the black inner city was a product, in part, of the catastrophic demise of manufacturing industry in the older industrial cities, but it was also a function of the particular *concentration* of other exclusionary effects that have operated on urban blacks in America, for example in the housing market. The general effect of current logic of the inner-city labour market, which holds out little opportunity for black men of any age, is to underwrite the reproduction of black men as a permanent kind of underclass, excluded more or less by definition from the legitimate labour markets of the broader society.

Many of the developments in the 'family form' in America, and the relationship of the family to the broader civil society, have been repeated elsewhere, though it is important to note the unevenness in the developments across different societies, and to try to understand the sources of this unevenness. The increase in divorce in Britain, for example (a *sevenfold increase* between 1962 and 1992; Utting, Bright and Henricson 1993) was a significantly higher rate of increase than in most European societies (and was measured in 1993 at 2.9 per 100,000 people in 1992 compared to a European Union average of 1.6).[38] Britain also has a far greater number of single-parent families than most other member-states of the European Community (see

Table 3 Percentage of women aged 20 to 39 living alone with children, European Community, 1991

	%
Italy	2.3
Greece	2.4
Spain	2.9
Luxembourg	3.4
The Netherlands	4.5
Portugal	5.7
Ireland	6.2
France	6.6
Belgium	7.1
Germany	7.7
United Kingdom	10.1

Danish figures not available.
Source: Eurostat, 2 Dec. 1993

table 3). The condition of young people (and the relationship of young people to crime in market societies) will be discussed in more detail in chapter 3. For the moment, let us consider four connected difficulties that are involved in any purely 'familial' explanation of crime.

It is important, first, to be aware that the attempt to *explain* crime in terms of a child's experience of socialization has been associated, historically, with a simple-minded version of positivistic psychology, in which the 'presenting behaviours' of a difficult or delinquent child are denied any contemporary rationality (like 'poverty') and almost always located in the 'psychic disturbances' of early life.[39] This emphasis in such positivistic accounts on 'the primacy of primary socialization' was first noted, with characteristic panache, by Jock Young in 1975:

> Deviancy [is seen as being] determined by factors operating in the far past of the individual. There is a split between 'real time' and 'actual time'. Real time has causal significance and is located in the traumas or deprivations of the past which are repeatedly enacted in the future. Actual time is relevant only to the extent that the individual encounters 'precipitating circumstances' which bring out the underlying 'real-time' predispositions. Thus, if we can explain deviant behaviour in terms of events which happened ten years ago, we are doing well;

if we can explain them in the first five years of the actor's life we are doing excellently, but if we can do so in terms of the individual's autonomic nervous system or chromosome structure, that is science! (Young 1975: 65)

Closely associated with the often spurious claim to scientific neutrality in such positivism, of course, was a programme of correctionalist intervention into the lives of delinquent individuals and the problematic families from which they were said to come, always conducted, it was argued, 'in the child's own best interests' (Schorr 1974), though other studies suggested that the altruistic interventions very often intensified the commitments of individuals so identified to delinquent or institutional careers (see e.g. Lerman 1975).

What has become clear in the 1990s is that the earlier disavowal by critical commentators of the positivistic approach to the 'measurement' of social and individual problems – born, as this was, of a political and moral objection to the 'oppressive' therapies and systems of correction with which these approaches were historically associated – may have involved some over-reaction. One of the potential strengths of positivist quantification is the way in which it can dramatize the 'organic character' of particular social processes – that is, the ways in which certain effects (for example, the predictable reproduction of inequality itself or, for that matter, the reproduction of the tendency to violence in particular neighbourhoods or socially situated households) may be a given – organic – outcome of these specific social and economic arrangements. One does not have to accept positivism's claim to the status of science to see the utility of Harvey Brenner's work in the United States in the 1980s, exploring the highly patterned effects, in terms of physical illness and early death, of the spread of unemployment (Brenner 1971, 1977, 1978). So also one can see the importance of the statistical evidence being collected by psychologists, psychiatrists and others in Britain linking the rapidly increasing rates of bullying and conflict in schoolchildren, and assaults and violence amongst adolescents, not simply to the overall loss of employment possibilities, but quite specifically to the stressed and troubled relationships that characterize the parental home (James 1995, ch. 1).

But the second problematic aspect of the positivistic identification of 'primary socialization' or the 'problem family' was the moral absolutism built into such accounts. Nearly always the assumed model of appropriate or adequate socialization was the patriarchal nuclear family, dominated for practical purposes by a male breadwinner, sequestered off from the intimacy of the family in the real world of mental or physical work outside the home, but held together in emotional terms by the mother.[40] What this kind of theological celebration of the 'nuclear family' always ignored was the potentiality or the actuality of violence (frequently, though not exclusively, directed at women) and other abuse (especially of children) within the 'private sphere' of the 'conventional' nuclear family itself. What it also dismissed were the critiques of 'the family' that were mounted both by the anti-psychiatrists in the 1960s and by feminists in the 1970s, identifying the institution of the family as a source of oppression and inequality of respect and value. In this literature, the 'bourgeois family' was often subjected to more scathing critique than the less-fortunate families from elsewhere within the social formation. The attempts taking place in most market societies in the 1990s to re-establish the family as an all-encompassing, protective shield for children from a threatening outside world are troubling, not least for their undemocratic character (artificially protecting the next generation from the experience of sharing public space and 'collaboration' with mixed and diverse cross-sections of the general public). Nor either is it clear what those celebrating the nuclear family *per se* as a hedge against crime would say about the spate of murders and other incidents of violence (committed for material gain or simply 'for thrills') that have been reported in California,[41] Italy[42] and Scotland in the 1990s, committed by young people *within* extremely well-established and 'respectable' nuclear families. In 1993, in the United States, the attempt by one fourteen-year-old in Florida 'to divorce herself' from her biological parents was accompanied by a pained national debate over 'the implosion' (*sic*) of 'the traditional family unit', born of the excessive stresses being imposed on this kind of family unit to carry the burden of broader social change.[43]

To allude to these incidents is to identify the third major problem in the particular, contemporary celebration of 'the family' and 'parenting' as a hedge against youthful crime and disorder. James Q. Wilson in the 1970s was clearly aware that this delegation of responsibility for socialization of children in High Modern America to the family alone placed a very heavy burden on the family institution. What he could not do – since he believed so little in the capacity of government and was not very obviously a theologian – was to think of an alternative. If the family was failing in the 'magnitude of socialization tasks' imposed upon it in the 1970s, however, how much more difficult are those responsibilities in the postmodern, privatized and fearful 1990s? A host of studies in the United States, Britain and other Western societies have highlighted the intensification of fear and anxiety associated with the use of public space in general, but specifically with the use of public facilities for leisure (the public park, public playing fields) or travel. Young children's travel to and from school is increasingly undertaken by car rather than unaccompanied on foot. The leisure life of the young child is increasingly focused inwards on the private sphere of the household, whether around the television and video, or (in the middle-class household) computer games and the World Wide Web). The 'public world' is increasingly experienced only at a distance or else in a mediated form, especially via an increasingly postmodernist mass media, in which the previously separate worlds of the child, adolescent and adult are increasingly elided or effaced. In the late 1990s, it really is *not* clear what 'the family' is being recommended to be, and it is no surprise that in these circumstances, in the United States but also in Britain and other societies, there is a strong, in part nostalgic, support (but no clear social-structural set of supports) for a 'return to basics',[44] that is, for 'traditional' or past family forms.

These are some of the problems in the current refrains indicting the family for its failures in the struggle against crime and individual trouble. The constant theme in the literature on the family and on parents' responsibilities with respect to children and individual trouble is the *quality* of the parent–

child relationship. The reference to 'quality of relationships' is a common feature of all such literature – from the positivistic and behaviourist analysis of the Gluecks (1950), through the psychoanalytically influenced work of Urie Bronfenbrenner (1976), and on into the urgent policy thinking of contemporary crime-prevention 'experts' (Utting, Bright and Henricson 1993). Literature outlining the really appropriate socialization of children and young people for life in market society is rather harder to come by. But, as I will argue in chapter 2, it is that transition – to 'life in market society' – which is having the most fundamental impact on the social relations and the personality-formation of the young in the last years of the twentieth century.

2

THE NINTH TRANSITION: THE RISE OF MARKET SOCIETY

As was described in chapter 1, there are several different accounts of the 'ground shift' that has occurred in many Western societies during the 1980s and 1990s (perhaps most notably in the United States, the United Kingdom and New Zealand) in the direction of 'free market' economic policies (see e.g. Hall and Jacques 1990). All these different accounts would recognize the forceful development of a new 'policy consensus' amongst most political and economic elites during this period – namely, that the days of the centrally managed Keynesian mixed economy, tied into a set of corporatist arrangements with individual national governments or public local authorities, were numbered. This wisdom seems to have received additional encouragement after the 'oil shocks' of the early 1980s (Piore and Sabel 1984) and, later, by the anxieties being experienced over the capacity of Western economies, as then organized, to compete with the then fast-developing 'tiger economies' of South-East Asia.

It will be an important future project for historians to trace the different trajectories of the emergence of 'free market' thinking and policy-development in different Western societies. In New Zealand, for example, the sudden strong articulation of a version of market thinking into national policy occurred as a result of struggles for leadership taking place within the organized Labour Party, and the subsequent experiment in free market policy-making (signified, in that country, as the 'User Pays' philosophy) occurred within the New Zealand Labour Party itself – without there being any major pressure group or social movement activity in support of such 'reforms' (Shirley 1990). In the United States, by contrast, the vastly increased emphasis placed during the 1980s on 'liberating' 'the market' from the constraints of Big Government was very evidently the result of some years of activity by a 'Free Enterprise' lobby (Steinfels 1977; Edsall 1984). This massive lobby of business interest organizations and committedly liber-tarian and individualistic spokespeople engaged in intense ideological work over many years – attempting, above all, to equate all societies where there was almost any form of State involvement in economic activity with the old and decaying Soviet Union, with its self-evident lack of (American-style) democracy and its failing economy. In Britain, in the late 1970s and early 1980s, the transformation was accompanied by similar kinds of ideological work – orchestrated, in part, through the leadership of the new Thatcherite government itself, extolling the value and potential of market libertarianism and coercive statism to be found in the writings of Ferdinand von Hayek and Milton Friedman, as an answer to the problems of an ailing British economy (Gamble 1979). In the nervous cultural climate and the fast shift of political priorities that characterized the Western world generally in the early 1980s, there was at least one crucial elision. Social-democratically minded economists like Alec Nove (1983) were arguing that a 'market economy' (rather than command economy) was now the only conceivable arrangement for the organization of productive activity in a modern society, and also the only way of ensuring efficiency in the distribution and consumption of goods.[1] Following the earlier example of Karl Polanyi in *The Great Transformation* (1944), however, great care was being taken to distinguish between socially embedded activities of trade and exchange which ought to be left to the market, and the issue of the provision of essential services (for example, in health, education and fundamental welfare) which should always be publicly provided as a form of 'social insurance' in the strong sense of that term. A 'market economy' must coexist with, and perhaps prosper on the back of, a publicly organized form of civil society. For many pure free market theorists of the 1980s, however, it was clear that the objective was actually a fully-fledged 'market *society*', in which:

> all other principles of social or institutional organization become eroded or subordinated to the overarching one of private gain. Alternative sources of livelihood, of social support, and of cultural value – even of personal identity – become increasingly obliterated, so that individuals, families and communities are more and more dependent on what we sometimes misleadingly call 'the free market' to provide for ... human needs – not only material needs, but also cultural, symbolic and psychic ones as well. (Currie 1990: 1)

Currie's idea of a 'market society' is a general reference, therefore, to a society in which *everything* (from consumer goods to public good(s), like health or educational opportunity) is 'for sale' (cf. Kuttner 1996). In a series of important papers, Currie has offered the additional argument – that it is precisely in societies which have embraced the idea of 'market society' that the level of dislocation to civil society (as expressed, most specifically, in the level of crime) has been most marked (Currie 1990, 1995a). In particular, he argued, the United States in the late 1980s constituted a kind of negative exemplar of what happens in a society when its leadership embraces the full range of free market ideas, including the liberation of market forces into civil society itself. There were five dimensions to Currie's formulation in 1990 of the indictment of market society, which can be paraphrased as follows.

1 'Market society' had promoted crime through its production of significant increase in inequality, in the process generating quite destructive concentrations of very pronounced economic deprivation.

2 'Market society' had eroded the capacity of local communities to provide support for people on an informal basis or through municipal or civic provision. One expression of this absence of public facilities and public provision is the ongoing production of a population of young people in public spaces (supermarket parking lots or neighbourhood street corners etc.) contributing to local fears and anxieties.

3 The advance of 'market society' is a key factor, in ways discussed in the last section of this chapter, in the stresses and strains imposed on the family unit, especially in respect of child-care and the socialization of children. In the United States, a larger number of studies point to the destructive consequences of the 'acceleration' of domestic life, on the one hand, and an explosion in the number of 'latch-key children', on the other, produced by the continuing struggles of two working adults to maintain what is thought to be an adequate domestic income.

4 The advance of 'market society' in the United States has been accompanied by a continuing and apparently unrelenting campaign either to withdraw public provision of different kinds of welfare or to offer such forms of welfare through the private market (see Block, Cloward, Ehrenreich and Piven 1987). This 'privatization of welfare' has been particularly marked in the sphere of care for the elderly, but has spread outwards to many other areas of welfare provision which, in the earlier, Fordist period, would have been offered through local or national government.

5 Currie argued that the advance of 'market society' had been accompanied by the development of what he called 'a culture of Darwinian competition' for status and resources – a competivity that was particularly apparent, he argued, in the sphere of consumption but which was also evident in 'the struggle for position' in the established labour markets (career struggles) as well as in young people's struggle to enter such a market.

Currie's arguments here have found an echo in the work of the British psychiatrist Oliver James, highlighting the recent, rapid emergence in Britain of a 'winner–loser culture' (James 1995). Associated with this, however – in ways which Currie does not discuss – is a much more general cultural (and actually political) process which works to *naturalize* the generalized extension of market competition, and therefore market provision, into many different spheres of life as a kind of *modern-day common sense* – a measure of the spokesperson's 'realistic' grasp of the modern world. I can allude only briefly to the way in which the development of this form of market common sense has worked, in a society like Britain, to produce certain ideological effects. As Raymond Williams argued in *Towards 2000* (1983), market common sense has worked to place the idea of 'consumption' at the centre of everyday lived experience. So advertising has become at least as important a cultural script, for example, as the evening television news. In the meantime, real problems in the organization of work – skilling up the labour force with the new technology – are ignored, except through the imposition of punitive sanctions resulting from different kinds of performance measures or league tables. The elevation of the consuming individual as the new sovereign subject of capitalism is also accompanied by new discourses of freedom and 'entitlement' – for example, 'the right to buy' public housing through to a range of new charters of consumer rights and entitlements, which legislate in the abstract for the provision of services (for example, public transport) via cut-throat competitive markets. These 'discourses of freedom' organized around the sovereign consuming individual have an expansionist and colonial character, working outwards from the traditional locations of consumption – the shopping centres or the high streets – via other areas of life that have historically been dominated by private purchasing (accident and life insurance) to other spheres of social activity now being made available for 'commodification' (the purchase of private education, private sports and leisure facilities, and, of course, the purchase of private security at the place of work and in the area of private residence).

With Elliott Currie, Oliver James, and very many others, I want to direct attention to these different *disabling and disorganizing features of the 'market society'* rather than simply being distracted by its rhetoric of liberation. I would argue that this particular dimension of recent social change in Western societies – that is, the crisis in previously existing forms of corporatist economic organization (the planned mixed economy, dominated by national governmental input, and the replacement of such economic arrangements by 'the free market') is, in two different senses, the most definitive of my nine social crises of the late twentieth century. First, as will be argued later, 'the market' is now a *fundamental* motor force in contemporary social and political discourse and practice, in a way that it was not in the 1970s. 'The market' is *hegemonic* in the realm of discourse, and in very many practices (including some domains of that most resistant area of all, the public sector). To draw on Raymond Williams's way of thinking the dynamic character of cultural shifts, 'the market' has moved from being the *'emergent'* or indeed *'oppositional'* culture it was in the late 1970s (opposing the discursive formation associated with the mixed economy and the welfare state) into a position of *dominance* (Williams 1974). What were identified in the 1970s as 'progressive' ideas (and also as a given feature of future social life) – for example, the idea of 'public service' itself (out-of-hours activities by teachers, *pro bono* work by lawyers, voluntary work by citizens in the broader community) – have now been reconstituted in everyday common sense as *'residual'* ideas, out-of-date and out-of-place.

A second important consequence, I want to argue, of the emergence of market society is the development of new forms of social inequality. Individual citizens of market society can simultaneously occupy a range of different positions within market society and the source and provenance of these different market-positions may not be explicable in terms of the traditional determinants of class, gender and race. Individuals' positions of disadvantage within the labour markets of market society, for example, may still be a function, to some degree, of a lower class position as traditionally defined within the old Fordist manufacturing-based economy, but they may also be a function of geography (and, in that sense, accidents of birth). This disadvantage may be more pronounced in some urban regions than others, depending on the strategy of re-industrialization being attempted in different regions (Lawless, Martin and Hardy 1998). In some local labour markets, for example, women are very much more successful than men in the search for employment. But women's escape from the subordinate position they occupied within the gender order of the broad Fordist society may simultaneously be subject to significant challenge in the culture – as in the manufactured revival of 'laddish' culture in Britain in the late 1990s. As suggested in some recent research in North of England cities, however, the extent to which women can advance within a local labour market is likely to be a function of the resilience of locally hegemonic gender orders. The general marginalization and subordination of people of colour within societies like the British may be reproduced within the everyday culture even of a marketized society, but self-reliant, well-educated and technologically sophisticated British Asians may have a much enhanced position within the new market society. Just as Ulrich Beck, in his analysis of social patterns in what he calls 'the risk society' (which I will discuss in chapter 7), wants to recognize a great plurality of new 'risk-positions' produced by recent social transformations, so we should recognize the existence of a range of different market positions within market society itself, which cannot be read off in any one-dimensional fashion simply from the facts of class, gender or race. I do not believe that positions of disadvantage all collapse into each other, to produce a shared sense of disadvantage at *discrete social positions* within market society, though I do believe there are areas in most market societies in which there are very dense concentrations of disadvantage. I have no illusions about the difficulty of specifying the range and the variation in the character in such 'market-positions' within the new market society.

The analytical challenge involved in thinking about such different market-positions is immense and may be one reason for the general absence of any such formal sociological account of these newly emergent 'frameworks' of life in market society, and especially for the absence of any attempt systematically to relate patterns of crime and 'anxieties about crime' in the late 1990s to the idea of 'market-position'. There remains a widespread tendency amongst critics of a progressive persuasion to address these issues one-dimensionally – in terms of a critique of the destructive effects of marketization in all different respects. Commentators working in the area of public health, for example, point to many different sets of data showing the return of ill health and illness, including outright malnutrition itself, which can be linked with the rise in inequality that has been produced by 'marketization'. The Canadian public health commentator and moral philosopher John McMurtry makes direct use of a medical analogy to describe in some detail the likely consequences of the withdrawal of public support from 'society's essential support system' and speaks of the advance of the free market as 'the cancer stage of capitalism' (McMurtry 1995). There are several different problems with this kind of account. The recitation of these and other pathological aspects of the process of marketization does not find broad expression, in any Western society, in the emergence of any developed 'anti-market' movement. We need to understand – if not the popularity of contemporary life in the market – then certainly its acceptability. Amongst young people, it has been argued, there is a real difficulty in transcending the immediate challenges of survival and/or self-advancement in market society, in order to think any alternative. Amongst older commentators, themselves the product of anti-capitalist activity during the Fordist period, the rise of a confusing, de-centred market society is associated with what Jürgen Habermas has called 'the exhaustion of utopian energies' (Habermas 1989). But there are other issues – not least to do with the 'cultural logic' of what I call market society, and also to with the very sharp impacts on the material realities of life (the struggle for a wage). The reduction in rates of crime known to the police in the United States through the 1980s and 1990s, coinciding as it has with the unfolding of the post-Fordist labour market of part-time or short-term employment – provides a real challenge in terms of explanation, though, as James Austin and Robyn Cohen (1996) remind us, the reported rates of violent crime as a whole continue to increase, and overall crime rates in the United States are still twice as high as they were in the 1960s. One important part of the explanation of declining crime rates in the United States is demographic (there have been far smaller cohorts of Americans in the vulnerable age groups of 16–24). But a full explanation might involve an understanding of the fundamental 'privatization' of personal and household life, and the sequestration of such private life from public gaze and surveillance. This may mean a reduction in the rates of publicly recorded crime, but, if commentators like Pfohl (1992) are to be believed, this is not a measure of a tranquil and ordered society 'at ease with itself' and secure about its future direction and development. Not the least of the concerns about this particular form of market society, indeed, is that it is a society with no sense of a future, other than the constant present (of everyday consumption).

I want here to offer an analytical description of some of the defining features of market society, to be understood alongside the eight other transitions of the late twentieth century discussed in the last chapter. I want, first, to identify key features and consequences of the process of economic transformation of the 1980s and the 1990s – the 'restructuring' of the taken-for-granted organization of everyday work, the labour market and the distribution of wealth within and across civil society. We can speak of these developments as the evolution of 'market structures'. Then, secondly, I want to consider 'market society' as a 'discursive formation' – that is, as a set of images, aspirations and desires with respect to the rewards of life in market society, as well as a body of ideas about the socially authorized definitions of conformity in such a society. We can think of these in terms of the evolution of a 'market culture'.

MARKET STRUCTURES

The 'material reality' of market society in part finds expression in the accelerating inequality discussed as the second of the nine late twentieth century crises in chapter 1. This inequality of economic prospects and life-chances finds its own expression in some market societies (Britain) in an explosion of reported rates of property crime or, as I will explore in chapter 5, the broader and increasingly transnational 'hidden economies' of survival and capital accumulation. In many different market societies, the inequality of material struggles also finds expression in the rapid development of a range of sensory or escapist crimes associated, for example, with drugs, alcohol or sexual pleasure (which I will discuss in chapter 3, the consumerist and individualistic logic of the market place). The new inequality of 'market society' also finds important expression in the accelerating influence and power of a population in many market societies of those who are economically successful within the new market society and who are then able, in effect, to 'buy themselves out' of society, through their purchase on the private market of their various needs (from schooling and health through to policing).

I will want to speak about the cultural effects of this kind of privatization of personal position later. It is important to register that one of the defining material aspects of the market society (very often sequestered from public view, except in the case of those individuals whose wealth depends on 'public celebrity') is the presence within (or, in a critical sense, 'outwith') civil society (in fortified or sequestered spaces or, periodically, 'offshore') of citizens with extraordinary and frequently visible levels of personal wealth. In the American business journal *Forbes Magazine*, for example, one of the most widely cited expressions of the continuing superiority of American free enterprise is the increasing number of millionaires being produced within that society.[2] There is an important sense, in market society, in which these New Rich differ from the affluent and successful individuals who were the focus of discussion for Robert Merton and William Whyte in earlier moments in the history of American capitalism. For Merton, the significance of economic affluence lay in the expression it gave to the idea of freedom-to-achieve within America, and it carried with it the idea that the successful American entrepreneur would be expected to show gratitude for the opportunities provided by 'America' by the good works he undertook within the community. As William Whyte also recognized, the successful capitalist at local level would be expected to be a prominent member of the local Rotary or Kiwanis Club, whilst at national level he would be expected, like the Du Ponts, the Fords, the Guggenheims, the Mellons, the Rockefellers, the Vanderbilts or any other of the sixty families described by Gustavus Myers in his *History of the Great American Fortunes* at the start of the twentieth century (Myers 1909), to engage directly in 'public life' or in other 'good works' or to make massive donations for the foundation of universities or other publicly accessible institutions. The cultural expectations attaching to material success in

America (and in market Europe) in the 1990s, by contrast, much more closely exhibit a theme of escape from such kinds of civic or public responsibilities – so encouraging the sequestration and retention of private wealth in 'offshore' banking havens and other private strategies for avoidance of taxation (or other payment of monies in the public interest). Chapter 4 will pay specific attention to the continuing significance in contemporary cities of highly privatized residential developments and consumption facilities – which is the most obvious spatial expression of the domination over market society of the new market rich. This development has its particular criminological expression, of course, in the growing significance in many market societies of kidnapping of family members of the new rich conducted for purposes of ransom, and also of 'household-invasion crimes' in which the attempted institutionalization of the household as a fortress produces its own response from entrepreneurially minded members of the excluded populations.

The character of market society as a material structure is most apparent, however, for most citizens of such societies in the sphere of the 'labour market' itself. Importantly, it is with the marketization of employment opportunities that has occurred as a consequence of the withdrawal of the State and as a result of the demise of mass manufacturing that employment is now very widely experienced, quite specifically, as a 'market' phenomenon – and a market in which a relatively weak body of 'labour' tries to sell itself to bidders, with an intensity and a level of strategic focus that was never demanded of generations of young people encountering the transition from school to work during the Fordist period. The new post-Fordist labour market is a quite specific phenomenon in respect of 'opportunity' or 'career', radically different from the secure world of lifelong employment that defined the Fordist labour market, especially in the old public sector of employment in education, public services and the welfare state itself. It is a market, even for those 'in work', in which short-term and contractual employment predominates, and in which those currently in employment have to develop very focused strategies to secure follow-on contracts and continuing employment security. In North America during the 1980s, as already suggested, surveys showed that those in employment were spending increasing lengths of time in the workplace, in consequence of a 'macho' culture in which length of time at work was a new measure of competitive commitment (Schwartz 1989). There was and is a powerful sense that what is called by economists the 'flexible labour market' is actually the framework within which new forms of inclusive social structure are being developed, especially around workplaces, where those in insecure and competitive employment (a significant proportion of the 'included' population) spend increasing numbers of waking hours, leaving their places of residence unattended or attended only by some kind of new support staff (cleaners, child-minders and others). These 'home arrangements' have been identified by researchers as a new and contemporary form of feudalism, very often involving women 'labourers' from Third World countries. (There is an ironic sense, then, in which dual-income households with children in North America and Europe are being tutored in another of the realities of 'market society' – its escape from the confines of any one national society and its articulation across global spaces – through the direct employment of Third World labour.)

For a very significant proportion of the working population in market societies, however, who will not be contemplating the kinds of income enjoyed by the dual-income middle-class household, the 'choices' available in the market place look rather less rewarding. In many of the public housing estates and inner-city areas of the North of England, central Scotland or South Wales, for example, where there are official rates of unemployment at over 50 per cent, employment is often available only on a very short-term basis indeed, and there is no prospect, especially for unskilled men, of full-time employment with any kind of pension or social benefits attached. Similar circumstances have been reported for a vast range of 'deindustrialized' old industrial areas in Germany, especially in the Ruhr Valley; in France (Wacquant 1994) and in particular urban areas in Spain (Mingione 1994; G. Smith 1994). What has been in place in these locales is a relatively highly developed survivalist economy, in which goods and services are exchanged without the mediation of the cash nexus – forms of primitive communism; a *regulated* market of exchange sits alongside an unregulated set of alternative markets in economic opportunity – the local hidden economy of crime. The relationship between the formal economy of paid employment (in post-Fordist market circumstances), the regulated economies of exchange of the long-term unemployed and the illicit economy is a matter for local research and investigation. We will see in chapter 5 that there are intriguing parallels between the opportunities and risks thrown up at these levels of 'market society' and those which are which are usually discussed as 'white-collar' or 'economic crime'. They have in common their production according to laws of opportunity and demand at specific locations within market society.

One of the central thrusts of activity, in the construction of 'market society' as already indicated, has been the pressure towards the privatization of an increasing range of activities, including, as said earlier, the provision of services to the public. It is beyond the scope of the present book to provide an authoritative summary of the achievements of the privatization movement in different societies. There has been considerable unevenness in the development of this process in different societies (it remains very undeveloped, for example in a country like Sweden) and in the range of provisions that have been handed to 'the market'. In Britain, the range of privatized agencies now includes the rail system, the electricity, water and gas companies (the so-called privatized utilities), the steel industry, telephones, municipal transport, and the provision of care for the elderly. The privatization movement now also finds some expression in the toleration which has been given to the growth of private police forces (see chapter 7 below), sometimes in competition over particular urban spaces with regular, publicly funded forces, as well as to the introduction of private companies into prison-building and prison management. Not the least effect, however, of the construction of a framework of 'market society' has been 'the deregulation of financial services', legislated in Britain in 1986, and the associated campaign (as supporters of the then government would have put it) to create 'a property and share-owning democracy' – a society of investment- and market-minded individuals looking for services from a range of banks, building societies and insurance companies, offering a range of different products. In chapter 5 we will examine a sample of the different 'private temptations' which this new market place can generate and sustain. What is important for present purposes is to emphasize the fundamental transformation that has occurred in the institutional matrices of society (and, indeed, the functions of specific different buildings in the urban landscape) as a result of the advance of 'market society'. The sense of a city as a configuration of a few private buildings (shops, offices) inserted into a vast public territory (public parks, the high street, municipally owned bus stations, etc.) – usually built around a central public icon, like the town hall – has been replaced by a new 'urban imaginary' (in which a city is re-imagined as a configuration of self-contained corporate office buildings with their own fast food and leisure facilities, other self-contained and self-policing private shopping malls, private car parking lots, and a range of privately owned places of leisure and sport – nearly always adjoining a full collection of private financial institutions). In many such cities, the central iconic building, in practical and aesthetic terms, is the shopping mall itself, no matter that it may not be built in the 'traditional' centre of the city. The rich and fast-developing social geography of the post-Fordist or market city is, in this sense, a way of making sense, spatially, of the fast emergent *social structure* of market society itself, in which possession of one or other position in the private building (as an employee of a company in an office building, a cleaner working for the mall, or a shopper) entitles one to entry, provided one is not intercepted by the private security staff employed in those spaces at their perimeters. One inescapable feature (as will be seen in chapter 4) of the social geography of post-Fordist cities is the growth and development of a range of residual territories, or places of social exclusion, left over for the use of those populations who do not have claims to membership of the private spheres of work and consumption defined by market society (Sibley 1995).

Routine management of life in these marketized spaces and territories is increasingly undertaken by a range of representatives of 'private interests' rather than public authorities, and there is a significant reduction in the number of encounters between citizens and identifiable agents of public authority. In Britain, the widely heard refrain that 'You can never find a policeman when you want one' has a specific new reference in the relatively low numbers of uniformed officers that the police service, as currently organized and financed, can now put on the streets. In many suburban areas in large cities, the inability of local police forces to respond even to emergency calls with any speed is a major factor in enhanced local investment in private alternatives. Local authorities, under constant and continuing pressure of financial cutbacks over the last decade and a half – losing confidence in their ability or entitlement to act in the public interest – have very few well-known public representatives. Transport provision is increasingly delivered either by entirely privatized companies or by public–private sector consortia, in which the role of public authority or initiative is not obvious. Responsibility for maintenance of public spaces in British cities during the 1980s and 1990s shifted to partnerships of private and public authorities or to development corporations with a short-term mandate. Interim evaluations suggest that such partnership-arrangements often resulted in struggles to deny *de facto* or financial responsibility for such tasks. The advent of 'market society', in other words, involves a critical *process of withdrawal of public authority from the oversight and maintenance of the public spaces of the city*, which is in many ways an expression of generalized advance of the competitive market in the field of financial services, also marked by a decline in the role of any public regulatory institution.

MARKET CULTURE

It is important for our purposes to understand that 'market society' is lived as a culture – that is, within a general framework that places great positive value on certain personal attributes (dynamism, innovation, ability to live with constant change etc.) whilst also, by definition, identifying other personal or social attributes (habitual, routinized practice, loyalty, deference to authority, tradition etc.) as residual, outdated and/or unproductive. In this respect, we share the curiosity shown by sociological commentators like Tony Giddens, Scott Lash and John Urry in the development of those personal sensibilities and life strategies which Giddens (1990) first called 'reflexivity' and which he and Lash have now reconceptualized as 'reflexive de-traditionalization'. The interest here is in the ways in which individuals learn to live with what he calls the 'disembedding' of 'traditional' social relations of modern society, occasioned by the advent of speeded-up and increasingly dispersed high modern economic and cultural change (see also Lash and Urry 1994: ch. 3).

The entrepreneur as hero

One defining feature of the emergent 'market discourse' in the early 1980s was the lionization in the popular mass media of some of the young and prominent figures in the enterprise economy. In some societies, public opinion surveys suggested that these figures – like Richard Branson in Britain, Bernard Tapie in France, Silvio Berlusconi in Italy (especially after his creation of his own political party, making heavy use of the symbolism of football, *Forza Italia*), Ted Rogers in the United States – were better-known and more popular and more widely trusted than the leaderships of established political parties. In some instances (Tapie, Berlusconi), indeed, the new market entrepreneurs decided to move directly into politics to try to reconstruct the ways in which politics was represented in and through popular media.

This is not the place to enter into extended analysis of this lionization of the entrepreneur. I have already mentioned the heroic status sometimes given leading figures in business and in management in the United States in the 1950s, albeit on condition of the involvement of these successful individuals in public or political life. One of the defining features of this celebration of the market activists during the 1980s and 1990s, however, has been the representation of a range of youthful entrepreneurs, with *no* involvement in, or commitment to 'public works', as iconic role models for young people. This process of heroization is clearly connected in itself to the valorization of the fast-moving, multifaceted market place of media and consumption itself, with chosen 'celebrities' being represented, in almost a Marxist sense, as vanguards exemplary of the ongoing transformation of existing social arrangements. The lionization of a wide range of youthful entrepreneurs in modern media (from the fashion designer Gianni Versace, subsequently targeted by a youthful serial killer, to youthful 'television personalities', like Chris Evans in the United Kingdom) is now a routine feature of 'market culture'. It is also impossible to ignore the impact of this lionization of the entrepreneur even in the most benighted of inner-city or public housing areas, where crime prevention and youth workers complain of the problems they routinely encounter in establishing an imagery of 'realistic role models' for local children and young people. Not the least of the unexamined consequences of this unqualified celebration of the entrepreneur (as the rational choice theorists from classical economics partially understand) is the development of other local forms of business and enterprise in these areas, in which the defining feature is the grasping of opportunities and not, a priori, much anxiety about the legality of these enterprises *per se*.

The market not the nation-state

A second defining feature of new market culture is its international character. The ever-extending range of terrestrial, satellite and cable television channels are vehicles not necessarily of a better-informed or even more pluralist, less nationalist sensibility; but, as Abram de Swaan (1995), amongst others, has observed, they do produce and re-produce an ever-enlarging set of images (or 'circles of identification') beyond the immediate experience of the private household or local neighbourhood. That is to say, they give expression to a universe of 'signs' – the signifying images, for example, in television programmes or on television, magazine or billboard advertising of a range of different 'lifestyles'- from the warm suburbs of Melbourne, Australia to the enticements of life in San Francisco or Provence (as well as the mean streets of Los Angeles or Manchester). That is to say, 'market culture' trades openly with the idea and the range of possibilities of globalization, especially in the possibilities of an alternative way of life (even for the most deprived of individuals living in the most constrained of personal circumstances) to existing everyday constraints. This is the production of a fantasy of a very particular and contemporary kind – namely, that the 'solution' to problems of material poverty and/or wealth may live not within individual nation-states but *within a global market place*, particularly through a flexible involvement with international opportunities. Commentators in the field of cultural studies write about the emergence of what they call 'glocalization' – where even people spending the majority of their waking hours in very limited and specific localities begin to negotiate or make sense of their local circumstances according to some global or international script (Robertson 1995). The anthropologist Arjun Appadurai (1996) suggests that this imaginative re-negotiation of local constraints may be particularly marked amongst those millions of migrant peoples located away from their societies of birth – a new 'diaspora' of transplanted and creative imaginations. One particular instance of this rethinking of borders has been evident for many years among minority peoples living near to international borders – like the Iroquois peoples living on both sides of the St Lawrence Seaway in North America, and engaging in a wide variety of cross-border trades (Jamieson 1998b). Other populations in North America and Europe who have come to think in this way in the 1990s include those thousands of people who are engaged in the routine trans-shipment of contraband goods, like cigarettes and alcohol, across national borders. The British television audience in the 1980s was acquainted in programmes like *Auf Wiedersehen Pet* with the movements of these new nomads – unemployed workers, moving across the continent of Europe in search of work. In the late 1990s, one of the most widely discussed issues in the popular press in France was the numbers of young French men and women engaged in a similar quest for work in London or in other parts of the European Union. Recent studies of the 'new migration' in Europe make clear that these movements of millions of people across this continent are to be understood not just as an effect of the demise of the Soviet Union or even as a mass escape from the new war-zones of southern Europe, but also as a vital contemporary version of the movements of peoples in the early nineteenth century in the search for material survival and advancement of personal life-chances (Koser and Lutz 1998).

The market and the discourse of choice

The emphasis placed during the 1980s in public political debates on the idea of 'the market' was frequently accompanied by refrains celebrating life in a market society as a life of freedom and personal choice (see e.g. Barry 1987; Rose 1992). The existing, dominant social and economic formation of a Keynesian mixed economy and a Fabian welfare state was indicted as a world of no-choice – as a world that was dominated, indeed, by monopoly suppliers who, by virtue of absence of competition, were unchallenged in the service or the goods they provided or produced.[3] At the core of these arguments in favour of Enterprise Culture was the insistence that the market would deliver competition, and that competition was the most reliable way of producing an improvement in overall economic performance of companies and of the country, in service to customers and, indeed, the more general issue of delivery of services to 'the public' by people employed within the bloated public sectors of established Fordist societies (Keat and Abercrombie 1991; Heelas and Morris 1992). The increasing acceptance of 'the market' amongst young people in societies like Britain's may have had much to do with the widespread recognition of a generation of young people, attuned to alternative ways of working and delivering services (for example, in North America or Europe), that the existing practices and common sense assumptions of the established public sector (and perhaps the broader society as a whole) in countries like Britain were, indeed, inefficient, badly managed and often simply amateurish. We will consider, in chapter 7 of this book, how this kind of sensibility plays into the rise of privatized alternative systems of social control.

The market and 'self-interest'

The new market society has been indicted by a wide range of classically progressive commentators, including, most importantly in Britain, the economist-cum-editor Will Hutton, in *The State We're In*, for its elevation of self-interest over public interest as a measure of the ongoing redevelopment and transformation of economic activity (Hutton 1995). There is no question, as Elliott Currie also observes in his commentaries on the United States, that the rise of market society *has* been accompanied by such an intensification of self-interest (or, at least, of sectional interest, in the interests of 'my family' or 'my tribe') and also, as is shown in the research enquiries of Robert Bellah and Robert Putnam (1996), by a quite startling decline in the level of voluntary activity (and, indeed, of any kind of shared public activities other than sport) 'in the community'. In the United States, a number of initiatives have been taking place, in the name of the so-called communitarian movement initiated by Amitai Etzioni's anxious extended essays on the crisis in the idea of a shared public good in America (Etzioni 1993). In Britain, there is talk at government level of initiatives to involve the citizen in new forms of 'stake-holding' in workplace or neighbourhood institutions. There is an unmistakable sense, in the meantime, that the 'genie' that is self-interest is out of the bottle, consequent on the success of the market's liberation of consumer desires during the 1980s and 1990s, and may not want to return (Bauman 1995). In the body of this text, my ambitions are to offer some speculations and observations with regard to the project of advancing a sociological account of life, but particularly with respect to crime, in such a market society. I will try to do this from a perspective of critique, of the kind outlined in chapters 1 and 2. That is to say, I do not want to reduce analysis of social conditions, or of all key social transitions, at the end of the twentieth century just to the fact of market society. Nor do I want to advance a critique of 'market society' (with all its implications for the social production of crime and of crime control and penal discipline) in which there is a self-evident alternative – a kind of return to Keynesian management of mixed economies at national level. But what I do want to argue, without ambiguity, is that the analysis of crime, in all its different local and transnational forms, must proceed in recognition of the social fact of our times – the demise of national Keynesian welfare states and the emergence of their successor, the post-Fordist market society.

3

YOUNG PEOPLE, CRIME AND FEAR IN MARKET SOCIETIES

My concern in this chapter is to provide an overview of 'the condition of youth' in market society in the late 1990s, and to use this framework as the basis for a grounded analysis of the problem of 'youth crime' itself. The organization of this overview will closely follow the order of the nine transitions of the late twentieth century discussed in chapters 1 and 2, with the exception that there will be no extended treatment of 'the crisis of the nation-state' as a process having direct impact on the condition of youth.[1] I have added an extended discussion of the issue of 'drugs and alcohol' – treated, in part, as a market phenomenon – as a discrete and specific aspect of the condition of youth. The overall objective is, of course, to ground discussion of the issue of youth crime and youth problems within the specific social and historical reality of post-Fordist market society.

I am aware that the account developed here could be regarded as too one-dimensional by some commentators, in accentuating the various different threats and risks confronting young people in market society and appearing to underestimate the new opportunities and freedoms which 'liberal' market societies may provide. The research report released by the Demos organization in Britain in 1995, for example, identified 'a generational shift in values' which, the authors of this report insisted, was evidence of the 'autonomy' and 'authenticity' made possible by life in market society. They also argued that 'life had improved compared to their parents' generation' (Wilkinson and Mulgan 1995: 3). This Demos report was particularly attentive, for example, to the increased power which young women were experiencing in the market place in Britain and also the increased opportunities for some form of education beyond that provided in school. My review of some other features of life for young people in market society is not intended as a dismissal of the Demos report, or of other analytical approaches which emphasize the new possibilities that are thrown up for some by the emergence of flexible and insecure labour markets, and other material aspects of life, in market society.

I am interested, however, in providing a clear sense of the material outcomes currently emerging from this competitive life in market society, and some sense of the particular stresses informing young people's lives at different levels of the social formation, that is, at different market-positions within individual market societies.

Unemployment and Insecurity

Since the late 1970s, all Western societies (albeit in different specific ways) have been experiencing the impact of the transformation of 'Fordist' systems for the organization of production and employment, regulated by systems for the welfare and support of individual citizens under the auspices of the national state, into 'post-Fordist' societies, as summarized in table 1. The *'Fordist culture' of work* can be understood as comprising five key elements:

- Paid work was an essentially *masculine activity*, frequently involving muscular effort.
- The workplace was essentially a male-dominated locale, excluding women and also operating as a sphere for *male-bonded socialization*.
- *Work* itself was focused on *production*, with no concern at the shop-floor level as to its sale or distribution. Workers were not directly involved in provision of services to customers.
- Training was mostly *informal*, although there was some development of apprenticeships in some Fordist countries (notably Germany). Formal accreditation of workers was uncommon.
- The domestic sphere was a sphere of *everyday social reproduction*, organized by workers' spouses. Leisure was organized around the rhythm of the male worker's week, with an emphasis on drink and sport.

The *Post-Fordist culture of work* is organized around an alternative set of dimensions:

- Work is increasingly *feminine* and *non-muscular*. (Some four-fifths of new jobs created in England in the mid-1990s were taken by women.)
- Work is increasingly *'decentred'*, carried out in small enterprises, offices, shops.
- Work is increasingly oriented to *consumption* and the *provision of service*.
- Entry into employment is increasingly overseen by systems of *accreditation*.
- In the domestic sphere, there has been a marked increase in *dual-career households*, especially amongst the professional middle

class. In such households, there is the widely reported phenomenon of *'accelerated'* daily life, and problems of latch-key children. In households hit by unemployment, there is frequently a reversal of the division of labour of the Fordist household, with only the woman in paid employment.

● In the employed middle class, 'leisure' is increasingly under threat or has been redefined as consumption, though there is evidence of widespread individual resort to sports and physical fitness activity, undertaken for stress-reduction reasons. In areas of high unemployment, there is a serious problem of *unwanted and over-extended leisure*.

The precise trajectory of the post-Fordist transition has differed quite significantly between different societies. Most obviously of all, the embrace of 'the market' at the political level has been much more marked in Britain and America than in most member-states of the European Community. In Britain, in the 1980s, for example – under the influence of its newly elected Conservative Government with its commitment to a rapid withdrawal from State subsidization of 'uncompetitive' industry and its messianic belief in the capacity of 'the market' to deliver a new period of capital growth and accumulation – unemployment soared. The impact on young people was unmistakable: 'By 1986 more than one-third of men and women in registered unemployment were under the age of 25, comprising some 1.37 million young would-be workers. Over 900,000 of these young people had been without work for more than one year, and one in twelve for more than three years' (McCrae 1987: 1–2). Closer analysis of the evidence by researchers at the Policy Studies Institute (White and McCrae 1989) confirmed that – for all the proliferation of different kinds of new training schemes and work-preparation programmes – larger proportions of 18–24-year-olds in Britain throughout the 1980s had experienced increasingly lengthy periods of unemployment. The 'cohort studies' conducted by the Department of Employment in the 1990s suggested that this phenomenon continued well into that decade, even during the period, from 1986, when official rates of unemployment had begun to decline (Courtenay and McAleese 1994; Park 1994).

Different processes of change and adaptation of 'national labour markets' were apparent in other societies. In France and Germany, for example, for different reasons, the advent of crises of unemployment was less apparent in the 1980s, but in both societies unemployment among young people began to attain the status of a fundamental national crisis by the mid-1990s. In 1997 survey research in France suggested that fully 28 per cent of the under-26-year-olds in that country were unemployed, compared with the national rate of 12.3 per cent: Labour Minister Martine Aubry announced a £3 billion subsidy for the creation of 350,000 new community service jobs (*Guardian* 21 Aug. 1997). In Spain and Italy, by contrast, relatively high rates of unemployment, as measured on official criteria, did not give rise to the same rate of anxiety – in part, because of the considerable spread throughout both these societies, especially in their rural hinterlands, of 'alternative economies' and 'lifetime strategies' revolving around unregistered part-time work and cultures of household and neighbourhood sustenance and survival (Mingione 1994; G. Smith 1994). In Spain, in the late 1990s, talk of an economic boom coincided with a reduction of the overall unemployment rate for all young people to a figure still above 20 per cent. It is, of course, vital to note how the reduction in the rate of unemployment in Britain in the 1990s, on official measures, coincided with the continued expansion in that country of the post-Fordist labour market of part-time and short-term work, as also was the reduction of unemployment in the 1990s in the United States, where – again on official measures – overall unemployment reached its lowest level for twenty-four years at 4.7 per cent.[2] The overall unevenness of the distribution of youthful unemployment across Europe should not distract attention from the scale of worklessness in the continent as a whole: in 1996 unemployment was officially measured at over 20 per cent of all under-25s in Spain, France, Ireland, Italy, Belgium and Greece, and, in an even more telling statistic, one-third of those under-25-year-olds had been unemployed for more than one year (Judt 1996).

POVERTY IN CHILDHOOD AND IN THE TRANSITION TO ADULTHOOD

In chapter 1 I outlined how the return of high levels of unemployment, and the emergence of long-term unemployment, has paralleled a return of poverty and a shift towards markedly increased levels of inequality in many of the new market societies. A series of research reports have highlighted the sudden and pronounced lurch towards greater inequalities of wealth that had occurred in Britain, in the United States, and in many other Western societies from the early 1980s onwards (Department of Social Security 1993; Rowntree Foundation 1994; Holtermann 1995). In each of these societies, but to differing degrees, the 'freeing of the market' has been accompanied by a persistent widening of the gap between the wealthiest and the poorest in the population. Between 1979 and 1992, in Britain, for example, the poorest one-tenth of the population experienced a 17 per cent fall in real income, and, although figures released by HM Government in 1996 suggested that some 400,000 less people were officially in poverty in 1993–5 compared to 1992, the fact remained that, on the Government's own figures, 13.7 million people in Britain were still living below the poverty line (*Households below Average Income*, HMSO, 1996). For our purposes, the interest here is with *the impact on young people* in two distinct (but connected) senses: the experiences of young people during the formative period of childhood itself and, then, in the context of adolescence itself (notably in its material constraints, which began to inform the period that, in Fordist societies, had been called 'the transition from school to work').

In 1994 a report from the Department of Health and Social Security concluded that 32 per cent of children in England and Wales under the age of sixteen (about 4.1 million young people) were living below the poverty line.

A report from Eurostat, the European Community's statistics agency, based on a comparison of this official statistic with those released by other member-states, suggested that Britain had more children living in poverty than any other European country, significantly above Ireland, Portugal, Spain and Italy: the European average was 20 per cent (*Guardian*, 28 Apr. 1997). Looked at over the period from the early 1980s, these and similar figures identify very large numbers of people (some of whom are now adolescents or young adults, and a few who are even adults into their early middle years) – some of whom, of course, will now themselves be parents – who have *never* known anything other than a relentless daily struggle with poverty,[3] but what is more, may never have even believed it possible to escape such poverty.

A more or less inevitable consequence of this new poverty has been a significant reduction in the quality of diet, and the health, of the adults and the young people in these households.[4] Research undertaken in London in 1991 suggested that malnutrition among 11–12-year-olds was such as to reduce resistance to infection and also to influence ability to learn (Newell 1994), whilst a National Children's Home study published in 1994 revealed that the basic social security benefit payable to 1.5 million families in Britain would not actually have been sufficient to cover the cost of the diet provided in the Bethnal Green workhouse in 1876 (*Guardian*, 1 Feb. 1994).

Other studies showed that the housing conditions in which many members of the new underclass in Britain were living were also in serious decline: national sample surveys suggested that a third of all dwellings were damp and that over half contained mould (Newell 1994). The overall set of living conditions of the new poor – the groups now so often identified as 'the underclass' – made it very difficult to understand how even the best-intentioned of parents would be able to pass on to their children any expectation of escape from such poverty, not least because they themselves could not imagine what such an escape would look like. In that sense I believe, as does Will Hutton for Britain and William Julius Wilson for the United States, that the experience of marketization in many European societies in part involves an increase in the numbers of very poor people, with little realistic chances of escaping their poverty through legitimate activities, living in 'enclaves' of heavily concentrated and long-established levels of poverty. This truth about free market societies is not accompanied – given the primacy to the larger market of private consumption – by any wider de-escalation of consumer appetites. The enlarging underclass of the newly marketized societies, especially its male population, has a declining position within the legitimate labour market, but, as will be argued later, it has felt the full force of the ideological offensive that has been mounted on hitherto existing State welfare schemes (in the name of removing the condition of 'state dependency').

During the course of the 1980s in Britain, young people (of different backgrounds, including the most deprived and difficult) have had to adapt to the withdrawal of 'exceptional needs payments' (for young people trying to set up a home), the loss of benefit for young people paying board at home (in 1983), the deregulation of the casual labour market for youth (the abolition of the Wages Councils in 1986) with its massive impact on the level of wages paid in casual and short-term work, the withdrawal of Supplementary Benefit from 16- and 17-year-olds (in 1986), the restriction of the rate for full benefit to over-26-year-olds and the introduction of the so-called Job Seekers' Allowance in April 1997, reducing benefits payable to under-25-year-olds by 20 per cent. In the meantime, the ever-increasing number of young people attending college and university in Britain have been asked to survive without the support of housing benefit (withdrawn in 1990), vacation grants (1991), full grants (transformed into loans as from 1993) and State support for the payment of college and university fees (ended by the Dearing Report in 1997). All of these material attacks on the living conditions of the young have occurred alongside the constant intensification of the emphasis on 'consumption' as the source of personal identity and well-being in a fast-moving culture. The range of consumer items may primarily be marketed at the increasingly rich 'overclass' which has emerged in most free market societies as an optional 'value-added' to the range of other alternatives, but for the underclass itself takes on a particular significance as a momentary distraction from the strains of everyday material realities.

There is an important sense in which this widening material distance between the poor and the consumption of goods in the market place should in itself be seen as a major contributory factor in the explosion of particular kinds of straightforward theft, burglary and other forms of property crime in countries like England and Wales in the 1980s and 1990s. In some local authority areas in Britain with a very large number of households and individuals dependent on State welfare, the constant cuts were guaranteed to produce significant increases in local poverty, at least in the short term, with all their consequences on health and well-being, as well as in different forms of criminal behaviour. In this sense the direct and indirect impact of these cuts would be particularly marked in areas already blighted by problems of poverty. A similar picture – with respect to the uneven geographical or local impact of the process of cuts in State welfare – has been apparent in the United States. Research by the Carnegie Foundation released in 1994 suggested that 3 million children (about one in four) were living in poverty (and also emphasized 'mounting evidence' that a children's environment in the first three years of life could help determine their brain structure and their ability to learn). Another report from the US Congress General Accounting Office, also released in 1994, suggested that the overall number of poor children under the age of three rose by 26 per cent during the 1980s, but that in some areas of the country the percentage of young people living in poverty was over 50 per cent. The National Center for Children in Poverty and other organizations within the American 'poverty lobby' campaigned for the adoption of the 'Carnegie agenda' in lieu of the market realism being pursued by the Clinton administration (*Guardian*, 13 Apr. 1994).

The transformation of material possibilities for young people in market societies is also apparent at the point of what used to be called the transition from school to work. The contrast with the experience of their parents' generation is clear: all things being equal, in increasingly competitive market societies, each new generation of adolescents faces a *harder time* in terms of the market place of employment and wage than the previous one. By 1987, for example, in Britain, the earnings of 18–20-year-olds (*excluding* those on Youth Training Schemes) had fallen from 74 per cent of average adult earnings to just 69 per cent (Wallace 1987: 3). This reduction in the overall material prospects of a youthful generation feeds into the embrace of the culture of enterprise and competitivity, not least at certain levels of the social formation, in the quest for any kind of employment or financial return.

YOUTHFUL INSECURITY AND RISK IN MARKET SOCIETY

I pointed in chapter 1, to the emergence of the new sense of insecurity and risk that has accompanied the rise of market society, not least amongst those adult citizens who were newly fearful of the riskiness of their own labour market position or their position in the housing market (Taylor and Jamieson 1998). Particularly in the aftermath of the publication in 1992 of Ulrich Beck's *Risk Society*, sociological writers have been interested in broadening the ways in which the concept of risk is applied in the analysis of contemporary daily life, and, in particular, to suggest that the current social, political and economic conjuncture involves strategic management of a qualitatively and quantitatively higher level and range of 'risk' than at any other historical moment. Beck's own analyses were activated, it should be said, by a recognition of a series of new problems in the spheres of natural and medical science – from the dangers presented to future food supplies to the challenge of AIDS – all issues of momentous significance for the reproduction and the integrity of the human species, to which 'science' as currently practised has no immediate answer. Other writers have been inspired to argue, however, that there is a new riskiness specific to social life itself, resulting in particular from the emergence and routine presence in everyday public space of a new and more extensive range of Dangerous Others. The attention that has been given to paedophiles and drug pushers in popular debate in the 1990s connects this new sense of risk, specifically, to the young.

There is a widely felt view, for example, that the problem of sexual abuse of children and adolescents is more extensive than ever was imagined (and therefore investigated), especially in the private sphere of the household, in earlier moments in the post-war period.[5] Detailed inquiries undertaken by Richard Kinsey and his associates in different schools and different areas in Edinburgh produced a remarkable summary of the routine experience reported by children aged eleven to sixteen of different forms of serious sexual abuse in the home and on the street, as well as other forms of serious crime (see table 4).

Mass media discussion in Britain, as in many other societies, focuses almost exclusively on the role of young people as *perpetrators* of crime – as also has conventional criminology itself – only rarely investigating the different ways in which young people are so frequently the *victims* of crime and of violence. A significant body of recent research with young people in Britain, however,

Table 4 Young people's victimization by crime, Scotland, 1990

Percentage	Offence reported
50	theft (without violence), assaults (with or without weapons) or threatening behaviour
39	assault
65 (girls) 53 (boys)	harassment (threatening stares, being followed on foot, followed in a car, asked things or called after)
66	verbal and non-violent harassment – **43 per cent** describing the circumstances as 'very frightening'
26 (girls) 9 (boys)	'importuning' behaviour by adults (attempts to touch, requests to be touched, asking children to go with them or indecently exposing themselves)

Sample of 892 schoolchildren in Edinburgh: reported incidents of which they had been victims.
Source: Anderson, Kinsey, Loader and Smith (1994)

reveals the extent of young people's experience of criminal victimization, and also points to the ways in which young people more or less knowingly negotiate the risks of crime, for example during school hours or during their leisure hours.[6] The riskiness of the urban environment in free market societies, I will argue in chapter 4, is no deceit: most free market societies *are* characterized by the expansion in the number and range of what Lash and Urry call 'ungovernable spaces' (for example, the 'sink estates' in Britain and the *banlieux* of France, but also, as will be discussed in chapter 4, a range of other residualized 'dead spaces' and 'hot spots of crime' in urban centres[7]). The crisis of the welfare system, alongside the libertarian critique of mental hospitals and other total institutions, has also resulted in the discharge into public territory over the last two decades of a number of individuals who are in need of care and support into the chancy networks that are called 'community care'. What is important analytically is to try to understand the relationship between all these connected marketizing logics – the demise of local authority 'civics', the crisis of a public police no longer tied into local neighbourhoods or communities and the overall, fiscally driven, process of withdrawal from welfare-state provision. From the perspective of many young people, the risks that may be encountered on the streets are well known, and factored into the 'street-wisdom' on which young people currently pride themselves. They also feed into a series of strategies routinely adopted to deal with such risks and threats (like the strategy of young women of only 'going out' in groups, and the routine pooling of resources for a taxi home at the end of an evening 'on the town').[8] Many of these youthful adaptations to life in free market societies operate entirely at the level of consciousness. But analysis must also be mindful of the ways in which such knowing and, indeed, reflexive adaptations may suppress more fundamental insecurities of life in market society, which are not so amenable to solution through the exercise of a cool postmodernist reflexivity. Ken Roberts make the important point quite straightforwardly:

> The [most] pertinent sense in which young people have to make their ways into risk societies is that they have to make decisions, to take steps, which will almost certainly affect their future opportunities, but where the outcomes are moderate probabilities at best. Unless a young German completes an apprenticeship it is most unlikely that he or she will ever become a skilled worker, but completing an apprenticeship will not make it equally likely that the person will obtain a skilled job. Even if such employment is obtained the occupation may not outlast the individual's working life. There is really no way in which anyone can be certain. An employer-based training scheme may lead to a good job or back into unemployment. A university degree may lead to high rising management or professional career, but an entrant into higher education would be unwise to bank on such a future. In a similar way, marriage may lead to lifetime domestic and emotional security, but it may also lead to personal despair. There is simply no way in which today's young people can avoid risk taking. (K. Roberts 1995: 117–18)

There is clearly much more that needs to be said about the play of insecurity and risk in the lives of the young in free market societies at the end of the twentieth century.

THE WAR AGAINST THE YOUNG IN MARKET SOCIETY

There is, of course, an important sense in which 'capitalist societies' in general have never been the most supportive and helpful environments for children and youth. Engels (1845) himself famously observed how the explosive growth of capitalism in Britain in the early nineteenth century witnessed the break-up of the extended family which had acted as an important source of support for the young in the last years of feudalism. This same explosion of capitalism also created the originating conditions for the employment of child labour – for example, in the coal mines of South Wales, northern England and Scotland – at very low rates of pay. Elsewhere within the world, similar moments of explosive capitalist development have been accompanied by rapid expansion in the number of young people put to work in 'sweatshop' conditions – from the point of view of capital, very usefully undercutting adult rates of pay in the local market place but, from the children's own point of view, radically undermining their prospects in life, through withdrawal from the benefits of education and through early exhaustion through physical labour. The later development during the twentieth century of high-modern forms of capitalist society, and, with it, the development of 'the welfare state' and of mass education, certainly transformed the 'pains of childhood' and adolescence in capitalist societies, but it is important, all the while, to recognize that the majority of such societies remained astonishingly unequal in absolute terms. There was also enormous variation in the degree of social provision and real opportunity created for young children and youth in

Fordist societies, like Sweden, at the one extreme, and Hong Kong, at the other. Throughout the post-Second World War period, there were radical differences between Western societies, in terms of young people's opportunities to enter into higher education on the one hand, or on the other to obtain entry into skilled or unskilled manual or professional occupations. These societies may have come to define themselves as modern and developed but, as many critics observed at the time, this did not mean that they had become sensitive to their own children or that they had institutionalized any sets of social or economic rights for generations of youth (Friedenberg 1959; Goodman 1956).

One important truth about the current liberalization of the world and of Western economies is the return of the 'sweatshop industries' thought to have been characteristic of a long-lost period of early capitalist growth. In the United States, in the late 1990s, according to one observer, 'tens of thousands of immigrant workers (mostly women) sew in tiny contract shops, with no guarantee of minimum pay, health benefits or safe working conditions' (Mort 1997). Two-thirds of all garment work in Los Angeles in the late 1990s is in 'sweatshops'. In the meantime, faced by attempts by State departments of labour to regulate these shops and/or illegal home working, many major corporations (including The Gap, Disney, Walmart and Nike) have relocated outside those countries where labour laws are enforced.

In the United Kingdom, in the aftermath of the deregulation of the labour market in the early 1980s, the earnings of young people actually in paid employment fell steadily from 82.8 per cent of adult rates in April 1984 to 66.3 per cent in April 1995 (Brinkley 1997: 165) and there has been a radical reduction of the number of full-time positions available (a loss of about 930,000 in the United Kingdom between 1984 and 1995) (Brinkley 1997: 167). In Britain, as in the United States and most European societies, very large numbers of young people who are technically in employment are actually in part-time and inherently insecure positions, paying significantly less than such work would previously have paid for young people doing similar work in an earlier post-war moment.

This is the same historical moment in which what looks like a war against the young has been launched in the public culture. In Britain, there has been an endless series of initiatives by leading politicians of both major parties focusing on behaviour of children in school (for example, requiring young children to enter into 'behaviour contracts',[9] or empowering head teachers actually to expel children from school[10]) or in public space (the use of curfews against children under the age of ten,[11] or the use of electronic tagging to monitor the movements of particular young people who have already been identified through the courts as 'children at risk' of entering further into anti-social behaviour). My concern here is not to suggest that these initiatives should just be understood as another instance of the unending 'moral panic' of adult authority over youth. It is far more important to understand the way in which these initiatives involve a concerted attempt by established political leaderships *to regulate the new social circumstances and the behaviours of the young within 'market society'* – for example, by making new demands on the probation or youth services to act as active additional agencies in the policing of a population of school-leavers rendered idle (and unquestionably frustrated) by the absence of paid employment. These initiatives are underpinned by the concern of politicians in market society somehow to respond to the anxieties of a larger voting public – especially what I have called the 'suburban social movements' of the 1990s (Taylor 1996) – who would like to believe in some policing solution to problems of youthful excess, disorderliness, frustration and/despair in market conditions: that 'order' can in this way be both realized and enforced, even in the nervous and endless transitions of post-Fordist market society.

THE ABSENCE OF SUBCULTURES

Many commentators in the field of cultural studies (Hebdige 1988; McGuigan 1992; McRobbie 1994) have pointed to the limits of a modernist subcultural theory in making sense of the contemporary condition of youth. One of the more obvious features of the condition of youth in market society, indeed, is that the formation of youth subcultures appears to have stopped, at least in the sense described in the classic literature. McRobbie and Thornton (1995) and Thornton (1995) go further in order to re-think the contemporary significance of talk about subcultures, as well as the connected critical literature which identifies all responses to youth trouble as an instance of 'moral panic' (an argument first elaborated by Stan Cohen (1972) in relation to the societal reaction to 'the Mods and Rockers' in 1962–4.) For McRobbie and Thornton, the significance of this well-established body of thinking lies in the way it is now drawn upon, in an essentially ironic fashion, in unending journalistic commentary on the market-driven recycling of youthful style and the (mis)behaviours of the latest pop music band. References to 'subcultures' or 'moral panic over youth' have significance – not primarily in terms of young people's attempts to resolve problems of unequal social position – but rather in terms of the endless attempt to create popular interest in each new commodity being thrown onto the youth market.

All this is to affirm, of course, that the sociological theories about social order from which accounts of subculture derive (for example, the sociological functionalism of Robert Merton) – and even those critical discussions over the panic-driven responses of Authority and the State to the perceived misdeeds of groups of marginal or unruly youth (moral panic theory) – are accounts of a relatively stable, orderly though unequal social structure in which personal advancement was still generally thought possible 'through legitimate means'. These kinds of sociological accounts have little direct relevance to the analysis of the expectations and the lived social relations of the mass of young people in market societies in the 1990s.

Informed commentary locates the death of subcultures in Britain in the late to mid-1980s, in the final but simultaneous 'retro(spective)' revisiting by teenagers in that period of the various youth subcultural styles of the entire post-war period: Teddy Boys, Mods, skinheads, Glam Rockers and even a few hippies could all be seen on the high street, sharing space with the only contemporary new variation of the times, the Goth. The subsequent history of 'youth culture', as Dick Hebdige (1988) has explained, is best understood as a history of heavily and speedily marketed styles, in music and clothing, with increasingly abbreviated half-lives, articulated through a newly emergent youth press preoccupied with issues of *individual* identity and also the rapidly changing 'gender experience' of adolescence in the new market society (breathlessly declared in the competitive market of new men's and young women's magazines). It has become clear in retrospect that the idea of subculture developed in modernist sociology, and then applied to the analysis of youth trouble, was a specific language for making sense of the routine transitions which were being experienced by generations of young people moving from school to work in high modern ('Fordist') industrial societies, characterized by relatively high rates of employment, but also by radical differences (notably in class, gender and ethnic terms) in the kinds of lifestyle or opportunities afforded by different kinds of job and different kinds of attainment at school or college. In place of that predictable social order, with its well-understood inequalities of position and its equally well-understood pathways for personal advancement and (limited) material reward, is an unpredictable, risky society whose future development is uncharted, and within which individual chances of success, at the one extreme, and survival, at the other, have become extraordinarily contingent matters. The majority of young people are likely to be worse off in material terms than their parents but, of course, in free market culture, the suggestion is always being made that a small number of individuals might be lucky and become very rich indeed.

If, in these new social circumstances, the 'subcultural form' is extinct, then so, one would think, is the capacity of the conceptual apparatus of subcultural theory to make sense of the troubles of youth in a society dominated, on its visible surface, by 'style', speed of change, and individualization. A series of studies of young people in Britain in the early 1990s (Wilkinson 1994; Wilkinson and Mulgan 1995; Hollands 1995) suggested routine organization of daily life and leisure of the majority of young people (for example, in evening 'clubbing') around friendship groups formed at school, rather than on 'the street', that most unvisited of social locations. The criminological logic is clarified: 'youth trouble' (what used to be called 'delinquency') – never, ever, simply and only the ahistorical 'behavioural' phenomenon identified by behavioural psychologists – has to be understood in the specific set of youth cultural practices of this particular historical moment (in a risky market society) and not in terms of the subcultural adaptations to an apparently entrenched modernist Fordist economy, dominated by the guardianship as well as the intrusions of 'the welfare state' and its representatives.[12] Youth trouble is somehow implicated, that is, in the pressures of the new labour markets and gender relations constructed in market society and, indeed, in 'market culture' itself; more specifically, it is implicated in terms of the types of recursive, daily activity that young people pursue – in relation to the employment they do obtain, and the markets of pleasure and leisure they do pursue in this kind of market society.[13] Before consigning subcultural theory entirely to the archives, however, we need to consider three other dimensions of the contemporary condition of youth.

PROTEST AND MARKET MASCULINITY AMONG THE YOUNG

Some space was devoted in chapter 1 to Bob Connell's theses with regard to the 'crisis tendencies' in masculinity in Western society at the end of the twentieth century. In particular, his notion on 'protest masculinity' is useful in understanding the aggressive colonization of contemporary street space by young men, the growth of an 'in-your-face' masculinism and also the heavy involvement of young men in particular kinds of 'crime' (notably car-theft and assault). Connell's object of analysis was 'masculinity' itself – rather than 'youth' or 'adolescence' – but his exploration of protest masculinity, drawing on the work of Alfred Adler, does strongly suggest that the current crises of masculinity arise in part out of the interruption in the process of psychological or developmental maturation – the transition from childhood to adulthood – that might have been taken for granted in earlier historical periods. That is to say, the crisis of the mass manufacturing labour markets of the Fordist period has involved the demolition of the systems of socialization of young men (including those provided within the family of birth) into the disciplines of factory life and the disciplines of working-class life itself[14] – leaving contemporary generations of young men, in particular, without those systems of socialization and symbolic affirmation. Connell also argues, however, that we are witness at the end of the twentieth century to the growth of another form of masculinity, very often situated amongst young managers, executives or entrepreneurs employed within the private sector organizations of market society, which he identified with the attempt to assert competitive or managerial 'rationality'. In this adaptation, the argument runs, older men, and/or men at some senior positions in a hierarchy, can be seen to be shoring up their authority in that hierarchy via a range of new kinds of 'rationalist' assertion. Younger men, at early stages in their careers within organizations, may attempt to establish and advance their position, especially vis-à-vis any female colleagues or competitors, through an assertive display of their own particular self-evident grasp of 'reason' (Connell 1995: ch. 7). In chapter 5 we will examine the particular forms which this display of forceful and risk-taking 'rationality' seems to have assumed in the stock market and other areas of the 'financial services industry', where the 'rationality' at issue, of course, is not 'hierarchy' and tradition, but market effectivity (profit) and innovative flair. Three connected observations are important here about this general 'crisis of masculinity' in the new circumstances of market society.

First, we are witness to what might be seen as a generalized 'reaction-formation' amongst very many young (as well as middle-aged) men. Following the pioneering analysis undertaken by Albert Cohen in very different circumstances, we can observe a variety of strategic attempts by young men in different positions within the post-Fordist social formation (with its ostensible gender-neutrality or alternatively its practical emphasis on a set of 'female' skills and talents, such as customer care in the service industry) to affirm their social value. We can translate this into Cohen's terms as a 'rejection of the rejectors' and a reaffirmation of the value of masculine talent (for example, as purveyors of humour). One of the most obvious resources in use in this process of reaction-formation in Britain is the fast-growing new market of men's magazines (ranging from *GQ*, *Loaded*, *FHM*, and *Maxim* at the expensive end of the market[15] to *Viz* magazine, at the other). *Viz* magazine achieved considerable success through the late 1980s via its celebration of the infantilist side of masculinism described by Adler. Most of these new 'lad-mags' cater for, and celebrate, a stereotypical and rigid version of masculinity, organized around sex, football, drink and leisure 'lifestyle', but they also position their reader in relation to the broader market society in very specific fashion (as irresponsible and hedonist consumers, still 'in the imagination' in a position of domination over women).[16] The explosion of this market of men's magazines runs parallel, in Britain, with the repositioning of football in the popular consciousness, as a form of everyday market culture – a cultural revolution which has worked to legitimize 'football-talk' (and therefore, primarily, the talk of men) as a form of everyday talk and conversation in different kinds of work environment. This process, of course, helps construct the terrain of the work environment itself – prioritizing the interests of men (even when these men's value and utility to an organization is in relative decline), and subordinating agendas of many women – precisely at a time when the composition of the workforce is changing, and women, both in numerical terms and perhaps in other respects, are threatening to achieve far greater power and financial recognition than in the earlier Fordist period. A variety of adaptations to such circumstances are available to young women. Not least, of course, they can learn masculinist roles (for example, as football commentators) but, in so doing, they contribute to the reinvention of new forms of hegemonic masculinity.

A second theme I want to highlight – though relatively underemphasized in Connell's account – is the contradictory relationship of this crisis of masculinity to the new realities of the market society. The issue here is the developing contradiction between traditional forms of male expression, where these still exist – the contemporary culture of 'laddishness' – and the actual disciplines, skills and aptitudes and cultural attributes ('social skills') demanded by the new market societies. This issue finds expression, for example, in the urgent debate now exercising the attention of national governments as to the failure of young men to keep pace with young girls in schools. A report from the Chief Inspector of Schools in England and Wales, released in March 1996, confirmed the conclusion arrived at by many educational researchers, namely that girls were now more successful in schools in every subject other than physics, and that almost all ethnic minorities were achieving better examination results than white boys from poor inner-city schools.[17] In the anxious journalistic coverage which followed the release of this report, commentators identified still other dimensions of this gender crisis in schools – for example, results from surveys of young men in schools who, in the face of all the evidence from examination performance, felt they were 'better than the girls'. The only barely suppressed issue here is the ability of boys and young men – as socialized not just by their families of birth but by the larger culture (for example in the reactive culture of laddishness in men's magazines and on football talk-shows) – to adjust to the technical demands either of the 'knowledge society' or the interpersonal skills involved in providing service in a consumer culture. The evidence is that this problem (of attachment to a rigid stereotype of masculinism) is more pronounced in some cultures (Britain, Australia) than others (France, Canada, the South-East Asian countries, Ireland) – particularly, perhaps, because of those societies' significant and lengthy history of mass manufacturing and, with it, of organized labour.

The third defining dimension of the crisis of masculinity amongst young men is the specific form which this crisis assumes at lower levels of opportunity – on what Miles (1992) would identify as 'the bottom rung' of market society. The emergence of protest masculinity is most marked, as Connell himself argued in respect of his own work in Australia, in circumstances of poverty. In Britain, Beatrix Campbell has provided a dramatic account of the depredations of the already-limited provisions and public spaces on benighted council estates (in Newcastle upon Tyne and Oxford) by angry young men cut loose from the disciplines and controls of the adult labour market (B. Campbell 1993). Similar processes of the cutting-loose of angry and disaffiliated young men 'in circumstances of poverty' and marginalization in the labour and housing markets are depicted with equal power in a French semi-documentary movie, *La Haine*. Bob Connell speaks of the public spaces of these residualized spaces as male 'zones of occupation', in which 'contests of daring, talk about sport and cars, drugs (mainly alcohol) and sexism provide entertainment in a bleak environment' (Connell 1987: 133). Also central to the activities of disaffiliated young men in these bleak environments, what Mike Davis, in the context of southern California calls the 'new bantustans' (Davis 1990: 223), is the everyday pursuit of money. Money is the entry-ticket to the consumer markets of the broader market society – clothing, for example (not just in drink or drugs); pleasure (drink, drugs, and sex, in different configurations, but also, as for example, in car-theft and so-called joy-riding, in 'fantasies of escape'); and excitement (very frequently, in the excitement of violence, so 'making a mark' in the local community by instilling fear or respect).[18] In many market societies, the attempt to control the activities of this new 'lumpenproletariat' (overwhelmingly composed of young men, sometimes of a very young age[19]) lies at the very core of Government investment in crime prevention and community safety schemes of many different descriptions – the new 'market in social control' to be discussed in chapter 7.

The masculinism of the new poor areas in free market societies has a particularly desperate quality. American researchers speak of an 'in-your-face' confrontationalism, not just amongst 'gangsta' young black males, but more generally evident on the street corners, supermarket parking lots and outside the all-night convenience stores that dominate many an urban neighbourhood. The few measures taken to try to improve the opportunities for work or for leisure in these areas meet with a violently negative response, as described in Jay MacLeod's ethnographic study of poor kids in an anonymous city in the American north-east, *Ain't No Makin' It* (MacLeod 1987). What little research has been completed in Britain into these residualized areas of major cities identifies what is now a long-established pattern of very high rates of unemployment amongst adult men, associated with a well-established and quite heavily patronized alternative economy catering to material needs and other pleasures, which increasingly has taken on the appearance and substance of a full-time business, dominated by a small number of leading entrepreneurs (Taylor and Walklate 1994; Hobbs 1997a). We shall turn to a more detailed discussion of these fields in chapter 5.

In the highly unpredictable alternative economies of 'opportunity', it is hardly surprising to find evidence of a new embrace – albeit in markedly different circumstances – of the 'focal concerns' of lower-class culture first identified in 1958 by Walter Miller; not least, the belief in toughness and in fate – highly accentuated renditions of what young men in these neighbour-hoods tend to buy into, as a way of making a symbolic connection to the lost world of muscular labour (for example, in the docks, in the steelworks, or the coal mines) with its widely mourned sense of comradeship and mutual assistance (amongst men).[20] What is also obvious, of course, is that this attempt to reinvent the male-bonded workgroups of Fordist industrial society in the urban wastelands of market society is a pathological process, in the specific sense of being a desperate attempt to shore up the power of working-class men with the attitudes, the language and folklore, and muscular capacities demanded of men in the Fordist factory *out of historical time* and entirely *in the wrong place* (in colonized public space rather than within the sequestered male space of the factory).

Household Formation, Household Non-formation and Homelessness

In Fordist societies, young people's entry into the labour market was frequently accompanied, sometimes within a relatively short period, by marriage and by moves made towards the creation of a new family home – the process known to social survey researchers as 'household formation'. There is evidence that many young people – unable to contemplate the long-term investment in mortgages – are postponing the prospect of household formation, except in the form of shared accommodation with a group of peers.[21] In Britain in 1997, for example, some 50 per cent of young people aged twenty-one to twenty-four were still living in their parents' home.[22] Research by Claire Wallace (1987) has suggested that the transition from adolescence to adulthood in post-Fordist societies has come to be reorganized around a range of more extended and discrete transitions, operating, first, between the school and the labour market, secondly, between the parental home and the housing market and, finally, between the family of origin and the 'family of destination' (which may not approximate a family in any of the familiar Fordist senses) – and that young people (competitively in college and in the labour market, and collaboratively in the housing market) are forging a range of very different biographical routes or pathways between these different points of departure and arrival (Wallace 1987: 2). In this sense alone, as will be argued later, any anxieties on the part of adult authority with respect to the development of collective subcultural adaptations by generations of young people as a whole to their 'shared' or unitary set of problems increasingly looks like an anachronism.

In the meantime, at the lower levels of most post-Fordist market societies, there has been a significant increase – again since the early 1980s – in the number of visibly homeless people, and of beggars, on the streets (a powerful signifier of material context within which young people's own consciousness of market-position is forged). According to one detailed investigation, there were some 150,000 homeless young single people in Britain in 1996 (Carlen 1996: 1) – a figure that has been increasing steadily though unevenly since the passage of the Social Security Act of 1988, which removed all housing benefit entitlements from 16- and 17-year-olds (1996: 29). In Britain the official figures on homelessness, collected by the Department of Employment, consist of counts of the number of individuals accepted into permanent local authority accommodation. These are widely accepted as involving a massive underestimation of the real number of actually homeless people: an independent research report released in December 1996 suggested that about one in twenty young people in British cities would be homeless in any one year (an estimate which included a count of those sleeping rough, staying in hostels, or living temporarily with friends) (*Guardian*, 10 Dec. 1996). The evidence of this homelessness is there on the streets for all to see, and my recent research in Manchester and Sheffield confirmed that this street presence operated as quite a fearful visual reminder to young people themselves of a fate that could befall them, if they fail to 'be lucky' in contemporary, post-Fordist markets for employment and/or housing (Taylor et al. 1996: ch. 11).

THE OMNIPRESENCE OF DRUGS AND ALCOHOL

One of the most critical issues, substantially ignored by modernist subcultural theory in the 1960s, preoccupied with young people's role in a society of production, is the extraordinary economic significance, in the sphere of consumption, of 'the youth market'. For all that young people as individuals may have been commanding lower wages in the post-Fordist labour markets of the 1990s, the overall size of the market for youth-oriented consumption products (from music and clothing through to new technology products, from CD players to computers) in most Western societies is enormous, and – as audience researchers have regularly confirmed – of vital importance for setting trends within adult consumption markets as well. In a number of powerful interventions, Zygmunt Bauman (1987, 1988, 1993, 1995, 1996) has discussed the inherent logic of this newly liberated market in consumption. It is a market that no longer has to confront the complex web of regulation imposed in the earlier modernist period – for example, regulating the public sale or intrusion of sexual commodities or clearly delimiting the limits of interpersonal violence, for example, in its representation on cinema.[23] This has helped launch the processes which have led commentators on contemporary Russia to identify it as *bespredel*, a 'society without limits' (Handelman 1994) – that is, a society in which 'everything is for sale'. The most prized commodities in such a society are those which appear to offer a temporary respite or escape from the sense of threat, the turmoil of constant change, the everyday striving and, indeed, the sense of defeat and despair that life in a competitive market society seems often to involve.

Not the least of the connections here is the question of young people's involvement with the use of illegal drugs. In Britain, in the late 1990s, the concern focuses on an apparent renewal of interest in drugs (after what was thought to be some reduction in use reported in the 1980s, after major government campaigns on heroin). The current preference is apparently for so-called dance drugs, sometimes used in combination with cannabis and/or with alcohol.

The market in cannabis and dance drugs for young people 'going out' on the weekend, in British cities like Manchester, or, indeed, the youth cities of 'middle Europe' like Berlin, Budapest or Prague, is enormous. About a quarter of all respondents (aged 16 to 29) in Britain admitted to Home Office Crime Survey researchers in 1994 that they had used prohibited drugs (overwhelmingly, cannabis or one of the dance drugs) in the previous year (Ramsay and Percy 1996). In the north-west of England further research, based primarily on 'self-report surveys', suggested that six out of ten 14–15-year-olds in the region reported being offered drugs, and 36 per cent admitted to having used drugs in the past month (Measham, Newcombe and Parker 1994). The same researchers' interpretation of other evidence on patterns of drug use in the region suggested that over 200,000 young people aged sixteen to twenty-four had used some form of drug – most commonly, cannabis or one of the dance drugs. On the basis of their survey research, they advanced the proposition that consumption of drugs, especially cannabis and Ecstasy, should now be regarded as a 'normal' feature of adolescence, at least in this part of England.

These generalizations about overall prevalence of drug use are controversial on various counts.[24] For many commentators, the most important interpretation of the recent return of cannabis use amongst young people and, in particular, the widely publicized explosion in the use of Ecstasy was that which emphasized the anti-depressant qualities of these two drugs (Keane 1997). It was in this way, in part, that one could begin to understand the *demand-side* of this particular pleasure market – particularly in the light of the depressing realities of the juvenile labour market itself, and the morose mix of authoritarianism and moralism which accompanied the treatment of the young in the last years of the Conservative administration. This would not be to ignore the presence in particular neighbourhoods or in places of youthful resort of the front-line salespeople (the 'pushers') involved in the trade in drugs (the 'supply-side' in this particular market), but it would be to insist that any adequate explanation of the success of these particular suppliers must first explain the conditions which gave rise to 'demand'. It is important, that is, to approach the analysis of the prevalence of drugs amongst young people in market societies in the late 1990s specifically as a phenomenon of markets: the marketing of pleasure, through purchase of a pleasurable item from a salesperson (albeit, in this instance, in formally illegal exchange). Vitally, as Dorn and South argued in a series of interventions in the late 1980s (Dorn, Murji and South 1991; Dorn and South 1983 and 1987), this particular market is a *mass market*, not just in terms of its overall economic significance but also in terms of its immediate impact on – and its widespread intrusion into – the lives of young people.

Research in the United States, in Britain and in other European societies amongst children of school age has confirmed a widespread acquaintance with illegal drugs, circulating amongst friends or on sale nearby. In this particular sense, of course, the drug markets of the 1990s are more 'democratic' (widely dispersed and available) than those described by Cloward and Ohlin in 1960, where drug-use was explained as the resort of the 'double-failure', moving on into the retreatist subculture. Analysis of the contemporary processes of recruitment of young people into drug-using careers, involving one substance or another, or a mix of drugs, would have to follow a different trajectory to that pursued in the 1960s – making sense, in particular, of experimental drug-use as a first resort on the part of young people in market societies. The relationship between experimentation with different kinds of drugs and involvement in other forms of criminality (especially theft) would involve much more complex lines of analysis than the straightforward sequences of career moves identified by either Cloward and Ohlin or Albert Cohen. Certainly, some forms of involvement with addictive drugs are closely linked to serious forms of theft and robbery. A research project in the north-west of England conducted by Howard Parker and his associates in the mid-1990s interviewed a sample of 82 heavy users of cocaine, who reported spending an average of £20,000 each on their cocaine supplies, as against only £6,000 on other domestic expenditures (Parker and Bottomley 1996). Not least because of its illegal status, but also because, as a mass market, it is concerned with its own survival in a volatile market place, the drug market 'naturally' operates as a supermarket for different tastes. In this fashion, hard drugs become more easily available to young people who might feel 'they have nothing to lose'. It is also important to realize how much of the consumption activity of a youthful generation working for low wages or in insecure employment is, in any case, connected with the illegal market – for example, in the market for replica clothing, running shoes or bootleg CDs and videos – and how drugs, especially when sold as a special deal or a bargain, present themselves as just another commodity on the market (Ruggiero and South 1997). In a number of other British research reports, significant numbers of young people are reported to be experimenting with combinations or mixes of drugs ('polydrug users'). It may be, indeed, that we need to retrieve at least one of the themes of the subcultural theory articulated by David Matza, in recognizing the existence of a very contemporary version of a 'subculture of delinquency' – that is, a loose and broad-based 'outsider culture', consisting of young people who have taken dance drugs and/or cannabis, or who know of those who do, and who therefore locate themselves outside of any identifiable and dominant moral sphere of strict legality. In some areas of youthful activity – for example, in clubbing – there may be a very close relationship between the commercial youth culture, sceptical of a purely legalistic idea of righteousness, and the broader body of young people as a whole. So we will need to understand that the distribution of 'outsider cultures' *per se* will not be a direct expression of social position and patterns of economic deprivation.[25]

The developments taking place in these markets in youthful pleasures and style in the late 1990s in Britain make it clear that any adequate explanation of that market has also to take into account the market in alcohol – and offer an explanation both of the demand for, and supply of, alcohol to young people. In 1997, the local and national press in Britain gave extensive publicity to the marketing by breweries and drinks companies of alcoholic soft drinks ('alcopops') in street-corner shops and supermarkets (where they were available for purchase by young people under the age of eighteen). The marketing of these new products to the youth market had actually been initiated (through an advertising campaign costing £190 million) in 1995, and by 1997 amounted to a £275 million.[26] Campaigns to market alcoholic lollipops ('popsicles' in American parlance) to children were also in active preparation (*Guardian*, 24 June 1997). The launch of these new youth products occurred in a context in which, according to other reports, increasing numbers of young children were starting to drink alcohol at an increasingly early age.[27] Average consumption of alcohol amongst young people as a whole was reported to have risen from 0.8 units per week in 1990 to 1.3 units in 1994.[28]

This occurred, it should also be noted, at a time in which alcohol use amongst adults was also significantly on the increase, and in which a significant number of adults (6 per cent of all adult men) were drinking to levels that were likely to damage their health (with 1 in 20 being alcohol-dependent, as against only 1 in 45 who were deemed to be dependent on any other kind of legal drug (from tranquillizers to Ecstasy), and at a time of increasing concern over the broader social effects of alcohol abuse. A report from the Alcohol Concern organization, *Measures for Measures*, released in 1997, graphically suggested:

> The link between violent crime and alcohol has a long history with recent research suggesting that drink is involved in 65 per cent of murders and 75 per cent of stabbings. Even more injuries and deaths are caused by drink-drive accidents which kill 600 people a year and thousands of injuries. The accidents do not end on the road. About 25 per cent of drownings and 40 per cent of deaths in fire are put down to drink. One in four acute male hospital admissions is related to alcohol. Young men are particularly vulnerable to alcohol-related violence. There are 5,000 'glassings' annually, in which a smashed beer glass is used as a dangerous and disfiguring weapon. All told, there are about 33,000 alcohol-related deaths every year in Britain. (Dean 1997, summarizing Alcohol Concern (1997))

The involvement of alcohol (and, particularly, of the kinds of strong lager marketed at adolescent young men) in some of the most horrific instances of youth violence in British post-war social history (from the Notting Hill race riots in 1957 to the Heysel disaster in 1986) is a matter of record. The 'excessive' use of alcohol by young British men is now widely recognized throughout many other European Union member-states as a symbol of a seriously problematic cultural adaptation. The challenge to social science and criminology, both politically and analytically, is quite clear, and it is irresponsible for populist commentators to take refuge in familiar mystifications of social scientists – operating within a framework involving a rather mechanical positivism, on the one hand, and relativistic appreciation of all things youthful, on the other – to cavil about the complexity of causal explanation and thereby clear British breweries or alcohol-abusers of any responsibilities in respect of the social consequences of alcohol abuse amongst British youth (Sumner and Parker 1995; Parker 1996).

In the general area of drug and alcohol abuse, the discourses of those health professionals and those social service workers who are still involved with personal and familial crises in the broad society speak urgently of the need for national (and, perhaps, international) strategies of *harm-reduction* – activated by a recognition, born of close observation, of the serious consequences of drug and alcohol abuse on individuals' lives, and the lives of their friends, families and (frequently) their neighbours and larger – perhaps already disadvantaged and disorganized – neighbourhood. Elliott Currie (1993a, 1993b)), in grappling with the drug dilemma in the United States and the prospect confronting young people in that society, recognizes that the launch of effective campaigns of harm-reduction might involve some of the elements that are currently being advocated by critics of current drug policies in the United States – notably, the decriminalization of minor drug-use, particularly, as in the Netherlands, the large-scale decriminalization of marijuana. Such a selective decriminalization of certain drugs could be one dimension in a serious campaign of hard-reduction, not least in disrupting the process of production of 'outsider cultures' of illegal drug-use. However, as Currie continues, in respect of the currently extraordinarily influential calls for the 'decriminalization' – that is, the 'deregulation' – of all drug-use (that is, the 'market solution') Currie observes:

> Proponents of full-scale deregulation of hard drugs also tend to gloss over the very real primary costs of hard drug use – particularly on the American level – and to exaggerate the degree to which the multiple pathologies surrounding drug use in America are simply an intended consequence of a 'prohibitionist' regulatory policy. (Currie 1993b: 68)

A central obligation of critically minded social commentators working in this area is to explain the 'conditions of existence' of the *apparently escalating demand* for both dance drugs and hard drugs amongst different fractions of the youthful population. In the sphere of alcohol abuse, the task is to explain the centrality of heavy drinking in 'British culture' generally – and, amongst many adolescent young men and 'young adults', the continuing play of the 'eight pints a night' culture – drinking into oblivion – as 'a measure' of 'the man', and other variations in the use of drink, and their consequences. One key issue here is to explore the reported new forms of transgressive 'excess' with drink, sometimes in combination with other drugs, and its relationship to the mass marketing of drink in youth magazines and also of the new 'laddishness'. In other European societies, the issue might be posed differently. For example, in Italy one serious issue is the use, not so much of drink, but of different varieties of drugs by young men, notably in the affluent North, in the course of different forms of 'excess', like the playing of 'chicken-games' on motorcycles on the motorways. The availability of drugs is also closely connected in with the emergence in that country of a range of alternative strategies for survival adopted by new immigrants into Italy – often operating under various degrees of duress in the drug trade as the front-line operatives for organized crime. In this instance, as in some of the heavily marginalized housing estates of Northern Europe, the significance of drugs as an item in the hidden economies of everyday survival is inescapable. But the analysis of the destructive personal effects of the use of such drugs on users, and on the neighbourhoods in which they live, is also a vital challenge.

Calls for the decriminalization of the drug trade – predicated as they are on the belief that 'the market' (unlike the State) has an inherent capacity to solve most social problems – may (contradictorily) forget the broader origins of the demand for drugs or alcohol – in particular, that is, their critical role as distractions from (as well as expressions of) the pressures inherent in competitive market society itself (not least a market society dedicated to the constant marketing of the short-lived pleasures of 'consumption').

WINNERS AND LOSERS IN MARKET SOCIETY: PRESENT AND FUTURE PROSPECTS

In the Fordist period (which formed the assumed, though usually unidentified, backdrop to the classic literature of subcultural writers on 'delinquency') the dominant assumption was that the mass of young people *would* be able, by means of merit and/or effort, to advance themselves in school, in the labour market and in personal life-chances. Critical commentary of the period focused on the ways in which the educational systems sometimes gave unfair advantage to privileged children in private schools. But the main emphasis in the critique of unequal opportunities in this Fordist period was on the relative underdevelopment of State systems of education, attended by the mass of pupils. One measure of the transformation of social possibilities in many contemporary market societies, even for children from 'privileged' backgrounds, is the rapid increase in the number of children who are now being educated outside any shared public facility – in private schools – in the hope, nurtured by their parents, that the purchase of this particular advantage 'on the free market' will advantage their children in the intensified competition for appropriate higher educational place and labour market opportunities that characterizes most market societies.

Living in market society in the 1990s is clearly not akin to living the 'market culture' of late nineteenth-century England, at the high point of industrialization or at the point of entry into Empire. As the architecture built in that period (for example, in the city centres of Manchester, Milan or Berlin) so clearly proclaims, the imperial period of high capitalism in Europe involved a massive level of self-confidence and of certainty with respect to future fortunes, certainly of capital itself, but also of the broader society. The grand self-confidence of a European capital class, drawing on the traditions of a landed aristocracy (along with some important instances of philanthropy and public works) is no longer an assured feature of most market societies in Europe. As also in the United States, there is an unmistakeable sense of a middle class 'under threat', engaged in a variety of strategic moves to shore up its position in the markets of housing, labour, education and health, and also in strategies to shore up a sense of personal security in its own residential neighbourhoods (Ehrenreich 1989; Taylor and Jamieson 1998).

Alan MacFarlane (1987) and Martin Weiner (1993) remind us how the unleashing of market forces was seen in Victorian times to have both liberatory and unsettling aspects. The 'liberation' consisted, primarily, in the consequences which apologists for the new capitalism hoped would flow from the general accumulation of capital and wealth, 'trickling down' to the population in general.[29] But anxiety was provoked, in particular, by the increasing encouragement which the power to consume might give to a population unattuned to giving expression to their impulses. Particular concern was expressed as to the ability of young people, in particular, to handle the 'social power' that this new purchasing power might give them (Weiner 1993: 137) – a refrain which has been frequently repeated at different moments in twentieth-century English history, not least during the 'affluent' 1950s and 1960s (Hall et al. 1978). Weiner argues that the social measures developed to guard against the unleashing of 'reckless passions' in nineteenth-century England entailed the massive expansion of the penal apparatus and, in particular, the controlling emphasis of a stern Victorian moral order, carefully delineating the appropriate limits of actual behaviour and expression. It needs little reflection to realize that these kinds of moral constraint have not been a powerful feature of free market culture in Britain or in any other identifiable market society at the end of the twentieth century. The articulation of a project of moral constraint was attempted at the national level in Britain during the second administration of Margaret Thatcher (Taylor 1987) but was quietly dropped during the mid-1990s, during the death throes of an administration itself beset by 'sleaze'. There is a sense, indeed, in which such a project of moral constraint sits uneasily alongside governmental or enterprise-led projects directed at encouraging the fearless entry of a population into the competition for world markets, oriented around the endless invention of new consumer goods (objects of desire), and consequent competivity of a national population in 'unregulated' global markets. The two key distinguishing features of free market societies in the late 1990s are the continuing emphasis on the common sense refrain that 'one must compete to survive' and, secondly, the recognition that this project of enhancing national competitivity may mean that 'the nation-state' cannot provide a universal protection for those who are said not to be helping themselves. In such societies, as Oliver James (1995) has so keenly observed, there will *by definition* be 'winners' and 'losers'.

The population of losers may potentially include very significant proportions of young people who have been excluded from the full-time secure labour market guaranteed to their predecessors in the post-war period, and who are now experiencing the full impact of the government campaigns, in the name of the market, against 'state dependency'. Oliver James argues that the increase that occurred in the prevalence of reported juvenile crimes of violence in England and Wales between 1987 and 1993, measured by him at 40.5 per cent, should be understood as a direct expression of the frustrations and difficulties faced by these cohorts of young people, attempting in vain to avoid the fate of being defined as 'losers' in a culture where 'winning' was the only apparently unchallenged value. In similar vein other commentators have pointed to the striking increase in suicides that has occurred in many Western societies – most notably amongst young men – as additional evidence of the impossibilist nature of the challenges facing this fraction of society in a rapidly changing post-Fordist and marketized society. According to a World Health Organization study, suicide rates amongst 20- to 24-year-old men have increased by an average of 20.5 per cent in fourteen selected countries in the period from 1970 to 1992 (see table 5).

Table 5 Suicide rates, young men aged 20 to 24, selected countries (per 100,000)

Country	1970	1980	1992	Change 1970–92 (%)	Change 1980–92 (%)
New Zealand	15.6	27.8	52.2	+234.6	+87.8
Norway	9.2	26.5	37.2	+304.3	+40.4
Australia	16.7	25.6	34.6	+107.2	+35.2
Switzerland	32.6	48.0	33.7	+3.1	−35.3
Austria	32.9	40.4	31.2	−0.6	−22.7
Ireland	6.6	7.3	29.2[a]	+342.4	+300.0
Canada	21.9	30.4	29.0	+32.4	−0.5
USA	19.0	26.6	25.4[a]	+40.0	−0.5
UK	8.5	9.6	16.9	+98.8	+76.0
Germany	24.6	27.0	16.0	+19.7	−34.9
Japan	18.8	24.1	15.3	+29.3	−18.6
Italy	4.5	7.6	8.3	+84.4	+0.9

[a] 1991.
Source: World Health Organization Database, reported in Blanchflower and Freeman (1997), recalculated

The increase in suicides amongst young men speaks to the way in which the crisis in Fordist labour markets connects to one of the other, previously discussed, defining crises of our time, the crisis in masculinity and the gender order. But, as an expression of the despair and the loss of self-esteem of the young men who kill themselves, these increases in suicide are also an index of a particular 'losing struggle' taking place in competitive market society. The statistical evidence on suicide amongst young men does not record the precise social position of suicides within labour markets or the broader 'social formation'. But counselling agencies and epidemiological researchers in the health field point to the increasing numbers of young men of lower- or working-class background committing suicide. A specifically psychoanalytical interpretation (of the kind encouraged by Bob Connell in his retrieval of the work of Alfred Adler) of the increase in male suicides, of course, would situate suicide on a continuum of behavioural adaptations amongst young men of different backgrounds. The 'protest masculinity' of young men imprisoned in desperate inner-city estates might result in suicide (for example, in a stolen car) but also result from acts of excess and transgression associated with the new 'laddishness' encouraged in different market-positions within market society, as well as from reactive bouts of desperation and despair. So whilst it is important, following the recent work of Chris Stanley (1995, 1997) into the 'transgressive' qualities of certain forms of youthful behaviour (he analyses 'computer hacking', 'raving' and 'joy-riding', in a post-Foucauldian sense, as a resistance to the 'discipline' of actually existing structures of opportunity and 'regulation' in market society), it is also vital to register the psychic and experiential limits of such behaviours as a 'magical resolution' of personal and social dilemmas (the classic approach of subcultural theory itself) – and, for example, in the case of 'joy-riding', a resolution which has potentially lethal consequences for self or others.

The medium- and long-term issues involved with survival of employment and growth within the European Union focus on the utopia of a highly skilled workforce, heavily involved with new technologies and especially new media, in which a longer-term strategy of survival demands a serious investment in education and training, especially in the skills involved in the explosion of high technology, multimedia etc. This vision of the economic (and cultural) future in Europe is, as already suggested, increasingly marshalled by a new transnational, multilingual business and political class, which routinely prepares its own offspring to take up key positions within this future society. The different societies which are now a part of market Europe are very differently placed in respect of this new economic market. Governments across Europe are frantically investing in the rapid provision of applied and vocational forms of 'skills' education, especially involving the application of computers and the Internet, thought appropriate for this new competitive global economy.[30]

The intriguing aspect of these new competitive pressures, as any Hegelian thinker would appreciate, is the way in which they contradict other aspects of market culture itself. In part, this is the classic issue, as first discussed by Daniel Bell (1976), in *The Cultural Contradictions of Capitalism*, of the contradiction between a culture that places emphasis on immediate gratification and reward (the consumerist market place), and an economy in which employment demands medium- or long-term investment of individual effort and labour. Another intriguing issue is whether such skills-acquisition is in practice a guaranteed or reliable route into employment, and whether it is widely believed so to be. In many market societies, there is a widespread belief, supported in the wider culture, that the attainment of employment and personal fortune is a function not of effort, in an ordered framework of organized education, but rather that such eventualities are a function of the contingencies of chance and the range of personal networks. For many young people living in what were once called 'transitional zones' – but which are now better described, following Mike Davis, as 'the new bantustans' or as residual territories, there is very little 'chance': there may be no escape. The experience of 'losing out' or 'falling' in a market society then becomes absolutely definitive for individual biographies (and the entry into alternative 'careers' in crime a serious possibility). For young people who, by fact of birth, gender, ethnicity, or area of residence, are better placed for survival in market society, the issue of chance or effort looms in a much more immediate fashion. Nowhere is this contradiction more forcefully proclaimed than in the 'wasteland' that is prime-time television in North America, where the marketing of undemanding 'entertainment' commodities have won out so unambiguously over 'education' and information. But it is also on television that the depth of the crisis of this aspect of 'market society' is powerfully glimpsed – on the one hand, in vicious irony (in *The Simpsons*) and, on the other hand, through the nostalgic or utopian imaginaries of alternatives (*Cheers, Northern Exposure*). The contradictions between the 'emptiness' and one-dimensionality of popular culture (and therefore everyday life) in market society in Europe and North America – and the challenges facing young people in the global market place – are inescapable, and make plain the limitations of a purely populist appreciation of market culture itself.

4

CRIME IN THE CITY: HOUSING AND CONSUMER MARKETS AND THE SOCIAL GEOGRAPHY OF CRIME AND ANXIETY IN MARKET SOCIETY

IMAGES OF CRIME, IMAGES OF THE CITY

The bulk of the crime and disorder that is the source of so much anxiety in market societies occurs, as a matter of personal experience or, more often, as a matter of report, in public space within cities.[1] This common sense connection has, of course, been in place, in the popular imagination, ever since the onset of mass industrialization and the explosive growth of the industrial cities in the nineteenth century (though it is worth remembering that the introduction of the 'nightwatchman' in English towns (and, indeed, of the jury system – understood as a group of witnesses to crime) dates from the Statute of Winchester in 1283 (Hibbert 1963: 27–9)). In Europe as a whole, from the early nineteenth century onwards, the 'image of crime' in the popular mind has been closely bound up with more or less dystopian images of the city itself as a place of threat or fear (Walkowitz 1992) – images that have been elaborated over the last 200 years, in a range of different ways, in crime fiction as well as in cinematic representations. Talking about crime in the late twentieth century is difficult to separate out from discussion of the condition of the city – and, indeed, throughout the last fifty years, during the high-point of the Fordist period, much of the criminological literature has overlapped with the literature of urban studies, and particularly with urban sociology.

In the literature on the city produced in the English-speaking world, in particular, there has been a consistent and recurring interest in the experience of one American city, Chicago, especially during the period between 1860 and 1920 – a period of explosive population growth (a sixfold increase) and also, of course, a period of enormous expansion in the geographical spread of that city and the mix and diversity of its housing areas. One important objective in this chapter, however, is to suggest that this continuing reference to one North American city whose origins and rapid growth can all be dated to the last 150 years (and understood as an expression of the explosive growth of American capitalism in that period) may be a misleading framework for the overall, comparative analysis of the urban condition and, in particular, the new struggle for position between cities in various ways in different parts of the world that is a defining feature of the transnational market society.

AMERICAN EXEMPLARS: CHICAGO TO LOS ANGELES

The continuing interest in Chicago has been a function, in large part, of the widespread availability of a literature of social commentary and analysis produced over a period of nearly thirty years in the Department of Sociology at the University of Chicago, providing a record of the effects of the rapid process of urbanization and industrialization taking place in and around that city in the 1920s to the 1940s, as well as making a number of recommendations for the amelioration of the 'social problems' such rapid change had produced. The prodigious output of ethnographic, statistical and analytic writing from this group of social commentators and reformists, in and of itself, has been an important factor in the continuing influence of 'the Chicago School' over twentieth-century thinking about cities.[2] The specifically ecological analysis of the Chicago School focused on the evolutionary logics thought to determine different uses of space amongst plant life as well as amongst humans – as developed by Robert Park in *The City*, but then by Ernest Burgess (1925) and later specifically applied to the explanation of patterns of 'juvenile delinquency' by Shaw and MacKay (1942) – has always been prominent in the accounts presented of the Chicago School in the field of criminology. Ernest Burgess's 'zonal theory of urban development' is one of the best-known legacies – a visual map or representation (see figure 1) of what were said to be five distinct concentrically developing zones around the 'central business district' (and 'the Loop' overhead railway) in Chicago itself. In one of a host of secondary commentaries, Bottoms provides a short summary of the Chicagoan model of 'axiate growth' of the city as follows:[3]

> According to this theory, the typical city could be conceptualized as consisting of five main concentric zones, the innermost of which was described as the non-residential central business district ... which was then circled by a 'zone of transition', where factories and poorer residences intermingled, and finally by three residential zones of increasing affluence and social status. New immigrants, it was postulated, would move into the cheapest residential areas of the city ... and then, as they became economically established, migrate outwards. This would be a continuous process, so that the 'zone in transition' would (as the name implies) have a high mobility rate. (Bottoms 1994: 588)

The driving forces of these processes of zonal development in the city were identified by Park and Burgess in terms of a biological analogy – that is, by reference to the ongoing struggle of 'different species' (in this instance, the cohorts of new immigrants from different parts of old Europe and the

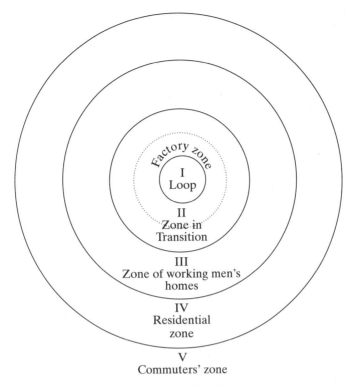

Figure 1 Ernest Burgess's zonal model of urban development
Source: Burgess 1925

American South and West moving into Chicago in search of work) for living space. Drawing on his reading of the German plant ecologist Ernst Haeckel, Robert Park (1967) wrote of a process of 'invasion, succession and dominance' in which new species of human being, transplanted into a new land, struggled for a place in which to settle, survive and grow. In his conceptualization of this struggle, the 'zone of transition' was seen as a kind of testing-ground of the strength and quality of each new 'species' – an examination of the ability of a species (an immigrant group) to thrive in a metropolis of opportunity and possibility. True to the straightforward evolutionary biology that underpinned this kind of analysis, some species would prove incapable either of advancement or progress in such an environment and would remain ensconced in certain sections of the zone of transition – and they would take up permanent residence in the mushrooming 'skid rows' or problematic zones of an expanding Chicago (including, indeed, the Wood-lawn area, close by the University of Chicago itself).

In the late 1960s, in one the most important re-formulations of Chicagoan axiate growth theory, John Rex and Robert Moore's study of the inner city areas of immigrant settlement in Sparkbrook, Birmingham, broke entirely with this biological and evolutionary approach and advanced an analysis of the struggle for living space in that city as a form of class struggle. This struggle was understood to be quite distinct from the direct conflict of classes in industrial production identified in Marxist theory, and derived instead from the classic analyses of class position, status and power advanced by Max Weber. The dimensions of the struggle took place between social groups occupying radically different positions in a market situation (that is, the market in housing). Rex and Moore argued, indeed, for the importance an outright 'class struggle' for housing, as a routine feature of all cities in industrial capitalist societies – but a struggle which would take on different particular forms in different cities in different societies at different times.[4] Rather later – in the 1970s – in France and in Britain, the work of Henri Lefebvre and David Harvey was to return to the Marxist tradition itself, especially the theories of property and value developed in Marxist political economy, seeking to explain the way in which the urban form (and, particularly, the radical differences in the quality of housing provision and of general life-opportunities within different areas of a city) gave expression to larger relations of social inequality in the capitalist order, and also contributed to their continued reproduction (Lefebvre 1991; D. Harvey 1973, 1989). The subsequent development in both these societies of what was then called a 'new urban sociology' was a measure of the extent to which critical social thinkers and social commentators wanted to move beyond the blinkered focus on the 'axiate growth' of cities developed in Chicago, elaborated as a 'natural effect', simply, of the rapid immigration and population movement into the ecologically patterned parameters of the urban region.

It is also important for our purposes here to register how much more recent sociological analysis of 'the city' and 'urban crime' in our own post-Fordist times, even in Europe, has relied on an American literature, focusing on another American urban conglomeration – namely Los Angeles. The inspiration of much such commentary has been the extraordinary study of that city produced in 1990 by Mike Davis – *City of Quartz: Excavating the Future in Los Angeles* (Davis 1990). This text has the overwhelming merit not only of understanding the city as a site of structured inequality but also of locating the unfolding destiny of the city within the broader set of dynamic and fundamental changes taking place in economic life – that is, in the crisis of the Fordist system of production, as it expressed itself throughout the southern Californian conurbation in the early to mid-1980s. It is a text that is able to retrieve a sense of the strong working-class and ethnic cultures, neighbourhood and work-based institutions and the sense of local identity that has grown up during the Fordist period, and to speak with great power and sensitivity about the significance of the loss of those strong communities (a city – and a set of places – which Davis was to identify in subsequent television documentaries as a 'warehouse of dreams').

THE CITIES OF OLD EUROPE

Over the years, many thousands of students of criminology outside America will have been asked to consider the applicability of an American urban literature to the understanding of cities in their own societies. Not least of the concerns of students of that American literature will have been that the processes through which cities emerged, with great speed, in the New World (in the case of Chicago, driven by a mass of commercial activities around the docks and, as described so graphically by Upton Sinclair (1900) in *The Jungle*, in the meat-packing and agricultural processing plants of Gary, Indiana, just south of metropolitan Chicago[5]) were very specific to America.

But this focus on the patterns of urban development in the United States in the early years of the twentieth century may be unhelpful as a way of understanding the evolution of cities in the Old World of Europe, or, indeed, the particular form and effect of the crises in those cities in the 1990s.[6] The transformation of the old medieval cities of Europe into heritage and tourist centres has been the subject of extended discussion by urban and cultural commentators. Arnold Toynbee's *Cities on the Move* (1970) reminds us of the continuing influence on the form and structure of cities in many different regions of Europe, of the city-states created over many millenia, but especially during the medieval period (see figure 2).

To this day, the built form, the street-scape and the social organization of daily living in many European centres of population (from metropolitan and capital cities like Barcelona, Rome and Vienna to cities like Cologne, Lucca and many other northern Italian cities) can only be understood by reference to the idea of a city-state, built around a central market and grand architecture of the sovereign prince, and surrounded by perimeter walls.

At the core of many such towns and cities, as Max Weber (1921) himself outlined, would always be a market place (in the Greek sphere of influence, the *agora*) which – according to many an urban historian (as well as to those modern-day philosophers revisiting the question of democracy: Habermas 1992; Sennett, 1970, 1990, 1994) – functioned not just as a place for the sale of agricultural and other produce, but also as a site of popular exchange of gossip, rumour and debate. According to some views, 'the market' was a kind of people's parliament in the street. For Weber, all cities of the occidental world exhibited some particular 'fusion of the fortress and the market' (Weber 1921: 77). Henri Pirenne (1925) argued that such market places were the node around which trade and commerce developed, expanding outwards beyond the city wall into a wider perimeter. Jane Jacobs was later to develop this argument, in her account of the development of the imaginary city of New Osibidian, whose early historical development was best to be understood, she argued, as a 'trading post' (Jacobs 1969: 23) – built around an empty space (a place where parties came together to engage in commercial exchange).

The lengthy history of the market city, and the different functions performed by these market places in different urban communities (what Weber would have called 'related forms of association') is a fascinating area of study (see Weber 1921: ch. 1) – not least in terms of the sociological queries that are always posed by such markets. Which fractions of the population make use in a particular historical conjuncture of the urban markets as consumers? What is the relation between the use of these markets and the ebb and flow of the business cycle? What is the relationship between these apparently legitimate

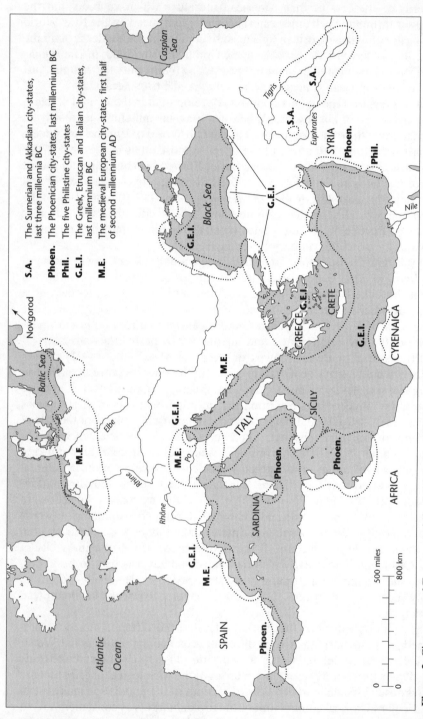

Figure 2 City-states of Europe and the Middle East (3000 BC–1500 AD)
Source: Toynbee 1970

Legend (from map):

S.A. The Sumerian and Akkadian city-states, last three millennia BC

Phoen. The Phoenician city-states, last millennium BC

Phil. The five Philistine city-states

G.E.I. The Greek, Etruscan and Italian city-states, last millennium BC

M.E. The medieval European city-states, first half of second millennium AD

instances of small business practice and the trade in stolen commodities or in commodities obtained by other means? Each and every one of these questions has enormous relevance in the understanding of 'the market', 'the city' and, indeed, the issue of community safety and 'density of use' of the city at the end of the twentieth century. In many different parts of Europe, for example, the return of a range of different kinds of 'street markets' is one of the clearest expressions of a more general process of marketization – whether the street markets in question are, on the one hand, the markets that have been built up (and then officially sanctioned) to cater for the new poor in some of the deindustrialized cities in the North of England,[7] the groups of kiosks that dominated the street-scape of Russia, Bulgaria, Romania and other ex-Communist societies undergoing the first years of 'shock-therapy' marketization, or, at the other extreme, the seasonal street markets that have been established to cater for the new rich in market Europe (like the summer market on Unter den Linden, opposite the Humboldt University in the old East Berlin – which specializes in the sale of extremely expensive bric-à-brac into the late hours of the evening, and which charges an entry fee). The issue of the relationship between street 'markets', urban space and the dynamic transformation of social structure (and of people's market-position) in market society is starkly posed.

There is certainly an important sociological sense in which the street markets of the poor are close cousins of other trading that is taking place on the street – particularly, of course, on the part of beggars, whose return in large numbers to city streets is one of the clearest expressions of the more general marketization of life at the centre of this analysis. The street markets of the poor, selling cheap items of food and clothing to those thousands of people in Western and Eastern Europe made poorer by the transformations of the 1980s and 1990s, are perhaps just one step away, in geographical terms as well as in terms of the potential of downward social mobility, from the street-corner which has become the established 'pitch' of the urban beggar – a colonization of public space for one particular commercial purpose. By contrast, the 'street markets of the new rich', and the pavement wine bars and cafés, involve the innovative colonization of what previously might have functioned as part of 'public space' to expand the numbers of sites available in a particular city for ostentatious consumption of consumer items. What is unmistakable, however, is the intrusion of capital (the possession or absence thereof) into different publics' use of urban space.

Just as we need to understand the continuing centrality of 'the market' to an understanding of cities, especially in the current period of market-liberalization, so also we need to understand the specific history – including the rise and fall, and the contemporary revival of the idea of a city as a fortress, derivative from the medieval period and earlier. The market towns and cities of the medieval period, importantly, *were* fortresses, surrounded by walls, and, in England, 'policed' at the perimeter by the men of the hundred, at the behest of the shire-reeve, with the streets inside the walls under the routinized surveillance of the nightwatchman. These 'community safety' arrangements, involving close partnership of the 'police' (the watch) and the citizen, which had been some considerable time in development, in different forms, in different towns across Anglo-Saxon England, were systematized for the entire kingdom by Edward I in the Statute of Winchester of 1283. Elsewhere in medieval Europe, similar developments were apparent – most notably, perhaps, in the broad belt of independent city-states – some 300 in all – which stretched across the territory that is now Italy. Operating under the hegemony of the Church or the Emperor, and dominated by different regimes of accumulation (the Medici in Florence, aristocratic patrons of the arts, or the more overtly mercenary families of Mantua and Ferrara), these city-states all had in common the construction of fortress systems for external defence and specified partnerships of the people and the principality itself.[8] Very similar forms of early 'urban development' were also occurring throughout the medieval period (from the twelfth to fifteenth centuries) across France, Spain and the rest of southern Europe. It is impossible to ignore *the return* in the late twentieth century of these forms of medieval thought, not least in the idea of a city as a fortress constructed *against* outsiders. But in recognizing this revival of the city-as-fortress, we should not forget the ways in which the rise of the modern industrial city in the nineteenth century very much coincided with the knowing and determined attempt to 'tear down' (or rethink the use of) the perimeter walls of the city, in order to create a body of shared public space even amongst the unequal citizens of early capitalist society.

So even the most cursory examination of the long history of towns and cities, from the early medieval period into the 'modernist' period of urban growth, prompted by the Industrial Revolution, acts as a kind of corrective to pragmatic and practical thinking about 'the city' and especially to the one-dimensional preoccupation of some twentieth-century urban sociologists (and criminologists) with the twentieth-century development of the new world cities of Chicago and Los Angeles. The model of the 'axiate growth of the city', expanding out in circles from a central business district (the centre of trade and commerce – a key spatial location in the city understood as a market in the use of space) makes retrospective sense *in a descriptive way* of the 'built form' of cities like Manchester, itself the subject of a famous extended commentary by Friedrich Engels himself in *The Condition of the Working Class in England in 1844*, except that (curiously) it does not see this struggle for spatial location as having any specific economic implications. Nor does it speak to the techniques which Engels attributed to the Manchester middle class for shielding nearby areas of poverty from view (Engels 1845) – the market in sequestered and protected space I will discuss in a little more detail later. There is no inherent reason why the pattern of urban growth in nineteenth-century London, as reported in the novels of Charles Dickens or the social commentaries of Henry Mayhew, or of St Petersburg, as recorded by Fyodor Dostoevsky, should be understandable only through the rigid prism of 'concentric zone' or 'axiate growth' theory. London as described by Dickens and Mayhew is a city divided, directly in class terms, from west to east, with a narrow strip of 'rookeries' (cheap lodging houses in multiple occupation) circling around the central core of London itself. This meant that the propertied middle class making its way into work in the City had to walk through a threatening and crowded corridor of street markets and narrow alleys, populated, at least according to the ethnographic observation (and fertile imagination) of Henry Mayhew, by a kaleidoscopic mass of 'costermongers', as well as women working the street market in sex (prostitutes), beggars, pickpockets, and others. Dostoyevsky's St Petersburg – a city built up by the Tsarist aristocracy between 1703 and 1796 around the Neva and a vast number of canals and rivulets – was (and is) a configuration of pockets of wealth and poverty in very close proximity, patterned primarily in terms of waterways and other features of local topography. The Haymarket area in St Petersburg, the dank and decrepit street market where Raskolnikov mingled with 'tradespeople and rag and bone men' in the opening pages of *Crime and Punishment* is only a matter of yards from the Marinskiy Palace to the north and the majestic Nevsky Prospect to the east. Some sixty to seventy years later, the urban form (and the social mix) of yet another old and majestic European capital city, Paris, was famously transformed as a result of the visions and commitment of Napoleon III's newly appointed prefect of the Seine, Baron Haussmann:

> In seventeen years [Hausmann] was responsible for a through-going transformation of the city. By 1870 one-fifth of the streets in central Paris were his creation, and the acreage of the city had been doubled by annexation. At the height of the reconstruction, one in five Parisian workers were employed in the building trade. In the name of slum clearance, some 350,000 people (on Hausmann's own estimation) were displaced from the *quartiers* of old Paris to make way for his new boulevards, parks and 'pleasure grounds'. These provided the illusion of social equality, but the practical effect – as in Engels' Manchester – was to raze working class neighbourhoods and shift the eyesores and health hazards of poverty to the suburbs. (Donald 1992: 438)[9]

St Petersburg and Paris were not typical examples, it should be said, of the emerging cities of the eighteenth or nineteenth century in Europe. Along with London (5.5 million inhabitants in 1890) and Berlin (2 million), Paris (also about 2 million) was one of the 'giant cities' that emerged as the capital city in the largest nation-states in Europe. Rome and Madrid, with only half a million inhabitants at the end of the nineteenth century, lagged behind, whilst the population of Vienna, the capital of the Habsburg Empire, at a million and half in 1900, was now slowing (Sutcliffe 1984: 5). The emergence of giant metropolitan cities was to be even more marked a feature of the processes of colonization of rural space, population growth and industrialization in North America that were to develop through the nineteenth century: New York had 4 million inhabitants in 1900, whilst Philadelphia and Boston had over 1 million. This unchecked growth of the vast metropolis, especially in North America, has, of course, given rise to a large and diverse literature, as well as other studies (for example, Fritz Lang's 1926 film *Metropolis*) on the amorphous, machine-like and impersonal character of urban processes. Marxist writers like David Harvey have wanted to see this vast expansion of the city as an expression of the inherent tendency of the capitalist mode of production itself to expand outwards in the search for new sources of capital accumulation (see Harvey 1973: ch. 6).

CITIES OF THE INDUSTRIAL REVOLUTION

The rapid development of capitalist industry during the course of the nineteenth century effected a fundamental transformation of the map of Europe itself. Economic historians identify the formation and consolidation of some twenty-five identifiable 'industrial regions', organized around fast-growing centres of heavy manufacturing industry and acting as a centrifugal force drawing populations into the cities in search of work and employment (see figure 3).

David Harvey's classic analysis (1973) elaborates how these industrial cities and regions were the sites of development of very specific sets of 'social relations'. These social relations (e.g. within the household) were in effect the processes through which industrial production itself was organized and reproduced. These processes might have a certain unevenness, dependent on the availability and level of development of the three crucial factors of production – land, labour and capital – and, in respect of the land that was available in a particular locale, on the natural resources obtaining in an area. The fast development, for example, of Manchester, in the North of England – the 'first city of the Industrial Revolution' or 'Cottonopolis' – was crucially dependent on its location at the confluence of three rivers, the canal system that linked it to the Atlantic Ocean, the abundant availability of wool for its textile mills from the sheep farms of the local countryside, and a climate that was beneficial for the craft of the cotton-weaver (Taylor, Evans and Fraser 1996: ch. 1). It also profited very quickly in the nineteenth century from a central position in the North of England and from an emerging system of rail transport that eased the emigration of workers into the city from outlying rural areas. Finally, it was enormously advantaged as a capitalist city by the fact of its early beginning in the process of industrial expansion and growth. The investment made by commercial interests in mills and warehouses helped to put in place an infrastructure which was to prove an attraction to many a wave of new capitalists from elsewhere in Britain and from Germany, Italy and other parts of fast-developing capitalist Europe. Manchester's rate of commercial and industrial expansion, and its growth of population (from 35,000 to 353,000 between 1801 and 1841 (Korn 1953: 57)), were a matter of international remark. But this city, the 'Shock City of the Industrial Revolution' was the same city, as indicated earlier (echoing the pioneering observations of Engels himself), in which quite unprecedented inequalities of living conditions and life-chances were unfolding, and grinding levels of poverty and ill health revealed. David Harvey reminds us how the bulk of the earnings of the 'free labourer' in these new capitalist cities would have to be spent on rent, and how those thousands and thousands who could not find employment would be left to their own devices on the streets. The central areas of these fast-expanding new cities of industrial capital became home to

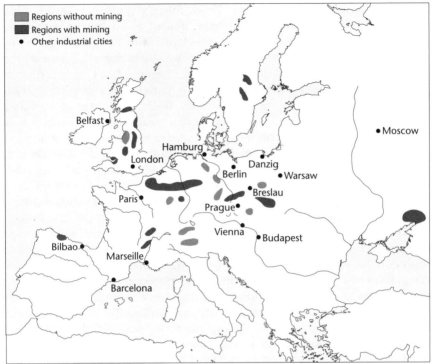

Figure 3 Industrial regions of Europe *c.*1880
Source: Hohenberg and Lees 1985 (© President and Fellows, Harvard College)

armies of beggars, pickpockets, vagrants and others – a 'residuum' that only later could seriously be described as a 'reserve army of labour', in that many of the urban poor (for example, in the 1840s) had *never* been in employment. It was not until the 1870s that any system of regulation of begging, and/or the other public activities on the street, which were so powerful a source of fear for the Victorian middle class, was created – in the form of the Charity Organization Society (Stedman-Jones 1971).

The new urban police

Properly speaking, the history of the regulation of the industrial capitalist city begins with the analysis of the development of the modern police force – in most European societies in the first years of the nineteenth century – a uniformed force, supported by public funds, given responsibility, alongside the army and militia, for the maintenance and enforcement of order in the public spaces of the exploding urban conglomerations. Allan Silver's classic study of the emergence of policing in England shows how policing developed specifically as a response to the anxiety felt by the propertied commercial and industrial classes over the security of their property, in the face of the explosive growth in the numbers of poor labourers taking up residence in the expanding industrial cities (Silver 1967). Silver's study has always been important for its depiction of the 'new police' as an instrument of the regulation of unequal class relations, developed with some nervousness by the newly propertied urban middle class, which, in the aftermath of the French Revolution, was anxious about the dangers of any such system of public policing, especially if organized as a national force (Ignatieff 1979).

The history of policing in England and Wales, and later in Scotland, therefore, is a history of the development of a local system of policing, with individual constabularies growing up in response to demands for policing in particular urban areas. There is an important sense in which this development of policing must be understood as an expression of the differential demands of different kinds of urban, semi-urban or rural areas for different levels or forms of policing (for example, the strategic capacities of individual metropolitan constabularies to undertake interventionist forms of policing in their local ghettos). The development of policing systems elsewhere in Europe and also in North America can also be understood as having this specific and distinctive local character, in which not only the culture but also the organizational form of a local police force can be understood in terms of the different demands made on a police force (in a direct and conventional sense, by locally powerful propertied classes but, more indirectly, by the particular configurations of inequality and deregulation – for example, the distribution of poor people's dwellings in juxtaposition with other areas of the city – determined, in large measure, by the built form of particular cities). In this sense, it is not surprising to observe the acquisition of quite distinctive reputations (and also quite distinctive organizational structures and capacities) on the part of different police forces in different countries (the Los Angeles Police Department as against the San Diego Police Department in California; Toronto Police as against the Ottawa Police in Ontario, Canada; the Greater Manchester Police as against the Lancashire Police in England).

The regulation of unequal industrial cities in the nineteenth century and in the twentieth century has certainly involved the periodic deployment of what now would be called a visible police presence – sometimes, in the form of preemptive interventions, especially in circumstances where 'working people' in the cities have organized collectively around some kind of reform (in England, the history would include the Peterloo Massacre through the 1929 General Strike to the Miners' Strike of 1982–4) but also police interventions into 'civil disorder' or criminal incidents, with the support of large sections of an anxious local population.[10]

Spatial and social sequestration in the industrial city

But, as many commentators have observed, the definitive dimension to the development of more regulated sets of social relations in new metropolitan urban areas of industrial society was the development of a system of social separation, or sequestration, of the classes. This process – focusing, in part, on the segregation of the propertied middle class – took specific and complex forms in different industrializing societies in the nineteenth century. In some regions of Britain, the sequestration of the commercial and industrial middle class took on a primarily symbolic and material form rather than involving radical geographical separation – many commercial and industrial magnates established their residence in large houses in close proximity to their factories or workshops, defended by a high front gate and equally high perimeter walls. In some British cities, other professional middle-class people chose to live close to their place of work (like, for example, the doctors of Manchester and Sheffield, taking up residence in Withington and Burngreave, respectively, close to the cities' major hospitals) – in close proximity to areas that would have been recognized by the Chicago School as 'the transitional zones' of the inner city.

Research into the development of 'residential segregation' in cities across Europe suggests that the development of a more radical separation of areas of class-based residence (in particular, the 'flight to the suburbs') first occur- red as a result of the development of new nodes of consumption (the suburban shopping street) in the later nineteenth century (Carter 1983: 190). In the United States, the work of Shevsky and Bell (1955), informed by a mix of functionalist sociology and classical geographers' interest in space, was to inspire an extensive research literature, in which was constructed a powerful and idealized image of the American city as a configuration of distinctive 'social areas', each characterized by discrete social functions (industrial production, commercial exchange, delivery of particular services (education, health, leisure and recreation, etc.), consumption, and areas for different forms of residential life (living close by the workplace, living in peace at some distance from the workplace, and living in retirement). In this idealized model, the American city was understood not just as a functioning social system, but also as the epitome of a fully developed modern urban civiliza- tion. An alternative variant of this vision was also to be found in the literature of urban planning with the planners' visionary commitment to the creation of new urban environments rationally built according to predetermined and specific social purposes. In the New World of North America, of course, given the availability of vast tracts of 'unbuilt ground', this envisioning of a planned city often had a very visionary and utopian character – the laying out on an open territory of a grid system of roads and highways, connecting different distinct areas of a territory in a rational pattern. This practice of claiming space was evident in both rural and urban settings. In cities, this rational organization of space and roads may (or may not) have helped newcomers navigate their way through that city making use of a geometric mental map (Indianapolis, in the United States; or Calgary and Edmonton, in Alberta, Canada), but its primary application was in planning of housing and industrial developments. This kind of a priori claiming of open territory in the name of the planned city was far less common in Europe than in North America,[11] and most often involves modification of the attempt to make a planned use of different areas in an already existing built form of the city, through the use of local authority powers (particularly with a view to 'zoning' a city for purposes of commerce, industry or recreation, or as residential areas). The chequered history of the attempt to re-plan the use of space in the crowded old cities and towns of 'old Europe' is far beyond the scope of this book, though it requires little reflection to understand that the challenges involved in this process of re-planning urban space will differ enormously in the older cities of medieval foundation, on the one hand, and the nineteenth-century industrial conurbations, on the other. What we can say is that the abstract conceptualization of all cities as planned and functional social systems is open to a mass of objections – not least, for an over-idealization of the ordered segmentation of the American city. It is also open, as I have suggested in two pieces on suburban areas in Manchester, England, in the mid-1990s (Taylor 1995a, 1996), to the empirical objection that it exaggerates the degree of separation between different social classes and different fragments of those classes that has been achieved in the twentieth century, in 'modern' industrial cities, especially in Europe. It may be that the idea of ordered segmentation of the classes and of different social areas is more accurate, descriptively, of metropolitan urban areas as they expanded outwards from their point of first settlement and commercial and industrial placement, on the vast land mass of North America, than it is for the crowded landscapes of old Europe.

The 'Modern City' – Twentieth-Century Processes of Urban Development

The most powerful memories of elderly Europeans still alive in the 1990s focus on the processes of urban development and rehousing that dominated the period after the Second World War. The removal of whole areas of poverty to 'the suburban edges' of cities, under the aegis, in particular, of central or local government planning authorities, was to be an absolutely definitive feature of social change in Europe for thirty years from the late 1940s. In part, this process of 'slum-clearance' and rehousing was the product of a particular political and moral sensibility born of the Second World War itself – the renewed commitment (first articulated after the first of the world wars in many European societies) to provide 'Homes Fit for Heroes'. But, in part, the commitment to the use of State investment and resources to rehouse the populations of the bleak terraced houses of industrial England, the estates of the Netherlands and Germany, the tenements and the 'projects' of Scotland and the *bidonvilles* in France was born of a memory of the 1930s themselves, and the brute inequality of the years of the Depression – the first experience, perhaps, during the twentieth century of the social effects of 'market failure' in capitalist economies. During the 1920s and 1930s, in Britain, millions of more fortunate people had been able to establish themselves in the expanding new suburbs – built to the west of the factories, enabling their residents to escape the effluence of the factories – and so begin the process of establishing their own private, utopian lives. But, as the residents of these suburban retreats were to discover during the common emergency of the Second World War, the majority of those defined as fellow citizens had remained imprisoned throughout the 1930s within the bleak and restrictive confines of 'the slums'. The process of slum-clearance that developed in Britain, and in many other European countries, during the 1950s, was, in this sense, a fundamentally utopian project – even a form of 'civic socialism' – in the sense of being informed by the commitment that 'the common people' should be accorded real opportunities in terms of shelter and space denied them, in free market circumstances during the first half of the century. In Sweden, this post-war civic utopianism was translated into a national project, as Gunnar and Jan Myrdal, amongst others, devoted their imagination to the design of whole suburbs, or residential communities, looking for a principled basis on which shared building and space might work to encourage more sociable and egalitarian forms of everyday life – as well as trying to think about the functional integration of transport, home and work (Harloe 1995). Across the whole of Europe, in the immediate aftermath of the Second World War, there was a perceptible desire – accepted even by the most conservative of organized political parties – not just to 'house the people' returning from the war, but, much more specifically, to rehouse the people in environments in which, according to the social wisdoms of the time, it was felt they could prosper.

Slum clearance and the new life

In England, this utopian sensibility found expression in the New Towns and Garden Cities movement. The underlying conception of this movement, with enormous appeal amongst planners and architects in the early post-war period, was not simply to replace the overcrowded environment of the slums, but more specifically to contribute to the general enhancement of the life of the people – for example, by separating children and play spaces from road traffic or by the provision, for the adult population or the elderly, of new and integrated systems of service and support, such as health centres, libraries, community centres and schools (Donnison and Soto 1980). In the late 1960s and early 1970s, in part as a result of the restriction of local authority finances, the utopianism that informed the Garden City movement was transferred into the aspiration to build new communities 'in the sky' (the catastrophic campaign to rehouse the urban poor in high-rise apartment buildings). In a rather formal analysis, Philip Cooke has identified the development of public housing (and other dimensions of the civilizing of the industrial-capitalist city during the early post-Second World War period) as the final maturation of 'modernity' in the sphere of urbanism. He continues: 'These locales express the transient ascendancy of the dynamic social strata of the time, namely the skilled and semi-skilled Labour-voting working-class' (Cooke 1988: 483). The 'socio-spatial' impact of this process of civilization and modernization – conceived of, in particular, as a project of the socially aspiring skilled working class (the labour aristocracy) – primarily involved, Cooke continues:

(i) the relatively even geographical spread to the periphery, semi-periphery and suburbs of modernization processes,
(ii) the partial convergence of income and employment indices between the classes and the regions,
(iii) a characteristic posture towards producing standardized products for volume markets, aiming for economies of scale,
(iv) economic developments in close proximity to new 'collective consumption' environments, and
(v) a characteristic demand for skilled and semi-skilled labour to fill secure, 'lifetime' occupations'.

The utopian aspirations that lay beneath this process of 'modernization' should be recognized and emphasized: on the one hand, the desire of many working people to escape proximity to the factory and, on the other, especially amongst working-class women, the desire to benefit from the 'modernization' of household economies that was promised by a house on the estates. This modern or, in our terms, Fordist city may have been spoken of, ideologically, as a sphere of egalitarianism and freedom, but it was also, of course, an urban social formation that expressed and helped reproduce very specific and structural inequalities in housing and space. The Fordist labour market itself – and therefore the larger Fordist housing market – subsumed a range of very different markets – with some more regulated than others – markets to which entry was by no means guaranteed to all 'free citizens'. The Fordist city was also, of course, a male-dominated urban formation, built around the divisions of labour in the home and the workplace that were demanded by the regime of mass manufacturing industry. So the city could be seen as a configuration of public spaces (factories, sports and playing fields, public houses, and even the public parks and the streets) dominated by men, whilst the home, and particularly certain spaces within it (e.g. the kitchen) was identified as women's territory (Common 1938; McRobbie 1980). In law, the domestic home was defined, above all, as a private place in which the writ of public authority did not run: the order of the household was maintained by the 'head of home'. Complicit in an acceptance of male authority (as a guarantee of the safety of women, children and other men in the private sphere), public discussions of issues of personal and community safety in the Fordist city focused almost entirely on issues of delinquency that intruded into *public space*. This kind of common sense about the security of the working-class household has recently been reinvented in a body of essentially mythico-nostalgic texts about the character of the mining communities of the North of England, by the ex-miner Norman Dennis, and then generalized to the Fordist social formation in general (Dennis and Erdos 1992; Dennis 1993). What Dennis's account so obviously suppresses is the understanding advanced long ago by John O'Neill with respect to the relation between the public and private spheres in the Graeco-Roman and modernist world – namely, that the existence of a formal, democratic system of regulation of the public sphere says little about the private sphere (the household) – an unfree, unequal sphere where the forceful reproduction of inequality between men and women, and adult men, especially, over children was unquestionable and necessary (O'Neill 1968: 70).[12] Robert Roberts's close description of the controlled violence of the working-class household in Salford, Manchester, in the 1950s – echoed in Bernice Martin's insightful reflections on working-class women's struggle in the same area to control their men and their drinking behaviour – is evidence of what sometimes went on within the 'sphere of necessity' in the working-class household (Roberts 1971; Martin 1981).[13] The gendered nature of public space in the Fordist city has been the subject of commentary by feminist social scientific commentators – for example, by Doreen Massey in her reflections on the taken-for-granted colonization of vast stretches of open field for football and other men's sports in Manchester during her childhood years (Massey 1994: 185). In some societies, like the Canadian, this colonization of playing space by young men has been the subject of significant practical challenge as well as legal challenges on the part of sports-minded young women.[14] Doreen Massey raises the fundamental issue, in respect of any celebratory accounts of the working-class household, as to who benefited most from such a structured form of social life. To make the point as directly she does, books with titles like *Coal is our Life* inescapably raise the question 'whose life'? So also, of course, do generalized disquisitions about the Public Sphere in modernist, Fordist societies (including Habermas's own enquiries) inescapably raise the issue, as posed by Nancy Fraser, 'which public ?'

Rex and Moore's pioneering research in the Fordist city that was Birmingham in the 1960s (Rex and Moore 1967) underlined the ways in which the demands of the organized and skilled working class for improved housing provision within the then-existing public sector of that city was itself a major contributing factor to the organization of the local 'class struggle' for space, especially in the way it structured the availability of housing by race and ethnicity. During the 1950s and 1960s, first- and second-generation immigrants of West Indian and Asian origins encountered a persistent system of discrimination, located in the Housing Department of the local authority, but driven by the post-colonial anxieties and aspirations experienced by the aspiring white working class of the industrialized English Midlands. The immigrants were driven back into the private markets for housing, especially the rented apartments of the inner city, where they had to battle for adequate and secure living space, in what was then a substantially unregulated market dominated essentially by 'rack-renting' landlords, preying on the weak position in which immigrants found themselves in a very restricted housing market. Within that private market in housing, immigrants had to compete with a range of other 'housing classes', including individuals expelled from the public sector by virtue of their criminality or anti-social behaviours. In the market society this book has been describing this private rental market for housing has become a contested space for a larger range of different groups competing for shelter and space – not least those young people in the post-Fordist labour market identified in the last chapter, unable to contemplate a long-term mortgage, and the expanding populations of students, struggling to enhance their position in the market through the acquisition of additional accreditations and qualifications. In Britain, many of these areas are the site of persistently very high levels of crime (especially burglary, theft and assault), as local young people, caught in relatively impossible positions in the labour market and imprisoned, possibly for life, in the locality of their birth, conduct a new form of 'class struggle' against an incoming, temporary student population which can rationally be targeted for their ownership of computers, hi-fi's and other consumable items that are easily sold on within local illicit markets.

The spate of nostalgic writing about working-class communities (and forms of family socialization) that has attracted a significant audience in the 1980s and 1990s is best understood, I would argue, as a nostalgia for *orderliness* (which is also to say the comprehensibility and the predictability) of such a lost set of social and domestic arrangements. This orderliness and predictability may even have some appeal for working-class women: for however much the Fordist cities may have been understood as 'male spaces' by subordinated women (largely inattentive to 'women's needs'[15]), dominated by places of leisure for men (the public house, the playing field) and however much the private space of the household was a place in which the use of force or violence was a possibility, there were also long-established strategies amongst working-class women of how to live with such routine masculinity. The strategies might range from the use of banter in the mixed-sex workplace to the protective groups of women that were formed in most working-class streets, policing the limits of acceptable behaviour on the part of their spouses. Few such informal strategies seem to be available for women in imposing closure or order on the 'protest masculinity' of young and middle-aged men in deindustrialized areas of post-Fordist society.

Post-war suburban utopias

The late Christopher Lasch (Lasch 1977, 1991) reminds us of the values and aspirations that were constructed and nurtured during the post-war period of Fordist development by another large fraction of the population in post-Fordist cities, the lower middle class. Lasch speaks of a segment of the population – especially that coming into maturity in the period around the Second World War – that was essentially cautious and sceptical of the changes and developments that were occurring through the years of the post-war settlement, and which, in particular, was sceptical of the 'modernist impulse ... for luxury, novelty and excitement' – the new enticements of post-war affluence. According to Lasch, this lower middle class was equally sceptical of the rhetorical emphasis on the benefits of 'community' that was so central an element in progressivist theories of social and urban reorganization in the aftermath of the Second World War. For the age-cohort which had lived through the Second World War, with its constant appeal to community (for example, of 'sacrifice') and its unending demonstration of inequalities of benefit and reward, 'community' had a double-edged appeal. A far more secure alternative was the personal investment made in the private life of the family, the personal home and a network of friends (Lasch 1994: ch. 4). Lasch's reflections can be understood as an exercise in nostalgia in a specific biographical sense (making sense of his own life as it was apparently led) – but it can also be read as an authentic expression of the forms of social and personal life that grew up in the suburbs of North America, and of some European societies, at the height of the period of Fordist development. David Chaney's recent analytic examination of 'the authenticity of the suburb' in the United Kingdom (Chaney 1995), and M. P. Baumgartner's studies of 'the moral order' of a suburb in an unnamed town in New York State (Baumgartner 1988) provide descriptions of particular parts of urban housing markets which (in part because of their social cohesion and orderliness) had a powerful appeal to large segments of the 'middle class' throughout the entire earlier post-war period. In Britain, to a very marked extent, as well as in North American cities, interest in a particular standard of suburban residence, like the interest in placement of children in particular schools, has always been an area of high social anxiety and personal investment for the urban middle class. The aspiration to live in housing built in the Georgian or Victorian period, set off from suburban developments erected in the interwar years, has been one of the most distinctive markers of social division in Britain – a marker of the elective affinity of the lower middle class for the gentrified status of the aristocracy and of Old Money. I have argued elsewhere that these areas has another social function:

> they also proclaim the residents' elective preference for the idea of what Patrick Wright has called 'living in an old country' (Wright 1985). They locate their owners within the long history of the nation. In John Betjeman's poetry of the 1950s, for example, areas like these (Broomhill in Sheffield being one of his preferred examples) were the quintessential definition of Englishness, resonating permanence and tradition, and thereby symbolizing the homeowner's taste and social standing. Many of the Victorian areas of our cities, developing as they have around a cluster of shops referred to as 'the village' have clearly wanted to encourage a definition of themselves as a kind of semi-rural retreat from the vulgarity and effluence of the industrial-commercial city around them. (Taylor 1995a: 264)

A key quality of the English suburb was always that of social segregation – 'the bourgeois' entered the suburban housing market, as Lasch also understood, to live apart from the rest of society. 'The price of such housing was one guarantee of such social exclusion, certainly of the working class and the underclass below it, but, also, in the first half of the century, of the commercial and industrial middle-class ("new money") itself' (1995a: 264). Sequestration in the suburbs was also motivated by the quest for a 'peaceful life' and a clear distinction between the world of work and the home-world: 'A particularly central role in the preservation of social cohesion and social peace was played by the local constabulary, and in particular by the local "bobby on the beat", with his antennae finely tuned to the intrusion into such areas of "suspicious" characters who "did not belong" ' (1995a: 264).

The social history of the English suburb has never been written, and we certainly lack good sociological accounts of life in the suburb, exploring below the appearance of suburban life into its inner core, unpacking the subtle role played in control and discipline of the local social structure (including its gender order and, certainly, relations of young people to adults) by the local shopkeeper, the publican, the railway stationmaster, or even the milkman or postman.[16] But, as I argued (1995a): 'the cultural significance of this version of the English suburb is well understood in the detective novels of Agatha Christie, P. D. James, Ruth Rendell and many others – all of which is now being recycled in the mid-1990s in the nostalgia-driven television-viewing of the English middle class'. So it is important, certainly for our purposes in this text, to understand the market for housing not just as a 'a struggle for space' – in the material sense of a struggle over bricks and mortar – but also, in a more symbolic and cultural sense, as a struggle for a social space in which an aspiring household, whether in public housing or the private market of sale or rent, imagines it might be able to pursue its preferred 'quality of life'. It is also important to understand that these struggles, and the cultural aspirations associated with them, evolve and take shape within particular historical periods characterized by different concep-tions of the 'ideal home'. In the last years of the twentieth century, particularly in North America but increasingly in Europe, the search for order among the suburban middle class and its desire to sequester itself away from the problems of the larger conurbation – especially from the predatory underclass – has found expression in the explosion of 'gated communities' – self-contained private housing developments, the polar example of what private developers in the United States refer to as 'common-interest develop-ments' (or CIDs) – usually set at some distance from the older 'modernist' city, surrounded by high perimeter walls, under the continuous surveillance of closed-circuit television, and policed by private security organizations. This process of sequestration was memorably identified as 'a wave of the future' in the opening pages of Mike Davis's extraordinary *City of Quartz* (Davis 1990). Davis angrily focuses on the reclaiming of the Mojave Desert outside Los Angeles by developers:

> Developers don't grow homes in the desert – this isn't Marrakesh or even Tucson – they just clear, grade and pave, hook up some pipes to the local artificial river (the federally subsidized California Aqueduct), build a security wall and plug in 'the product'. With generations of experience in uprooting the citrus gardens of Orange County and the San Fernando Valley, the developers – ten or twelve major firms headquartered in places like Newport Beach and Beverly Hills – regard the desert as simply another abstraction of dirt and dollar signs ... they christen their little pastel pods of Chardonnay life-style, air-conditioned and over-watered, with scented brand-names like Fox Run, Mardi Gras, Bravo, Cambridge, Sunburst, New Horizons, and so on. The most hallucinatory are the gated communities manufactured by Kaufman and Broad, the homebuilders who were famous in the 1970s for exporting Hollywood to the suburbs of Paris. Now they have brought France (or, rather, California homes in French drag) to the desert in fortified mini-*banlieux*, with lush lawns, Old World shrubs, fake mansard roofs and *nouveaux riches* titles like 'Chateau'. (Davis 1990: 5–6)

For the professional middle class in many different geographical locations in market society in North America and Europe, there is a new market of housing in which 'choice' is dictated more by the quality of the security and protection, and the level of sequestration provided by a particular housing development, than by considerations like the proximity of schools or even (given parallel developments in technology and the advent of new technologies of communication like fax, e-mail and the Internet) the length of the journey to work. The explosion in the number of such gated communities is particularly marked in the United States in southern California and especially along border areas with Mexico (there are half a million Californians currently living in gated communities[17]), where the physical presence of these communities takes on a powerful symbolic form almost as a series of encampments on the border, often with specific material expression in the form of moats and stockaded earthworks as well as gates which open only for the insider.[18] It is hard not to recognize the reinvention on the American suburban frontier of the fortress cities of the early medieval period in Europe (complete with their own systems of social control inside the fortification – nightwatchmen (the private security firms), individual stabling (private garages) and covered markets (the self-contained local mall).[19] There is some evidence of this process of suburban fortification and sequestration in Britain and elsewhere in Europe, though – not least because it is more difficult to create such homogeneous sealed environments in the more crowded urban settlements of a long-established European land mass – the process is not so advanced as in North America (where in 1997 some 8 million people were inhabiting such communities; Walker 1997). In Britain the key process still seems to be the refurbishment or gentrification of old-established suburban spaces. This is a kind of sequestration that only very partially immunizes its residents from the anxieties and concerns about crime and safety in the nearby urban environment. My own enquiries in South Manchester in the early 1990s underlined how the anxieties of the suburban middle class were constantly excited by what might be called a local noise-scape (loud gatherings of young people in the street or outside local pubs, activated burglar alarms or speeding ambulances and police sirens) from which there was no easy escape.

In both North America and Europe, these fortified spaces are frequently the subject of a bemused or dismissive critique, especially by a public space-minded academy. It is important, however, to recognize how these new private fortified spaces have become one of the most highly prized commodities on the housing market, especially, in fact, on the part of those fractions of the population 'doing well' in the accelerated struggle for accumulation in the market economy itself. They operate as places in which the tribes of the newly affluent professional classes can take up very private residence, in the knowledge that their neighbours will have a similar social background, with similar leisure and social interests. Precisely because they are so private, of course, they also operate to block any routine public scrutiny of what takes place in private in these suburban retreats – an issue taken up in chapter 5. For the moment, I want simply to register the appeal of these privately sequestered spaces (a) as a tribal settlement and (b) as a retreat from what may be thought to be the unregulated or dangerous public territory of market society.

THE PROBLEM ESTATE AND THE DEMONIZATION OF SOCIAL HOUSING

One of the defining features of the evolution of the housing market in the 1990s, in most Western marketized societies, has been the fundamental change in the cultural and social definition of public or social housing – what in England would be called 'the estates'. Philip Cooke argued, in the quotation on p. 105, that the first estates (and garden cities) built in Britain in the immediate post-war period were actually a utopian destination for aspiring 'upwardly mobile' households of the 'labour aristocracy'.'Slum-clearance', in this sense, was understood not just as the clearing of an old part of town – the industrial terraces – but the creation of new forms of community, which would give expression to the social solidarity of the working-class street but in another, better place. This 'ameliorist' refrain has been a constant feature of State housing policies during the Fordist period, switching focus sometime during the 1970s and 1980s from the straightforward project of 'slum-clearance' to the grander experiment in social engineering, in which residents from the 'zone of transition' were to be introduced into new forms of lived community. In the 1990s, references to 'the estate' either as social community or as an easy destination for residents of zones of transition no longer make sense of the actual operation of local housing markets. The literature on the inner city, certainly in England and Wales, provided a detailed account of the series of 'hollow promises' (about the prospects of the large majority of the poorer sections of society being rehoused in decent and affordable housing) that have been a feature of national and local government rhetoric and generally ineffective initiatives of the 1970s, 1980s and 1990s (see Keith and Rogers 1991) and provides evidence of the institutionalization of 'the inner city' as *a permanent feature* of the post-Fordist urban landscape. Priemus et al. (1994: 181) summarize a thirty-year process, which they claim to be very general throughout most European societies with a significant stock of social housing, in the following terms:

> In general it was not the original purpose of social housing to house the poorest strata of society, but from the 1970s onwards, social housing has been increasingly oriented in this direction: housing allowances have allowed the poor to gain entry; in some countries legislation has provided for a partial 'right to housing' and the range of alternatives for the poor (in particular cheap private rented housing) has diminished. Policy toward social housing has therefore become an important part of the 'fight against social exclusion'.

Priemus et al. focus on 'the entry of the poor' from run-down slum housing and/or the 'zone of transition', into the estates as the originating moment in the loss of a generic faith in the public housing estate *in general* as a new strategy in the creation and amelioration of community. This process is seen to have developed, though unevenly, over the last twenty to thirty years, as local authority housing departments and tenants have worked together in the protection of standards on some 'better estates' whilst engaging in benign neglect with respect to others. Bottoms and Wiles's various reports on the difference in crime rates of two adjacent council estates in Sheffield (Bottoms and Wiles 1986, 1988, 1992, 1997) – interpreted as a consequence of an unspoken policy in that city's Housing Department for the isolation and containment of 'problem families' on certain estates – suggest that an unspoken sub-text was operative in the bureaucratic-political organization of the public housing market, first evident in the early 1960s with the emergence of the 'sink estate' (R. Wilson 1963).

This process of social separation has assumed an increasingly desperate character in the public housing market in the 1990s, in part because of the reduction in the numbers of new houses being built and, in part, because of the broader spread of poverty produced by the market transformation. In Britain, the impact of this poverty amongst non-white sections of the population was concentrated in those areas of private-rented housing that had become the now permanent zones of occupation for third- and fourth-generation Afro-Caribbean immigrants (St Pauls in Bristol, Moss Side in Manchester and Chapeltown in Leeds).[20] The 1980s and 1990s were also witness to the emergence of estates and high-rise developments which could no longer be seen just as 'difficult to let' but which have become absolutely definitive 'symbolic locations' of Fear and the Urban Other. As early as the 1980s, indeed, some of these estates had already been designated in popular common sense as the home base of that new category of social life – the underclass – which, in part through the efforts of the American essayist Charles Murray (1990, 1994), was increasingly being seen in the nineteenth century – as the Italian legal philosopher Raffaele Garofalo would have seen it – as a category of people whose inherent failings and inadequacies 'rendered them unfit for social life' (Garofalo, 1914: 33). The identification in the 1990s of 'the problem family' – making life a misery for others on public estates – as something on which local authorities can take action (via exclusion) is a measure of the growing influence of this kind of Darwinian evolutionary thinking, not only as a way of 'making sense' of the travails of life on public housing estates in Western Europe, but also as a guide to local authority officials attempting 'to rescue' such estates from total dereliction by vandalism and crime. In 1996, for example, the Association of Metropolitan Authorities in England and Wales was successful in its campaign to have the Government include provisions in a new Housing Act for local authorities to be given the power to evict any public housing tenant during the first year of his or her tenancy, without having to go to court. One objective of this campaign (dramatized in a video, collaboratively produced by nine local authorities, *Winning Back Communities*) was to modify the security of tenure which had been a defining feature of British public housing policy since 1980. The other was to try to introduce a procedure for eviction of difficult tenants, accused of harassment of others, far more efficient than the existing legal system and therefore more immediately responsive to fears and 'demands for action' on the part of other tenants (BBC-Radio, *File on Four*, 9 March 1996). The attainment of this power of eviction of 'the problem family' was closely tied in with the continuing preoccupations of local crime-prevention 'partnerships' with the growing problem of intimidation and harassment of other citizens sharing their occupancy of these residual territories, the estates. The commentaries on the underclass which abound on television and elsewhere within popular culture in the 1990s[21] are evidence of the curious couplet of fear and fascination in respect of the underclass which underpins the agitated quest for security and protection amongst 'respectable' citizens. This fearful and fascinated contemplation of the underclass can also be understood, of course, as an imaginary exploration, at one remove, of the ongoing and real consequences of the immiseration of the bottom 40 per cent of the population that has been a specific consequence of market liberalization during the 1980s and 1990s (Hutton 1995). It operates, at its most conscious level, as a confirmation of 'the decline in civility' which popular common sense is convinced is a defining feature of that same historical period, and also as evidence of the personal failings and defects of the people in such a position. But, more subconsciously, it also operates as a measure of the fate that might befall any individual who failed to exhibit the right mix of enterprise and caution which survival in market society is thought to require.

The housing stock owned by public local authorities has been a sphere of reorganization and redeployment throughout the 1990s. In England, some of the most infamous problem estates or high-rise developments – like the Hulme Crescents in Manchester, the Kelvin Flats in Sheffield and many others – have been speedily demolished.[22] The management of other estates has been transferred to housing associations – 'partnership organizations' committed to the provision of affordable housing to different groups within the population, but working within the parameters of 'the market' (in the sense of having to raise their funding from sources other than local taxation). Other estates have been handed to new tenants organizations, assuming legal responsibility for their own building stock and surrounding territory, and introducing tenant leaders into partnership arrangements with local police or other 'service-providers'. This reordering of responsibilities for the routine management of public estates has run parallel in England and Wales with a process of 'privatization' of public housing – the sale of council houses to their sitting tenants, first legislated in the Housing Act of 1980 – and a general opening up of the housing market to private capital and to individual landlords (Forrest and Murie 1988; Power 1995). The overall objective of these changes in the bureaucratic and political management of entry into public housing stock, and the routine maintenance and management of such a stock, has been that of devolving responsibility to local agencies and partnerships – a process of devolution of power that is fairly general in most market societies, and a process, in this sphere as in others, that assumes the capacity of these local organizations to provide the services (such as policing, maintenance of the fabric of buildings and surrounding spaces), on at least as efficient a basis as the centralized local authority and local State itself. In this scenario of privatization and devolution of ownership and management to the local level, particular estates may – by virtue of their earlier history of development through the post-war period – have established advantages. Others may 'sink' further, in the sense of being managed only by whatever local partnership emerges in an area (a private security firm, some underpaid youth workers in the local youth club or, as Bea Campbell (1993) has argued in her study of Meadowell Estate in Newcastle in the early 1990s, groups of mothers or other determined women leaders in the locality).

In many such estates across Britain, and also in the broader Europe, there were and are, on official measures, heavy concentrations of unemployment, on a long-term as well as short-term basis, and also poverty that are quite without historical precedent in any 'developed' society this century. An analysis by the Employment Policy Institute of the British Labour Force Survey in 1997 suggested that half of all local authority and housing association properties were recorded as 'workless'. Half of those so classified had not worked for over three years.[23] Parallel processes of pauperization, evacuation and dereliction have been in full flow in the United States, as Camilo José Vergara's account (1995) makes clear, since the early 1980s, but these processes have been located not only within those very few publicly owned housing developments in the American inner city, but also in those areas of privately rented housing stock that have traditionally been the only place available for the poorer segments of American conurbations – the 'zones of transition' discussed by the Chicagoans and also the long-established inner-city areas 'on the wrong side of the tracks'. It is not just that the zone of transition has been transformed into a kind of permanent 'skid-row': it is also that the areas which are identified locally as 'ghettos' or no-go areas are engulfing adjacent areas and, in this process, contributing to the mass emigration from the city that has led many commentators in the United States to ponder whether the depopulated, untended and unsupervised post-Fordist city really has a future.[24]

In the United States, as in Europe, there is a widespread public and political 'discourse' which wants to attribute this process of urban decline to the activities of a parasitic underclass, which has somehow emerged in these locations in greater numbers in recent years. One defining dimension of this discourse – with its interest in 'blaming the victim' of the new urban ghettos for hyper-ghettoization (see the discussion later in this chapter) – can be seen in the rebirth of a psychological literature on crime and delinquency focusing directly on the personal inadequacies, for example, of young workless men, unmarried mothers and others whose failures to establish successful independent lives in the market society leave them dependent on the State for housing and other provision.

Two observations must be made at this point. The first is to emphasize the truth that, even in the aftermath of many years of 'privatization', demolition and sales of public housing stock, 'the estate', in many different European societies, remains the only available place of residence for large numbers of the population. In Britain, in 1989, some 24 per cent of the entire housing stock (of 23.1 million units) consisted of rented accommodation provided by local authorities or New Towns, as against 7 per cent which was privately rented, and only 2.8 per cent provided by housing associations (Power 1995: 235, table 24.1). Ten years after the election of a government committed to the creation of a 'property-owning democracy', the percentage of owner-occupiers had increased by 11 per cent to 68 per cent of the total housing stock. In Germany, in 1991, fully 35 per cent of all housing was State-owned, by comparison with 25 per cent in the private rental market, and a further 25 per cent owner-occupied (Power 1995: table 14.1). Some 15 per cent of the population lived in cooperative housing. In France, some 17 per cent of the population in 1991 were in rented social accommodation – including some 6 million people living in *grands ensembles* (peripheral estates on the outskirts of French towns and cities, estimated to total over 1,300 in number[25]) – as against another 35 per cent in the private housing market, with 53 per cent of the population owner-occupiers (Power 1995: 82, table 7.2). The evidence from many other countries in Europe suggests that the role of social housing, as some kind of residual provision for the new poor, will continue to be significant for very many years to come. Only in the United States, where public housing in 1990 constituted less than 3 per cent of the total housing stock, are the new poor of market societies restricted in choice to the privately rented housing market (housing 33 per cent of all American households in 1990; Hallett 1993: 3).

But, secondly, we need to underline how housing shelter in different, marketized post-Fordist societies (in their specific national mixes of public and private housing, in the rental markets and in the markets for private ownership) has been affected during the 1980s and 1990s by fast-developing crises in the availability of housing stock and also by a 'crisis of affordability' (see Hallett 1993). In the United States in 1990, after years of 'disengagement' on the part of the Federal Government from a direct-involvement national housing policy, the number of people in the market for low-cost affordable housing exceeded supply by a factor of 3 to 1 (M. Turner and Reed 1990). In newly unified Germany, very significant numbers of households in 1990 were spending nearly 40 per cent of household income on housing (Ulbrich and Wullkopf 1993: 119). In Britain, where there had been a doubling in the official rate of homelessness between 1978 and 1989 (from 53,100 to 126,680 households), a range of other crises has unfolded in the public housing market, not least in respect of the accumulation of rent arrears. In the private housing market itself, which had been celebrated by the Conservative Government in the mid-1980s as a measure of a newly propertied democracy and as a safe investment against the future, the emergence of the problem of 'negative equity'[26] in the early 1990s cut deeply into the confidence of the middle class itself.

Even this most cursory of examinations of some of the evidence about the housing markets of post-Fordist societies in Europe underlines an important truth about the housing markets of such societies in the 1990s – that, for all that post-Fordism may have involved an end to the war of the classes in the industrial workplace (in some instances, by closing the workplace), this had *not* put an end to what Rex and Moore in 1967 had called 'the class struggle for housing'. Many different groups within the new post-Fordist society (the young, many segments of the elderly population, immigrants and members of ethnic minority groups) faced a problem of obtaining affordable and acceptable accommodation. Many other groups – like the conventional middle-class family in North America – though apparently advantaged by virtue of their position in the labour market, have actually been facing serious problems (of cost, investment of time and attention, and strategic problems with respect to the everyday management of the household) which did not obtain in the earlier Fordist period. In North America, the 'dual-career' family, 'out at work' in the name of paying for accommodation, engaged in an ever more 'speeded-up' and stressful existence (with little time for children or personal leisure) was increasingly seen as the source of a raft of problems in respect of the socialization of young children and adolescents left behind in such households. This 'speeded-up' dual-career household would constitute one new ideal-typical 'housing class' of the new post-Fordist market society, in the sense described by Rex and Moore, following Weber. But so also would be the 'workless household' marooned on the public council estate or the declining areas of poor rental accommodation in American cities, constituting, in this particular sense, the lumpenproletarian fraction of the working class consigned for the rest of their lives to sub-standard rental property. Those whom housing officers and other local tenants call 'problem families' (and understood in terms of the 'presenting symptoms' of their personal inadequacies) can also be understood as individuals, families and households who have fallen foul of the competitive struggle for employment in post-Fordist society, the competitive struggle for housing shelter, and, indeed, the increasingly difficult struggle which faces those without saleable skills, personal advantages or connection for some kind of secure position 'on the bottom rung' of a market society. What is clear to observers of the public housing estate in Europe, and the declining rental stock of inner-city America, is that these areas have undergone a profound process of transformation since the 1970s. In chapter 5 I will draw attention to the 'alternative' or 'hidden' economies of subsistence and survival which have grown up in many of these areas (forms of 'primitive communism' involving exchange of labour as well as goods, but very little exchange of cash), 'alternative economies' which seem to be especially well developed in what previously had been strong communities of the semi-skilled manual working class. In the meantime, however, other forms of alternative economy, including the alternative economies revolving around car-theft, house burglary and the drug trade, have grown in significance. The detailed analysis by Anne Power and Rebecca Tunstall (1997) of thirteen urban riots in England and Wales in 1991 and 1992 confirms that these estates were the location of the vast majority of major incidents of social mayhem in these two years. Every one of these estates was home to large numbers of 'young, poorly educated, unemployed young men who have no stake or recognized role in their communities' (Power 1997a: 15). Many of these young men were routinely engaged in a process described by Jock Young (1993) as 'the long, slow riot of crime': attacking the police, intimidating local residents, or forming gangs to claim control of the streets.

The issue clearly posed in many such residualized public housing estates, in North America as well as in Europe, is the issue of whether these areas have become what Lash and Urry speak of as 'ungovernable spaces' (1994: ch. 6). Many of these areas (for example, in the most deprived areas of de-industrialized cities of the North of England) are certainly defined in practice as 'no-go' areas for police for a large proportion of 'the policing day' – that is to say, they are regularly denied the protection of a visible police presence, especially in the nighttime hours. The local population of many of such areas, particularly – but not exclusively – the elderly, spend enormous amounts of time sequestered in their own homes, periodically venturing out into the wider urban environment in order to complete the daily or weekly sub-sistence shopping. In some of the most de-nighted of such areas, even the completion of everyday subsistence shopping can become extraordinarily problematic – consequent, perhaps, on the closure of local shopping facilities (as a result of the constant predations of local 'criminal gangs') or the withdrawal of local bus services (as a result of the frequency of attacks on bus drivers). In many such areas, the dystopian images of the city in *Blade Runner* seem not too far away.

THE 'CITY CENTRE': URBAN PLEASURES AND PRECAUTIONARY STRATEGIES

I have left discussion of the 'city centre' until last, in order to locate understanding of city-centre spaces in an understanding of the mix of differ-ent people(s) who make use of those spaces. What may be called the 'city centre' is not just a configuration of buildings and streets (what architects call the 'built form' of the city centre) but is also a destination visited for different pleasurable and utilitarian purposes by people from very different social backgrounds and neighbourhoods. The 'city centre' can be a place that is visited, primarily, for work (for example, a set of office buildings linked to a set of auxiliary places for quick consumption (fast-food restaurants, bric-à-brac shops etc.). But the centre of long-established modernist cities has historically always been a 'shopping centre' – that is, the location of a number of major retail stores, markets, and a number of auxiliary shopping locales. The 'city centre' has been a relatively fixed and familiar centripetal point, often simply referred to as 'town', 'recursively' revisited by residents of the larger conurbation over a lifetime. The conurbation as whole could be thought of as a matrix built around that central area, involving some more crowded inner-city areas, industrial areas, and more spacious outer suburban neighbourhoods, sometimes reaching out to outer rural areas (places of leisure at the weekend). Over the last twenty to thirty years, however, as many social and cultural commentators have observed, the character of the modernist city and the patterns of use of those cities has been transformed. These changes may be summarized as follows:

(1) There has, first, been what Graham and Clarke have called 'a multi-plication of urban spaces' (1996: 172). That is to say, the long-established and familiar configuration of centre, inner-city terraces and 'slums' and suburbs has been modified by processes of development and change. Commentary in the late 1970s and early 1980s focused, for example, on the processes of 'gentrification' of some modest residential areas, re-positioning these areas in the overall housing market of the larger conurbation; and in the 1990s this process has continued, with the important consequence of reclaiming some office buildings in the traditional centre of the city as apartments for young professionals – the 'lofts' described by Sharon Zukin – places of residence and urban fantasy for the new professional middle class (Zukin 1989). Paralleling such gentrification, in or near to the centres of major old industrial cities, has been a continuing series of redevelopment initiatives and pro-grammes (for example, in Britain, under the aegis of the Urban Development Corporations, created by the Conservative Government in the 1980s to encourage the growth of enterprise zones in the old industrial areas). The effect of these initiatives to reclaim unused land and to regenerate abandoned building stock (for example, in the Docklands area in the East End of London; see Butler and Rustin 1996) has produced significant change in the longer-term sense of destiny of some of these inner-city zones and urban regions. Finally, the modern city has been transformed, especially in North America, by the development of residential 'communities' linked to shopping malls on the outer suburban edge of the major conurbations – the alternative 'edge cities' of the North American continent described in some detail by Joel Garreau (1991). In North America, these edge cities have come to constitute an alternative residential and leisure space for large numbers of professional people, and these locations have taken on life as places in which large amounts of what analysts call 'personal leisure time' are spent.

(2) Paralleling this reconfiguration of the city as a set of material spaces has been an important transformation of the ways in which such cities, and the mix of spaces within them, are understood and 'imagined'. A large body of cultural theoretical literature focuses on the transformation of cities from individual places organized around routine activities of production to a set of places organized around the pursuit of consumption. The emphasis in this literature in on the rise of new shopping malls and other places of consump-tion – the 'new cathedrals of consumption' first described in Gardner and Sheppard's analysis of the radical shift in retail culture in Britain in the late 1980s (1989).[27] Built into such a reinvention of the city-region as a set of consumption sites or locales is the recognition that these places – like the heritage homes, mansions and other tourist sights visited in search of 'authen-ticity' from the past or the cathedrals visited by the faithful in search of different visions of God – may actually have to compete for the continuing attention of their public, the new '*flâneurs*' of the late twentieth century, constantly looking for some new kind of transcendent shopping experience. The competition may focus on the size of new mall developments – a dimension of market competition first glimpsed with the opening in 1981 of

the West Edmonton Mall in Edmonton, Canada (with its own night-clubs, hotel, forty restaurants, a 10-acre water park and an eighteen-hole mini-golf course; Shields 1989). Throughout the 1980s and 1990s, many thousands of such self-contained shopping cities continued to open across North America and in some parts of Europe, very often publicized in terms of their size.[28] In September 1996, for example, the CentrO centre opened in Oberhausen in the Ruhr Valley in Germany (in the area of Germany most hard-hit during the 1980s and 1990s by the crisis of mass manufacturing in that country, with some 14.6 per cent of the local population unemployed), to the acclaim that it was now the largest in Europe. The CentrO contains 3 kilometres of shop frontage, 51,500 roses, shrubs and trees, an 11,500-seat arena, thirty restaurants, hotels, tennis courts and a business park.[29]

In the United Kingdom, only a small number of super-malls have been opened – the Metrocentre in Gateshead, Meadowhall in Sheffield, Merry Hill in Dudley, near Birmingham, Lakeside in Essex, the Trafford Centre in south Manchester – each claiming, on opening, to be 'the largest in Europe'.[30] But, consistent with the restless search for markets, there has been a rapid increase in most urban regions in the number of smaller self-contained shopping cities and malls, as well as of more specialized shopping malls and territories (for example, directed at families with children, built around a Toys 'Я' Us store; at sporting enthusiasts, built around a retail store for athletics wear and equipment; or at gardening and/or Do It Yourself hobbyists). The location of these different new retail outlets across an urban region works to produce new 'mental maps' of the region for different publics in that region – that is to say, new 'indicative' guides for the imagination and memories of a consuming public of the location of particular sites of leisure and consumption and of the transport routes that lead to these locations.[31] These are 'selling places', that is to say, which are premised on there being significant numbers of monied consumers, whose locations and design were chosen by market entrepreneurs with a view to encouraging maximum use of these new facilities – that is, to 'include' precisely these publics and, if necessary, to exclude any Other who might interfere with the efficient operation of these particular private markets.

(3) This reorganization of urban regions as a new mix of residential and working places and spaces, and the overall reconfiguration of cities in market society into a new mix of consumer market places, has run in parallel with a reorganization of the management of public interaction (and indeed inclusion within such an authorized, overseen interaction) in such regions.

We will be discussing some of the developments in the management of social control of market societies in chapter 7 and we will see how the development a private market in the sale of security runs alongside the development of multi-agency partnerships and competition between 'the private' and 'the public'. The policing of many new palaces of consumption in our cities (whether in the centre or on the periphery of cities) now exhibits a range of exemplary partnership arrangements between public police and private security firms, operating with very different levels of official accreditation and professional qualification, remuneration and reliability.

Nearly all researchers investigating these new consumer environments have noted how the glossy friendliness of the new markets of consumption, like the gloss of Disneyland itself (Shearing and Stenning 1985d; Zukin 1995), betrays a highly controlled discipline of social control. At its most obvious, this system depends on the presence and surveillance of highly trained and effusively friendly uniformed staff adept at the identification of potentially difficult individuals, who might disrupt the routine functioning of consumer exchange, and the quiet removal of such individuals from the consumer space. The additional reassuring dimension usually is the background presence of closed-circuit television (CCTV) cameras and recording technology. As Graham and Marvin (1996: 225) have noted, the installation of such technology in shopping centres and their surrounding urban street-scape was pushed high up the agenda of many commercial companies and local authorities by the extraordinary murder of the three-year-old Jamie Bulger in Liverpool in 1993: his two young assailants were identified and arrested from the images of them on the centre's CCTV system. By November 1994, it was reported that 95 per cent of local authorities were contemplating the installation of CCTV in city-centre locations and the size of the market for such systems was estimated as having increased from £170 million in 1989 to £300 million in 1995. There were over 150,000 professionally installed systems in British towns and cities in 1995, with new systems being installed at the rate of 500 a week (Graham and Marvin 1996). Over and beyond any measurable impact which are claimed for such systems in actually occurring rates of 'crime', and over and above the utility of CCTV images in retrospective detective work, the introduction of such systems is usually described as an exercise in the enhancement of 'the public's sense of security and well-being'. This managerial attention to the well-being of the citizen-consumer is also evident, even in cultures (like Britain) where there is no tradition of service, to 'user-friendly' design features and to the (re)training of staff in American-style service skills and sociability. Many of these new consumer palaces also include play-areas and supervision for children as well as special facilities for the disabled or the elderly; and many more are wanting to expand directly into the leisure industry, to include cinema, video and theatre within the new consumer cities.[32] These new urban locations increasingly include within their perimeters, that is, facilities for the provision of many of the 'goods' (including those of leisure, entertainment, care and attention for the elderly or the infirm) that in earlier post-war utopianism about the Garden City and the New Town were to be offered, in public space, to citizens as a whole. But now these facilities are on offer only as part of the contract with the consumer allowed into these new locations.

Residual Space in the Market City: Questions of Definition and Strategies of Negotiation

Mike Davis's classic account of the rapid restructuring of the physical or built form of Los Angeles will probably be most often remembered for its graphic description of the 'destruction of accessible public space' (Davis 1990: ch. 4) – visually signified in the photograph of the 'bum-proof' bus bench, designed to deter overnight sleeping by vagrants (1990: 235). 'Public space' in what Davis calls 'post-liberal' Los Angeles has been relocated inside the postmodern buildings of 'the downtown' and suburban edge cities – the super-malls and other temples of consumption. The routes between these buildings – most often, in Los Angeles (as in other Californian and North American cities), around the edges of major parking lots or urban highways – may have been subject to some beautification and/or landscaping – and, in particular, there may have been some attempt to create sets of urban squares or Italian-style piazzas, complete with a range of fast-food 'alternatives' to serve as a public space for office workers during the lunch-time hour (a public space which is then usually locked away from the public at the end of the working day) – for example, the Harvey Milk Plaza in San Francisco, in front of the Moscone Centre. The rest of the city – the residual space – is left to the devices of 'street people', and, as Davis observes:

> The contemporary opprobrium attaching to the term 'street person' is in itself a harrowing index of the devaluation of public space. To reduce contact with untouchables, urban redevelopment has converted once vital pedestrian streets into traffic-sewers and transformed public parks into temporary receptacles for the homeless and the wretched. (Davis 1990: 226)

European discussion of these developments in North American cities sometimes mistakenly reduces these developments to the 'North American love of the car' – and it is true that there are cities in North America (for example, Calgary, Alberta) in which walking through modernist public space is now almost impossible, given the abolition of footpaths (sidewalks) in the outdoor spaces.[33] In urban contexts like these (which are not confined to North America), one of the most routinized ('normal') forms of social interaction is the exchange of glances and looks between passengers of cars. In such cites, criminologists interested in regulation and rule-breaking in public space ought perhaps in principle to re-focus on issues of road-design, highway-policing and 'road rage'.

The concern of the rest of this chapter, however, is to try to think the relation between 'the urban' question and the broad range of behaviours in urban space that get to be defined as crime, especially in the competitive market societies of the 1990s. The 'objects of analysis' here certainly ought to include the widely discussed 'decline of incivility' in everyday urban life that has been an active topic of public and political debate in North America since the publication in 1982 of the classic 'Broken Windows' article by George

Kelling and James Q. Wilson. There are few observers who would now challenge the empirical importance of the 'Broken Windows' article as a description of the neglected and dilapidated condition of many parts of many American cities, and the common-sense argument that these kinds of urban 'stigmata' act as evidence of the neglect of such spaces by public authorities and a general absence of public custodial supervision and oversight. What is, of course, contentious in the Wilson and Kelling article (now developed further in an extended monograph by Kelling and Coles (1996)) is the argument that the neglect of public space in American cities is best understood, on the one hand, as an effect of the instability of family life, or, on the other, of the prevalence of over-permissive systems of policing in nearby neighbourhoods – as distinct from being an expression of a political antipathy to the exercise of an effective public custodianship of shared public spaces and facilities.[34]

The analysis of 'the urban' and 'the social', and the relationship between these levels of personal experience and 'crime' (and the fear of crime) in the late 1990s cannot proceed without regard to the larger logic of economic change with which this book has been preoccupied. The focus of official criminology in North America and in Britain on urban matters in the 1990s – attentive, as official criminology always is, to its auxiliary role in the maintenance of order or the reduction of anxiety within existing relations of social inequality – is currently focused on particular sites within the city which are thought routinely to function in the local mind as 'symbolic locations of crime',[35] or which appear in police records as what Sherman et al. (1989) have called the 'hot spots' of crime, especially of 'predatory' forms of crime. Sherman and his colleagues analysed a total of 323,979 telephone calls to police in Minneapolis in 1985–6 and discovered that just over half of all calls resulted in the dispatch of police cars to only 3.3 per cent of a possible 115,000 'places' in that city (street intersections, parks, hospitals, large department stores, City Hall etc.). Further analysis of their Minneapolis data-set suggested a distinct patterning of different offence-behaviours being reported to the police in terms of place: domestic violence appearing to be concentrated in a very small number of addresses, for example, and street assaults occurring around a relatively small number of bars, homeless shelters, record stores, adult bookstores etc. (Sherman et al. 1989: table 5). In Britain, the thrust of Sherman's work has been taken up or echoed in the use of computer-generated analyses of patterns of reported crime in different local police force areas (so-called Crime Pattern Analysis), drawing attention to a patterning of certain kinds of offence behaviours.[36]

Wesley Skogan's *Disorder and Decline* – a study of perceptions of neighbourhood decline in Chicago – identifies a series of 'public locations' like a poorly maintained neighbourhood park, with its children's playing areas outside the line of vision from the parental home, abandoned and decaying buildings left behind by private and public sector interests, and particular stretches of graffitied and vandalized local landscape – as the places which are most often cited as evidence of a generalized experience and feeling of decline (Skogan 1990: chs 1 and 2). My own ethnographic observations of the suburban area of Hale, south Manchester, in the early 1990s also high-lighted the importance of the neighbourhood park, of a particular public house and a specific late-night fast-food outlet as the main symbolic locations on an indicative map used by most local suburbanites in their agitated discussion of crime, as well as being frequently referenced in the equally passionate discussions of crime in the local community newspaper (Taylor 1995a).

The analysis of the city as a matrix containing particular concentrations of such symbolic locations or 'hot spots' can, of course, have important implica-tions for the organization of police resources, in terms of the increased level of policing of certain areas and the reduction of policing in others. But it can also contribute to the development of a new sensibility amongst the broader population of a local area, in helping to inform the construction of a practical and strategic everyday knowledge put to use in the everyday navigation of public space.

The attention of criminologists in the United States has been drawn to this dimension through the attempt by Lawrence Cohen and Marcus Felson (1979) to apply a version of neo-classical economic thinking – so-called rational choice theory – to the analysis of the purposive and/or opportunistic use of places for criminal gain. As with all such neo-classical analyses, the analytic focus in such an approach is of a highly rational and calculating individual criminal, as if he or she is in possession of a stock of more or less accurate and factual information about a specific choice-making location or context. Felson developed these themes further in his text of 1994, but was concerned here more specifically to identify what he sees to be a number of 'good practices' that are available to all rational individuals and rational organizations in the project of reducing opportunities and criminal tempta-tions in the broader environment (Felson 1994). As with all such utilitarian accounts, however, the individual under discussion in Felson's world of everyday 'routine activities' seems to live in a historical, cultural and social vacuum, without any particular identifiable personal biography or identity. Such actors in the urban drama are, in the abstract, more or less identical 'calculators', whose behaviours can be analysed (on an analogy, perhaps, with those calculating players of the financial markets, whose widely reported daily movements are an important background item in the recursive life of market society).

In research recently completed in two large old industrial cities in the North of England, for example, my co-investigators and I were frequently told by our informants about the 'strategies of avoidance' which they adopted in relation to key 'symbolic locations' in the centre of those cities, or in the informants' immediate neighbourhood. Informants nearly all spoke of 'hav-ing their routes' for walking through particular parts of the city, or for using public transport, or even a car, from one point to another. Sometimes, these strategic decisions would be informed by practical experience – a product, perhaps, of a particular encounter, for example with an aggressive street beggar or with groups of young men taking up possession of a particular urban location (Taylor, Evans and Fraser 1996: 221–4). In this sense, the broad outlines of 'routine activities' analysis were confirmed: that city-users engage in decision-making about the ways they make use of the space and the built form of the larger city. The problem is, of course, that the particular strategies adopted by 'different publics' in these cities were *quite different*, not least in respect of the traditional sociological categories of class, gender, ethnicity and age,[37] and in no simple sense reducible to a single 'rationality'.

Many of the people we encountered in these two cities whom we would describe as the 'new poor' of market society in Britain had had *no* choice, in fact, but to develop strategies which encompassed the careful use of those more fearful parts of those two cities (the badly lit city-centre bus stations in Manchester or the covered markets in Sheffield which specialize in selling cheap food and everyday provisions), precisely because they had no choice in economic terms but to make use of these locations. Some elderly people in Manchester reported in some detail as to the extended routes they normally would take in order to avoid Market Street, the pedestrianized street in the city centre which, in the 1980s, has become the main gathering-point for the city's beggars, homeless youth, 'crusties' and other street people. Young people's strategies for the use of the city centre, however, might involve direct avoidance of certain places (and also certain situations of perceived risk or danger (the use of unlicensed taxis), but more frequently involved strategic arrangements to ensure that the use of the city, especially in the evening hours, was organized with a group of friends (see Hollands 1995). As we saw in chapter 3, following the work of Kinsey et al., young people are the most frequent victims of assaults and thefts in the cities, as well as being the group most widely perceived by other publics to be the source of the problems of crime in the city (see also Stenson and Watt 1995; Brown 1995).

Young professionals, in complete contrast, reported on a use of expensive private urban locales and spaces, which in many ways approximated the casual style of Walter Benjamin's *flâneur*, but with the qualification of being interested in the proximity of the nearest car park. Chinese immigrants in the Manchester area reported on their own use only of those parts of Manchester that catered for the kind of foods and provisions in which they were interested, whilst also reporting on their regular wistful visits to the international airport to gaze at 747s flying off to Asia. Young men of Afro-Caribbean background in Sheffield spoke with some anger about the amazingly restricted amount of urban space and territory available for their use, indicating that they were routinely evicted from the massive Meadowhall shopping centre by the mall's own private security officers and how, equally routinely, in the city's older-established shopping centre, they were subject to harassment by shopkeepers, police and the broader public. There was, in this sense, evidence of a distinct indicative map in use on the part of young blacks, informing their strategic use of the broader 'white city', in the name of their own avoidance of harassment and safety. In both cities, gay men also spoke at length about the routes which they would use in the hope of avoiding harassment or 'bashing'.

In further discussions about the wider city, we also heard evidence of the development of new mental maps, in which certain areas of the city which had attained a demonic status in local newspapers and other media (Moss Side in Manchester, Burngreave in Sheffield – in both instances, as the home base of 'Yardie'-type criminality and violence) were clearly identified in the memory, with transport routes being adopted for their avoidance. Even in this instance, however, the negative labelling of areas was in no way unanimous, as specific groups (for example, of students) admitted to a preference for living in such ostensibly dangerous areas, on the grounds that they were cheap and also exciting. These young people were showing an elective preference for living in what Antonio Arantes (1996), following the work of the anthropologist Victor Turner (1967, 1969, 1982), calls a 'liminal zone' – a zone in which the familiar or routine activities and conditions which define and contain normality are absent, and the excitement of uncertainty prevails.

DIFFERENCE AND POVERTY IN THE MARKET CITY

We can begin to identify, perhaps, some of the key dimensions of the fearful and strategic choice-making (what some analysts, again a little too abstractly, would speak of as 'the minimization of risk') entered into by these different publics making use of urban space and urban facilities in a market society. Most importantly of all, perhaps, are the issues of *difference* and widening *inequality* of persons – underwritten, however, by what I will call a *crisis of public custodianship* in market society (an aspect to be discussed in more detail in chapter 7 of this book). But a fourth and defining feature of the post-Fordist urban reality of vital importance is the unevenness of these processes of transformation in different cities, and the very different prognoses for different cities of Fordist origins in confronting the challenges of post-Fordist competition, in local, national and international competition.

These developments in the pattern and framework of 'the social' and 'the urban' are not reducible to the transformation of Fordist society and its replacement by a post-Fordist society of market competitivity and personal uncertainty, but neither are they unconnected. There is clearly an important sense in which the increasing emphasis placed in all political discussion and public discourse on 'international competition' produces its own defensive responses in different societies. This return of what Maffesoli (1995) and Walzer (1992), independently, have referred to as 'the return of tribalism' can take specifically nationalistic forms, as in the responses of large bodies of opinion in Britain to the prospects of an accelerated move towards greater economic union with the rest of the European Union. But they can also take the form of a tribalism within national societies, concerned to elaborate and celebrate the fact of *difference*, very frequently defined in ethnic terms but also, sometimes, defined in terms of the particular interests of particular territories within a nation which claim (and then elaborate) a claim to 'special status'. This claim to exceptionalism is particularly important a feature of the continuing post-war political debates in Canada (around the continuing claims of the Province of Quebec), in Spain (around the claims of the Basque country), but also the prosperous northern provinces of Italy (home to the Northern Leagues, articulated around the fantasy of Umberto Bossi of creating a new independent state of Padania). In its most lethal form, of course, the return to tribalism at the level of 'national politics' has found expression in the bloody civil war in Bosnia. It seems self-evident that the reassertion of this tribalism – or of what Michael Ignatieff refers to as the sense of 'blood and belonging' – is decipherable, in the form it assumes at all levels of any social formation, by reference to the broader development of competitive global economic logics, born of the demise of nationally organized Fordist economies, in which national governments were implicated not only in the management of the beneficial impact of economic activity (for example, in tax policy) but also in the management of the negative impacts which such activity might have on the broader citizenry.

The assertion of 'difference' is clearly linked, too, to the unfolding inequalities of outcome that are a feature of the transformed post-Fordist economies. In the United States, in particular, the new competitive market realism of the 1990s, the framework within which have occurred a massive explosion in part-time and short-term contract employment and a continuing acceleration of the working week, is itself colour-blind. It is also blind in formal terms to the subtle pressures of class and status – career outcomes of individuals are seen to result from individual luck, hard work or talent. But the constantly advancing hegemony of market-liberalism in the United States during the late 1990s has nonetheless been associated with determined political moves, at both federal and state level, to unpick Positive Discrimination legislation passed in the early 1970s – not least, for example, in the quotas reserved for African-Americans in America's universities and public sector employments markets. The continuing withdrawal of the State from interventions in the housing market in favour of the poor, and the ongoing 'disinvestment' from American cities (new post-Fordist processes that are complicit, internationally, in the production of inequality in different cities described, for example, by Sassen (1994)) are leading to a process of what Wacquant (1994) has called 'hyper-ghettoization' in some post-Fordist American cities. This process of hyper-ghettoization involves a fundamental transformation in the character of earlier forms of inner-city life. Wacquant identifies the 'enduring' and 'communal' ghettos as being 'compact' and 'sharply-bounded' and also as being characterized by 'a full complement of black classes bound together by a unified collective consciousness, near-complete social division of labour, and broad-based communitarian agencies of mobilization and representation' (Wacquant 1994: 233). The *hyper-ghetto*, by contrast, involves a fundamental dislocation and fragmentation of each of these enduring features of the 'communal ghetto'. The 'compactness' and 'boundedness' of the ghetto are unpacked, on the one hand, by earlier attempts at redevelopment, and, on the other, by the spread of poverty within the broader locality. The collapse of employment cuts deeply into the capacity of local institutions (bars, union halls etc.) to sustain a sense of a local class identity. Patterns of emigration and flight reduce any sense of belonging and place that used to characterize the communal ghetto, and, in the case of the black ghetto, to feed into its sense of local pride (the 'soulful' dimension of urban black consciousness). Confronted with local labour markets that do not easily provide young men with any sense of pride (for example, as a righteous breadwinner), and by local communities imploding into themselves in destructive recrimination, young blacks have somehow to invent a livable sense of identity which endows them with some sense of self-respect. Hebdige (1988b), Cooper (1989), Bhahba (1994), McLaren (1995) and many others have written on the role of 'gangsta rap' culture amongst young African-Americans ('Niggers with Attitude') – offering close and detailed analysis of its in-your-face confrontationalism, the 'pimp-roll' walking style, the specific choice of clothing, trainers and headwear, the ostentatious display of firearms – as a coherent set of signifiers of what Wacquant thinks of as new and advanced forms of marginality in post-Fordist America – signified in the widespread perception amongst younger black and Puerto Rican young people in such areas that 'there ain't no makin' it' in the legitimate world of market liberal America.[38] In many African-American and Puerto Rican areas, as Philippe Bourgois's powerful ethnographic study of East Harlem graphically reveals, the only source of respect which is felt to be available is the efficient operation of the neighbourhood 'crack house' (Bourgois 1995). We should never be so distracted, however, as to forget how the rise of gangsta rap confrontationalism, on the one hand, and the growing entrepreneurialism and competitivity of the illicit markets of crack, on the other, have coincided with a steep increase in the numbers of blacks aged fifteen to twenty-four being killed by guns across America, as well as a significant jump in the number of suicides in this age group.[39]

The responses of 'white America' to the confrontational identity-politics of some young black men have clearly to be understood in terms of the continuing history of America's racial politics. But they also need to be connected, interpretatively, to the intensifying inequalities of post-Fordism, in its specific American expression. This management of inequality involves preoccupation of social control agencies in America with street curfews, zero tolerance policing, radical revision of the sentencing powers of the courts ('Three Strikes and You're Out') and a continuing expansion of the range, and the reach, of different forms of social exclusion, not just of a black Other, or indeed of troublesome young people (the 'War against the Young' discussed in chapter 3) but generally in relation to the new poor of market society. The 700,000 people who, on estimates at the end of 1995, were sleeping rough on American streets have increasingly been cleared away by forceful police action, and the places which they have used for sleeping have been placed off-limits.[40] The rapid development of what has been called 'incivility policing', particularly (but by no means exclusively) in New York City – targeting the offensive behaviours of 'the people on the street' – is an unmistakable dimension of the management of urban life in America and of many other major conurbations in other societies in the late 1990s. But so also is the development of a range of new personal strategies that are adopted, in fragmented and unequal urban spaces, for safe navigation and travel through those cities. Antonio Arantes's ethnographic observational study in São Paulo, the booming centre of growth and inequality in Brazil, reports on the elaborate practical strategies and 'presentations of self' (or displays of different identities) that different sections of the public utilize in traversing the central areas of that city, all the while crossing the subtle, locally understood boundaries between different urban territories and places (Arantes 1996). Intolerant and exclusionary responses to the homeless and to beggars has been less clear-cut in Britain (in part because the homeless have achieved a degree of public support through the *Big Issue* magazine). Our research in Manchester suggested that the larger population operated with clear mental distinctions between the deserving and 'undeserving' people on the streets of that city. What was evident in Manchester, however – as I suspect it would be in most large British cities in the 1990s – was a deeply felt, widely expressed fear of the groups of aggressive young men ('yobs') that were routinely to be encountered in any excursion into public space. This was not 'a section of the public' that any other fraction of the urban population, including, indeed, other young people, wanted to share the city. It was a section of the urban population who were assumed to have come into the centre of the city from their 'base camps', on the sink estates, so introducing another (post-Fordist) reality into territories that should be reserved for the pleasures of post-Fordist existence – untroubled individual consumption.

THE URBAN SPECTACLE IN THE 1990S

Grasping the specificity of the use of urban space in competitive post-Fordist societies involves a range of theoretical issues, and an awareness of publics other than just 'the *flâneur*'. The sharing of urban space by rich and poor is no new phenomenon: there is a considerable literature in Britain, for example, on the fear (as well as the fascination) that accompanied the bourgeois use of urban territory in the Victorian period (Stedman-Jones 1971; Walkowitz 1992). One of the defining anxieties highlighted by Stedman-Jones's retrospective historical enquiry was provoked by 'the plague of beggars' that seemed to be engulfing London in the middle years of the nineteenth century, underwritten by the anxiety that many of these beggars were prospering from their activities, to the point of undermining the incentives felt by the larger working class to engage in paid labour. An agitated debate ensued as to whether the giving of money to street beggars then constituted a self-defeating subsidy of the idle and undeserving ('a deformation of the gift'). The resonance of this Victorian debate in respect of the everyday use of public space in post-Fordist cities in the 1990s is unmistakable. So also, it should be said, are the discursive attempts which were being made by social commentators like Henry Mayhew in this same period to construct a kind of practical and indicative taxonomy of the contemporary people of the street – written, in part, to inform the 'avoidance strategies' that might be deployed by 'respectable society'. Mayhew's taxonomy of the London poor derived from his observation of the structure of the casual labour market in London in the late 1850s, focusing on fine distinctions between the appearances and potential behaviours of window-cleaners, costermongers, building labourers, unlicensed ('butterfly') cab drivers, messenger boys, and people involved in various 'scavenging' activities, such as rag-collectors, street-sweepers, 'sand-wichmen' etc. (Mayhew 1861, as discussed in Stedman-Jones 1971: ch. 3). Our own research in Manchester and Sheffield in the 1990s produced many examples of such taxonomies being developed and deployed by different publics, as a personal aid in the use of these cities. Mayhew's writings on the poor of industrial London, like the later writings of Charles Dickens, and many other social commentaries of the time, also gave rise to an elaborate 'cultural geography of place' (P. Jackson 1989) – in which the character of particular locations in the city was seen to be given by the particular character of the people who were likely, by virtue of their casual employment or their residential concentration, to be encountered there. Particular sections of the East End of London were constructed in the mind of respectable society as 'rookeries' – overcrowded tenements full of full-time professionals, especially 'pickpockets', con-artists or prostitutes. Particular fears were excited by the idea that certain locations were the preferred territory of the pickpocket specializing in the use of 'garrotting' (the use of a wire around the neck of the chosen victim; Hall et al. 1978: 4).

Our North of England research in the 1990s confirmed the use of such indicative maps of places and of social types within the city on the part of different users of those cities. There was a widespread belief amongst many adults that the city-centre branch of Boots the Chemists was a chosen locale (i.e. a routinely revisited place) for significant numbers of drug-addicts. Particular streets and particular intersections or pavements – often the residual spaces left after particular reconfigurations of urban street-scapes – were identified as the places in which encounters with aggressive beggars or alcoholic vagrants were possible. What was not clear, however, is the extent to which these different 'peoples' and 'places' were connected (like the rookeries of Victorian London) in the minds of different sections of the public with the empirical possibility of assault or other forms of predatory crime, or the extent to which the avoidance of such places was provoked by a perceived risk of 'crime' or violence. Elderly Mancunian women spoke of the 'sadness' of drug-addiction, and of the sympathy they felt for the young people they assumed to be victims of such addiction, but there was little sense of 'risk' or 'fear' attaching to this particular locale. What was unwanted was a direct, uninvited and intrusive encounter with such a young person, in which the elderly person felt that he or she might somehow have to take some personal responsibility of care for the Other. Some young people spoke of their encounters with beggars and street people of their own age as an ominous signification of 'the fate' that might await them in competitive market society – a measure not of their fear of immediate personal danger, so much as their medium-term anxiety about the destiny awaiting them in the post-Fordist struggle for survival and position. Young women alluded to their encounters with young men – for example on late-night public transport – as involving not simply the traditional rituals of sexual exchange, but also a heavy overlay of aggressive banter about the different opportunities available to women in the recently reconstituted local labour markets. There is a strong sense, then, of the urban space not just as a playful place of pluralistic tribal difference (which can be one way in which the city spaces are experienced) but, with a rather more specific sense of caution or foreboding, as a place in which the symbolic aspects of individual destinies (or market positions) within post-Fordist markets are played out. Similar sentiments to those expressed about the intrusion into personal space of 'beggars', the mentally ill and alcoholic street people were given voice, especially by middle-aged and elderly citizens, in our research discussions, coupled with the widespread sentiment that these unwanted encounters somehow resulted from the failures of local councils and government to take responsibility for these 'casualties of life'.[41] What I want to suggest here is that this sense of the city, outside and beyond the various private temples of consumption, constitutes a map of places in which the human casualties of contemporary post-Fordist change are likely to be encountered, and the absence of care and custodianship of people and spaces that is a characteristic of so many cities in market society revealed.

The drama of the sharing of public space by 'the respectable' and 'the poor' in post-Fordist cities generally takes place against a widespread assertion as to the loss of a governing custodial authority over such space, and an anxious concern to avoid the intimate encounter in which responsibility for the Other is demanded. But this drama takes place, as I now want to show, against different specific local contexts in different post-Fordist cities.

URBAN FORTUNES AND FUTURES

The crisis of the Fordist system of mass manufacturing is nothing if not a crisis in the prospects of the individual Fordist city as well. The industrial cities built up during the Fordist period have demonstrated very different capacities, institutionally and strategically, for responding to the challenges of a post-Fordist world. Logan and Molotch's analysis of the political economy of American cities, published in 1987, led them to develop a taxonomy of different 'urban fortunes' apparently on offer to local city leaderships.

For some of the more dynamic and diverse metropolitan cities – particularly those with a well-developed infrastructure in the field of communications and the new technologies – the prospect obtained of becoming what Logan and Molotch called a 'headquarter city', attracting massive inward investment and further development opportunities. Other cities might not obtain quite this status but, by virtue of pioneering work being undertaken in local science and business parks, and/or the leaderships provided by those whom Logan and Molotch called the 'local growth coalition' they might come to be seen as 'innovation cities', with a bright future within certain sectors of the new post-Fordist market place.

Other cities might take advantage of their particular geographical location – on the coast or at other border-crossing points – to develop a new destiny as an 'entrepôt city'. Some towns and cities, without these other given features, might trade on their rural hinterland or other natural attributes to try to reconstruct themselves as 'retirement centres'. For the powerful coalitions giving leadership to the mass of the larger industrial cities in the United States, however, there was little possibility of such a re-positioning of the local economy, and the future of these cities (like the steel cities of the Northern states) would in some way derive from what had been the staple industries of the locality (they would remain as what Logan and Molotch called 'module production cities').

From the point of view of what Logan and Molotch call the urban growth coalitions, who in market society have a considerable *de facto* responsibility for the management of a city's fortune(s), these processes of re-imaging and reorganizing local economic activities are precisely concerned to re-position these cities in the competition for inward investment – in the market, that is, for finance capital. At any time, as the creators of a computer software game, Simcity, very well understood, the continual redevelopment of a city's real and symbolic economy may work, along with other subjective and 'objective' measures (including its rate of reported crime), to re-position the city fundamentally in national or international leagues tables measuring 'urban quality of life'.

As with so many of the other league tables of performance measurement in market society, these representations of quality of urban life may then have their own independent effects on the perceptions of investors, as well as of other influential sections of the mobile professional classes as to the future market-position of particular urban regions. Officially recorded crime rates in American cities in the late 1990s took on a rather different pattern to the organic patterns of crime that had characterized America in earlier periods. Where criminological commentary had focused for many years on the continual production of higher rates of violent crime, especially homicide, in Western states in general (by comparison with the Southern states, the mid-West and the eastern seaboard),[42] much more complicated patterns were beginning to emerge. So also with cities; where in the 1980s cities like New York, Washington, DC, and Miami were vying for the title of 'homicide capital' of the United States, in the mid-1990s attention was increasingly focused on urban centres where previously there had been little sense of such 'criminal notoriety'. In 1995, for example, Minneapolis, widely known throughout the United States for its liberal and relaxed atmosphere and Scandinavian quality of life, there were 97 murders, more than twice the number of each of the previous four years, and for that year the official murder rate was higher than in New York City.[43] The two top cities for homicide in the United States in 1995 were Gary in Indiana (with an incidence of 116 per 100,000) and New Orleans (73), some way ahead of the more familiar 'homicide capitals' of Washington, DC (62), Detroit (46), Atlanta (45), Chicago (29), Dallas (26) and New York (16).[44]

The history of many English cities in the 1980s and 1990s can certainly be understood as a history of continuing struggle, by local growth coalitions, to re-position these cities in the broader imagination (especially of potential investors), but the struggles may have been more urgent in the old industrial cities, for example in the North of England, than elsewhere. The port city of Liverpool was reconstituted for a time as the Garden City (by virtue of the hosting of the International Garden Festival in 1984); Newcastle upon Tyne as the city of shopping (by virtue of the opening of the Metrocentre in 1985); and Sheffield, the City of Steel, was momentarily constructed, during the World Student Games of 1993, as the City of Sport. This period of 'urban booster-ism', in the period between 1983 and the early 1990s, appears now to have been superseded by a new mood of urban realism, in which the routine management of post-Fordist realities (not least, the policing of the city centres and the suburbs) is higher on the agenda of locally powerful politicians.

In the meantime, a focused recognition has emerged with respect to the very different prospects confronting different urban areas. In England and Wales, for example, in July 1996, the rate of unemployment in fourteen major cities varied on official measures from some 5.8 per cent to 12.9 per cent (see table 6), whilst the numbers of those who were being defined, officially, as the 'long-term unemployed' (i.e. unemployed for over a year, and not yet discouraged from registering for work) varied from between 1.9 per cent of the local labour force to 5.5 per cent. These were post-Fordist cities, then, within the relatively small area of the North of England which were home to very different numbers of unemployed and long-term unemployed people (31,154 in Birmingham and 24,397 long-term unemployed people in Liver-pool as against only 3,261 in Norwich) and a connected sense of economic prospect. But they were also cities – like most cities in market society – in which discussion of the prospects confronting the local urban region – for

Table 6 Unemployment and long-term unemployment on official measures in four-teen major UK cities, July 1996

City	Official unemployment (%)	Long-term unemployment (%)
Norwich	5.8	1.9
Bristol	6.5	2.3
Southampton	6.9	2.3
Leeds	7.2	2.6
Manchester	7.8	2.7
Cardiff	8.0	3.0
Nottingham	8.9	3.5
London	9.2	4.0
Birmingham	9.4	4.1
Glasgow	9.4	3.1
Newcastle	9.7	4.0
Sheffield	10.0	4.0
Middlesbrough	12.4	5.3
Liverpool	12.9	5.5

Source: City of Sheffield *Economic Bulletin* (July 1996)

Table 7 Rates of recorded crime in fourteen North of England police force areas, 1988, 1995

Police force	Largest city	Total reported crime, 1988	Total reported crime, 1995	Change 1988–1995
Cheshire	Chester	49,044	71,427	+45.7
Cleveland	Middlesbrough	58,474	73,447	+25.6
Cumbria	Carlisle	26,107	39,168	+50.0
Derbyshire	Derby	43,204	80,610	+86.6
Durham	Durham	44,381	67,180	+19.3
Greater Manchester	Manchester	293,785	299,412	+1.9
Humberside	Hull	85,113	127,439	+49.7
Lancashire	Preston	96,500	109,405	+13.4
Merseyside	Liverpool	149,954	151,901	+1.3
Northumbria	Newcastle	160,708	171,408	+6.7
North Yorkshire	York	34,686	59,543	+71.8
South Yorkshire	Sheffield	89,292	149,764	+67.7
West Yorkshire	Leeds	175,825	283,044	+61.0

Source: Criminal Statistics, England and Wales (1996) Cm.3764 table 2.4

example, in the pages of the local newspapers or on local radio and television – focused heavily on issues of crime and disorder in the locality. Official police statistics on crime, as gathered by police forces in the fourteen police force areas in the North of England, however, suggest that the cities in these areas were experiencing quite *significantly different fortunes in respect of the levels of crime*, at least as reported to the police (see table 7).

There is surely no simple relationship between overall levels of unemployment and overall levels of crime, but there is certainly a suggestion that the highest rates of increase in reported crime have occurred in those industrial areas, like South Yorkshire, with the most recent loss of what was locally assumed to have been a secure labour market, where the smallest increases in crime have occurred in areas like Greater Manchester, the 'youth capital' of the North of England with one of the largest post-Fordist labour markets in the North, not least in its night-time economy. In 1995–6 and 1996–7, when officially recorded rates of crime nationally registered a decrease, those decreases were less pronounced in the older industrial areas than they were elsewhere. Assuming that a significant proportion of the offences reported to the police were for 'offences against property' – a measure, that is, of the level of theft, burglary and other activities conducted in search of financial resource – these figures may cautiously be read as some indication of the level of development of 'hidden economies of crime' in particular localities and regions. This in turn may perhaps be read as a measure of the extent to which particular localities and regions are being successful in the embrace of post-Fordist market society, and in the creation of a significant range of labour market alternatives, especially for young people caught on the cusp of the transition. Social scientific commentators have only recently come to grips, analytically, with the different impacts which the first Industrial Revolution, from the early years of the nineteenth century to the post-war period, has had on different geographical spaces and localities. Thus some towns and cities were more affected than others by the concentration of mass employment in cities, and by the creation of what John Urry called 'local class structures' – expressions of the particular mix of industry and other employment in particular localities (Urry 1981). Commentators now confront the challenge of understanding the unevenness of opportunities and life-chances that face individuals in the headquarter cities or purely 'local branch-plants' of the global market economy.

5

FRAUDSTERS AND VILLAINS: THE PRIVATE TEMPTATIONS OF MARKET SOCIETY

I: FRAUDSTERS

PRIVATIZATION

One of my primary concerns in the last chapter was to investigate the ways in which the advance of 'market society' encourages the advance of different kinds of private space (especially for purposes of consumption) over shared public space and territory. This enhancement of 'private experience' and especially private consumption is a very general feature of life in market society. As long ago as 1974, Raymond Williams coined the concept of 'mobile privatization' to describe one of the defining dimensions of the *emergent culture* of market society. In 1983, he revisited the concept in the following way:

> It is an ugly phrase for an unprecedented condition. What it means is that at most active social levels people are increasingly living as private small-family units, or, disrupting even that, as private and deliberately self-enclosed individuals, while at the same time there is a quite unprecedented mobility of such privatized privacies. (Williams 1983: 188)

In the 1990s, we could argue that such a 'mobile privatization' finds an intensified expression, on the one hand, in the renewed voyeuristic interest shown within popular culture in the lives of wealthy individuals or, on the other, in the widely discussed phenomena of 'road rage' or 'in-your-face' aggression so often exhibited in public places.

The continual advance of the primacy of 'the private' (private institutions, private spaces, private consumption) over their public alternatives has many different genealogies. So, for example, the 'privatization' of transport provision in Britain in the 1980s, under the name of 'deregulation', had a specific history and a specific set of effects (a specific *genealogy*, to borrow Michel Foucault's term) – the handing over of a guaranteed market (that is, a market in which there will always be some consumer demand and some necessity to pay). This distinguished it from other privatizations (for example, social care of the elderly) where there is no generalized ability to pay. The general emphasis on strategies of 'deregulation' – advanced in the name of providing space for entrepreneurial initiative to advance, untrammelled by the bureaucratic intrusions of state, may potentially have created space for such creativity at some levels of the social formation, whilst simultaneously laying the basis for benign neglect of key areas of social management elsewhere.

The almost unqualified ideological emphasis on the sovereignty of the consuming individual ('the rights of the customer') in the 1980s and 1990s – coupled with the continual nervous expansion of different consumer markets, especially in leisure and entertainment – has produced a range of curious effects. So, for example, the endless continuing search for new products with which to entice the attention of the satiated consumer is now heavily implicated with the re-marketing of sexuality, in most highly marketized societies, as a consumer item in many different markets (for example, on video, television drama, teenage magazines etc.). In this sense, the private pleasure of sexuality, in its most elaborate and varied expressions, gets to be increasingly publicly marketed (to be mobilized as a form of public entertainment of the global market place) rather than being sequestered, as in earlier forms of State-regulated Fordist societies, in *private* markets away from places of public resort. What cannot be anticipated, in such a public marketing of sexual desire – and the refrain that sexual pleasures, of all kinds, are a kind of consumer entitlement – are the ramifications of such a liberalization in people's personal biographies or 'lifestyles'. The continuing pressure to deregulate the consumer market in sexuality, is expressed in the slow demise of the systems of censorship previously operated by the State 'in the public interest' and, as many commentators have observed, the explosion of what in an earlier post-war period were seen as adult films or other material into mainstream, prime-time television. The 'freeing' of the market in this sense unpacks the distinction between what previously were taken-for-granted adult and adolescent worlds. This process runs *in direct parallel* in most market societies with an unending series of 'moral panics' about the dangers posed to children and adolescents from sexual predators of one kind or another. This is not to suggest that there is a direct connection between deregulated markets in sexual materials and 'actually occurring' sexual behaviour (as behaviourist proponents of the 'media effects' argument would want to argue). But it would be a curious kind of social analysis that did not want to explore the social consequences (including consequences in terms of the development of people's personal 'sexual scripts') of this marketization of sexual pleasure as a consumer entitlement.

I do not have space in this book to go further into this particular aspect of market society. I want to concentrate instead on territories that have been more central to criminological concern in the Fordist period, with a view to (re)thinking their significance in the new post-Fordist market circumstances – namely, the spheres of 'economic crime' and 'street crime'. I particularly want to offer a focused discussion of the issue of fraud in the post-Fordist market place, on the one hand, and of local, neighbourhood-based, organized or professional crime, on the other. I recognize that the choice of these two topics for focused discussion excludes many other areas of empirical analysis, but hope that my discussion might be helpful in rethinking these other areas. My main concern in the ensuing discussion is to try to understand 'financial frauds', on the one hand, and neighbourhood organized crime, on the other, as explicable choices by individuals and social groups *at particular market-positions in market society*, not least in the light of a market culture which places such a primacy on the entitlement and necessity of individuals to be active consumers, and which simultaneously withdraws legitimacy from those institutions set up in another historical conjuncture to subject such market activity to the constraints of 'the public interest'. Analysis of post-Fordist society must never neglect the truth that significant and increasing proportions of people currently 'in work' are dependent on post-Fordist forms of employment. This is not just a matter of the explosion in the numbers of people so employed in the well-known centres of financial activity – like the 415,435 people, for example, who were employed within the Square Mile of the City of London in 1987 at the start of the 'Big Bang' (Thrift and Leyshon 1994: 284) – an increase of nearly 10 per cent on the early 1980s. The impact of market change on employment markets in other cities, including the mainstream cities of manufacturing Fordism themselves, cannot be ignored: in Leeds, the erstwhile centre of the West Riding textile industry, employment in the financial sector increased by a factor of 67 per cent between 1981 and 1991, as a result of the development of national telephone banking in that city (Tickell 1996).

Over and above its importance in 'job-creation', the financial market has been playing an increasing role in consumers' attitudes towards their 'personal finances'. In early 1998, about 9.5 million people in Britain (some 23 per cent of the population) were *directly* involved in the ownership, exchange and sale of private shares,[1] whilst a further 6 to 7 million were *de facto* share-owners as a consequence of the 'de-mutualization' of building societies.[2] By contrast, there were in 1998 only 29.5 million direct private shareholders in the whole of the United States – only 19 per cent of the population.[3] Involvement with the financial markets in post-Fordist Britain is no longer simply an elite activity, of marginal interest to all other citizens.

FRAUDSTERS IN THE POST-FORDIST MARKET PLACE

I recognize that the distinction I have offered between Fordist and post-Fordist society in this volume will have been far too sweeping for many economists and other analysts of the changing forms of political economy. Not least of the issues suppressed in generalized discussion of 'Fordism' are the distinctions made by Esping-Anderson (1990) between different types of organized social and institutional forms of governance within Fordism – the liberal welfare state (the United States and the United Kingdom, especially after Thatcher), the corporatist-conservative state (Germany, Japan) and the social-democratic model (Sweden)). I certainly recognize the utility of this categorization, and many other detailed analyses of the specific forms of Fordist society (Amin 1994: ch. 1) in understanding the specific recent history of individual societies entering into the experience of 'marketization'. So also would I want to recognize the importance of understanding the many different 'trajectories of development' of societies moving between Fordism and the post-Fordist global market place.

1   A key issue here, undoubtedly, alluded to in chapter 1, is the extent to which economic development in a particular regional economy now depends on the adoption of what are assumed in the abstract to be key practices (just-in-time-production, flexible and multiply-skilled work-forces, flattened managerial hierarchies etc.) (*homogeneous* economic practices) or the extent to which the provision of space and opportunity for diverse and specific practices may help a corporation to respond to the need for new products in a fast-changing consumer market place (*heterogeneity* of production).

2   A closely connected issue, of long-term significance even within the last years of Fordism itself, is the significance and influence within national societies of multinational corporations (MNCs) and the extent to which these MNCs, in the light of their many involvements in horizontally and vertically integrated producer and consumer markets across the globe, have now to be rethought and understood as global or transnational corporations (TNCs) (Harvey and Quilley 1997).

3   Another vital aspect of this globalization of transnational corporations is the 'outsourcing' of the productive process itself (the exportation of employment) into the cheap labour markets located in the Third World – and, indeed, in some cases, the increasing use of 'sweatshop' or child labour.

Encouraging further investigation of 'post-Fordism' in understanding the social context of crime, I would also point to two other theoretical arguments being advanced in contemporary analytical work on international political economy. One key argument focuses on whether current transformation and change now *necessarily* involves national states within the older-established Fordist societies moving towards the creation of 'workfare' models of welfare provision, along the lines described by Joseph Schumpeter (see Jessop 1994). The other is concerned with the question of whether the convulsions of the 1980s in the Fordist systems of production and social organization should be understood as a momentary readjustment – a period of crisis repositioning economic actors for *a new phase* of relatively orderly and coherent capital accumulation ('an institutional fix') or whether we have to understand the transformations of that period as a precursor – a first sighting – of what will continue to be a period of *continuing chaos* (or 'disorganization') in the history of international political economy (Lash and Urry 1987; Peck and Tickell 1994).

These are not matters I have the space to explore here, and I am not convinced that these questions can be answered in any final fashion simply through the elaboration of formal theoretical models. There is, however, a widespread consensus that a key and defining feature of the post-Fordist transformation of the 1980s (extending into the 1990s 'with a vengeance') is the emergence of vertically and horizontally integrated regimes of productive activity involving what is called 'flexible specialization' across a range of economic areas. According to Piore and Sabel in their pioneering analysis of 1984, the new global economy is indeed as the opening-out of a 'second industrial divide'. The *first* industrial moment, obviously, was the rise of mass manufacturing in the early nineteenth century, and Piore and Sabel remind us how this actually suppressed a considerable diversity of skills that pre-existed mass industrialization, and also institutionalized a rigid form of competition. The second and contemporary divide, they argue, will unleash a diversity of skills and talents, but also provoke much less predictable 'competitivity' (Piore and Sabel 1984: chs 1, 10, 11). These new regimes of flexible specialization are observable in the film industry in the United States (Storper 1994) and, indeed, in most television and media production companies through the world, but they are also easily identifiable in most other consumer industries (like the international Benetton corporation, with its commitment to increasingly rapid chains of production and sale) as well as in what are now called the 'financial service industries' (banking, mortgage companies, insurance). What is also quite clear to any thoughtful observer is the way in which these post-Fordist organizations are now engaged in an unending daily struggle for 'market advantage' within particular 'niche markets' or, indeed (in the European 'theatre' through the auspices of an enlarged European Union, for whole new markets as such). This endless competitive struggle frequently involves the mobilization of managerial struggles to reduce the agency's labour costs, alongside further creative investment in cost-saving technology dedicated to the replacement of human labour in the performance of particular market functions (Talahay et al. 1997).[4] Where Turner and Hodges in 1992 spoke of the late 1980s and early 1990s as involving a 'global shakeout', Tony Judt in 1996 was speaking of the new global capitalism as developing an essentially 'turbo-charged character', whilst William Grieder (1997) spoke of the 'manic logic' of 'global capitalism' and McMurtry (1995) went even further in speaking of capitalism having entered a 'cancer stage'.

The convulsive changes of the 1980s were associated, as described in chapter 1 of this book, by continuing discursive struggles and campaigns within the public sphere of the mass media and organized national political debate, especially in the United Kingdom, prioritizing the importance of 'enterprise', initiative and self-interest, as the key ingredient in a new period of economic growth and innovation. This was also a period, therefore, of 'denationalization' of industries and services that (in Britain) had previously been in 'public ownership' – that is, under the supervision and centralized regulation of the command State. This rapid 'privatization' of economic activity occurring in Britain and many other old Fordist societies paralleled a more generalized move towards 'flexible' specialization and accumulation. The London banking and investment markets were opened up to international players, large public utilities (gas, water, electricity, telecommunications, and rail) were rapidly privatized and other commercial and financial interests subject to complex processes of take-over, merger and buy-out. Christopher Stanley (1992a, 1992b, 1994, 1997) discusses many of the key structural and cultural aspects of this process – not least, the central role played by the national state itself in the construction of a new 'liberalized' (i.e. de-centred) financial market 'free' from centralized regulation. One of the main consequences of the UK's Financial Services Act, legislated in 1986, for example, was to replace the system of oversight over banking and investment provided by the gentlemen's clubs of the Bank of England and the Council of the Stock Exchange by a series of self-regulatory organizations (SROs) largely funded by the different commercial and financial sectors over which they were to provide some oversight.[5] This new post-Fordist 'City of London' was no longer dedicated primarily to the provision of long-term support to capitalists involved in mass industrial production. It was now centrally involved in a capitalism which, in Rothman's words, was distinguished 'not by the buying and selling of goods, labour and services, but of money itself' (Rothman 1987: 87). This reorganization of 'the City' was in itself an example of the general move taking place towards 'flexible specialization' and 'accumulation'. But Stanley's analysis of this transformation is particularly important (after the example of Tom Wolfe (1987) in *The Bonfire of the Vanities*) for its grasp of the 'culture' through which the new regimes of finance capital were actively lived and embraced in the 1980s, in everyday work-life and leisure, by the fast-witted young brokers (the Young Turks – the vast majority of whom are male) employed by the hundreds of new financial houses thrown up in a 'liberalized' financial market. This was a culture constructed around the highly competitive daily struggle for advantage in a range of increasingly fast-flowing markets, in which the absence of regulation (other than of the agency itself, whose self-regulatory commitments were always mitigated by the broader search for market position) allowed for the elevation of 'profit' and return above most other considerations. It was also a culture in which playing with 'other people's money' built in an ethic of individual irresponsibility. The 'subculture' that emerged in the vanguard positions within this newly globalized financial services industry has also to be understood – as suggested in chapter 1 – in relation to the crises taking place in the forms of masculinity in this period. And it must also be understood in relation to the organic transformation of the labour market (where most new employment opportunities were short-term and insecure, but with some paying significantly higher salaries than others). Stanley echoes Connell (1995) and Messerschmidt (1993, 1997) in glimpsing the presence here of new forms of forceful managerial masculinity at work – in this instance, in the mushrooming financial service industry.[6] This aggressive,

nihilistic masculinity (inattentive to any larger conception of 'public' responsibility) is clearly exemplified in the 'private language' in everyday use in the
post-Fordist financial markets:

> [The language of the young City professional] is . . . self-referential because it is
> almost always shouted. [It makes full use] of animal metaphors (bulls, bears,
> stags), of sexual metaphors (Big Bang, Big Swinging Dick), of suicide met-
> aphors (poison pills, golden parachutes); and it relies on acronyms: LIFFE, SIB,
> DTI. (Stanley 1992a: 149)

City Scandals in the 1980s

One of the definitive aspects of the 'frauds' and other financial crimes that
attracted public attention in the United States, in Britain, and in other major
developed capitalist societies in the late 1980s, was the sheer scale of the
depredations in question. Table 8 recalls a few of the more famous cases in

Table 8 Some major reported frauds in the United States in the mid-1980s

Instance		Type of fraud	Yield
June 1986	**Dennis Levine**	insider trading	pleaded guilty to earning $12.6 billion on insider information
1986	**Ivan Boesky**	insider trading	agreed to repay $50 million in illegal profits, $50 million to US Securities and Exchange Commission
Dec. 1988	**Michael Milken**	junk bonds	paid $650 million in fines for violation of securities law

the United States in the mid-1980s. Publication of major frauds during the
1980s was in no way confined to the United States, or to individuals employed
within American finance houses.[7] Public concern over such massive frauds
was excited in the late 1980s in France by reports when close associates of
President Mitterand, like Roger-Patrice Pélat, were charged with making
massive personal gains on 'insider trades' in shares of Péchiney-Triangle
Industries in advance of a take-over bid worth over $1.26 billion known only
in high circles of government. The interest excited in the emergent relationships of individuals in government and politics with the new globalized
regime of finance and enterprise were to lead, in 1995, to the arrest and
imprisonment *inter alia* of Bernard Tapie, erstwhile Mayor of Marseilles, and
also a former Minister of Communications (Alain Carignon), as well as to
charges being laid against the mayors of several other significant cities
(Montaldo 1993). In the Netherlands and Canada, in 1988, attention focused
on the activities of a group of young Canadian entrepreneurs, led by Irving
Lott, in a 'boiler room' operation 'flexibly' located in a number of different
rented offices in Amsterdam: in a period of five years, this group of five young

Canadians accumulated personal fortunes of over $6 billion by selling phoney or over-priced stocks and shares through telephone marketing to elderly people living across Europe (Francis 1988). In Italy, continuing concern over the penetration of the Mafia into many different aspects of life took on a new particular form in the early 1990s, as a result of testimonies by the *'pentiti'* (informants guaranteed protection by the newly reforming judiciary), in discussion of the direct or indirect involvement of so-called business-politicians in major economic criminality (Della Porta 1996; Paoli 1998), as well as in the more routine systems of corruption that had been institutionalized in the earlier, Fordist period.

Individual incidents of major fraud reported to the press and receiving public attention in Britain during the 1980s included some instances of 'insider-trading' personal gains, notably by an elected MP and a senior executive of a City of London brokerage. Concern was sufficient to give rise to the establishment of the Serious Fraud Office in 1988, though the creation of this agency is best understood as an artifact of the Financial Services Act of the previous year (a 'compensatory measure' to accompany the 'Big Bang' of deregulation). But the scale of 'the financial revolution' which liberalization of financial markets had unleashed – and the size and scale of the financial risks and temptations which had effectively been handed over for 'market competition' – only really became apparent during the 1990s in a series of well-publicized instances of fraud. These cases are summarized in table 9.

The amount of attention that has been given these massive frauds, in Britain and in other societies, is important,[8] but in two different senses. On the one hand, the scale of the losses to companies and, indeed, to individuals (for example, the 32,000 employees of the *Daily Mirror* newspaper who lost their pensions, or the many thousands of elderly people defrauded of their savings in phoney investment schemes) has provoked action on the part of national governments. The effectivity of these responses of national governments (for example – in Britain – the 'track record' of the Serious Fraud Office, as currently constituted, or the value of the various inquiries initiated by the Department of Trade and Industry – the responsible government department) is a different issue.[9] The broad 'social response' to these massively publicized frauds also involved some scholars in the fields of criminology and jurisprudence revisiting the spheres of company law, with a view to a reassessment of the relative value of approaches based on a theory of deterrence, retributiveness and/or some notion of 'compliance' in the name of equity and social justice (see Levi 1987a, 1987b).[10]

But the attention which has been given to these well-publicized frauds may also have been *deceptive*, in encouraging a conception of financial crime in post-Fordist market society as the activity only of small numbers of parasitic and amoral *individuals*. There is a persistent presentation of such cases in the mass media as transgressive behaviour on the part of a small number of individuals who have somehow 'gone too far', taking selfish advantage of the complexity of the regulatory environment of liberalized market society. There can be no escaping the highly ambiguous response in the popular media in Britain to many of those prominent individuals who have been

Table 9 Some major reported frauds in market Britain, 1988–1998

	Individual case	Loss (to company/ investors)	Summary
1986	Guinness affair		four senior executives eventually found guilty in 1992 of complex and fraudulent 'share-support' arrangement facilitating £2.35 billion take-over of Distillers
1988	Barlow Clowes	£190 million	17,000 elderly small investors defrauded by Peter Clowes
1989	Blue Arrow affair	£65 million (1987 only)	eleven executives charged with 'deliberate deception' of investors with respect to progress of sale of a £837 million shares offer: County Natwest failed to disclose its own share in Blue Arrow shares
1991	Bank of Credit and Commerce International	£760 million (£100 million lost by UK local authorities)	monies laundered out of BCCI HQ bank in London through subsidiaries in fifteen countries by eight senior executives; BCCI shut down by Bank of England
1991	Polly Peck	£450 million	Asil Nadir 'jumped bail' May 1993 to Northern Cyprus, charged with misappropriation of money belonging to creditors of Polly Peck International
1991	Maxwell pensions affair	£450 million	fraudulent investment of occupational pension funds belonging to 32,000 *Daily Mirror* employees
1995	Barings	£800 million	revelations that trading by Nick Leeson in the futures market had led to collapse of Barings, Britain's oldest bank
1996	Morgan Grenfell	£438 million	monies belonging to Deutsche Bank and three investment funds defrauded by Peter Young and five senior managers within Morgan Grenfell
1997	Natwest	£89 million	Natwest invests £89 million in vastly overrated options on advice of own trader, Kyriacos Papouris, with a view to personal gain

Sources: Langan 1996; Hunter 1997

accused of such frauds (especially 'celebrities' like the comedian Ken Dodd or the jockey Sir Lester Piggott, both accused of tax avoidance on quite a systematic and significant scale). Similar ambiguities of popular response have attended the jailing in Australia of Alan Bond, one of the leading entrepreneurs of the 1980s and the founder of Bond University. In the United States, the 'junk bond king' Michael Milken, released from jail in 1995, very quickly re-established himself in the favours of leading agencies of opinion formation, being immediately given a $50 million contract by Ted Turner's CNN Television to act as a financial adviser.[11] There is a suspicion that 'the culture' of market society has a powerful short-term memory and that it remembers to show gratitude to entrepreneurs and other celebrities who were active during earlier moments in the development of the enterprise society, acknowledging their investment of themselves as 'heroes of the hour' in this earlier creative period. It is certainly not clear that bodies like the Securities and Exchange Commission in the United States, the Financial Police in Italy or the Serious Fraud Office in Britain can point to a clear national-popular consensus of values, around which it could mount a moral campaign against such 'frauds' or other forms of financial crime 'in the public interest'.[12] To say this is to raise the issue as to how far such morally ambiguous activities are in fact restricted, in market society, only to a small number of well-placed individuals within corporate or media elites. I want to turn to the vast range of 'economic crimes' which now attract the attention of 'city journalists' and other commentators on the economic life of market society in the late 1990s, especially in the pages of the specialist financial press. In so doing, I should immediately remark, I am not intending to argue that any or all of these different kinds of economic crime, with their distinctive individual histories or genealogies, are straightforwardly the creature of 'market society'.[13] What does excite my interest, however, is the ways in which the social and economic significance of these different opportunity-crimes may have been transformed by the advent of a market culture which places such a high value on individual independence and entrepreneurial creativity.

AN INVENTORY OF FINANCIAL 'CRIMES' IN MARKET SOCIETY

I alluded earlier to the increasing significance, within market society, of 'the market' in finance and investment to individual citizens of such societies. I was thereby in no sense suggesting that the character of contemporary market society approximates in reality the utopian vision of apologists for 'popular capitalism' like Milton Friedman – a kind of open playing field for the 'small man' (or woman) as much as for the major investment house. Participation, through investment, in the competitive practices that are central to market societies – as some of the advertising reminds 'the punter' – is an activity endowed with many risks. One critical area of research specialism for investment houses, insurance companies and banks is the continued mapping of the patterns of risk within market society as a whole, and within particular segments of economic activity within market society.

I want to retrieve some examples of some of the more important areas of financial and economic crime currently under discussion amongst those whose responsibility it is, in market society, to map the risks. This sample of instances of financial crime, drawn from a close reading of many sources in the financial press, is not intended to be comprehensive or final (such a notion may indeed be an oxymoron in what Judt calls a 'turbo-charged', fast-moving market society). But what the taxonomy is intended to suggest is the importance of an analysis of the range of what Ulrich Beck (1992) or Richard Ericson and Kevin Haggarty (1997) might refer to as 'risk-positions' within market society, but which I might simply to refer to as 'market-positions within market society'.

The empirical area I want to visit in this section is to some extent occupied territory, dominated by analysts employed by the financial industry itself (for example, by insurance companies, in the constant appraisal and refinement of actuarial models of 'moral hazard' pertaining to particular categories of individual, social group or types of employment or leisure pursuit). It is also an empirical field that has been visited with increasing frequency by economists and political scientists, as well as a small number of criminologists, working in the tradition of neo-classical utilitarianism or 'rational choice theory' (see *inter alia* G. Becker 1968; Cornish and Clarke 1986; Cook 1986; Pyle 1993), all wanting to resolve the complexity of the challenges involved in the analysis of an apparently 'chaotic' market change, by focusing only on the hypothetical situation of a knowledgeable and free-willed individual responding rationally to a set of different 'opportunities' to maximize personal advantage.

These searches for a formal model of 'rational action' is not the starting point for the approach I am trying to develop in this volume to the reality of market society – for me, 'the market' is a much more complex and difficult object of analysis, acting to obscure as well as to clarify the choices available to individuals. 'Market society' needs itself to be critically examined at least as closely as the responses of the individual to opportunities thrown up within it. Not least, of course, 'market society' works to magnify some existing forms of inequality (especially at the level of the old manufacturing working class) whilst also actually generating a range of new inequalities of life-chances and position. So my concern, in speaking in this chapter of different forms of financial crime, is predominantly sociological. That is to say, I seek to provide an introductory map of different forms of financial crime – primarily, here, in terms of the 'conditions of existence' of such crime (who is engaged in these different financial crimes, and where?).[14] I want to recognize the situatedness of the different kinds of activities that get to be discussed as 'crimes' at different levels and locales in market society. In each and every instance, of course, the application of the label of 'crime' to their sharp-witted or far-sighted appropriation of capital will be contested by the different actors involved (from welfare 'fraudsters' and tax evaders to corporate executives 'going offshore'), and there might be conceptual and practical problems in confirming the illegal status of many of the activities I want to discuss. My warrant for discussing these areas of financial activity as 'crime' is precisely that 'societal responses' to these behaviours (albeit that these 'societal responses' might be the voices of a modernist citizenry, still committed to a notion of social equity and a social contract between the citizens and the State) will frequently speak themselves of these behaviours as 'criminal' – parasitic in different ways on the idea of a just society. That said, of course, it is also important to register that the activities I want to discuss can include those committed at very privileged levels of 'market society' (in the board-rooms and suites of major corporations) all the way down to the local street-market and car-boot sale. It can easily appear, from one perspective, that 'everyone is a capitalist' (M. Clarke 1986) or, from another, that everyone – 'from petty crooks to Presidents' – is 'on the take' (Chambliss 1978). The task of a criminology interested in the kaleidoscopic presence of financial and economic crime is to try to describe the picture which appears when looking through the viewfinder. That is not the position adopted here: my view is that the analysis of the complexity of different forms of financial exploitation and appropriation in market society should be undertaken from a perspective that does *not* see this way of organizing economic life as inevitable, and which also recognizes the substantive injustice, not to say massive human costs, that can be involved in local forms of life and work in a liberated global market.

Part of what I want to advance here involves a retrieval of the kind of work and insights undertaken by a number of prescient scholars in North America and Europe in the late 1970s and early 1980s into the growing significance of what variously was called 'the hidden' or 'black' economy. Some of that literature (Ditton 1977; Henry 1978; Mars 1974, 1982; Mattera 1985) focused primarily on the great variety of strategies which workers employed during the Fordist period to enhance their wage-packets, to alleviate the boredom or length of the working day or simply to engage in a highly individual form of class struggle (through theft from the workplace). Other commentators (Mingione 1983; Gershuny 1977, 1979) focused more on the unfolding of the crisis of mass manufacturing industry – that is, in a period in which the escalation of unemployment, understood largely as the reduction of the numbers of unskilled men in full-time employment, was the critical issue. Much of the research ethnography produced on the 'hidden economy' of this period focused on the different strategies utilized by the newly unemployed, like the miners of northern Kent – many of whom expected a return to full employment 'after the recession' – to enhance the income received from unemployment benefits (Pahl 1984b). This earlier literature has the impor-tant quality, that is, of recognizing the ways in which everyday economic life, even during 'late Fordism', was much more complex and varied than the student of 'the industrial wage' and the 'official' labour market would ever recognize. It also had the important quality of wanting to understand the socially patterned character of the different forms of economic strategies being pursued and the fact that these strategies were unequally effective in the 'solution' they offered to personal or household economic problems. Perhaps the most important contribution made to this developing literature, as the logic of the transition into a post-Fordist economy became more and more clear, is the work of Enzo Mingione (1983), outlining how the collapse of the Fordist labour market in many southern European societies in the early 1980s was producing the conditions for a revival of different 'survival strategies' based around the extended household.

I am concerned here to understand 'financial crime' as a particular response to opportunities for economic gain or simply for economic relief taken by individuals in particular biographical or structural situations within 'market society'. I want to encourage a view of 'financial crime', that is, not as the *abstract* recognition of opportunity, and the *abstract* freely willed calculation to take opportunity (as described by rational-choice theorists) but rather as a socially situated 'drift into delinquency', as classically described by David Matza (see chapter 2) that operates in particular ways in different levels of constraint or inducement. At certain higher levels of market society, those constraints and pressures will focus on the demands for continuing capital accumulation and at others there will be continuing pressures simply to survive, or somehow to do better than survive, at levels of the market society in which full-time employment is no longer a realistic option.

Welfare fraud

The notion that criminological discussion of 'the problem of fraud' might proceed without the troublesome intrusion of moral or political discussion or argument is dramatically challenged in any examination of fraud and abuse of the welfare system. Conservative critics of 'the welfare state' concept, from Hayek to Charles Murray – concerned to identify and challenge the encouragement which 'welfare' was alleged to give to individuals to pursue lives of 'state-dependency' – have also pointed to the opportunities which an impersonal and bureaucratic system of financial support can present for fraud. In the 1970s and 1980s, the attack on welfare which unfolded both in the United States and in Britain had the issue of 'welfare fraud' as one of its central themes.

Criminological discussion of 'welfare fraud' in Britain, during the last years of Fordism (D. Cook 1989) was very largely concerned to highlight the 'differential responses' of the State, through its revenue and welfare agencies and the courts, to offences of welfare claimants, on the one hand, and offences of tax evasion by individual taxpayers on the other. Cook's analysis of government ministry annual reports in England and Wales for 1987–8 revealed a total of 9,847 prosecutions by the Department of Health and Social Security for 'welfare fraud' as against a grand total of only 322 Inland Revenue prosecutions for tax evasion (D. Cook 1989: 120). Subsequent analysis of the data for 1988-9 revealed a total of 14,625 prosecutions for supplementary benefit fraud compared to 363 prosecutions for tax evasion by Inland Revenue (D. Cook 1991: 3).

The primary thrust of the analysis of the differential prosecution of tax evasion and benefit fraud, like the work conducted by students of differential enforcement of the law against 'the powerful' in many different areas in the late Fordist period, was to unpack and demonstrate the *substantive injustice* in legal proceedings and outcomes that underlay the formal equality of Law itself. This was an entirely noble and vitally important project – not least in the way in which scholars were able to highlight the means by which executives and managers of private corporations were so frequently able to avoid any personal legal responsibility and accountability even in circumstances causing massive loss of human life, for example, on the oil platforms of the North Sea during the 1970s and early 1980s (Carson 1982) or around the Union Carbide chemical plant in Bhopal, India, in 1987 (Pearce and Tombs 1989, 1992).

This was not a literature, therefore, that engaged in unflinching investigation of the role of welfare fraud in local economies. A survey of 4,350 welfare recipients by the Department of Social Security in Britain in 1996 did confirm that 79 per cent of those surveyed were entitled to the benefits 'at the rate they were receiving them', but it also found evidence of 'fraud', however that might have been defined, in about 11 per cent of cases, involving *£1.77 billion* of public monies.[15] The great danger is that any careful analysis of the role that is played by state benefits, on the one hand, in local economies of survival or, on the other, in local forms of organized crime may fall foul of a broader, political attack on the idea of welfare provision as such. In 1998, the new British Government's first moves towards a rationalization of the welfare support system for the disabled were accompanied by the release by the Department of Social Security, to the dismay of the disability groups themselves, of internal reports (based on 'spot checks') which claimed that 17 per cent of claims made by the disabled were fraudulent.[16]

Tax fraud by individuals and businesses

The avoidance and evasion of tax by individuals and businesses has a lengthy history, which I do not have space to rehearse in any detail here. One of the important developments in this sphere in the 1980s and 1990s has been the outright avoidance of taxation by wealthy individuals and corporations moving their persons or personal accounts 'offshore' to one or other of the growing number of tax havens in different locations within the global market place: the movement of money 'offshore' is one of the new opportunities provided to mobile individuals and corporations by the globalization of markets.[17] In the political climate of 'possessive individualism' encouraged by free market rhetorics, underwritten by a populist disregard for Big Government and the Public Interest, the avoidance and evasion of tax sometimes take on the appearance of a new social movement. In this context, government authorities in most advanced capitalist societies have increasingly turned away from the systematic investigation and prosecution of fraud on personal tax returns by individuals, and have increasingly urgently moved to systems of self-regulation or self-completion of taxes, in which the objective is *compliance*. This concept of 'compliance' in the governance of tax returns is a close cousin to a notion of trust that is emerging (alongside the couplet of 'high risk–low risk') in other areas of national and international governance of the movement of people and money – for example, in the distinction now being encouraged in nearly all customs and immigration agencies in advanced societies, with the encouragement of the World Customs Organization, between Low Risk Travellers, who should be allowed across boundaries without hindrance, only on advance completion of a form mailed into appropriate agencies, and High Risk Travellers, who are the subject of elaborate and multifaceted surveillance and tracking (Jamieson et al. 1997).

The importance of tax fraud in the personal lives of individuals, or the financial resilience and market position of business and corporations, is a major field of enquiry, noticeable for its almost complete absence from study in criminology. The Inland Revenue of the United Kingdom in 1997 reported that its various initiatives with clients in the field of compliance 'had brought into charge' a total of *£4.3 billion*: this presumably referring to taxation owed that might otherwise have not been available to national government (Inland Revenue 1997: 21). Specific investigations by Inland Revenue investigators into 4,743 companies and 41,186 individual businesses has yielded £51.2 million and £211.2 million respectively (1997: 4). Some of these investigations will have involved enquiries into the prevalence and scale of evasion of Value Added Tax by business involved in commerce and trade. In 1996 HM Customs and Excise Department's enquiries identified a massive and increasing 'shortfall' in VAT payments by businesses in the United Kingdom, consequent, it was argued, on more elaborate tax evasion strategies entered into by business.[18] In its 1997 Annual Report, it also highlighted the increasing evasion of VAT revenue by transit companies operating through the Channel Tunnel and across the broader European Union, which it estimated at £900 million for the year (Inland Revenue 1997: 10). Like customs agencies throughout the world, Customs and Excise were no longer operating a regime which contemplated the control of the many different forms of evasion being initiated in the market place. The new strategic plan of the agency (operating under the rubric of 'Spend to Save') promised national government only the attainment of certain specified targets of performance, such as interdictions of smuggled goods (Customs and Excise 1997).

The stock market

We have been made most aware in recent press discussion of forms of financial crime associated with the stock exchange and, specifically, with the now-international system of stock exchanges around the world, through which international investment now moves (for example, via Electronic Trading) at the touch of a button.[19] Four particular forms of 'market crime' have attracted attention during the 1980s and 1990s.

Perhaps more than most, *money-laundering* is and had been identified as a definitive crime of the new global post-Fordist market place. Money-laundering involves the movement (and 'cleansing') of monies initially earned in the 'dirty' market of the drug trade, often on a massive scale, through extended chains of accounts in the newly established and rapidly expanding 'offshore' banking systems of the global market place into accounts in mainstream banks, the stock market or other financial institutions in such a way as to disguise the originating source of these monies. The first mentions of money-laundering in the international financial and business press date from the early 1980s. By 1989–90, estimates that monies to the value of £49 billion were being laundered through 'the Western bank system' were encouraging the belief that a threat was now posed to the bank system itself, and fifteen different Western governments agreed to participate in the creation of an ad-hoc Financial Action Task Force (*Independent*, 12 Apr. 1990): in the UK alone, authoritative figures estimated that over £1,800 million of deposits were monies earned in the international drug trade in process of being laundered into legitimate accounts (*Guardian*, 8 Dec. 1989). By 1996, it was being estimated by the head of the United Nations Crime Prevention and Criminal Justice Division, Eduardo Vetere, that some $1,000 billion was now being laundered through the global banking system (*European* 22 April–1 May 1996). In their analysis of the conditions of existence of this trade in 'hot money', Piore and Sabel (1984) had already argued that such monies were of an enormous and disproportionate value compared to monies locked *within* deposits made in individual nation-states, in that, like the much celebrated 'Euro-dollar' (deposits made in American monies outside the well-regulated banking systems of America) they were almost by definition located, at least *ab initio*, 'offshore' *between* different regional markets (Blum 1984; Naylor 1987; Piore and Sabel 1984). In this sense, successfully laundered money was 'post-Fordist money' *par excellence*, with good potential for investment, both horizontally and vertically, in different legitimate markets. The explosion of money-laundering (at both a sophisticated and an unsophisticated level – for example, in the use by some Third World drug operatives of 'mules' (carrying either drugs or money on the person across national borders) – is one of the important dimensions of the transformation of global transnational crime in the 1980s and 1990s.

Insider trading is a particular reference to the use of confidential information acquired as a result of occupying a position within a company, for purposes of making a personal profit through sale or purchase of shares in the stock market. There was growing awareness of individual instances of this kind of profit-making in the 1980s,[20] encouraging the belief among commentators that insider trading, like money-laundering, was a new phenomenon of individual market societies, and, in particular cases, of the global market place. There is evidence, however, of quite significant instances of 'insider trading' in the earlier post-war history of commerce and finance (for example, in the stock exchange in Toronto, Canada, in the 1960s).[21]

Other forms of *stock market manipulation* by individuals with access to such markets which have been under discussion in the 1980s and 1990s include the kind of fraudulent manipulation of an individual company's market-position of the kind that was revealed, in Britain, by the inquiry into the Guinness affair. These forms of market manipulation have included *wash sales* (where attempts are made to inflate the value of shares in particular companies on an artificial basis, by creating a series of phoney transactions without there being real change in beneficial ownership) or *matched orders* (where 'pools' of traders pre-arrange the sale and purchase of stocks to each other, again with a view to creating the impression of considerable interest in the market in a particular company). A *cross trade* occurs when a trader moves monies between a personal account and that of a customer, again with a view to deceive the wider market. All these three forms of 'market manipulation', it should be said, have long been defined as crime within the company and securities legislation of individual nation-states. It was precisely this kind of market manipulation, after all, which had led to the infamous crash of the South Sea Company in 1720, consequent on investors – including the Government itself – attempting to gather the high-yield returns they had so enthusiastically been promised by this early example of a venture capitalist company. The 'South Sea Bubble' affair, in the words of George Robb (1992: 14), 'exercised a psychological restraint on joint-stock organization for over a century'. From the middle of the nineteenth century, in England as well as in many other capitalist societies, a series of Companies Acts have laid a number of obligations on directors of newly formed companies as to the publication and auditing of accounts. Other legislation has imposed further requirements on the leading institutions of the financial world, including the stock exchanges, as to the 'proper conduct' of trade. It is no part of my concern here to rehearse the history of regulation of commerce and the City, but, in the British case, we can follow Michael Clarke (1986) in recognizing an uneven history of regulatory 'development' during the twentieth century in which national governments seem to have taken interest in the aftermath of particularly well-publicized individual scandals and in which a taken-for-granted reliance on the existence of trust between gentlemen (for example, amongst the leadership of the Big Five banks or the council of the Stock Exchange) was increasingly put under strain. The encouragement given to different kinds of 'stock market manipulation' in the liberalized and self-regulated environment created within the British-based market place by the Financial Services Act of 1986, especially perhaps during the 'recession' of the early 1990s,[22] is a matter for dedicated research. The variety and the value of stock market manipulations being conducted transnationally in the late 1990s, through the network of stock exchanges open twenty-four hours a day, is a different matter again.

A fourth instance of the kind of opportunity which the liberalized Stock Market presented for massive private gain, on the part of prescient and entrepreneurial individuals like Michael Milken in the United States, involved the so-called *junk bond* market. These were investments marketed to private investors, in the context of the fast-moving financial markets opening up in the early 1980s, on the argument that they constituted an unprecedented opportunity to take ownership of companies that had been massively undervalued in the previously regulated market place. The investor was being encouraged, in effect, to take part in a buy-out of these companies organized, in this instance, by the well-reputed brokerage firm, and the funds which were so generated were the 'leverage' through which reinvestment was to occur in the firms which had been so identified. The concept of the 'junk bond' entirely depended on the investors' being persuaded of the under-valuation argument, and in the euphoric market deregulation in the 1980s, this argument did succeed in creating an enormous new segment of the market, worth over $180 billion (Stanley 1992a: 154). Michael Milken was eventually accused in the criminal courts not of an illegal business practice *per se*, but of the use of fraudulent information (deceit) in the marketing of the junk bond shares. Persuading investors to part with their money for shares in 'new opportunities' in the global market place – from buying shares in retirement or holiday homes or investing in very fast-growing banks and other financial institutions – was quite a widespread phenomenon in the liberalizing 1980s, not least in the elusive and very mobile 'boiler houses' (quickly removable rented offices used for telephone selling across national borders).

Fraud in the financial services market: pensions, mortgages, insurance

Some of the other 'frauds' that come to light in different ways within the newly deregulated market societies within institutions directly involved in the sale of money – for example, for purposes of *insurance* or for *pensions* and other investment now constitute a complex field of enquiry in their own right.

The history of the insurance industry is, in part, a history of a private market selling protection and reassurance, in the form of financial compensation. It is also a history of an industry heavily involved in the understanding, and financial assessment, of different kinds of risk, as well as being a history of an industry that has been involved with the identification and control of different types of fraudulent claim, by individuals or by different kinds of socially organized conglomerates or cartels, on its resources. Importantly, this history of fraudulent activity in and around insurance is very often a history of coordinated schemes of fraud committed – not by the transnational Mafia that is so central to orthodox discussion of economic crime – but by 'home grown' groups of citizens of entirely 'respectable' professional backgrounds.[23] In 1991, for example, a report by a consultancy organization in London, the Access Parliamentary Public Affairs Group, concluded that one in twenty mortgages in Britain were fraudulent – the results of the coordinated efforts of 'rings' of local solicitors, mortgage brokers and valuers, entering into schemes (double mortgaging the same property etc.) with a view to defrauding banks and building societies for personal gain.[24]

A key feature of the contemporary enthusiastic embrace of the opportunities of global markets, as already suggested, is the passage of legislation to revise the set of regulatory instruments that have been in place, over some two centuries, to regulate and protect the specific local provenance and market hegemony of individual insurance, banking and mortgage companies, as they had developed within particular localities. So, for example, in Britain the Financial Services Act of 1986, among many other things, legislated for the first time to allow 'door-to-door' selling of insurance to citizen-consumers, on a competitive (free market) basis. The oversight (or 're-regulation') of this revolutionary and extensive new market for insurance salespeople was to be provided by the Financial Intermediaries and Merchant Bankers Regulatory Association (FIMBRA) and the Life Assurance and Unit Trust Regulatory Organization (LAUTRO), the new semi-autonomous and self-regulatory bodies financed by the insurance industry itself, in the form of guides which were produced for the use of salespeople and clients alike.[25] Not the least of the issues addressed in these guides were the problems which the client might face – for example, in buying pensions or life insurance – in ascertaining whether the salesperson in question was a 'tied agent' (an agent of the company selling its own insurance) as distinct from an independent adviser, actually earning commission from different companies. Many other issues regarding 'disclosure' of the expenses and fees of the individual insurance agent surfaced during the late 1980s, and in the early 1990s a large number of cases of fraudulent selling of insurance received public attention.[26] Examination of the market in *pensions* itself quickly identifies the very large financial resources that are deposited in different unit trusts, securities and other locales (larger in size than most other segments of the futures market). This market has indeed proven irresistible to a number of individuals like Robert Maxwell in advantaged market-positions. In January 1998, for example, pension funds constituted some 27.8 per cent of the entire equity market in the United Kingdom.[27] Where for many years the idea of 'risk' had primarily been applied within the insurance industry itself, in carefully calibrated actuarial tables ('risk profiles') of the population, alerting insurers, in particular, to *clients* making fraudulent claims, in the competitive market environment of the late 1990s there has to be an increasing interest in the activities of the salespeople and agents themselves, and the entrepreneurs and other individuals with any kind of market access to the pension funds.

Bank fraud

Some re-focusing of analytic interest was also to be recommended, in the new circumstances of the late 1980s and 1990s, in respect of bank fraud. The banking industry has been very seriously concerned itself over many years with problems of client fraud, on a range of different fronts – from the use of deceit in obtaining loans all the way through to the disguising of the origins of particular funds (an issue which has reverberated in the banking industry throughout the 1980s and 1990s, with the growing threat posed by 'money-laundering' – resulting in some relaxation, even in Switzerland, of very long-established practices regarding the protection of privacy of individual accounts). But other students of banking and financial institutions have paid attention to the growing significance of fraud within the banking industry itself – in part as a consequence of the decline in morale of employees threatened by the continuing 'downsizing' of this employment market as a result of technological development (cf. also Friedrichs 1996–7), and also as a result of the fudging of the boundaries between legitimate banking practice (for example, investment on the futures market) and outright involvement in ongoing and systematic fraud. Other commentators on the banking industry, especially during the transition to liberalized global markets, would want to identify the new set of dangers posed to depositors and customers by the banks' various moves, with greater or less degrees of sophistication, training and experience, into the 24-hour global market (M. Clarke 1986: ch. 6; Stewart 1982). Very little of this particular 'exposure' of bank depositors to new risk in the new global market feeds into popular political discussion of bank fraud.

The expansion of automated banking and the increased use of 'plastic money' has added a further, explosive dimension to the challenges facing the private banking industry, and one which is more widely understood by the mass of customers. The fraudulent use of stolen credit and bank cards was one of the fastest-growing, and most favoured, of financial crimes at local or street level in many societies in the late 1980s (Tremblay 1986). By the early 1990s, the fraudulent use of credit and bank cards was estimated to be costing banks in the United Kingdom about £100 million a year,[28] and politicians concerned about the role played by such frauds in the wider 'black market of crime' were pressing for the introduction of new bank cards with photographic or other identifiers.[29] By 1996, the banks' Association for Payment Clearing Services and the Credit Industry Fraud Assurance System were reporting significant increases in the systematic 'impersonation' of individual victims of credit card fraud.[30]

Counterfeiting and piracy in the global market

We mentioned earlier some of the extended research enquiries that took place in North America and in Britain in the 1970s and early 1980s into the character of local hidden or black economies. The existence of these local traditions of the black economy is a continuing feature of life in most market societies, but, as suggested in many different places in this book, the overall trajectory of these local economies has now been heavily influenced by the general opening out to new opportunities which present themselves in the local-national Fordist economy, on the one hand, and, on the other, by the process through which full-time and permanent opportunities in the labour market have been replaced by insecure and contract work. The 'casualization' of the 'official' labour market in itself works to produce horizontal contact and overlap with local hidden economies of crime, producing a range of local labour market situations in which the returns to 'labourers', in particular, may be considerably more attractive in the illicit than the licit markets, or in which the illicit trades are the only ones a local labourer 'naturally' encounters in his increasingly desperate search for 'work'. Other opportunities to work within local illicit labour markets – for example, in organized rings of car-thieves – may function as an apprenticeship preparatory to recruitment into more elaborate and flexible forms of post-Fordist 'employment' in the interstices of the licit and illicit markets (in this instance, in cars). So also may post-Fordist labourers in particular local markets find it necessary and possible to supplement a primary income with a secondary return – for example, in the local night-time economy (bouncers, fly-posters etc.) – but soon discover that these desirable alternative markets are themselves the site of struggle between locally ambitious street-level entrepreneurs.

The ongoing and restless development of these local markets of enterprise is one of the very distinctive features of a post-Fordist market place, in the specific sense of elevating market-competition (akin to the kinds of struggles that have accompanied primitive capitalism in other societies at other times) into primary and determining features of the local labour markets, along with the inevitable conflicts and struggles over territories of influence, and markets of distribution and sale. It is also, however, a struggle in which the broader logic of market activity (expansion of markets, understanding fast-moving consumer trends, cutting costs) – well disseminated throughout the culture of the broader market society – have their own echo within the illicit economy.

One of the best-known contemporary examples of such market enterprise involves piratical raids on the licit market with a view to the production of 'counterfeit' copies (for example, of CDs, cassettes or videos). This kind of piracy, of course, runs alongside the attempts of legitimate manufacturers themselves to clone the products of 'market leaders', like the trainers produced by the Nike corporation). Authoritative commentators on the international music industry currently point to the entrepreneurs setting up their own manufacturing plants in Eastern Europe and Latin America, where they can produce extremely cheaply: the trade in such counterfeit commodities in early 1998 was worth about *£3 billion a year*.[31] Given that one in three CDs, cassettes and records being sold were counterfeit, the threat to jobs in the legitimate industry was considerable. The return of this form of piracy (like the return of industrial espionage in the broader legitimate market place) is a defining feature of the new global market society, somewhat removed from the gaze of orthodox criminology. In 1998, research by Andrew Clark suggested that 'counterfeiting entrepreneurs' were now involved in the production and sale of brewing equipment, computer central processing units, medical equipment, nautical parts and car vehicle parts: the best estimate of the total value of this market were that it was now worth some £300 million a year.[32] A defining feature of these products, emblematic of the risk-productive dimensions of market society, is the fact that the consumer could not know whether the safety of the product had been subject to any examination. But there was also an important sense in which the counterfeiting trade posed a real threat to the employment securities of those involved in the relatively regulated legitimate trades in these different kinds of goods.

The Criminological Classic: E. H. Sutherland and *White Collar Crime*

Students attempting to make sense of financial or economic crime in the 1990s are still very frequently directed to the classic text by Edwin Sutherland, first published (in a highly edited form[33]) in 1949. As Geis and Goff remarked in their introduction to the published 'uncut version', *White Collar Crime* was identified, as early as 1965, by Hermann Mannheim as a pioneering piece of scholarship which – if there were such a thing as a Nobel Prize in criminology – ought to have earned the author the award (Mannheim 1965: 470). Primarily, this was because of the way in which the text – nearly ten years in the writing – by virtue of the sheer range of its detailed research, established its fundamental argument (first voiced by Sutherland in 1940 in his presidential address to the American Sociological Association), namely, that 'white-collar crime' was indeed *serious* crime, whose absence from discussion in conventional criminology was a scandal (Sutherland 1940).

'White-collar crime' – 'crime committed by a person of respectability and high status in the course of his occupation' (Sutherland 1949: 9) was serious in two discrete but connected senses. It had enormous consequences, as Sutherland's own extensive research was to demonstrate, in terms of financial costs – losses were very nearly always passed on by corporations or businesses to the rest of the citizenry. Writing in 1949 – a historical moment in which America was about to embark on an unprecedented post-war recovery and growth – Sutherland insisted that: 'The financial cost of white-collar crime is probably several times as great as the financial cost of all the crimes which are customarily regarded as "the crime problem"' (1949: 12). But the costs of 'white-collar crime' were also moral and social: 'The financial loss from white-collar crime, great as it is, is less important than the damage to social relations. White-collar crimes violate trust and therefore create distrust: this lowers morale and produces social disorganization' (1949: 13).

As Geis and Goff make clear in their fascinating introduction to the 'uncut version' of *White Collar Crime*, Edwin Sutherland was no old-style socialist, intent on the regulation of a rabid capitalism in the name of some other political objective (for example, a 'command economy' dominated by a Keynesian State). (Geis and Goff, 1983) Sutherland's anxiety about the range and the depth of malpractice and corruption within American corporations was mounted in the name of 'free competition'. Absence of regulation of free enterprise by the State, Sutherland was convinced, would mean that corporations – like the robber barons of late medieval Europe – *would* engage in 'cut-throat predatory activity to the disadvantage (specifically) of customers' (Geis and Goff 1983: xvi).[34] The body of *White Collar Crime*, with its extended examination of the vast range of practices of corporations acting as corporate entities and of individuals employed within corporations (touching on price-fixing, anti-trust violations, violations of workers' safety legislation, bank frauds, infringement of patents, trademarks and copyrights, financial manipulations, war crimes, and very many other instances of corporate and individual 'malfeasance') is testimony in support of Sutherland's critique, specifically, of the unregulated corporation.

But the second vital aspect of Sutherland's work in this field is his attempt to think through a theory of white-collar crime as interpersonal activity and 'social learning' at work. Geis and Goff's enquiries for the introduction to the 'uncut version' reveal that the final 'theoretical' chapter was added at the last moment by Edwin Sutherland, in 1948–9, as he laboured with the demands imposed on him by Dryden Press (and also came to feel that the mass of empirical material he had gathered needed some theoretical synthesis). It is in this final chapter that the seeds of Sutherland's theory of *differential association*, as an approach to the explanation of white-collar crime, are first laid out, but it was only with Sutherland's collaboration with a graduate student, Donald Cressey, that the theory was fully elaborated. The organizing propositions, as advanced in *White Collar Crime*, are:

1 'that criminal behaviour is learned in association with those who define it favourably and in isolation from those who define it unfavourably' [and]
2 'that a person in an appropriate situation engages in criminal behaviour if, and only if, the weight of the favourable definitions exceed the weight of the unfavourable definitions' (Sutherland 1949: 234).

In his collaboration with Cressey, these raw generalizations were to be further elaborated to embrace the important additional propositions that the 'learning of criminal behaviour', taking place in 'appropriate circumstances', also specifically included the learning of:

3 'the techniques of committing the crime, which are sometimes very complicated, sometimes very simple ... '[and]
4 'the specific direction of motives, drives, rationalizations and attitudes' (Sutherland and Cressey 1966: 81).

Sutherland himself never succeeded in theorizing the range of 'appropriate circumstances' that might develop, for example, in the life of an individual or a corporation – to encourage the initial exploration of new 'associations' and learn new forms of behaviour. The parallels with Robert Merton's description of 'the innovator' adaptation in his classic essay of 1938, 'Social Structure and Anomie' – for example, on the part of ambitious young executives experiencing blocked opportunity – have always seemed pertinent, except that Sutherland's emphasis was not so much on the mismatch between a set of dominant goals in American society and the distribution of opportunity, as they were on the general absence of regulation and control *per se*. What Sutherland and Cressey did go on to argue was that it was important to explain the continuing attraction of individuals to 'white-collar crime' and their continued involvement with it as a function of the '*frequency, duration, priority and intensity*' of individuals' association with 'definitions favourable to the violation of law'. What was required, therefore, in the analysis of patterns of white-collar crime within corporations, from the highest to the lowest level, was a kind of social network analysis attentive to the transformation of such networks and their associations from what students of youthful street-corner delinquency in the United States would have seen as 'near-groups' (Yablonsky 1959), in which occasional rule-breaking is a matter of common knowledge, into a full-blown subculture in which the neutralization of the normative force of criminal or securities legislation is routinely demanded as a condition of acceptance within his or her new network.

The adequacy of Sutherland's theory of differential association, with its attendant focus on the application of a behavioural 'learning theory' to small group formation in the world of commerce and business, has been the subject of a continuing debate in criminological literature (Pearce 1976; Box 1983). David Nelken, however, in a more recent and telling assessment – in part as a result of writing in the late 1990s (in the context of global economic transformation and 'the crisis of Fordism') – raises a fundamental set of issues. He notes, first, how charges have been laid at Sutherland for conceptual ambiguity: not least, a continuing slippage of attention between 'white-collar crime' defined as 'crimes committed *by individuals* in the course of their occupation' (for example, frauds by bank-tellers) and coordinated and systematic activities which many other commentators would prefer to identify as *corporate crime*, committed, usually, in and through groups and networks. Closely associated with this ambiguity in Sutherland is a continuing ambiguity as to whether the objects of his attention are crimes committed *against* corporations or crimes committed *by* them, like the famous Tennessee Valley Authority conspiracy of 1961 in which twenty-nine major corporations, including GEC and Westinghouse, involved in the sale of electronic equipment were found to have been engaged in systematic fixing of artificially high levels of prices (Pearce 1973: 27–8). But, thirdly, according to Nelken, there is a further ambiguity in Sutherland as to the relationship between 'white-collar criminality', broadly and discursively understood – defined only, by him, as criminal activity committed during the course of one's occupation – and 'organized crime' *per se*.

Recent developments in the global market place – in Europe, South-East Asia and North America – have thrown up a range of situations, and instances, in which 'legitimate businesses' appear to have been subjected to *de facto* control by 'organized crime' – however invisible this process may have been to many employees within such business institutions. In the 1980s, some individual branches of major national banks were a particular target: in 1982, the Banco Ambrosiano, one of Italy's largest banks, was closed for some months, after it was discovered that individual branches had been taken over as conduits in major international money-laundering schemes (Paoli 1995; Santino 1988). In the same year, the United States Department of Justice demanded the closure of the branch of one of Canada's Big Five banks, the Bank of Nova Scotia, in the Cayman Islands, after evidence that the branch was playing an active role in the initiation (and protection) of a series of tax and mail frauds (Taylor 1989). The explosive migration of banks and other financial institutions in the 1980s and 1990s 'offshore' to dedicated 'tax havens' fuelled widespread suspicion amongst the small number of commentators who were closely observing this trend that these movements may have been informed by a generalized interest in the avoidance of supervision and scrutiny by any national state and its regulatory organizations, and not simply the management of tax exiles (Blum 1984; Naylor 1995–6).[35] Much more recently, in a different area of legitimate business activity – international transit of goods – a special inquiry by the European Parliament has concluded that the records pertaining to about 3 million individual shipments of goods within the European Union were now 'going missing' annually, and that the vast bulk of these 'incomplete shipments' involved organized fraud, conducted with different degrees of sophistication (European Parliament 1997). Given that the lowest possible estimate as to the value of these lost shipments from 1990 to 1997 was about 1 billion ecu, the parliamentary commission had no hesitation in concluding that transit fraud was contributing in a massive degree to 'the development of a grey market throughout Europe's economy' (European Parliament 1997: para. 4.1.1.1). The returns involved in smuggling of cigarettes, alcohol and many other commodities into and across the European Union are now high enough to have attracted the attention of organized crime cartels, but, equally importantly, as the commission itself observes: 'the organizations . . . involved are often companies based in non-EU countries offering favourable tax regimes and secretive banking laws' (European Parliament 1997: para. 5.3.2.3). Scrutinizing individual instances of the cross-over between 'legitimate business' and 'organized crime' – in which, undoubtedly, individual agents *were* and *are* actively involved in the commission of crime 'in the course of their occupations' – suggests, as Nelken also recognizes, that the ambiguity in Sutherland's classic account of 'white-collar crime' is a faithful reflection of the dynamic and changing character of such 'crimes of the powerful'. The question that is increasingly starkly posed, however, as Nelken goes on to enquire, is whether 'white-collar crime' (especially understood in such a fluid and dynamic sense) can 'be explained using the normal frameworks of criminological explanation' (Nelken 1997: 901). It is clear that the questions posed do *not* reduce to the kind of social psychology of individuals' membership (and 'differential association') within specific networks. What need also to be explained are the wider sets of relationships, of an economic character, and the broader set of cultural imperatives that are hegemonic over these particular workplaces, such that they can become active and significant nodes in the cross-over between business and crime.

In part, the transformation of the business world in the new global context raises the issue of whether such kinds of business activity are to be thought of as *marginal and deviant* within the broader business environment or whether they are to be understood, in more enquiring a fashion, as having a *critical role* in the recent hyperactive development of enterprise culture. As all the most perceptive commentators observe, one definitive feature of this new post-Fordist culture of enterprise is the restless search for new and larger markets and, indeed, for higher levels of profit and return beyond the parameters of the individual nation-state. Piore and Sabel (1984) outline how this imperative must also inform the everyday work, not just of those involved in the front line of commerce (international transportation of products and goods) – for whom the question of the markets in which goods are sold, and the returns which are gained, is at least as important as the question of excise and tax avoidance – but also all those who are involved in the trading of money (and investment itself). In the volatile international circumstances (notably involving constant change in the exchange value of different national currencies) that have dominated the world markets since the demise of the Bretton-Woods agreement in 1971 – where there is no longer any one 'safe store of value' (the gold standard) – there is constant pressure on any individual or institution involved with investment and banking to grasp any opportunity that arises to move capital around the global markets in search, if not of safety and security, then certainly of the highest possible level of return (Piore and Sabel 1984: 105–11). In such circumstances, a particular premium is placed on the capacity of key actors within institutions of finance and commerce to think and act in the global rather than the local or national market place, and there is also a real sense in which particular 'local' demands (for example, national legislation in the field of securities and investment) may become an obstacle ('a threat' in market-competivity terms) to a larger situation of 'opportunity'.

One of the defining features of this increasingly internationalized set of circuits of business and financial activity is, of course, the increasing frequency of commerce, in the traditional descriptive sense of that word, between transnationally important businesspeople, on the one hand, and new operators in the market of unknown background and origins.[36] We are witness to the emergence of new 'subcultures' of finance, commerce and trade of an essentially transnational character, with their own particular definitions of good or effective business practice – very much at odds with definitions held within individual national societies in a different historical period (the London Stock Exchange before the 'Big Bang' of 1986, for example). Within such subcultures, a particular premium will be placed on the capacity of individuals to 'do business' within the new transnationally organized free market areas, in different cultural and interpersonal contexts, in which relationships are based not on the certainties deriving from personal acquaintance and a relatively predictable business environment – as in the Fordist era – but on much more risky or speculative calculations, dependent on ad-hoc judgements derivative from the persuasiveness of particular individuals or their proximate relationship to particular 'markets of opportunity' (see Stanley 1994). Analysts of this new global market society – like those social theorists and economic historians (Weber, Braudel, Marx) who paid attention to variant forms in the nineteenth-century development of a capitalism based on mass manufacturing, need to consider whether the development of practice and culture in the global market place assumes different and identifiable forms within the different free trade areas (the North American Free Trade Area, the European Union and the South-East Asian region) that have developed in the 1980s and 1990s.

One important question here concerns the relationship between business cultures in which the exchange of presents and personal favours is a normal practice, deeply embedded in larger social practices, and the anxieties about corruption and, specifically, bribery in the global market place expressed by other agencies (like the European Parliament and Commission and the Organization for Economic Cooperation and Development (OECD)). The prevalence of bribery within the newly liberalized global market is thought by close observers to be particularly important, for example, in the international arms business (Naylor 1994–5). The pressure that has been placed since 'the end of the Cold War' on the arms-producing industries in this respect has been considerable: in the United States, nearly 1.1 million jobs have been lost in Pentagon contracts between 1987 and 1997 (*Guardian*, 10 Jan. 1997). Some measure of the different stratagems at work in the marketing of new arms contracts came to light, in Britain, as a result of Sir Richard Scott's inquiry into the 'Matrix-Churchill affair' – the sale, in direct contravention of national Government declarations of policy, of a 'Supergun' and a massive number of arms by British manufacturers to Iraq during the course of its war with Iran and its domestic campaigns against the Kurds. In the late 1990s, specialist researchers on the arms trade suggested that the volume of arms sales throughout the world was once again on the increase, and that the governments of France, Russia and the United States were giving active support to new campaigns of publicity and export. Analysis of the prevalence of bribes to gain competitive advantage in this market would be an important, though undoubtedly very difficult and dangerous, project of contemporary research in the criminological study of economic crime, as well as the criminology of war (Jamieson 1998a).[37] Students of fraud would also want to pay attention to the more routinized, and continuing, issue of fraud committed within the established institutions of national defence, which in many different societies have been the subject of continuing anxiety on the part of civil servants attempting to oversee expenditure of public monies within these inherently secretive institutions.[38]

Fraud is also widely reported in respect of civil engineering contacts being conducted in Africa or other parts of the underdeveloped world.[39] In 1997, for example, after nine years of deliberations, the OECD finalized a major convention which would make it a criminal offence, in all signatory countries, for a public official to accept payment, directly or indirectly obtained, from any foreign business organization in respect of international business transactions.[40] Discussion of the prevalence of bribery in the new global market place, however, highlights only one of the dimensions that need to be understood in respect of the new global market place – not least, the extent to which 'market' or 'enterprise' culture is now *hegemonic* within different national societies, or regional free trade areas, as a kind of 'common sense' delimiting (or, more often, expanding) the boundaries of normal everyday practice, not just of 'men of business' but of citizens in general, depending on the different relationship their daily employment or their saleable skills and attitudes may have to the new global market. In the second section of this chapter, I will focus on what sometimes in criminology is called 'crime in the streets', and we will see that the inescapable issue that is thrown up for examination is that of *the increasingly intimate relationship between legitimate and illegitimate activity* in specific 'subordinate social worlds' within this new global market in its particular local expression, that is, at *local and subordinate* 'market-positions' within international market society (see also Hobbs and Dunningham 1998). The analysis of this new set of economic relationships and market cultures clearly demands something other than the social psychological analysis of small networks that informed Edwin Sutherland's classic analysis of *White Collar Crime* in the particular historical moment of the 1940s.[41] It is to that level of everyday activity – the level of recursive daily activity and social life which has recently been called (albeit by a writer restricting his vision to a neo-classical economic kind of analysis of 'opportunities', 'costs' and 'benefits') the sphere of 'routine activities' (Felson 1994).

II: VILLAINS

THE 'FULL-TIME MISCREANTS' OF FORDIST SOCIETY

Even at the high point of Fordist society during the 1960s, a certain proportion of the lower or working class, especially men, was routinely involved in 'organized' or systematic criminality, especially in different forms of theft and burglary. In Canada, in the early 1970s, Peter Letkemann's study explored the world of the 'rounder' – the individual property thief with an all-round set of skills and interests in opportunistic forms of crime, and argued for an analysis of this kind of crime *as a form of work* – a career choice taken by certain people at the level of 'the street' (Letkemann 1973). In Britain, attention was given to this kind of professional street-level criminality primarily by crime journalists or by police officers when writing their autobiographies, rather than by scholars. The exceptions in Britain in the 1960s and 1970s were John Mack (1964, 1975) and Mary McIntosh (1971, 1975). This small body of work laid the foundations for the more extensive scholarly investigations into street-level professional criminality in Britain (Hobbs 1988, 1995, 1997a) and in North America (Åkerström 1993) and Europe (Ruggiero 1996) in the 1980s and 1990s.

John Mack's importance in this field derives from a small-scale study in the early 1960s of twelve 'full-time miscreants' in an anonymous British town of about 100,000 people. These 'full-time miscreants' or 'full-time criminals', all interviewed by Mack at length (1964: 39), exhibited three defining characteristics:

1 'that although the people concerned have some nominal occupation which they practice more or less regularly, they are known to be engaged in or available for criminal activities at all times';
2 'the main classes of crime in which they are engaged are crimes against property, or, more generally, crimes of dishonesty. Some of them are also violent, but the violence is marginal to their main activity';
3 'they have been engaged in continuous criminal activity for a considerable period of time'.

Mack also observed how local police discussion attributed the bulk of the organized crime in the region to these men and also suggested that such police discussion echoed broader discussion of such criminal involvement as a product of personal psychopathology. Mack's own enquiries suggested, by contrast, that the recruitment of these men into lives of full-time crime was best understood as a subcultural phenomenon, 'not unlike' the process operating, in this period, to recruit young people into specific types of trade (like the docks) as 'a way of life'. Mack's account echoes accounts of the ways in which locally organized forms of full-time professional criminality in Russia have developed, and been sustained, through both the Tsarist and Soviet periods (Handelman 1994; Rawlinson 1998). That is to say, it speaks of professional semi-organized crime as a life-option that may emerge in specific local situations of opportunity and constraints, but which then takes on an autonomy and a local provenance of its own, sustained over time by processes of recruitment and renewal. In Russia, during the nineteenth and twentieth centuries, this form of life has been institutionalized in the form of the so-called Thieves' Code – a code of ethics for professional criminals – and the extended subculture known as the *Vorovskoi Mir* (the 'Thieves Society' or 'Thieves World') – which outlines the boundaries of permitted and pre-scribed behaviour for full-time criminals and sometimes imposes penalties on those who break the rules of the society (Handelman 1994: xx). In southern Italy, of course, similarly routinized processes of recruitment of new appren-tices and inculcation of subcultural values have been evident in the generational renewal of the Sicilian Mafia (Ianni and Ianni 1972; Gambetta 1993; Hess 1970), the Camorra of Naples, and the 'Ndragheta of Calabria, with the crucial difference that such professional criminal associations engaged in enforcement by elimination, and often without fear of retaliation by the force of State (Falcone 1992).

According to Mack, writing on the ordered world of mixed-economy Britain in the early 1960s, regulated by a well-established state police force:

> It is perfectly feasible to hold that the same process is at work in the production of normal criminals as operates in the manning of the ranks of sociologists, or policemen, or decision-makers, or any other more respectable social group. It is simply the process of social selection which is to be found in all social systems, and which in our particular social system works by a combination of chance, choice, or personal cheque-book. (Mack 1964: 53)

What Mack did not go on to argue – though he could have – is that this reproduction of 'professional crime' could be thought of simply as a kind of social deviance – to be understood, like some kinds of hobby activity (trainspotting, mountaineering, etc.) as a departure from the dominant forms of work and leisure in 'modern industrial society' and their normal cultural or value expressions. In no sense, in Britain or many other industrial societies at the time, were these organized behavioural systems as extensive or violent as were, for example, the behaviours of the *mafiosi* in the distinctive social circumstances (absence of regulation, underdevelopment of the State etc.) obtaining in southern Italy. Even so, however, it made sense to understand the processes of reproduction of professional crime at local level, like the reproduction of 'deviant' hobbyists, *as a situated social process* – than it did to conceive of these processes in clinical or psychopathological terms. Like the Fordist industries that dominated each local working class area of residence, the local 'economies of crime' were highly regulated structures, with their own developed hierarchies and systems of recruitment, operating on many

Table 10 Four varieties of professional criminal organization

Ideal type	Exemplars	Organizational characteristics
picaresque	pirates, brigands	fairly permanent one-man leadership; some supporting 'officers'; profits shared according to rank
craft	skilled small-scale thieves; confidence tricksters; burglars	small, fairly permanent; usually 2 to 3-people task groups each with specific role; teams of equals, profits shared
project	robbers; smugglers; fraudsters	large-scale crime, complicated techniques, advance planning; ad hoc teams, gathered by entrepreneur; profits shared on agreed, a priori basis, some participants working for 'flat fee'
business	extortionists, suppliers of illegal goods and services	largest in scale; most permanent; hierarchy of participants engaged in specialized tasks; payment *either* from superordinates in hierarchy *or* on a share-out basis, frequently weighted in terms of specialization

Source: adapted from McIntosh 1975: 28–41

different levels (for example, in gendered terms – these structures were heavily masculinist) as a mirror of the broader social order, other than in the preferred area of trading. As many participants in the criminal trade of the Fordist period observed, the main difference between themselves and other skilled and intelligent members of the local labour aristocracy, the craftsmen, was in the level of return and the excitement attaching to their respective crafts. What both these fractions of the local working-class 'elites' might share was a disdain for the mass of the employed working class, 'wallies' 'slaving away' 'for peanuts' (L. Taylor 1984).

THE ANALYSIS OF PROFESSIONAL CRIME IN FORDIST BRITAIN

The closest approach to a formal sociological analysis of the different forms of local organized crime that have developed in Britain is to be found in the work of Mary McIntosh (1971, 1975). McIntosh adopted in effect a Weberian analytic strategy in identifying four 'ideal types' of professional crime group, which she fully recognized can be understood in terms of their different specific histories and their specific contemporary provenance. This is expressed in table 10. Over and above her objective to offer this kind of analytic taxonomy of organized crime, McIntosh was also concerned to recognize that different mixes of these kinds of criminal organization might be subsumed beneath any discussion, in newspaper discussion or in police discourse, with respect to organized crime. In McIntosh's more extended account she presents a picture of organized crime in Britain in the post-war period as having an essentially rather stable genealogy – predominantly local in character, with the concentrated mix of illegal activities in each locality being a function of the kind of opportunities thrown up in the area, alongside the particular specialisms of the criminal trade that had been locally developed, especially within small numbers of 'criminal families'.[42] The vast bulk of professional crime, in numerical terms, in the early 1970s consisted of small-scale craft crime, though popular attention remains preoccupied by some high-profile examples of 'project crime' – most notably, the 'Great Train Robbery' of 1963 (Fordham 1965), which, McIntosh argued, was likely to be increasingly thrown up, as a form of criminal enterprise, in response to the more organized and secure forms of security adopted, nationally and internationally, by both public authorities and private corporations. There was also a sense in which this stable 'criminal underworld' – rather like the broader society within which it existed – was seen to be relatively effective in the regulation of its own activities, generally without the need to resort (like the Sicilian Mafia or the Colombian drug cartels in the 1990s) to the use of elimination or terror in dealing with competition.[43]

The Villains of Market Society

My interest here is to think how the advent of 'market society' conditions in the 1990s has contributed to a revision of the relationships between organized and professional crime, as North Americans would put it, at the level of 'the street'. One issue is the continuing utility of the taxonomy advanced by Mary McIntosh in the 1970s: analysis of 'the structures' or 'the patterns' of professional crime in contemporary market society confronts a vast range of different reality. We would not expect, that is, to encounter simply a small number of professional criminals, routinely and recursively engaged, in a knowing and businesslike fashion, but in largely invisible a way, in a form of parasitism on the margins of a cohesive and orderly Fordist economy. Nor either would we reasonably expect to encounter simply a local or neighbourhood-based set of criminal practices, of the kind described by Mack and McIntosh, with what seems in the 1970s to have been a rather limited involvement in *international* racketeering, in such a way as to weaken local supervision and control.[44]

Just as one should not expect to find a Fordist logic in contemporary organized crime, so also one should not expect to encounter the 'abolition' of the impact of practices, values and assumptions that had been built up over long periods of time during the Fordist period in respect of professional or organized crime. Steve Hall (1997) has suggested that the 'capacity for violence' which is associated with some specific forms of organized crime (for example, in the specific sub-trade of 'enforcement') – which, after Bourdieu, he calls 'the visceral habitus' – may in fact 'be durable in the sense that it is quite capable of surviving through shifts in the social order'. Indeed, he continues:

> If a durable violent habitus has been established in specific locations of the productivist order, it may well be that, under the prevailing material conditions, a more convivial life cannot be engineered ... or [be] expected to emerge organically from some suppositious 'interstices' in a fragmenting social order. (Hall 1997: 462)

There is a widely voiced suspicion in the 1990s that 'organized professional crime' has a much more widespread presence in Western societies than in earlier periods. It is important, of course, to recognize that this same widespread common sense might have a metaphorical quality – that is, that the talk of 'organized crime' (or indeed 'the local Mafia') might be a shorthand that is used, especially by police officers and by local crime reporters – in some societies more than others – as a way of alluding to a perceived internationalization of economic and social activities. There seems little question, too, that the more frequent discursive reference to the presence of highly organized criminality at work in different national societies coincided historically with the impact of the increasing prevalence of an international trade in drugs, especially heroin, in the mid-1970s, and that this discourse has been given further force, in societies like Britain's, as we will see in chapter 6, by the sudden increase in the numbers of crimes involving the use of firearms.

Petrus van Duyne, an internationally known specialist in the field of 'organized crime', has written about the continuing reinvention of powerful myth that is promulgated, especially in international police circles, about the amoeba-like influence of a transnationally organized hierarchy of professional criminal enterprise (the Mafia of Italy or Russia), and contrasted the power of this myth with a range of empirical research into 'organized crime' which emphasizes its essentially local, opportunistic and entrepreneurial character (van Duyne 1996). Van Duyne's own characterization of 'organized' or 'professional' crime itself suggests that participation in different forms of professional crime ('planned violation of the law for profit') is no longer confined to groups of lifelong professionals, and that the vast bulk of the professional crime taking place, for example, in Western Europe – for example, the smuggling of contraband cigarettes through the territories of the European Union (avoiding local taxation and selling on in high-cost market places) – is the product of opportunistic initiatives on the part of small groups of entrepreneurial-minded 'locals' with no ties to international organizations of any serious character (see Hobbs and Dunningham 1998). It is only when these local entrepreneurial initiatives (establishing secure new cross-border routes for smuggling contraband cigarettes, alcohol, or computer software; successful new locations for gambling; or efficient 'boiler houses' selling fraudulent house-shares in Mediterranean retirement resorts) show evidence of having established a lucrative market for themselves (a new niche in the survivalist economies of market society) that the traditional international crime organizations start to show an interest.

So the emphasis in much newspaper and police talk as to the international source of organized or professional forms of criminality (suggesting that the emergence of such a phenomenon at local level is the product of international 'corruption') might work, at the level of discourse, as a displacement of other truths about particular localities in market society – not least the issue, so frequently raised in this book, as to how working class men, nurtured in the traditions of peer group, neighbourhood and local school for work in the manufacturing trades, are indeed 'to employ themselves'. Many of the new organized crime 'syndicates' have developed in areas which have experienced long and sustained periods of intense and deepening disadvantage in respect of the changing local economy. That is to say, in particular, that several cohorts of local young men have now experienced adolescence without experiencing this age of life as a transition into the ordered and regimented workplaces of a Fordist society. In Britain, these cohorts of young men have been the target, from the early 1980s onwards, of a continuing sequence of government-led job-training and job-creation initiatives and programmes – from the Manpower Training Programmes of the early 1980s through to the Welfare to Work programme of the new Labour Government in June 1997.[45] A continuing feature of these programmes has been the idealist project of trying to disseminate the basic ideas of the 'enterprising culture' to a population that might otherwise become surplus to requirements in the new market society. The mantra has been that of encouraging the realization of an 'enterprising self' – individuals who are capable of glimpsing and grasping opportunities to help themselves, rather than remaining within the 'dependency culture' of the welfare state (P. Cohen 1990; Rose 1992). Studies conducted by Craine (1997) and many others show that attempts made to help themselves by young people living in benighted localities of very high unemployment – for example, by entry onto local training and enterprise schemes – very often result in what Craine nicely calls the 'magic roundabout' experience. The whole of the period of late adolescence and early adulthood, that is, gets to be spent 'going round' a succession of different 'schemes' rather than in paid employment itself. No amount of commitment seems to produce viable or desirable full-time work, or anything approaching the lifelong career that was taken for granted by earlier generations of adults living in the same locality. Janet Foster's study of one such neighbourhood in South London draws particular attention to the emphasis on local young men's increasing sense of reliance on their own devices, working alongside long-established conceptions of working-class patriarchy, to legitimize their routine involvement in different kinds of 'rackets' (Foster 1990). Philippe Bourgois's stunning ethnography of young Puerto Rican men involved in the trade in crack in East Harlem, New York City (Bourgois 1995) provides further illustration of the desperate character of the 'search for respect' by young men confronting not only the universal reality of post-Fordism (in the continuing absence of sufficient viable employment in the unskilled labour market for men) in the specific and severe form this crisis has assumed in the

1990s in New York City (Fitch 1994), but also confronting this challenge as the first generation of offspring of the most recent groups of aspirant migrant peoples attempting to 'make it' within the melting pot of New York City and the United States. Accounts have been presented of the emergence of a mass underclass population of unemployed young men in a permanent position of marginality vis-à-vis the Fordist labour market of opportunity and routinely seduced by the alternative opportunities of local hidden economies of illicit activity in most of the old 'Fordist' societies of Europe and North America (Mingione 1994; Wacquant 1994, 1996). It may be that analysis now needs to proceed a little further in order to outline the range of opportunities that are being thrown up in different market societies, other than of remaining dependent on the unemployment or welfare benefits provided by the State which (following the example of the Clinton Administration in the United States) seem about to be significantly undercut in most advanced societies. To put this point differently, it may be helpful analytically to try and draw up a kind of 'business-plan' – or an indicative map – of the different kinds of business opportunities that may be presenting themselves to subordinated groups (included the unemployed who may no longer have the option of 'welfare') within market society. In the final section of this chapter, I want to outline some aspects of such a business plan 'in draft form'. I do not want to suggest that this is a complete and comprehensive analysis, and further work along these lines is enthusiastically encouraged.

THE MARKET IN PROTECTION IN MARKET SOCIETY

I introduced some discussion, earlier in this chapter, of the significance of fraudulent activity in and around the insurance industry. But the insurance industry is only one growth point in a fast-developing market in the provision of protection in insecure and competitive market societies. The growth of a range of different forms of privately provided protection has been most dramatically illustrated, of course, in newly liberalized market Russia, especially during the immediate aftermath of the privatization reforms of 1992–4 (Gilinsky 1998; Rawlinson 1998; Lloyd 1998). But the logic of marketization and private protection has a more general provenance. Even the most cursory examination of the new marketing of 'protection' in Western market societies, experiencing the full impact of transition to free market competition, is instructive.

Table 11 is an attempt to identify the wide range of different sites in which 'protection' is demanded in 'market society'. Some of these sites (for example, army camps) have been in need of specific protection over a long period of time: they continue to have their protection provided by their own dedicated forces of 'protection provision', delivered more or less as it has always been in earlier historical moments. Others (some government agencies and buildings) have, however, added extra dimensions in relatively recent years to the ways in which they try to guarantee protection for themselves, notably by the addition of increased numbers of private security

Table 11 The markets in 'protection' in market society[a]

Locales, sites	Provider	Agent	Payment	Regulation?
army camps, defence facilities, secret State institutions	army	military police officers	–	internal to State
other major institutions and buildings of State	State police, state's own agencies	local security staff/police	–	internal to State
major (national, multinational) commercial and industrial sites	national or international private security industry	local/regional staff of major national/ international companies	contracts	'self-regulation'
local commercial and industrial sites (incl. 'shopping malls')	local security 'firms'	locally-recruited trained security staff/local 'hard men'	contracts/ one-off fees[b]	no
private land, private estates etc.	private landowners	retainers[c]	feudal obligation (tied cottages etc.)	no
local sites of leisure consumption (clubs, pubs etc.)	local security firms	'doormen'	short-term contracts	no

[a]Terrestrial sites only (i.e. excludes market in security in computer data).
[b]In 'free-market Russia' in the 1990s, bribes.
[c]Cf. the '*Bravi*' employed by feudal landowners in Sicily through the late Middle Ages, released from baronial control in the early nineteenth century, and seen by Gambetta (1993) as a key element in the development of the Sicilian Mafia – 'providing security' to local traders and citizens in a society in which State-provided alternatives have been consistently underdeveloped.

staff. Major private sector organizations, especially those which are active in the consumer market place (like shopping malls) now depend heavily on the provision of protection by private police or security agencies.

Anticipating more detailed discussion of this 'privatization of social control' in chapter 7, we can identify the demand for provision of protection as one of the largest growth-markets in an uneasy market society, but also as an arena in the provision of 'security' which is full of internal contradiction. The rapid growth in the use of private security staff acting as door staff for clubs, wine-bars and other outlets in the urban night-time economy of major British and European cities (itself a major growth area for temporary post-Fordist employment) is widely thought to have played a critical role in the institutionalization of locally organized drug-trading activity, under the protection provided by private security staff whose salaries are easily augmented by 'backhanders'. Activists in community crime prevention in Britain are also alarmed by suggestions and demands that the provision of protection for schools and hospitals might also soon be provided by private security agencies, from one of the most unregulated industries in the whole free market society, employing many thousands of individuals whose personal backgrounds (and 'criminal histories') have not been subject to any systematic and disinterested kind of scrutiny.

Protection is only one of the commodities around which we might expect to see some market growth in the immediate future in market societies. I have tried in table 12 to provide an assessment of the prospects for a selection of different 'criminal markets' in the last years of the twentieth century. This assessment derives, like most market assessments, from the internalization of a mass of information about levels of activity within these market areas in one particular region of the global economy (the North of England) and no doubt would require modification for other regions. It is certainly not exhaustive: the World Ministerial Conference on International Organized Crime in Naples in 1994, for example, focusing on the European theatre as a whole, identified a portfolio of activities of 'organized crime' ranging from the rustling of cattle, through piracy, kidnapping, smuggling of rare animals and objets d'art, terrorism, 'baby-trafficking', prostitution, trading in bodily parts, smuggling of nuclear material, car-theft and smuggling, money-laundering, to the well-known trades in drugs, arms, and people (*European*, 18–24 Nov. 1994). The market assessment set out in table 12 is a little more restricted.

The development of models and analyses of these new markets in crime is replete with difficulties. Not least is the problem that very many of these new markets involve forms of forceful and entrepreneurial conquests of new markets, involving significant levels of risk and danger.[46] Bourgois's study of crack cocaine sellers in Harlem, New York, is one of the few genuine and reliable ethnographies of street-level markets we have – in that Bourgois seems to have been able, like the best of anthropological fieldworkers, to establish a relationship of trust with the local community, by living there for nearly three years and also by speaking the local patois of Puerto Rican migrants (Bourgois 1995). There is an understandable reluctance in some circles to undertake enquiries which might contribute to the further institutionalization of crude mythologies, of the kind identified by van Duyne (1996), in which 'the world' (or 'respectable society') is somehow seen to be threatened – routinely and primarily – by a world-wide international conspiracy called 'the Mafia'. This kind of thinking (mobilized as it is by certain powerful police agencies, international police magazines and journals) is a very poor substitute for concrete and specific analysis of the many different forms of organized criminality that currently cut across the body of market

Table 12 Project and craft crime in market society

Commodity	Yield/return[a]	Agency (firm/individual)	Essential players	Provenance (local/national/international)	Market analysis (1998)
stolen cars		local firms and apprentices	local car-theft specialists[b]	local to national	falling[c]
computers	medium		professional burglary teams; drivers	local to international (theft of computers in West for Russia/eastern Europe)	steady
computer data		individual entrepreneurs	hackers	international	excellent
drugs	low but reliable at local level[d]		suppliers; salespeople, local protection	international to local	?
contraband cigarettes; alcohol	medium	underclass entrepreneurs esp. near borders	drivers	international to local	steady to good
transit frauds	high	legitimate businesses	drivers; international collaborators	international across national borders	good
pornography	low	traditional craft criminals involved in smuggling	airline or shipping company employees?	international to local	declining[e]
firearms	high		long-established smugglers & fraudsters; new market entrepreneurs esp. ex-USSR/Czech.	international to national and local	good
people (refugees, asylum-seekers)	low locally (but high returns for firms)	transnational 'firms' esp. in shipping	sailors; shipowners	international to national	good

[a] Relative to alternative sources in the legitimate local markets.
[b] In the UK, local slang = 'TWOCers' ('taking without consent').
[c] Car-theft in Europe declined between 1994 and 1996, especially because of introduction of electronic demobilizers. Reductions varied between the UK, the 'car-theft capital of Europe' (4.6 per cent), France (5.4 per cent), Germany (9 per cent) and the Netherlands (13 per cent). (David Harrison 'Europe's thieves forgo Ferraris for old bangers', *Observer*, 16 June 1996).
[d] Bourgois's close analysis reveals how little income actually accrues to crack cocaine sellers in Harlem (Bourgois 1996).
[e] As a consequence of market competition (satellite television).

society, and the many different (both vertical and horizontal) relationships that may develop between different sets of entrepreneurial individuals and groups in particular locales and regions and the better-established and experienced professional criminal organizations, but also with different local legitimate businesses. In the next chapter, I want to provide an initial exploration of a key area in which the cross-over between different forms of market activity are of particularly pressing contemporary significance – the market in guns and other firearms.

6

LETHAL MARKETS: THE LEGAL AND ILLEGAL ECONOMIES IN FIREARMS

In many 'advanced' and increasingly 'liberalized' societies, general public anxiety over crime has quite suddenly come to a head in a more specific agitation – focusing on the apparently increased use of firearms in crime. I use the term 'focus' here with some reluctance, since, as I will want to argue throughout this chapter, public anxiety over firearms has a different meaning in different market societies (as well as some shared or 'hegemonic' features). It is by no means clear that the anxiety over guns is reducible (as some victimologists and government researchers would have us believe) to the citizen's calculation that he or she is ever likely personally to be a victim of any criminal assault with a firearm.[1] Indeed, my major purpose in this chapter is to argue that the anxiety over firearms in crime speaks, by analogy, to more generally fearful aspects of competitive and risky conditions of life in market societies – fears about risks and dangers which are increasingly widely recognized at the conscious level by the citizens of many such societies. The icon of 'the gun' evokes powerful memories of what, for many of us, is a classic source of childhood learning – the Hollywood gangster movie – where the significance of the gun was well understood. It was an instrument for 'taking out' 'the opposition' – a way of 'enforcing a contract'. In other filmic representation of gangsterism in America of the 1930s, there was further graphic depiction of the gun's importance in the enforcement of social and economic exchange, that is, in market relations.

For most of this century, common-sense belief in Britain and many other societies has assumed that the use of guns in civil society in peacetime is largely restricted to the United States, though it is important to understand that this common sense has always suppressed recognition of the scale of firearms ownership and the routine use in 'normal circumstances' by certain groups (farmers, the sports-shooting community and others) in those societies.[2] We shall return to these themes later. In Britain, the 'spree-killing' of sixteen people at Hungerford in 1987 and the massacre of sixteen pre-school children at Dunblane in 1996 has severely challenged that popular common sense. In Sweden, a series of lethal firearms incidents, beginning with the assassination of Prime Minister, Olof Palme on a public street in 1986, and culminating in the random machine-gun murder of customers at a wine bar on the stylish Stureplan, in central Stockholm, in 1993, has also provoked anxiety over the prevalence of firearms in private hands. Fear about 'the gun' and also about other potentially lethal or disabling instruments (flick-knives, the 'combat knives' on sale in army stores,[3] laser-beam lights) now impinge on the taken-for-granted sense of safety in everyday life in many market societies. Alan Hunt (1997) has argued, in rather Durkheimian a vein, that these different campaigns implicitly reference the sudden emergence of a 'new' and threatening range of individuals. The mass media are implicated in a constant demand for some kind of regulation and control of these threatening individuals. The objective of agitated attention is to try to shore up a beleaguered 'community' or anxious individuals, in the name of social reassurance. I want to open discussion in this chapter by focusing on the conditions – and, indeed, on some of the specific events – which are making for the new level of concern, or anxiety, over firearms in specific market societies. I will start with the country which is, on so many different dimensions, the exceptional case, the United States.

THE UNITED STATES: GUNS AT THE FRONTIER

The United States is, of course, a state that was founded upon, and created through, violent conquest – first, the conquest of nature across a vast and initially inhospitable land (a 'settler society') and, secondly, the conquest of the founding peoples themselves of North America, the Indian peoples.[4] This first victory of pioneer Americans, of course, depended in no small part on their use of firearms, including the mythological Colt 45[5] and the Winchester rifle[6] – and this victory of American firepower has subsequently been elaborated through a series of connected mythologies (the Seventh Cavalry, Custer's Last Stand, Davy Crockett, the Alamo etc.) which have had enormous purchase on the American imagination, as well as on the minds, mostly, of young men in other societies. Less than two centuries after this pioneer settlement, the majority of the population in the US show little active interest in wanting to live without guns. According to estimates in 1993, some 57 per cent of all households in America contained at least one firearm, and there were thought to be some 211 million firearms in circulation. American public opinion seemed at this time to be unmovable, especially on the idea of restricting private ownership of firearms, even in the aftermath of a number of massacres of innocent citizens committed with guns.[7] Some commentators have suggested that the continuing opposition shown by the majority of Americans to a stricter regime of firearms control was primarily encouraged and legitimized by the campaigns of the National Rifle Association and, in particular, by its regularly recycled refrain that 'it is people who kill, not guns'.[8] This slogan has worked, over many years, to displace discussion away from the lethal character of the firearm as a piece of technology, especially in the private home,[9] onto the much more congenial, popular-criminological terrain of searching for and controlling 'the psychopath'.

Other commentators on the stubborn commitment shown by American gun-owners to their weapons have underlined the importance for Americans of these privately held guns as a symbol of the deeply ingrained distrust in the American psyche of 'the State' as such. In this perspective, 'the right to bear arms' is the right of all 'free' and independent citizens of the United States, enshrined, as the NRA and other like-minded commentators so often proclaim, in the Second Amendment of the United States Constitution. The Second Amendment proclaims that:

> A well-regulated militia being necessary to the security of a free state, the right of the people to keep and bear arms shall not be infringed.

A small but influential group of lawyers, NRA supporters or sympathizers and politicians in the United States have for some years been active in developing what is called a 'Standard Model' for the interpretation (for example, in the courts) of the Second Amendment,[10] suggesting that the intentions of George Washington and other architects of the US Constitution were always that the average citizen of America should have lawful ownership of arms – first, for purposes of common defence (the idea of a republican militia of all the people) and, second, in order to deter any 'oppressive' government somehow wanting to exert its power through its monopoly of armed force.[11] Deeply embedded in the arguments of the Standard Modellers – some of whom, it should be noted, would describe themselves as 'radicals' (in the sense that they are committed to an essentially libertarian ethic) and others of whom would see themselves as exemplary conservative-republicans – is a shared common-sense commitment to the sovereignty of the individual as the bedrock of civil society. This is closely connected to a deep distrust of State provision or regulation – at least in any form that might be described (for example, in many European societies) in civic or collectivist terms.[12]

Three developments may be said to have given strength in the very recent period, however, to advocates of stricter regulation of firearms in the United States. First and foremost – especially for students of the politics of legal reform and 'moral crusades' (H. Becker 1963; Gusfield 1963) – is the example of individual 'moral enterprise' set by James Brady, the erstwhile Press Secretary to President Ronald Reagan. The so-called 'Brady Bill' or Crime Control package, passed by the American Senate in November 1993, has many critics amongst advocates of even stricter regimes of control, but the legislation *did* ban the sale or production of semi-automatic assault weapons and, at least in theory, also banned the sale of handguns to juveniles. It also required all intending firearms-purchasers to wait five days after their first and original enquiry in a firearms dealership before obtaining their firearm of choice – the hope being that this measure would reduce the numbers of firearms-homicides resulting from the 'sudden, temporary impulse to kill'. There is no doubt that the fact of this campaign being led by a stalwart, upright member of the Reagan Administration – himself the accidental victim of an attempted assassination of the President – helped endow the Brady campaign with a special legitimacy for majority opinion in America. It is noticeable, however, that the 'Brady Bill' made no attempt to make any legislative inroad into the millions of firearms that were already in private hands in America.

A second development in the enhanced American concern over firearms – which clearly touches on the raw nerve of 'the liberty of the individual' in America, and which in many ways threatens to open up issues which the governing classes in America would prefer not to have to negotiate – has to do with the recent rebirth and rapid growth of religious and political fundamentalism in the United States. If 'the (constitutional) right to bear arms' extends to *all* Americans, then this would, of course, include the leadership and membership of religious sects like the Branch Davidians holed up in Waco, Texas, in 1992–3,[13] as well as the different kinds of militia groups which have been emerging, notably in Montana and other Mid-western and Western states, during the 1990s. These groups are the product, on the one hand, of the residualization and immiseration of many thousands of farmworkers and other working people, dependent for their livelihood, in these parts of the United States, on forms of agricultural production and cattle-farming increasingly left behind by mechanized alternatives and also by competition from the world market, but, on the other, of an angry reassertion of the kind of white, male, individualistic fundamentalism which fuelled the original pioneer settlement of America in the early years of the nineteenth century. The power of the cultural myths describing 'America' as a pioneer society run deep, and they certainly do not constitute the cultural or political terrains with which the contemporary market-liberal politicians in Washington, in sun-belt California or the Eastern seaboard want to do battle, or for which they have any answer on which they would like to 'go public'. The only answers available – prioritizing the retraining and flexible reskilling of the worker spoken of by Robert Reich (1991) and other anxious commentators on the problem of the future competitivity in the American economy – are not the kind of answers which are likely to win votes in 'Marlborough Country', where cattle- and other forms of farming, or masculinist work on the land or with machinery, are an assumed individual male destiny. Television images of the militia groups in the 1980s and 1990s – where they are not of young men accused of the bombing of the federal building in Oklahoma City – are almost invariably pictures of groups of angry young and middle-aged men – taken at some distance from their retreats – usually referred to as a 'compound', and always accompanied by the display of the iconic handgun or rifle. In media images of this kind, importantly, I would argue, the gun acts no longer (as the NRA would prefer) as a signifier of peace, order and responsible individualism, so much as it resonates the deeply felt sense of segmentation, break-up and disorder in what Americans desperately want to believe is still an organic and inclusive Republic (the idea of America whose other defining symbol, of course, is the Statue of Liberty).

The third development of importance in the current anxiety about firearms in America, I would argue, is the developing and fearful sense that guns are now getting into the hands of another, inappropriate, section of the population – namely the young. It would be reassuring to say that this anxiety was born of a concern for *the fate of others* – that is, on the part of a relatively affluent, dominant, and white middle class for the fate of whole sections of black America (especially, young black males), who are overwhelmingly the most likely victims of firearms crime, including homicides, in the United States. Recent data shows, in fact, that homicide is now the absolutely leading cause of death amongst black American men: the lifetime risk of being murdered has for some years been over six times higher for young black men than it is for young white Americans (Fingerhut and Kleinman 1989) and this massive discrepancy continues to grow – consequent, in particular, on the prevalence of handguns in black urban areas. Of those treated in US hospital emergency departments during 1992–3 for gunshot wounds 52 per cent were black males, about half of whom were under twenty (Zawitz 1996).

It is not clear that this holocaust is a matter of general concern in America. It would be more accurate to identify the anxiety of the dominant middle class of America, especially those who are parents, as arising out of the fear that 'the gun' might make an entirely unwanted appearance, directly or indirectly, in the lives of their own children, and thereby, indirectly, in their own lives. Widely publicized reports regarding the number of school-age children carrying guns (especially, in media reports, in the public school system) engender fear in many parents for the safety of their children within the public school and are one factor in the escalation of private education. So also is there some fear (fuelled by sensational homicide cases, like the Menendez brothers in California) that children could take to arms as their own (Tarantino-like) solution to domestic strife. Given the fact that a small, plastic-covered 9 millimetre handgun can now be bought in American firearms-dealerships for some $50 (so that an absolutely lethal small handgun is a relatively cheap item available, as the anxious commentators so often suggest, as a 'fashion accessory' from a local, publicly accessible market place – the firearms store[14]) the anxieties of parents are entirely understandable. What is at issue here, however, we should note, is *not* the idea of a 'gun culture' *per se* – which remains more or less unproblematic within dominant American culture – but rather the idea that an accessible *market for guns* has been allowed to develop amongst inappropriate sections of the population – the young and immature. There is a closely connected worry amongst concerned agencies in the United States (like the Bureau of Alcohol, Tobacco and Firearms) as to the relationship between the expanding private market in firearms (especially the numbers of legitimately held firearms) and the appropriation of these firearms through theft, or different kinds of business transactions, by groups of organized criminals active in particular localities. The role of stolen firearms in crime as a whole was underlined in a number of surveys amongst inmates of the ever-expanding prison population in the United States.[15] There is, finally, significant anxiety in the United States over the medium- to long-term impact which this spread of firearms is having on the ghettos and barrios of the American city and the possibility of continuing to guarantee peace and order generally in major racially divided American cities.

BRITAIN: SOCIAL DIVISIONS WITHOUT FIREARMS

In the anxious public debates that emerged over firearms in Britain in the 1990s, especially in the wake of the Dunblane Massacre,[16] and also in the aftermath of continuing reports about the use of firearms in bank robberies and other thefts, there were some apparently very 'fundamentalist', though entirely comprehensible, public responses. One of the initial demands of one coalition of concerned citizens, the Gun Control Network, called for 'a gun-free society', whilst its ill-fated (and short-lived) competitor organization, established by an American confidence trickster (in the interest of attracting public donations), launched itself as the Society against Guns in Europe (SAGE). This 'gun-abolitionist' response made sense, I would argue, in terms of the horror felt at the multiple-murder of young infants at Dunblane, and also as a response to what was sensed as a growing gun-culture, in a society in which, *mirabile dictu*, the police are still not routinely armed and in which it is rare to have sight of armaments at all (except perhaps at Heathrow Airport and similar 'high security' locations). Firearms have not been seen in any significant numbers on the streets of Britain since the immediate aftermath of the First World War, when there were many reported instances of soldiers demobilized from the war making use of the weapons they had smuggled home, either in robberies or in shows of bravado at Football League matches.[17] The rapidly growing anxiety over firearms in public circulation gave rise to the Firearms Act of 1921, which is the originating legislation in a series of measures passed in Britain to restrict and control the private ownership of firearms. Each of the subsequent revisions of the legislative regime – the Firearms Act of 1968 and the Firearms Amendment Act of 1988 – had resulted from 'sensational' individual incidents of firearms use,[18] given headline coverage in the press precisely because of their atypicality.

The general absence of firearms from everyday 'popular' experience in Britain has a long history – dating at least from the Restoration in 1660 and the determination of the Crown and the ruling nobility that firearms (and other weapons) would no longer be so widely disseminated amongst the lower orders as they had been during the tumultuous period of the Civil War (Kennett and Anderson, 1975: 24). A statute of 1670 closely linked the ownership of firearms not just to annual income (which had been the regulatory regime developed during the early Stuart period, in order to ensure the right social composition of the militia, whenever it was called to the defence of the peace in local or national emergencies), but also to the right to hunt. Henceforth, firearms ownership and use in England was as much an effect of the game laws as it was any more formal or national set of criminal or civil law. Historical research suggests that the ownership of firearms, outside the nobility, was in practice uncommon through the sixteenth, seventeenth and the bulk of the eighteenth centuries. This was not primarily a matter of the presence or absence of a strict common law: firearms were simply too costly, and, in any case, inefficient and unreliable. Even the improvement wrought by the development of the flintlock system of ignition at the end of the eighteenth century seems to have had little effect on ownership or use of firearms in England; a defining feature of the popular revolts of the period, from the Luddites to the Chartists, is the infrequency of any use of firearms.[19]

In the agitated debates over the creation of a 'new police', in the first years of the nineteenth century, the English aristocracy and the new *rentier* and commercial classes – fearful of the examples unfolding in revolutionary France – organized with great commitment against the creation of a national structure of policing as such (Silver 1967; Ignatieff 1979). The idea of the new police being armed was simply off the agenda. The extraordinary paradox of nineteenth-century English history, therefore, was that such an unreformed and unequal society, dominated by the 'Old Corruption' of local aristocracy and local commerce, should succeed in institutionalizing itself without much resort to armed suppression. In this sense, there is a heavy irony in the familiar refrain of American visitors to London, used to the policing of an open and democratic republic with armed local, state and federal forces: the unarmed British police are 'wonderful', precisely inasmuch as the broader society does not throw up the same, unlimited but restless, set of economic and social expectations that are the stuff of the American dream, and precisely insofar as it continues to reproduce a general culture of deference, underpinned by the respect for tradition and order.

In the mid-1990s, seventeen years into a fundamentalist government-led experiment in free market economics in Britain, this culture of deference and tradition was under significant threat – not least, it should be said, from an outgoing Conservative Government itself, which (as discussed in chapter 1 of this book) continued to release a series of new and radical measures of marketization and privatization on the economy and to issue continuing demands for innovation and change in the overall conduct of economic affairs in the life of the country. This constant appeal to the need for intensified investment of popular commitment in the post-Fordist market place has had radical consequences within what, we should remember, is a very 'old country'. The promises held out in Britain in respect of the *social* benefits of enterprise (that is, in some sense, the promises of a *better* society) have, however, constantly been challenged 'in the public mind' by developments in the domain of crime and social order. The horrific massacre at Dunblane had actually been preceded by a series of well-publicized incidents involving the use of firearms in public places and also by a sharp increase in the number of crimes involving firearms being reported to and by the police, and regularly recycled in the press. The Criminal Statistics for England and Wales for 1993 reported a total number of firearms-related offences of 13,300, compared to 8,500 in 1988, with a particularly marked increase in the number of armed robberies reported to the police:

1981	1,790
1991	5,140
1992	5,827
1993	5,918

By comparison with the United States, of course, these numbers were and are minimal. What was at issue, however, was the *level of increase* in the number of reported incidents (187 per cent between 1981 and 1991, and then 1.5 per cent in the two years from 1991 to 1993), as well as the perception in many urban areas in Britain that these incidents could potentially occur in any suburban high street, as distinct from being confined to traditional crime areas in the city.

The growth of this perception of a changing social geography of crime in British cities, associated with an increased use of lethal firearms, is difficult to demonstrate, though analysis of local community press is instructive (Taylor 1995a; Williams and Dickinson 1993). So also is it difficult to quantify any evidence about a parallel, widely reported perception, of there being a sudden growth of interest in firearms – not only among the committed 'criminal fraternity' (that beloved object of discussion on the part of Britain's police), but also amongst other identifiable social groups. In the early 1990s, the sudden emergence of a 'gun-culture' in Britain was variously attributed to the Yardies (violent ex-convicts and professional gangsters from Jamaica, who were allegedly exerting considerable presence in Brixton, South London, and Moss Side, Manchester); to American Gangsta Rap music, with the influence it was having in similar (racialized) areas of British cities as well as in other heavily deprived areas of social exclusion; as well as to the growth of professional crime on a serious scale in major British cities. The anxiety felt in many quarters about the growth of this new culture of guns, not least amongst police, was informed, to no small degree, by a sense that the prevalence of guns introduced an entirely unfamiliar and random element into the project of maintaining social order in Britain – that 'New Times' had arrived for the British police force.[20]

Overlapping in some quarters with the sudden and mounting anxiety about the growth of a 'culture of guns' was a fear that the increased use of firearms was in some way an expression of problems being generally experienced by many men in respect of their assumed role, not least by men whose sense of self was bound up with concepts of muscular labour on behalf of self and a dependent family in the lost manufacturing trades. Some commentators observed in the growth of membership of gun clubs,[21] as well as the increasing circulation of survivalist and firearm magazines,[22] the same kind of 'protest masculinity' which was fuelling recruitment to the militia movements in the United States.

The anxiety of some sections of the public about the increased prevalence of firearms in Britain was no doubt also informed by a developing concern about the moves taking place within the European free trade area, driven by particular divisions of the European Community, towards full realization of a 'free market' within it – and, in particular, by the concept of abolishing internal border controls. Some sections of the Community had determined on 1 January 1992 as the start-date for this project of full-scale market liberalization, with no interceptions of European citizens and radically reduced numbers of searches of movements of goods across national borders (frontiers on land, ports or airports). The national governments of France, Germany, Belgium, the Netherlands and Luxembourg in 1985 signed the Schengen agreement, declaring their intention to substitute a series of 'counter measures' internally within their own countries (especially in respect of police surveillance and exchange of criminal information) to compensate for any sense of lost control over trans-border shipments of illegal goods or undesirable migrants.[23] There could not fail to be a commonsensical concern in many quarters that the outright removal of border checks might constitute an irresistible invitation to serious criminal organizations – in terms of easing very substantially the movements of illicit substances or persons across the vast swathes of territory of free market Europe. Reports released to the press in the early 1990s by customs authorities in Britain (no doubt concerned for their own employment futures) suggested that the continuing level of transshipment of drugs, on the one hand, and firearms, on the other, constituted a significant and present danger. In 1994, a Customs and Excise report to the press quoted an overall number of firearms seizures at British customs of 8,674 items (an increase of 508 per cent on the 1,427 seized the previous year). Periodic individual news-stories in the national press of seizures of major shipments of Czech, Russian, Eastern European and other firearms shipments, including machine guns, will have done little to assuage this kind of anxiety amongst attentive readers of these stories.[24] Further investigation of this trans-national trade in conventional or small firearms, of course, would have revealed a situation of a keen and continuing search for market-share on the part of arms manufacturers all over the world, in the context of the end of the Cold War and a steadily declining overall market size.[25] In East European countries like the Czech Republic, where the arms industry had been one of the main employers of labour during the 1980s, the governments have been giving very serious encouragement to renewed export drives on the part of local arms manufacturers. In Russia itself, reports suggest that the new circumstances of marketization have created a whole new market for firearms, not only to enforce contracts internally within market Russia, but also for purposes of both the legitimate and illegitimate export trade.

FIREARMS FEAR IN OTHER MARKET SOCIETIES

A heightened popular anxiety with respect to 'the return of the gun' as an element of risk in everyday life was also observable in many other Western societies in the 1990s, precipitated, to a significant degree, by horrific individual incidents. In Canada, a major national debate was initiated in response to the machine-gun murder on 6 December 1989 of fourteen young women engineering students in the Ecole Polytechnique at the University of Montreal: the young gunman, Marc Lepine, accompanying his actions with declarations of 'death to feminists', then turned his guns on himself.[26] A year later, a disgruntled professor at the downtown campus of Concordia University in Montreal decided to resolve his differences with a colleague with a gun. Throughout the early 1990s a determined campaign for a tightening of firearms ownership was pursued by a Coalition for Gun Control based in Toronto, and 6 December was marked by many Canadians by the wearing of white ribbons, as a statement against 'male violence' and also as a personal commitment against firearms. In November 1995, the Canadian Parliament finally gave approval to a revision of the Criminal Code to enshrine a new Firearms Act. This act established a national registration system for all firearms in Canada; instituted a four-year minimum sentence for use of a registered firearm in a violent offence; and also considerably stiffened penalties for illegal import of firearms. To the dismay of the Canadian Coalition for Gun Control, the Firearms Act of 1995 did not make ownership of handguns illegal, but firearms owners were now to be required to demonstrate their continued need to have such guns on a regular, five-yearly basis. Public anxiety over firearms in Canada will not have been assuaged, however, by the killing of nine people with rifle and handguns at a wedding party in Vernon, British Columbia in April 1996.

In the very same month – in another frontier and pioneer society, in which rifles had also played a role during the nineteenth century in the conquest of both nature and the aboriginal peoples – firearms were taking on another symbolic significance. In Port Arthur, Tasmania, a young man called Martin Bryant, later revealed to be a gun collector, mowed down a total of thirty-two people – with the bulk of his victims being Australian families, including children, on vacation. This massacre followed three other incidents of multiple-killings, on a smaller scale but in three much better-known public places (a residential suburb in Melbourne,[27] a shopping mall in Sydney,[28] and a prestigious office building address in Melbourne City Centre), and precipitated a very rapid response by the newly elected National Liberal (conservative) government.[29] The new gun control legislation in Australia required that all new gun purchases be registered on acquisition; those wanting to buy a gun had to show a genuine reason (for example, proof of membership of a gun club, or proof of permission from other gun owners to hunt on their land). 'Self-defence' was not to be allowed as a genuine reason.[30]

GUN ANXIETIES IN THE 1990S

The public anxieties expressed in different surveys over the apparent increase in availability and use of firearms, as I indicated earlier, have several different dimensions, not least with respect to the generalized insecurity felt with respect to security of self, friends and family. In this last respect, fears about firearms are connected with a broader set of anxieties about the security of everyday social life and, indeed, the fractured condition of social life in market society *per se*. Jon Stratton has recently offered an analysis of the widespread contemporary 'fascination' with serial killers (as evidenced, for example, in the success of a modern (1989) horror story by Thomas Harris (as translated into a movie), *The Silence of the Lambs* (Stratton 1996). Stratton's argument is to interpret this fascination as an effect of contemporary perceptions of citizens with respect to the rupturing of the social bonds that held Modernity itself together. In Stratton's own words:

> In modernity the general assumption was that crimes had motives. Disregarding crimes committed in the emotional heat of the moment, the modern understanding of crime thought of it as a deviant form of instrumental rationality. The idea of a motive highlighted a means–end relation. From this perspective the crime, as a designated non-legitimate act, was a practice which took place within a pre-given rationally ordered society. (Stratton 1996: 80)

The appeal and importance of this ordered set of relations (actors with motives, mostly working within a given set of rules) is most clearly revealed in the detective story – organized around 'narratives [that make visible] a series of logical connections which ultimately link crime and criminals ... by means of a motive which [gives] meaning to the criminal act in the context of the social' (Stratton 1996: 88). This search for motives and rationality also characterizes police practices of detection, as well as official and governmental responses to sensational criminal incidents reported in the mass media.

Stratton's critical concerns are threefold. He wants, first, to argue that this particular conception of an ordered social whole should be understood as what, following Baudrillard, he calls a 'discursive construct' – that is to say, as a particular set of practices, ideas and institutions first constructed in the late eighteenth and early nineteenth centuries, replacing a discursive formation (late feudalism) in which there was no such given, or clear understanding of 'the social'. In the nineteenth century itself, the new discipline of sociology, not least in France (for example, in the writings of Auguste Comte) played an important role in this development of the idea of the social. It is important to note the central role accorded the family in this tradition in producing a fully socialized being (therefore, in the task of social reproduction). So Stratton argues that: 'The conservative belief in this view of the "family", for which we should understand the bourgeois, affective, privatized family form, reified in much sociology as the nuclear family, helped to establish it as central to the practices of the modern state' (Stratton 1996: 78). For Stratton, therefore, the historical construction of 'the social' in the period that others call the Enlightenment is to be thought of, primarily, as the period in which bourgeois domination over social life was first established, and also key bourgeois values (like the privileging of private life within the family) institutionalized. Importantly, this particular 'moral order' was also given force and legitimacy by the modern State – not least in the development of systems of discipline and policing, defined in the broadest possible sense (as Foucault and Donzelot have discussed) to underwrite this particular ordering of social life. Drawing on the exhaustive empirical work of Elliot Leyton (1989), Stratton notes how frequently the 'serial killer' comes from marginal social strata –

especially the lower middle class; he also observes, without developing the point very far, how the universe of serial killers is dominated by men, and how far the fantasies of the serial killer are those of the un-socialized man.

Stratton's second concern, however, is to interpret the fascination with 'serial killers' as being a dramatic shorthand expression for a broadly perceived breakdown in the security and given-ness of this particular bourgeois social order. Foucault himself had raised the spectre of the 'great crimes without reason' in the nineteenth century and the horrors they provoked (Foucault 1988). The 'serial killer' is the most modern expression of this same fear – the term itself being as recent as 1992, coined by the FBI's Robert Ressler as an alternative to earlier conceptualizations like 'the stranger killer'. Stratton examines the accumulating body of theory and technical knowledge that informs police detection of the serial killer and concludes that 'the new serial killer is the isolated individual, an individual who feels excluded from the social' (1996: 84). In this sense, for Stratton, the 'modern serial killer' (which means the serial killers of the nineteenth or twentieth centuries, whether or not they were so identified), were products of the particular form of 'the social' – they came, nearly always, from the most isolated and excluded locations within the bourgeois social formation, and their acts could be seen as acts of angry revenge.

Stratton's third concern is to argue that even this modern horror has been superseded by the emergence of the 'postmodern serial killer'. The postmodern serial killer, he argues, 'takes the social for granted and acts on it as a reification' (1996: 84). That is to say that the postmodern killer's 'motivations', if that is still an appropriate language, are to play a (starring) role within contemporary, postmodern social life – that is, the aestheticized (and amoral) society of consumption, entertainment and diversion which was most effectively described, ahead of his time, by Guy Debord (1977) as 'the society of the spectacle'. Hannibal Lecter, in *The Silence of the Lambs*, was putting into practice what had been identified, in 1827, by Thomas De Quincey, in an ironic essay on the limits of aesthetics in the critique of everyday life as 'Murder Considered as one of the Fine Arts'. In this tradition, that is, murder *can* be carried out for personal pleasure, particularly if undertaken as a kind of art form (that is, with *jouissance*). The serial killer claims not only his day in court, but also several weeks' coverage in the ever-attendant popular media.

Stratton's argument has appeal as a way of approaching not just 'serial killing' but also the broader sense of uncertainty (and even panic) that is identified by many social and cultural critics as a defining feature of contemporary experience. The missing element in Stratton's account might be said to lie in its failure to discuss the material contexts of contemporary uncertainties – not least with respect to 'the labour market', narrowly defined in terms of the availability and sustainability of paid employment, but also the more general shift to competitive individualism as the common-sense culture of free market societies. This, in turn, suppresses the kind of issue I want to address in the final chapter of this book – the extent to which it remains politically possible in market society, through the initiation and coordination of new forms of social movement,[31] to regulate the growth of private markets of individual choice or consumer entitlement, when some of these markets are exposed in terms of their public consequences.

7

THE MARKET IN SOCIAL CONTROL

THE EXPLOSION OF PENALITY IN MARKET SOCIETIES

The transformation of Fordist societies, and their displacement by competitive market society, has been accompanied by three definitive developments in what sociologists have been used to speaking of as the institutions or the structure of social control.

There has, first, been an extraordinary expansion, especially since the early 1990s, in the scope and the scale of 'penality'. This expansion of penality is most obvious in the expansion of the prison populations of most Western societies (see table 13). But this continuing increase in most Western European societies in the numbers of citizens being sentenced into prison, as a proportion of the population of those societies, suddenly and sharply accelerated in the early 1990s. The overall prison population of the member-states of the European Community, for example, expanded by the extraordinary figure of 23.6 per cent in the four years from 1991 to 1995 (see table 14). The prison population of England and Wales subsequently increased (between September 1995 and November 1997) to 63,271 (an increase of over 22 per cent in just over two years).

The explosion that has occurred in the prison population in the United States over the last twenty-five years is already well known: the population of state and federal prisons in the United States has increased more than fivefold during the period from 1970 to 1996 – from less than 200,000 inmates to 1,182,000.[1] In 1995, according to one of the most definitive international comparisons, the rate of incarceration in the United States (at 600 people per 100,000) was second only to that of Russia (690) in a cluster of countries from the old Soviet bloc (Belarus, Ukraine, Latvia, Lithuania, Moldova, Estonia and Romania) with incarceration rates at over 200 per 100,000. The only other countries from outside the old Soviet bloc with anything approaching these rates of incarceration were Singapore (with an incarceration rate in

Table 13 National rates of imprisonment, Western Europe, 1985, 1995

Country	Prison population per 100,000 people (1985)	Prison population per 100,000 people (1995)
Belgium	65	75
Denmark	65	65
England and Wales	90	100
France	75	95
Germany	90	85
Greece	35	55
Ireland	55	55
Italy	n/a	85
The Netherlands	35	65
Northern Ireland	n/a	105
Norway	45	55
Portugal	90	125
Scotland	100	110
Spain	60	105
Sweden	50	65

Source: Roy Walmsley, *Prison Populations in Europe and North America: Some Background Information*, Heuni Paper 10 (1997) (http//www.penlex.orga.uk/hlfact31.html)

Table 14 European prison populations (excluding Luxembourg), 1991–1995

Country	Prison population September 1991	Prison population September 1995	Prisoners per 100,000 population 1995	Per cent change 1991–5
Spain	36,562	40,157	122.0	9.8
Portugal	8,092	11,829	119.0	46.2
Scotland	4,860	5,657	110.0	21.4
Northern Ireland	1,660	1,740	106.0	0.5
England and Wales	44,336	51,265	99.0	15.6
France	48,675	53,178	86.0	9.1
Italy	32,368	49,102	86.0	51.7
Germany	49,658	68,408	84.0	37.8
Austria	6,913	6,180	77.0	− 10.6
Belgium	6,035	7,561	76.0	25.3
The Netherlands	6,662	10,329	67.0	55.0
Denmark	3,243	3,421	66.0	0.5
Greece	5,008	5,878	60.0	1.7
Sweden	4,731	5,794	66.0	22.5
Finland	3,130	3,132	61.8	0.06
Ireland	2,114	2,032	60.0	− 0.2

Sources: Prison Statistics, England and Wales, 1991; *The Prison Population in 1994* (Home Office Statistical Bulletin 8/95); Criminal Statistics, England and Wales, 1995 (Cm 3421)

1995 of 287 people per 100,000), South Africa (265) and Hong Kong (207).[2] Most Western European societies, along with the United States, are committed to a further expansion during the foreseeable future of 'the penal estate'. In the United States, in 1995, some $55.1 billion was spent on new prison construction (at an average cost of $58,000 per medium-security cell).[3] In the United Kingdom, where the prison population reached 55,300 in 1996 (a new record), the new Government was not slow in announcing an additional $43 million for the building of new prison accommodation during 1997–8.[4] I will be discussing this expansion of the prison population, and other developments in the expansion of penality in market societies, in the next section of this chapter.

A second definitive feature of this expansion in the use of prison has been the radical change in the discourses which have surrounded (and are thought to legitimate) this exercise of intervention and social control. In particular, there has been a generalized shift away from the concepts – like rehabilitation, resocialization and even 'correction', applied to individual rule-breakers in the situation of custody – in the direction of conceiving of the whole penal and justice system as an instrument in the policing (surveillance) and minimization of 'risk'. This rapid transformation of the role and mandate of a set of social institutions involved with the care and rehabilitation of individuals into a set of institutions involved, in an actuarial fashion, with the defence of the social fabric against 'dangerous individuals', in societies that continue to become ever more unequal in material terms, is a penological phenomenon of quite fundamental proportions.

The third inescapable feature in the structure of social control in market societies, unsurprisingly, is the rapid increase in the involvement of private organizations and individuals in the provision of services in the field – or, indeed, 'the market' – of social control. In the United Kingdom, the development of 'partnerships' between long-established public sector organizations (including the police itself) and local private sector organizations (often with their own privately provided security) is particularly obvious in the new 'palaces of consumption' discussed in chapter 4, especially in the deterrence of shoplifting and the general oversight exercised over public space and behaviours occurring within it. This increased involvement of private bodies in the provision of security and social control is a phenomenon of major proportions in the last years of the twentieth century, and, in Britain as in the United States, has now extended to include private commercial organizations which advertise their product as the management of prisons, on the one hand, or, on the other, the policing of residential neighbourhoods and other urban spaces as well as commercial premises.

EXPLOSIONS OF PENALITY: OLD ORTHODOXIES

Rusche and Kirchheimer: the political economy of prison and the reserve army of labour

The extraordinary increase in the numbers of citizens of Western societies being incarcerated in those societies' prisons is clearly in need of explanation. For many left-minded commentators writing over the years about the beginnings of this upturn in the 1980s (Quinney 1980; Sim et al. 1987; Sim 1987; Spitzer 1983), the temptation has been to advance such explanation from within the familiar formulae of orthodox Marxist theory. Growths in the prison population are to be understood, more or less directly, as an effect of the latest crisis in capitalist economy, and, in particular, the explosive increases in unemployment that have occurred in many Western capitalist societies in the period since the late 1970s.[5] Interpretations of this kind usually make reference, more or less explicitly, to the pioneering investigation undertaken in the 1930s into the political economy of imprisonment – first conceived by the German Marxist scholar Georg Rusche, and later written up, with the assistance of Otto Kirchheimer, and published (through the auspices of the exiled Frankfurt School for Social Research) in New York, as *Punishment and Social Structure* (Rusche and Kirchheimer 1939). In chapters 2 to 8, Georg Rusche provides a detailed analysis of the relationship between labour markets and the exercise of penal discipline in Western European societies in three discrete periods or 'epochs'- the early Middle Ages (characterized by penance and fines), the later Middle Ages (a harsh regime of corporal and capital punishment) and the Age of Mercantilism. Later chapters, probably primarily written by Otto Kirchheimer, focus on the Industrial Revolution and the period from the late 1880s to the early 1930s, which they identify as 'the modern period' of planned Monopoly Capitalism (characterized by rising living standards and some moves towards 'reform' of the injustices and inequalities of the nineteenth century, like the welfare state itself).

Adrian Howe provides the following helpful and succinct summary of Rusche's argument:

> an abundance of land and a labour shortage gave rise to a relatively lenient penal system in thirteenth-century Europe. By the fifteenth century, however, the beginnings of a capitalist form of production led to a drop in wages, intense class conflict and an increase in crime amongst a newly emerging impoverished urban proletariat. Because there was now a labour surplus, labour, and therefore human life, was no longer valued. Consequently, punishments became harsher, with mutilations and death sentences increasing markedly over the sixteenth century. With the rise of mercantilism in the sixteenth century, the conditions of the labour market again changed fundamentally. New labour shortages and increased wages led capitalists to turn to the state to find new means to control and exploit labour. New forms of punishment – galley slavery, transportation and penal servitude at hard labour in houses of correction –

therefore focused on enforcing labour. The emergence of new capitalist labour market conditions in the eighteenth century, however, forced further changes in penal forms. The prison emerged as the dominant mode of punishment. (Howe 1994: 16–17)

Rusche and Kirchheimer argue that the emergence of these different forms of penality should be understood, above all, in terms of the changing character of the labour market (what orthodox Marxists would call the developing 'means of production') in each particular period. So 'transportation' of convicted criminals (initially to America and, from 1787 onwards, to Australia) emerged as a favoured form of punishment in England in the early eighteenth century primarily because this was 'a time when the labour market was over-supplied' (Rusche and Kirchheimer 1939: 122) but also, in part, because of the colonizing impulses of a commercial and industrial ruling class intent on expanding its sphere of influence. In the first years of the twentieth century, prison populations declined in many Western societies, and the use of the fine by the courts increased, specifically in consequence of the general expansion taking place in economic activity in Western capitalist societies, and the overall demand of capitalist employers for labour.[6]

In their later commentaries, Steven Box and Christopher Hale summarized Rusche and Kirchheimer's account as involving what they call 'a workload model' of prison (Box and Hale 1982, 1985), that is, the prison performed different specific tasks for the powerful in different historical moments. In the various periods of crisis endemic to industrial capitalism, especially in its chaotic *laissez-faire* development during the nineteenth century, the task performed for Capital was that of incarcerating increasing proportions of the unemployed or under-employed underclasses – the 'reserve army of labour' – in response to the social strains produced by economic recession. Importantly, this process of incarceration and containment within the prison of a fraction of the unemployed working class in a capitalist society also worked, according to Rusche and Kirchheimer, to underline what other commentators have called the principle of *less eligibility* so vital to the management of inequality in capitalist societies – that is, the principle that 'the standard of living within prisons (as well as for those dependent on the welfare apparatus) must be lower than that of the lowest stratum of the working class' (Rusche and Kirchheimer 1938: 108). Only this could help to ensure, especially during these times of recession and crisis, that the broad mass of workers will continue to work.

Rusche and Kirchheimer provided a detailed account of the ongoing development of policy discussion in France and Germany in the nineteenth century, always organized around the assumption that prisoners (even when engaged in repetitive and extended labour) should be paid 'the barest minimum' (Rusche and Kirchheimer 1939: 107). So in this argument, the prison, as it developed in capitalist societies, through the nineteenth and early twentieth centuries, is to be understood not simply as a warehouse for the temporary confinement of a portion of the otherwise unruly and politically and socially unpredictable underclass, significantly increased in size in periods of economic downturn. It also performed two other vital roles. On the one hand, it made a contribution to the 'process of reproduction' that is always problematic in unequal capitalist societies (by presenting the labouring masses with the vision of an even less desirable alternative) and, on the other, it contributed to the practical tutelage (the 'retraining')[7] of the prison population.[8] That is, the prison functioned as an instrument for the (coercive) inculcation not just of the skills and habits of work, but also as a means of disseminating an acceptance of the work-discipline demanded by the wider, unequal capitalist market place.

There were always problems with Rusche and Kirchheimer's account, especially if understood only as a deterministic application of a Marxist political economy.[9] Some of the problems were empirical. Box and Hale, for example, noted that the increases that took place in the size of the prison population in the modernist period never 'took up' or incapacitated (removed from civil society) more than a small proportion of the newly unemployed 'reserve army of labour'. Anticipating later theoretical discussion, they argued that what was important about the increased use of prison sentences during such periods was the role such sentences were perceived to play in respect of *ideological* work with respect to social control of the broad society. That is to say, the concern was that the judiciary and magistracy *were seen to* be responding, with *appropriate severity* of sentence, to 'the perceived threat of crime posed by the swelling population of economically marginalized persons' (Box and Hale 1982: 22); whilst the popular mass media (including, in Britain and the United States, the 'Yellow Press' and the paperback books with their overwhelming preoccupation with crime) should be seen to be giving due publicity to this unflinching exercise of their sentencing powers by determined and responsible magisterial and judicial authorities. It is curious how insulated the debates between scholarly criminologists have been from relevant research in other disciplines. The classic essay by the social historian Douglas Hay (1975) on the expansion of capital punishment in the eighteenth century – an expansion, by all appearances, of 'rule by terror' on the part of the landed aristocracy over thousands of landless poor – shows how such sovereign power was frequently subject to mitigation in practice, through the exercise of mercy. This exercise of clemency, particularly evident in cases where the lord of the manor would appear before his fellow members of the local gentry to speak to the character of a tenant at risk of severe punishment (for example on a charge of poaching), was seen by Hay to be a crucial element in the construction of the *culture of deference* so evident amongst the rural peasantry to this day. So social historians like Hay were certainly alert to the broader cultural and ideological impacts of law, in a way that rarely excited the interest of orthodox criminology or jurisprudence.

In a later re-formulation of the more narrowly political-economic rendition of the issue, Dario Melossi suggested that shifts in the frequency and severity of use of penality ought properly to be interpreted in terms of shifts taking place in 'the political business cycle' (Melossi 1985). David Greenberg had already addressed this issue in one fashion, through his analysis of what he called the 'oscillatory punishment processes' in relation to shifts in the business cycle in Canada in 1945–59, hypothesizing, correctly, that the use of prison would increase during periods of unemployment, independently of the volume of crime (Greenberg 1977: 648). Colvin (1981) raises a separate, potentially more sophisticated argument – suggesting that there might be radical differences between business organizations' orientations to the issue of the control of 'the surplus population' and that larger, more monopolistic organizations might be more likely to favour the use of welfare provisions than prison in the effective regulation of this surplus population. The issue posed for analysts was that of providing some firm foundation for the analysis of shifts in 'ideology', as these constantly reappeared as the new common sense of different historical periods. In his *Punishment and Modern Society* (1990), the historian of penal ideas David Garland raises a number of other essentially empirical objections to what he sees as Rusche and Kirchheimer's 'reductionist' political economy (not least the considerable variation in the use of different forms of penal punishment and lengths of prison sentence as between 'different capitalist societies'), and he also insists that the Rusche and Kirchheimer thesis is flawed 'because it fails to address the internal dynamics of penal administration and their role in determining policy' (Garland 1990: 108).[10] Not least, according to a number of 'revisionist' histories of prison, published during the 1970s and 1980s (most notably, Rothman 1971, 1980; Ignatieff 1978), is the fatal problem of the materialist approach adopted by Rusche and Kirchheimer – that is, its failure to explain the persistence of the prison institution, in circumstances where 'the labour market' or 'the economy' no longer necessitates the application of such a form of penality. Garland also highlights a number of different dimensions in the development of the prison institution and 'the penal estate' in the eighteenth, nineteenth and twentieth centuries – not least the continuing reappearance of 'reform' as an answer to various different problems presented by the prison at different moments to different constituencies of opinion and power, and the constant modification of the issue of the problem in need of reformative correction. Richard Sparks's recent overview of prison histories argues for the continuing value of four different perspectives to the understanding of the prison – the Whig interpretation of the prison (as a place of benevolence and philanthropy); the approach of the 'disillusioned liberal' (a system always in process of reform, always with unintended consequences); the orthodox Marxist account (prison as a warehouse for the reserve army of labour and a place for retraining of capitalist labour forces); and the 'revisionist' version, in which the continuing expansion of the subjugated population, never an openly stated objective, is the real truth about the prison – its 'true rationale' (Sparks 1996: 193). The advantage of recognizing these four different perspectives on the prison, according to Sparks, is that they enable us 'to deconstruct' (*sic*) different aspects of penal discipline. The problem with such a pragmatic and pluralist position, of course, is that it does not identify *any* overall logic to this situation of coexistence, and also that it seems doomed to speaking of the problem of prison – in the characteristic common sense of such liberal sociology – as one ingredient, in particular, in the (abstract, ahistorical) analysis of the practice of 'social control'. It is arguable that this over-generalized notion of social control itself, derivative as it is from an idealist tradition of liberal sociology in the United States, is itself of limited value in understanding the content or meaning of social regulation in different social formations in different historical conjunctures. Certainly, the attempt to identify the prison simply as an instrument of social control disconnects the analysis of prison as an institution from the specific historical and social location (Elizabethan England or post-Fordist America) through which one can understand its particular practices and form.

Dario Melossi's review of *Punishment and Social Structure*, published in 1978, is critical of that text for its excessive (and eventually incoherent) reliance on the concept of the 'labour market' as an instrument for the analysis of the expansion or decline in the use of penal discipline. Anticipating the release of his volume with Massimo Pavarini (1981), Melossi argues, instead, for an understanding of the organic connection that has to operate in capitalist societies between the disciplines of *the factory* and the disciplinary logic of the prison, and for the overall interconnection of these disciplinary sites and the broader sets of institutions and practices that helped to sustain and reproduce the unequal social relations of capitalist society, especially in the nineteenth century. But he also makes the important observation that the final manuscript version of *Punishment and Social Structure* bore the imprint of Rusche's distant collaborator, Otto Kirchheimer,[11] and that in this respect the book, when released (by Kirchheimer, a key member of the Frankfurt Institute for Social Research, now in exile in New York) was intended as a contribution to the Frankfurt School's *critique* of the bourgeois order of 'monopoly capitalism'. That is to say, the objective was precisely to rescue a generally Marxist perspective (with its continuing focus on the dynamic effects of a changing political economy) from the debilitating effects of a mechanical form of 'dialectical materialism' where everything was reducible to a series of law-like processes, ultimately dependent on developments in 'the means of production'. Under the influence of Max Horkheimer, the founding figure of the Frankfurt School from 1931, the objective was to try and understand 'the manifestation, management and rationalization of the crisis of culture during this transition (from laisser-faire, competitive capitalism to monopoly capitalism)' (Melossi 1978: 74).

The Frankfurt School's exploration of changes in the family form and also 'the authoritarian personality' were important examples of this project in action. In the intriguing chapter in *Punishment and Social Structure* on 'New Trends under Fascism', for example, Otto Kirchheimer pays attention to the tendency in some of the statutes to conceive of law as a field in which the moral and social character of 'the people' (*das Volk*) left over from the Weimar Republic could be challenged and re-worked. He references, in particular, a statute constructed in response to continuing prevalence of 'begging' and vagabondage, in which such behaviours were re-constructed as criminal felonies, on the grounds of their exhibiting 'a decomposition of the racial will to work (*völkische Arbeitswille*)' (Rusche and Kirchheimer 1939: 182). The contemporary echoes of this particular statutory initiative are hard to escape, and I will return to these issues in the final section of this chapter.

There is an important sense in which I am trying in this chapter to retrieve and defend some dimensions of Rusche and Kirchheimer's thesis – for all the critiques that have been made by liberals of its tendencies to 'reductionism' and 'materialism', and for all that it ignores the analysis of reform and modification of the prison institution – in three crucial respects:

1   It does try to advance some conceptual framework for understanding the dynamic relationship between the provenance of the prison and 'penality', on the one hand, and the character of broader social and economic order, on the other. It does not think that the prison is merely an empirical institution, whose emergence can be taken for granted (or left to social historians), whilst its contemporary 'application' is assessed and measured in terms of the blinkered methodologies of 'Evaluation and Audit'. In contrast to so much penology in contemporary market society, that is, it tries to *explain* the phenomenon in question.

2   The elemental and flawed conceptual framework that is offered in *Punishment and Social Structure* does nonetheless have a specifically socio-logical, rather than metaphysical or moral and religious, character (the struggle against 'evil' etc.). That is to say, it conceives of the prison, and of the broader 'penal system', as having some specific and identifiable function (that is, of control, repression or incapacitation in a contradictory and unequal social formation, whose specific character is, in principle, open to description and explanation).[12] This conceptualization of the prison – as part of a structure of social control framed by specific changes in the broader social formation – is challenged by other conceptions of the character of discipline and order in a social order, notably those deriving from the work of Michel Foucault. No matter how these perspectives result in a different stance on the question of prison and penality, they do, however, have in common the claim to advance a sociological account.

3   A third and vital feature of Rusche and Kirchheimer's account of the prison is their insistence on seeing the prison as an institution which functions, primarily, as a place for the containment and marginalization of 'the dangerous classes'. The population of the earliest forms of prison in the late Middle Ages consisted primarily of the most feared and disruptive of the landless poor – the wild vagrants and footpads on the risk-endowed highways and byways of medieval Europe. Some of the best-known instances of law-making in the Middle Ages are the statutes passed to control the volatile population of vagrants, vagabonds and bandits (Chambliss 1964). The prison populations of early industrial England were swelled beyond capacity by the massive crisis of rural poverty and migration, urban overcrowding and unemployment that was the 'hungry forties', and the mushrooming popula-tion of thieves, prostitutes, beggars, and semi-organized groups of criminals on the street. In the post-industrial new market conditions obtaining in the United States in the late 1990s, the primary source of clientele for the ever-expanding penal apparatus is that main source of social anxiety and fear in public places in the United States – the young black male. In 1996, almost one in three black males aged 20 to 29 was under some form of correctional

control (incarcerated in prison, on probation or on parole) in the United States (as against only 1 in 15 young white males and 1 in 8 young Hispanic males).[13]

Michel Foucault and Stanley Cohen: the carceral and disciplinary society

The most widely available alternative orthodoxy for the understanding of prisons, over the last twenty years, has derived from the analytical framework developed by Michel Foucault, especially in *Discipline and Punish*, first published in English in 1977. *Discipline and Punish* is an extended analysis of the fundamental shift in emphasis in the systems of social control and regulation during the eighteenth century into the early years of the nine-teenth century – from the insistent use of capital punishment as the ultimate form (or 'end-point') of punishment to the increasingly common reversion to the use of prison. Central to this process was a reconceptualization of the whole project of punishment – from ideas of physical punishment of the felon (for example, 'branding', a common practice in many feudal societies) to ideas of moral re-socialization. The prison – first spoken of in France and the United States, in particular, as 'the penitentiary' – was increasingly put to use (and the numbers of such institutions expanded) as a place of solitary contemplation, behind walls, of 'wrongs done', and a place in which new moral commitments were to be forged. Foucault identifies this extended and halting process as just one dimension of an overall shift taking place, over the *longue durée* of the eighteenth and nineteenth centuries, towards the seques-tration from the society of a number of identified populations in a linked and connected set of incarcerating institutions:

> Incarceration with its mechanisms of surveillance and punishment functioned ... according to a principle of relative continuity. The continuity of the institu-tions themselves, which were linked to one another (public assistance with the orphanage), the reformatory, the penitentiary, the disciplinary battalion, the prison; the school with the charitable society, the workshop, the almshouse, the penitentiary convent; the workers' estate with the hospital and the prison).
> (Foucault 1997: 298)

Foucault's description of the range of such institutions of incarceration closely echoes the descriptions provided by Erving Goffman in *Asylums* (1961) of the emergence of a number of 'total institutions' – all characterized, as he put it, by 'barrier[s] to social intercourse with the outside and to departure [which are] often built right into the physical plant, such as locked doors, high walls barbed wire, cliffs, water, forest or moors' (1961: 4). Goffman (1961: 4–5) identified five 'rough groupings' of such total institu-tions:

1   'institutions established to care for persons felt to be both incapable and harmless' (homes for the blind, the aged, the orphaned, and the indigent);

2 'places established to care for persons felt to be both incapable of looking after themselves and a threat to the community' (TB sanitaria, mental hospitals and leprosaria);

3 '[institutions] organized against what are felt to be intentional dangers to it, with the welfare of the person thus sequestered not the immediate issue' (jails, penitentiaries, POW camps, and concentration camps);

4 'institutions purportedly established the better to pursue some work-like task and justifying themselves only on these instrumental grounds' (army barracks, ships, boarding schools, work camps, colonial compounds, and large mansions from the point of view of those who live in the servants' quarters);

5 'establishments designed as retreats from the world even while often serving as training stations for the religious' (abbeys, monasteries, convents and other cloisters).

What is particularly striking about this wide variety of different 'total institutions' are their shared organizational and social features, particularly their sequestration from the broader society and also the intense discipline that is exercised over their members, not least in terms of the totalitarian organization of time. Goffman writes with extraordinary insight on the different rituals involved in total institutions in 'stripping' the individual of any obtrusive features of personality ('the mortification and curtailment of the self' (1961: 45). But at no time does Goffman generalize out his perceptive account of these features of life in total institutions to a kind of political critique of institutional purposes: there is no theory in Goffman, for example, after the fashion of the famous 'Anti-psychiatrists' of the 1960s of the essential inauthenticity of mental illness.

Michel Foucault's approach to the institutions of incarceration (which, he argues, emerged in Europe during the period 1760–1840) has a rather different trajectory. He insists, first of all, that the rise of these incarcerating institutions is to be understood in terms of a transformation in the form and the purpose of punishment. Punishment of the body, as signified, for example, in the use of torture and capital punishment as a public spectacle, is replaced by a new and more complex 'penality' – 'the carceral' – in which the new institutions of incarceration function as instruments for the containment of the human body. 'The body', in turn, is then subjected – not to physical punishment, except, he allows, in terms of the fact of spatial restriction of the body and the rationing of food and sexual contacts – but to a range of projects of correction.

> Beneath the increasing leniency of punishment . . . one may map a displacement of its point of application: and through this displacement, a whole field of recent objects, a system of truth and a mass of roles hitherto unknown in the exercise of criminal justice. A corpus of knowledge, techniques, 'scientific' discourses is formed and becomes entangled with the practice of the power to punish. (Foucault 1977: 22–3)

So, secondly, Foucault wanted to argue, the imposition of correctional practices that goes on within institutions of incarceration (via a vast range of 'constraints and privations, obligations and prohibitions') is not in fact a punishment of the body, so much as it addresses 'the soul'. *Discipline and Punish* very quickly moves from being a description of the steady replacement of torture and other forms of physical punishment by 'the prison' to the development of a historical analysis outlining the emergence of 'new tactics of power'– that is, 'a correlative history of the modern soul and of a new power to judge, a genealogy of the present scientifico-legal complex from which the power to punish derives its bases, justifications and rules, from which it extends its effects and by which it masks an exorbitant singularity' (1977: 22–3). It also becomes clear, as Foucault's narrative unfolds, that *Discipline and Punish* is to be understood not just as a history of the emergence of the 'modern' prison (the prison in the form it assumed in the bourgeois era) but also as a history of the emergence of a more generalized regime of discipline and control common not just to institutions that incarcerate the human body, but also to a range of other disciplinary occupations (doctors, psychologists, teachers, and many others). The analytic focus is on the emergence of what Foucault calls 'power-knowledge' – that is to say, on a complex range of practices and schemes of professional wisdom and forms of practical common sense that were increasingly being put to use in the control of unruly, difficult or simply disturbingly different populations. Foucault's student, Jacques Donzelot, was soon to follow up his master's work, in an extended study of the forms of what he called 'psy-knowledge' developed and put to use in France during the nineteenth and twentieth centuries by generic social workers, family caseworkers, health visitors and others (Donzelot 1979). Foucault's own explanation as to the origins of the new regime of 'power-knowledge' (and the historical agencies involved in its production) seems to vary in the vast range of scholarly work he completed, in an abbreviated but highly intellectually productive life. He essentially wants to argue that the coercive and punitive character of the incarcerating institutions has its origins in the rise of a new bourgeois sensibility emerging, in different specific forms, across Europe in the eighteenth and nineteenth centuries. It was in this period, for example, that new and narrow definitions began to emerge as to the character of individual mental health and presentation of self, and therefore the redefinition of 'insanity', according to more finely graded distinctions of mental ill health (Foucault 1967, 1973); it was in this same period that more specific and repressive definitions began to be placed on individual sexual expression (Foucault 1980).

Foucault's interest in power-knowledge has been particularly influential in the social sciences, in the 1980s and 1990s, in the development of the field of social enquiry known as discourse-analysis, focusing on the close analysis of specific sets of practices and ideas in very specific spheres of social life, understood as performing their function within the 'micro-physics' of the Disciplinary Society. The Italian Foucauldian Pasquale Pasquino has developed an argument to the effect that 'criminology' itself should be understood as a particular integral element (a 'special *savoir*') whose very existence and substantive preoccupations (with social control) identify that professional field as a child of the Disciplinary Society (Pasquino 1980). But perhaps the most effective and influential application of Foucauldian ideas is the attempt made by Stanley Cohen in England to apply Foucault's notion of 'the carceral' to the understanding of the explosion of interest, in the late 1970s, in ideas of community control and community treatment (S. Cohen 1979a; 1979b). Cohen's curiosity was excited, in part, by the growing movement taking place in most European societies in this period in the idea of 'de-institutionalization' – especially, the de-institutionalization of the mentally ill (cf. Scull 1977). But his curiosity was also informed by the release of data and information displaying the increased use of non-custodial sentences in the sphere of criminal justice itself. Where other commentators might have been content to understand these developments, at least in part, as an expression of a new-found humanitarianism in the broader society and/or as an effect of the widespread critique in both popular and social science literature of the human effects of 'total institutions',[14] Cohen interpreted 'de-institutionalization' and the expansion of community alternatives as an overall expansion of the reach of 'social control'. He saw evidence of three discrete developments:

1 Blurring of the boundaries of social control

The rise of a range of new measures of social control in 'the community' (for example, probation officers with a wandering brief to operate with children on the street) was symptomatic of a general shift of emphasis away from the prison or the juvenile institution in the sphere of control activity. In American states like California, the development of a range of different alternative measures 'in the community' for young people had been particularly speedy, and programmes now existed for identifying and dealing with 'the pre-delinquent' young person, at one extreme, and young people on parole from a penal institution, at the other. Official reports spoke of 'a correctional continuum' or 'spectrum'. The contrast with the nineteenth century is fundamental:

> Whether prisons were built in the middle of cities, out in the remote countryside or on deserted islands, they had clear spatial boundaries which were reinforced by ceremonies of social exclusion, such as the criminal trial. Those outside could wonder about what went on behind the walls; those inside could think about 'the outside world'. Inside/outside, guilty/innocent, voluntary/coercive, formal/informal – these distinctions more or less made sense. (Cohen 1979a: 610)

Now, argued Cohen, 'social control' was based not in institutions but in a bewildering range of different community programmes, in which, indeed

> A halfway-house or 'residential treatment centre' or 're-integration residence' may be halfway *in* for those too serious to be left at home, and not serious enough for the institution and hence a form of 'diversion' – or halfway *out* for those who can be released from the institution but who are not yet 'ready' for the open community, hence a form of 'after-care'. (1979a: 610)

2 Thinning the mesh and widening the net

Cohen's reflections on developments in the field of community control also encouraged the recognition of two overlapping processes – of 'a *decrease* [in] the amount of intervention directed at many groups of deviants in the system', on the one hand, and 'an *increase* in the total number who get into the system in the first place' (Cohen 1979b: 347). He famously referred to these two processes through the metaphor of 'thinning the mesh' and 'widening the net' of social control. His exploration of these developments, as taking place in the United States in the 1970s, was underwritten by a range of important insights – not least, the appeal to childcare and youth workers of any idea of non-custodial alternative and their willingness to make use of any programme that presented itself in benign and attractive terminologies. Some children and young people may have been helped and even encouraged by their teachers, care workers or even their parents – in their own interest – to enter into specific programmes, usually as a result of problems occurring in school. Others may have been directed towards these agencies and processes by police or the courts, very specifically as an alternative to explicitly 'legal' and penal procedures. The overall consequence was an increase in the total numbers of young people, in particular, who were inducted into the surveillance and oversight of an expansive system of social control:

> whatever the eventual pattern of the emergent social control system, it should
> be clear that such policies as 'alternatives' in no way represent a victory for the
> anti-treatment lobby or an 'application' of labelling theory. Traditional deviant
> populations are being processed in a different way or else new populations are
> being caught up in the machine ... [There is] a more voracious processing of
> deviant populations, albeit in new settings and by professionals with different
> names. The machine might be getting softer, but it is not getting smaller. (Cohen
> 1979b: 349–50)

3 Masking and disguising

Like Goffman in the early 1960s, and also like many other liberal social scientists of the 1970s (Kittrie 1971; Pearson 1975; Schorr 1975; Schur 1980), Cohen was particularly concerned to penetrate beneath the benevolent surfaces and discourses of these programmes of social control and treatment. He discussed two such programmes in the United States – the 'Community Correction Facility' in Fort Des Moines and the Adolescent Diversion Project in Urbana-Champaign – and showed both such programmes, described in their own literature as non-secure, friendly and informal alternatives to institution, were actually very carefully regimented and ordered environments in which very specific behavioural demands were imposed on their clients. The Adolescent Diversion Project, like many such programmes in the United States at the time, was working with a form of 'behavioural contracting' between staff and clients, involving a particular version of conditioning theory. The use of this kind of behavioural regimentation was in no way apparent or openly declared: here, as with a vast range of the new community control initiatives across the United States, the actually occurring processes (as Cohen would see it, of 'social control') were 'blurred' and 'disguised' from the scrutiny of any interested member of the larger public. Other studies completed in the 1970s, like that by Paul Lerman on the California Youth Authority's Community Treatment Project, showed how the experiment conducted with young people, sentenced into the community as an alternative to institutionalization, very often resulted in those young people spending much longer periods of time in institutions in the long run, as Youth Authority workers, nervous of community reaction, made forceful use of their power of 'revocation' (revoking a community treatment order and returning difficult young people to the courts; Lerman 1975).

Cohen's own analysis ranges widely over a range of other developments then current in the treatment and justice systems in the United States (including, indeed, the increasing entry of private agencies into the public system – a point to which I will return in the final section of this chapter). But his main concern in the extension of his analysis, very much after the example of Foucault himself, was to find evidence in all these different developments of a set of connected processes – *absorption*, *penetration* and *reintegration*. Cohen's argument here is that the expansion of social control in the late twentieth century has to be understood as an attempt to bring all offenders, rule-breakers and deviants out of the wilderness and back into the symbolic surveillance and care of 'the community'. He quotes Empey, as arguing that:

> we are in the middle of a third Revolution in corrections – the first from Revenge to Restraint (in the first part of the nineteenth century), the second from Restraint to Reformation (from the late nineteenth century to the early twentieth century) – and now from Reformation to Reintegration. (Cohen 1979b: 356)

In this current period of Reintegrative activity, Cohen believed, we could expect to see an expansion in the use of different kinds of substitute family settings in the treatment of juvenile offenders (including perhaps the increased use of fostering and family placements) – a development which Cohen seemed to want to suggest was to be understood as a part of the proliferation of Discipline and of Power/Knowledge. Discipline was likely, he thought, to 'disperse' and penetrate ever-extensive areas of social life, 'spreading out' throughout 'the city' to different 'carceral archipelagos' and therefore no longer confined within particular institutional or other physical locations. What Foucault had called 'the project of docility' would be evident across the whole 'Punitive City'.

Liberal social science, and cultural studies, have for some time been entranced by what has been called 'the Foucault Effect'. The legacy of Foucault's exemplary endeavours is a continuing production of critical studies of different forms of discourse and practice as evidence of the play of power-knowledge within the Disciplinary Society, or alternatively of the effectivity of different forms of applied academic writing itself as exemplars of 'the special *savoir*' (the technicist forms of knowledge) that hold the disciplinary society together. There are at least four observations to be made about this continuing industry of critique vis-à-vis the disciplinary society:

1   Most obvious of all are the empirical queries. Foucault's vision of a highly organized and integrated system of Discipline and Control has always carried strong traces of the sociological functionalism of Talcott Parsons, and there has always been the suspicion that the picture it paints of a strongly controlled and disciplined culture makes more sense of the culture of *that* society – the society classically described by Herbert Marcuse (1964) as the home of 'repressive tolerance' – than it does of fractured and conflictual societies like those of old Europe. The characterization of the social welfare and justice organizations of the older European societies (and their difficult relations with police and prisons) as an efficiently integrated 'system' would come as a surprise to most people employed as practitioners within them. As the economic crises of the 1980s and 1990s unfolded, and the unending series of cuts made in public sector finances continued to unfold, the fragile character of this 'system' was increasingly revealed, and new regimes of ad-hoc 'crisis-management' initiated – for example, in the management of the adult and youthful populations. By the mid-1990s, indeed, according to many inside observers, the prison service in England and Wales had actually given up on the attempt to maintain an up-to-date register of the location of individual inmates.

Elsewhere, the increasing importance of private agencies (for example, private police) in the management of social space was often the occasion for conflict and competition, as much as it was the occasion for systematic cooperation. I will argue later that such conflicts often created new 'jurisdictional vacuums' (deregulated spaces) in which 'in-discipline' rather than discipline was the norm. The emergence of such an ad-hoc set of arrangements may not be an argument in principle against the visionary conceptualization of a Disciplinary Society, but it certainly suggests that the earliest formulations 'over-rationalized' the move to some coherent overall system of practical discipline and social control.

Equally importantly, the argument which seems so central to the Disciplinary Society thesis – of a society that was increasingly capable of reintegrating its problematic populations through different strategic exercises of 'power-knowledge' in the carceral field – seems not to make sense of the logic of the new penality of the 1990s, with its emphasis on extended incarceration, on the one hand, and residualization and 'social exclusion', on the other. So far from becoming the norm in the last years of the twentieth century, programmes in the justice system aimed at the reintegration of young people in trouble with the law within their own communities of origin through dialogue and interpersonal counselling have lost ground to programmes which foreground alternative notions. Among these are restitution – as exemplified in the Community Services Order in the UK and the recently introduced 'Travail d'Intérêt Générale' in Belgium (Taylor 1998) or 'community-shaming', evident in some smaller townships in Australia, with

substantial aboriginal populations (Braithwaite 1993). Each of these programmes is underpinned by the threat of some kind of banishment from 'the
community' of those young people who do not fulfil the individual behavioural demands that have been placed on them.

2   It is vitally important to see the conflation – and some would say
confusion – in Foucault's work between the *critique of bourgeois society* as
such and the critique of a disciplinary society. There is no specific attempt in
Foucault's work – as there is, for example, in the work of Jürgen Habermas –
to identify the new forms of discipline and control that emerged in the late
eighteenth and nineteenth centuries in Europe as being an expression of the
Enlightenment conception of social justice *per se* (the bourgeois concept of a
Public Sphere, identified in formal terms as a sphere of equality and liberty
for all, but often operating in a substantive sense in very different ways). The
emergence of policing, for example (never really directly dealt with at all in
Foucault), is not analysed as a contradictory institution responding, on the
one hand, at the ideological level, to the abstract and universalist demand for
the *preservation of the peace and community safety*, whilst also always
responding, in everyday practice, to urgent demands of the propertied middle
class for *protection of property* as well as person. Nor is there any attention
paid in the Foucauldian critique to the gendered character of the Enlightenment project, and the issues that are thrown up through recognition of the
gender inequalities of nineteenth-century social order.
    Adrian Howe makes the point very clearly:

> The 'spectre' of expanding social control is not self-evidently regressive for
> women. Their experience in the family, a site of oppression and control for
> many women, has demonstrated that there is nothing inherently progressive
> about the defence of a 'sphere of private, individual relations, autonomous of
> regulation'. (Howe 1994: 115)

So the *contradiction* between the Enlightenment 'discourses' surrounding the
rise of the new industrial societies (and their formal commitment to 'liberty'
and 'equality') and the mobilization of social control in practice in those
unequal societies never becomes a part of the analysis. The analysis of the
contradictory character of the Enlightenment (and, in particular, the unfin-
ished character of an industrial social order which spoke in terms of 'freedom'
and 'justice' but lived with massive structural inequality) is not Foucault's
project. His project, instead, is the critique of all structures and systems of
control, from a premise which identifies the idea of freedom as the freedom of
the solitary Ego, rather than the enlargement of the sphere of social life and
the full realization of the Enlightenment ideal, through the development of a
more inclusive form of Social Contract such as to embrace the range and
diversity of citizens (women, working people) who, under existing conceptions of the Enlightenment project, were subordinate or invisible.

3   It is important to observe how the embrace of the Foucauldian critique
in the 1970s and 1980s by students of 'the social' has had the effect of

rendering these 'critics' silent or mute – during a period in which the institutions of the welfare state have been under vigorous and fundamental attack by the free-market Right. The critiques made by discourse theorists and Foucauldians with respect to practical policy developments during the last years of the Fordist period were few and far between, not least because for Foucauldians the institutions of social welfare (including, as in Donzelot (1979), agencies working with troubled families) were seen as integral elements in an oppressive Disciplinary Society. It is unkind to suggest that there is no difference *in principle* between the free market libertarian critiques of State provision and the Foucauldian critique of discipline (since they do operate from different versions of libertarianism – the freedom of the 'soul' as against the freedom of possessive individualism) but, as perspectives on the social world, they have had in common a lack of care for the potential or actual benefits of social welfare, directly or indirectly provided by the modern State.

Cohen's application of the Foucauldian vision to the analysis of youth provision in and around the justice system in the United States at the end of the 1970s is a case in point. Like Foucault's own work on the prison, Cohen's analysis of the juvenile justice system is noticeable for its generally anti-institutional posture and its unswerving dislike of all forms of social control – often on the fundamentalist premise that social control is in some sense inhumanitarian, and always underpinned by a libertarian assumption that seems unable to countenance any form of institutional restraint of individuals under any circumstances. It is also notable for a tendency to generalize out from a Foucaldian vision, applied selectively to a small number of cases in the United States, to a critique of the character of youth work in the justice field or in youth work in that or any other society. This is, *inter alia*, open to the criticism that it unwarrantably generalizes out from a society in which individual and social problems are understood, in a liberal-pragmatic tradition, as matters of individual pathology (in principle soluble through the exercise of professional expertise) to other societies in which such a liberal-professional approach has rarely attained the hegemony it has in the United States. In Italy, for example, during the 1960s, the movement to 'de-institutionalize' the mental hospitals was very much influenced by the thinking of a Marxist psychoanalyst, Franco Basaglia, for whom the issue of treatment within the community was a class issue, posing collective challenges for the institutions of local working-class neighbourhoods and institutions (see Ciacci 1975). In Britain, in the 1970s and 1980s, the social work and juvenile justice system professions were dominated by people whose commitment was to 'forms of community' (and, it could be argued, social control) which were under direct attack from the government of the day. The defence of these different, more or less coherent, notions of 'community' and 'public life', with their origins in Enlightenment social thought, was certainly not helped by the unending libertarian and Foucauldian critiques of 'social control'. The critique of daily life in free market societies of the 1990s, in which, for many observers, the presenting issue appears not as an excess of social control, would certainly also elude a

Foucauldian critic. In the meantime, those institutions and agencies left with the project of preservation of peace and order in the troubled cities of America and Europe (the police, the court systems, and youth workers) are left to struggle to identify a basis on which to proceed.

4   Finally, I want to advance the central proposition that the Foucauldian critique of a hypermodern society organized in and through a configuration of disciplinary discourses and practices, largely centred on 'the State' and the public professions, seems unable to make much sense of the everyday mobilization and specific effects of 'marketization' on social life, and, in particular, the connected logics of 'deregulation' and privatization. This is an issue to which I will return in the final section of this chapter.

Contemporary Discourses of Social Control: The Management of Risk

Over and above the explosion of penality, the other fast-growing dimension of social control practice in marketized post-Fordist societies is 'the management of risk'. The increasing importance of 'risk management' is apparent in a very wide variety of contexts, and, importantly for my argument here, is evident as much in international exercises in social control, broadly understood, as it is in national or local initiatives. So, for example, ideas of 'risk assessment' and 'risk management' are absolutely central to the new strategies and tactics of international police organizations, customs authorities and immigration agencies in 'policing' the movement of people and goods through the newly created free trade areas in North America and Europe (Jamieson et al. 1997). Large numbers of key operational decisions about the deployment of police resources are now made by local police forces by reference to data on patterns of criminal offending (*Crime Pattern Analysis*) produced through a software computer program delivering such information at the level of individual beats. Information being released by the New York Police Department suggests that the use of a similar instrument was important in the reorganization of policing initiated in that city in 1992–4 by Commissioner William Bratton (New York City Police Department 1995).

The rapid emergence of talk of Risk Assessment and Management of Risk amongst these different organizations of social control has, in many societies, run in parallel with the continuing development of a connected set of 'discourses of risk' – most notably, in Britain, in the launch, since the late 1970s, of endless 'new initiatives' by national government departments or by the two auxiliary organizations of Crime Concern and NACRO in the field of crime prevention, Safer Cities programmes, community safety programmes, and many others. Parallel refrains (focusing on the development of personal strategies for minimizing a sense of risk or even the statistical probability of the kind of victimizations which individuals feel they routinely risk) are apparent in the mushrooming, and equally endless, literature on the Fear of Crime. These applied criminological literatures have a close – not to say symbiotic – relationship with the increasing number of victimization surveys that are now undertaken by national departments of justice (e.g., on the UK, Maxfield 1987; Mirrlees-Black and Aye Maung 1994), and seems particularly concerned to measure and to reduce rates of victimization from different offences and also different levels of fear.

So it requires little reflection – as any Foucauldian analyst (and, indeed, any student of 'moral panics') would know – to understand that we are now witness to the creation and the elaboration of a new 'discourse of risk' which has the potential to explode out from the original point of its creation across the whole body politic. Jon Bright, Director of Field Operations for Crime Concern in Britain, has recently argued in a *Demos* pamphlet for the knowing adoption by all kinds of professional organizations and associations of a 'culture of prevention' – dedicated, in particular, to the prevention of crime but also equally knowingly dedicated to the prevention of a vast range of other dangers, threats and social problems, for example, in the fields of health and early childhood education (Bright 1997). Not the least of the consequences of such an explosion of discursivity, especially in the field of applied criminology, renowned for its impatience with theoretical and political dispute, may be a real ambiguity as to the definitions of terms. In most of the empirical studies that have been conducted into the levels of fear of crime being reported in Britain in the 1990s (see e.g. Varnava 1995; Pain 1995), references to 'risk' faithfully echo and rather uncritically reproduce the complaints of the researchers' own respondents – in affirming that everyday experience of local neighbourhoods and public spaces has recently become somehow more nasty and uncivilized,[15] and indeed, by implication if not in terms of direct experience, more dangerous and more 'risky'. All too often, researchers on the 'fear of crime' lose understanding of the truth, neatly summarized by Ian Loader, that these admissions to fear are 'defensive, individuated responses to a host of structurally generated public insecurities' (Loader 1997b: 156), which require careful 'deconstruction' by researchers.

Theorizing Risk i: Ulrich Beck's Phenomenology of the 'Risk Society'

Inasmuch as this applied criminological literature tries to venture into the field of explanation, it often does so, in rather inchoate a fashion, by reference to the emergence of what is said to be a new set of 'risky' social circumstances, which are in some way feeding into people's practical consciousness, and the precautionary strategies adopted by some and the transgressive strategies adopted by others. The implicit or explicit reference is sometimes to the recently published work of Ulrich Beck (1992), though very rarely is the full import of this reference spelt out. Beck's *Risk Society* is not a text in criminology at all and it certainly does not offer any direct discussion of the range of interpersonal threats and fears which routinely find their ways into reports on community safety and/or crime prevention. At one level, Beck's analysis is about the fearfulness of the present moment of transformation –

most notably, in respect of ecological dangers and the risks involved in contemporary medical research. But Beck's purpose is also to grasp the overall character of the different, connected transformations taking place in modern industrial society and, in particular, the emergence of a 'new' or 'reflexive modernity' that is exploding the old boundaries and patterns of industrial society.

Beck offers an open, non-reductive account of fundamental changes taking place in the character of modern-industrial life, in the spheres or work, class relations, family life and gender relations, as well as in the realm of science and knowledge. He pays particular attention to changes that have occurred to undermine the essentially feudal status of women: the technologically driven transformations of housework, the construction through family planning and abortion of *intentional* motherhood and the opening-up of the labour markets producing some kind of liberation of women from their 'modern female status' (Beck 1992: 111). This transformation in the gender order *runs parallel*, however, with the reconfiguration (or the 'reconstitution'[16]) of just about every other 'ordering' mechanism that was involved in the formal and informal organization of social control in modernist industrial society. Familiar structures of superordinate and subordinate populations (especially the employing and labouring classes) are increasingly being replaced, according to Beck, by much more diverse 'subject positions', in which an individual's sense of personal worth and security, or anxiety and fear, may be a function, primarily, of the specific culture of these different organizations. Beck suggests that we should think of the high modern social formation as consisting of a complex range of 'social risk positions', and also recognize, in constructing such a map, that 'some people are more affected than others by the distribution and growth of risks' (Beck 1992: 23).

The risks attending high modern society are quite different from the risks involved in life in the earlier modern period of 'industrial society'. In that period, according to Beck, the struggles were over the attainment and retention of social wealth (consumer goods, incomes, educational opportunities, property etc.) which were 'desirable items in scarcity', whereas in high modern society, by contrast, 'risks are an incidental problem ... in *undesirable abundance*' (Beck 1992: 26).

Beck argues that high modern society is riddled with sets of new opportunities (for example, for women or for cultural professionals) and also new hazards (global warming, nuclear contaminations, AIDS, crises over food hygiene etc.), which both call forth new risk-aware strategic sensibilities from citizens. The risk-avoidance strategies are seen to be the province, in particular, of specific new social movements and bodies of professional expertise which have emerged to 'take ownership' of these different issues and to mobilize a kind of political as well as a personal response (for example, in respect of the ecological environment).

Beck's analysis is clearly an important contribution to the contemporary understanding of 'risk' – not least in respect of the overall trajectory of the whole society itself (he does see 'risk society' as involving a universalistic (rather than an essentially fragmentary or sectional) sense of threat). But

Beck also offers a 'phenomenology' of risk in high modern society, which may be a way of understanding the kinds of patterned meanings that a risk society can involve for people in different risk-positions. So we can understand, for example, how the 'liberation' of women from the subject-position to which they were consigned in industrial society, in moments of both work and leisure, produces a form of liberated womanhood which still recommends the carrying of a rape-alarm in public places. We can understand how *reflexive modernity* might begin to throw up the demand for alternative styles of 'policing' of public spaces, like the proposal made in 1996 by Network SouthEast rail service in England that regular commuter passengers should organize to police their daily journeys themselves. Beck's idealist vision seems to consist of a new form of political community in which the new social movements, enlightened (or alarmed) experts and government come together, in a classically rationalist fashion, to deliberate the management of such a risky set of social challenges, and attempt to advance practical solutions. This may be the kind of idealist vision which, unspokenly, informs the daily work of the many thousands of practitioners who are now involved in high modern (post-Fordist, marketized) societies in trying to assess, manage or diminish people's sense of being at risk from crime.

I want to associate myself here with some of Beck's analytic project, not least his awareness of the great range of different 'social positions' that have been thrown up by recent social and economic change, and also his recognition of the enlarged range of individual sense of 'risk' as well as personal opportunity that obtains in the new social circumstances (for him, high modern; for us, post-Fordist, market society). But I also want to be critical in two key respects. As Michael Rustin has observed in an extended review essay, there can be no doubting the essentially idealist character of Beck's project. That is to say, Beck's desire to encourage 'reflexivity' in the interpretation and in the management of the wide range of new risks confronting high modern society seems to be predicated on the power of such ideas themselves, and on the possibility that such ideas could distil in the form of 'a universal subject' (a whole new powerful cadre of reflexive subjects menaced and activated by different sets of risks). Rustin simply observes:

> There is a danger that the theory of 'risk' is being unduly driven by the immanent concept of agency; that is, by the hope of the universal social subject that it promises to construct. 'Reflexive modernity' is here ushered into existence before its time, because if it can be imagined, it may generate active, discursive, participatory citizens as its natural concomitants. (Rustin 1994: 10)

Rustin's criticism here is contingent – in the sense that he is unpersuaded of the existence of any such agency under present historical circumstances. More fundamental in a theoretical sense to Rustin's critique (and to the question of Beck's idealist project) is his anxiety about 'the centrality given to the individual, "post-class" subject [in Beck] and the extent to which rational self-determination is located in such subjects and in whatever associations they choose freely to enter' (1994: 10). The theoretical argument here is that the 'reflexive subject' in Beck's account of postmodern society may just be one socially situated expression (a particular phenomenology, put to use in thinking about present dangers and risk) in an accelerating process of individualization of subjects, resulting from the generalized demise of collective alternatives in earlier moments in the development of a bourgeois order. This demise of 'collectivism' and social provision is not simply the result of a lost battle of ideas: it also arises out of the developing logic of the economic order itself and, in particular, the increasing competitivity of the global economic order.

In the meantime, however, Rustin throws up a set of irresistible queries:

> will individuals released from the unquestioned roles and obligations of families, and free to negotiate their own fundamental relationships, escape loneliness and expendability? Is the serial or multiple choice of partners by individuals who may deploy different bargaining resources necessarily an improvement on conventional monogamy, which demands at least some formal reciprocity of obligation? Does the flexibilisation of employment mean that material existence and employment will be structurally separated from each other (for example, via a basic income entitlement), or merely that large minorities will once again be forced into economic uncertainty and intermittent poverty? Isn't the present erosion of 'Fordist work patterns' in the West leading mainly to social polarisation and the expulsion of a significant part of the population from any economic role whatsoever? How is the ethos of 'flexibilisation' not to lead merely to the casualisation and atomisation of a previously more solidaristic and mutually-supportive workforce? (Rustin 1994: 5)

THEORIZING RISK 2: THE POLITICAL ECONOMY OF PERSONAL AND SOCIAL INSURANCE

The return of a conception of everyday life as involving risk, which seems to be common to all market societies, has given rise, as I began to investigate in chapter 5 of the market in protection, to a practical renewal of interest amongst individuals in the possibility of insuring themselves against different kinds of risk. It has given rise to a renewed interest in the history of 'insurance' (Ewald 1991; Simon 1987, 1988) as well as in the application of 'insurance' to crime prevention (Feeley and Simon 1992; O'Malley 1992). The strategic search for different forms of insurance can clearly be understood as a response to a range of different anxieties associated with life in market society, especially that of insuring accumulated personal property and indeed, for some, the possibility of trying to insure one's investments in the financial markets. In a society like Britain's in the 1990s, there has also been a marked expansion in the variety of products on offer by insurance and investment companies. The market has in this sense recognized and responded to the many different challenges facing newly propertied individuals involved in the competitive struggles of life in market societies – for example, the availability of sufficient funds for sending offspring to private schools. Alongside these kinds of investment for competitive survival and advancement, however, there has been a significant increase in different types of insurance for personal protection, with the explosive growth of private pension companies being one measure of this development. Taken together, these new types of financial investment (for competitive advantage and for protection) can be seen as attempts 'to resolve' (or to assuage) some of the insecurities associated with life in market society. Insurance is, in part, what François Ewald has called a 'moral technology'. That is:

> To conduct one's life in the manner of an enterprise ... begins ... to be a definition of a morality whose cardinal virtue is providence. To provide for the future means not just living from day to day and arming oneself against ill-fortune, but also mathematizing one's commitments. Above all, it means no longer resigning oneself to the decrees of providence and the blows of fate, but instead transforming one's relationship with nature, the world and God so that, even in misfortune, one retains responsibility for one's affairs by possessing the means to repair its effects. (Ewald 1991: 207)

In that sense, contemporary developments in insuring against risk are in part explicable in terms of a grasp of Beck's phenomenology of life in a risk society. But the recent literature on insurance reminds us of a rather more cold-blooded issue, which we may see as *the political economy of risk*.

Insurance in 'the modern sense', that is, as involving, on the one hand, individual payments to private companies in exchange for compensatory financial payments in the event of specific events, and, on the other, socialized systems of insurance lodged in the State itself, to cover individuals or groups in the event of other events (like industrial accidents) is a child of the nineteenth century. The origins of many private insurance schemes can, however, be traced back to the mercantile period and, in particular, to the attempts made by enterprising merchants to insure their galley ships setting out on the high seas in search of plunder; it is possible to trace the first articulation of many of the 'actuarialist' systems of risk calculation in the kinds of payment demanded, to insure against different kinds of eventuality, in negotiations conducted between merchants and usurers. Prior to the development of mercantilism – that is, in late medieval society – the 'insur-ance' investment of men of wealth and property (for example, the princes of the Italian city-state) would have taken on a more direct and human form – in the hiring of a large retinue of bodyguards and of guardians of the landed property itself. As mentioned in chapter 1, Diego Gambetta argues that the origins of the Sicilian Mafia lie in the purchase of 'private protection' by the owners of the large estates of Sicily in the early to mid-nineteenth century, in particular the *bravi* (armed feudal tenants) who had been released from the service of the nobility (Gambetta 1993: ch. 4); and, indeed, that the Mafia should itself be understood as 'a business in private protection' in a society in which the development of any alternative system of protection, as provided elsewhere by the public authority of the State, has failed to develop (see also Varese 1995). Of course, the object of such a direct retention of private protection was actually to prevent specific events rather than guarantee some financial or other compensation.

The development of State-sponsored socialized systems of insurance is a product, according to most accounts, of the rise of the organized labour movement in Europe in the nineteenth century and the demands for a system to cover workmen for industrial accidents. The development of such schemes of socialized insurance ran parallel with the development of a mass of private companies selling 'insurance' as an individual form of investment, in which individuals would invest in order to minimize a variety of threats to their persons and property. Central to the development of such schemes was the development of what Ewald calls an economic and financial technology (whose specific forms of expertise are explicable in terms of the kinds of mathematical knowledge accumulated through the historical development of usury). Implicit in such knowledge were models for the calculation not just of the level of compensation or reparation, but also models for the calculation of the levels of risk associated with different kinds of social practice (such as different kinds of employment). These calculations were associated with the development of a specific system of knowledge, which functions around the classification of risk and indemnity – an *actuarial* system. Actuarialist knowledge has been important in the nineteenth and twentieth centuries not only in the pursuit of successful private insurance business, but also, of course, in the practices of the State itself, in determining the level of investments to be made in different kinds of social insurance and, indeed, the taking-in of responsibility for such schemes (for example, in Britain, the National Health Service).

Central to much of the recent rebirth of interest in the political economy of insurance, and the specifics of actuarialism, is the recognition that socialized insurance was a specific creation of the modernist period, the period of welfare-state mixed-economy, managed by a national State (in part through its investment of monies raised in taxation). The transformation of modernist and Fordist societies and the rise of market society has, on the one hand, encouraged individual citizen-consumers to see appropriate levels of insurance (for example, to underwrite a pension) as a personal responsibility, and, on the other, has 'problematized' in public-political discourse the capacity of nation-states to continue providing universal or socialized insurance (including, in Britain, the universal health service itself). So also, however, there has emerged a widespread recognition, at the level of taken-for-granted knowledge, in a range of 'public service occupations' – especially, perhaps, the police – that the provision of such service on a universalistic basis (if ever it really was so provided) is no longer possible.

The history of public policing in most Western societies in the 1980s and 1990s is the history of the development of some form of actuarialist form of knowledge – that is, of new systems for classifying and rationing the investment of resource (money and staff) and of measuring the impact of the use of these resources in relation to different orders of threat. In Britain, the advance of such an actuarial approach has been the imposition on the police forces of 'performance indicators' for individual officers (in the Sheehy Report of 1992); the introduction of comparative measures of performance for police forces themselves for example, in 'clear-up' rates or in measures of crime rate in relation to overall staffing levels), the development in the 1980s of so-called

Police by Objectives (PBO) schemes and, in the 1990s, the use of computer-ized Crime Pattern Analysis systems in order to direct police resources to particular areas of a police force area rather than another. The introduction of such systems for targeting the use of a declining level of resource is a common feature – and perhaps a defining feature – of the management of the public service sector in many market societies in the 1990s.

Feeley and Simon want to identify the way in which this rebirth of systems for the classification of risk and threat, and the responsive deployment of public resource to the control, deterrence or the minimization of hazard and its effect, as the 'new penology' (Feeley and Simon 1992). The absolutely definitive feature of this new penology is the rapid shift that is taking place, or has taken place, from the surveillance or punishment of individuals to the surveillance and control of individuals in aggregates: 'the new penology is markedly less concerned with responsibility, fault, moral sensibility, diag-nosis, or intervention and treatment of the individual offender. Rather, it is concerned with techniques to identify, classify and manage groupings sorted by dangerousness' (Feeley and Simon 1992: 452). The actuarialism of the 'discourse' of the new penology is an expression of a broader project – the project of identifying the most rational, and especially the most cost-effective, system for the management of public life in market societies. The objectives of this project are *not* the punishment or the rehabilitation of individual offenders *per se*, but the task of identifying and screening the most disruptive and/or dangerous of such individuals. The nearly universal shorthand for this project – whether adopted by an individual police force, an individual company involved in some local crime-prevention partnership, a national customs and immigration service, or an international police collaboration exercise, is that of *risk assessment*.

Feeley and Simon point out how there is now little interest amongst penal system managers in the United States as a whole in any national project of crime prevention in 'recidivism', that is, in measuring the success of pro-grammes in reintegrating individuals into the community. The managerial interest in recidivism would now focus on the measurement of the ability of the probation service to identify individuals returning to the courts through the constant surveillance of these courts in relation to computerized data banks. The interest in the effectivity of surveillance is part and parcel, especially in the United States, of a larger managerialist interest in the capacity of such a system to 'monitor' its client populations. The objectives of such a managerialist project, moreover, are not the identification of such populations specifically to be punished: Feeley and Simon argue that the new penology is concerned, in part, to identify areas of activity where minimalist forms of policing and punishment might be rational and strategic, as much as to identity other areas where heavy deployment of police resources would best be advised. The 'new penology' in this sense can coexist with 'the return of penality' identified at the beginning of this chapter, but is not reducible to it. A true market rationalist would want to undertake a cool analysis of the costs and benefits of the apparently irrevocable explosion of prison ware-housing in market societies in the 1990s.

I do not have the space to offer an analysis of the relationship between different kinds of market rationality and the continuing thrust to penal incarceration taking place in the courts, which might be seen by the new analysts as an irrational response to developments in market society. However one might contemplate such an analysis, one point is inescapable. The idea of a monitored society – as in George Orwell's dystopian vision in *1984* – is here; but that monitoring does not result in forms of policing that intrude into *every* instance of rule-breaking or deviant behaviour. The other important irony is that the monitoring gaze is directed not by a 'Big Brother' State (the State *is* complicit in the process, for example, in state-sponsored CCTV schemes – a State which is nonetheless in the process of being 'downsized' and 'rationalized' according to market rationalities) but rather by a 'free' and liberal market.

THE NEW INDUSTRY IN 'CRIME PREVENTION' AND DETENTION IN MARKET SOCIETY

Many years ago, in a short and ironic disquisition on what he saw to be mistakes of 'bourgeois' thinking on the sources of innovation and development in capitalist economic production, as exemplified in Bernard de Mandeville's *Fable of the Bees*, Karl Marx observed how:

> A philosopher produces ideas, a poet poems, a clergyman sermons, a professor compendia and so on ... The criminal produces not only crimes but criminal law, and with it the professor who gives lectures on criminal law and in addition to this a compendium which this same professor throws onto the general market as 'commodities'. This brings with it augmentation of national wealth, quite apart from the personal enjoyment which ... the manuscript of the compendium brings to the originator himself. (Marx 1969: 375)

The ironic character of Marx's concerns become more clear as the passage proceeds:

> The criminal moreover produces the whole of the police and of criminal justice, constables, judges, hangmen, juries etc., and all these different categories of the social division of labour develop quite different capacities of the human spirit, create new needs, and new ways of satisfying them. Torture alone has given rise to the most ingenious mechanical inventions, and employed many honourable craftsmen in the production of its instruments.

He continued:

> The criminal produces an impression, partly moral and partly tragic, as the case may be, and in this way renders a 'service' by arousing the moral and aesthetic impressions of the public. He produces not only compendia on criminal law, not only penal codes and along with them legislators in the field, but also art, belles-lettres, and even tragedies ... the criminal breaks the monotony and everyday

security of bourgeois life. In this way he keeps it from stagnation. and gives rise to that uneasy tension and agility without which even the spur of competition would be blunted. *Thus he gives a stimulus to the productive forces.*

I need to clarify Marx's concern here, as being to identify and ridicule what he called 'the vulgar bourgeois apology' wherein 'society' is conceived of as being divided, on moral grounds, between the 'the upright', on the one hand, and 'the depraved' on the other. Paul Hirst suggested that Marx's short disquisition was an attempt to 'tease these vulgarians with the proposition that the most upright citizens depend for their livelihood on the criminal classes' (Hirst 1972, in Taylor, Walton and Young 1975: 223). The Marxist argument, of course, was one which understood these differences as a product of the logic of capital itself, and specifically the production of class division (not least the division between the bourgeoisie and the proletariat, but also the production of the residual reserve army, the lumpenproletariat) through the ongoing organization of material production. But Marx's essay continued:

> The effects of the criminal on the development of productive power can be shown in detail. Would locks ever have reached their present degree of excellence had there been no thieves? Would the making of bank-notes have reached its present perfection had there been no forgers? Would the microscope have found its way into the sphere of ordinary commerce (see Babbage) but for trading frauds? Doesn't practical chemistry owe just as much as to the adulteration of commodities and the efforts to show it up as to the honest zeal for production? *Crime, through its constantly new methods of attack on property, constantly calls into being new methods of defence.*

In his assertive observation in a famous essay of 1972 that torture or the production of locks have 'in no period [constituted] a major branch of capitalist production', Paul Hirst concluded that the control had no critical role in the development of Capitalism, writ large.[17] In these last years of the twentieth century, it must be said, the extraordinary expansion of the whole criminal justice system, involving *inter alia* the rapid development of a whole new private industry of crime control and employing ever-increasing numbers of people in the protection industries of market society, restates this issue in a particularly challenging fashion.

'The public interest' in policing and punishment

I want to introduce some discussion of this growth of the private industry in crime control. A number of criminological scholars in Britain and North America (Loader 1997a, 1997b; Sparks 1994, 1995; Schihor 1995) have paid more extended attention to this development, and have focused, in particular, on the 'normative implication' of the ever-extending intrusion of a 'private (commercial) interest' into the spheres of policing and punishment (a sphere which these authors also insist must be a central sphere of public concern and deliberation).

The influence here of the thinking of Jürgen Habermas and other commentators on the fate of the Enlightenment idea of 'the public sphere' is clear. The absolutely fundamental assumption of the ideological settlement constructed within unequal societies in nineteenth-century Europe, and the body of law associated with that settlement, was the argument that the use of police or of penal punishment would be undertaken only by a democratically constituted State, and only within the parameters of a popularly understood contract between free individuals and that State, overseen by an independent judiciary. In chapter 5 I referenced Allan Silver and Michael Ignatieff's essays on the reluctant support given by the commercial and industrial middle class in England for the introduction of a uniformed police (Silver 1967; Ignatieff 1978). The history of the development of policing in other European countries in the early nineteenth century and in the United States is, in part, a history of struggle over rights and entitlement of a public police force vis-à-vis the rights of the private propertied. Central to the Enlightenment view was the insistence that the judiciary, the magistracy and Parliament would all contribute in different ways to law-making and enforcement so as to give expression to some notion of 'public interest' in policing. This idea of a general 'public interest' (for all the difficulties which critics have subsequently highlighted in that notion, not least with respect to the democratic representation of all citizens in the idea of 'the public') was absolutely non-negotiable in the Enlightenment. In England and Wales, for example, from the late nineteenth century to the early 1960s the specific 'operational' decisions as to what places and people are to be policed was ceded to Chief Constables, but only within a regime in which the general direction of policy on the part of a local constabulary was kept under the constant oversight of local Watch Committees, responsible for the interpretation of 'the public interest' at local level, along with the police department of the Home Office. A similar division of public and institutional responsibilities and roles (between the Governors and local Committees of Visitors) has underpinned the management of the prison system throughout the nineteenth and twentieth centuries.

By contrast, the arguments advanced during the 1980s and 1990s for the privatization of prison services – notably by Charles Logan (1990), a leading American proponent of such 'liberalization' – have assumed what Richard Sparks (1995) identifies as a strictly and narrowly 'consequentialist' character – as distinct, that is, from any argument articulated in the name of 'a public interest'. The arguments for privatization have focused on the efficiency and, especially, the financial cost of a 'governmental service' (that is, a function of the State), rather than in any assessment of the legitimacy of this 'service' continuing to be provided, in a jurisdictional sense, by the government or the State.[18] Sparks goes on to argue, however, that the continuing advance of privatization of prison functioning has a series of other consequences which in themselves cut away at Enlightenment principles. Not least, he argues, the increasing growth of a private interest, for example, in the management of prisons works to remove routine practices within the prison – an institution dedicated to the 'deprivation of liberty' from many hundreds of citizens – from public scrutiny and accountability or control. The advance of specific managerial and commercial considerations within the prison also poses issues for the legitimacy of such regimes in the minds of the inmates themselves. Sparks summarizes the argument by reference to David Garland's earlier expressions of concern over the challenges increasingly being posed to punishment as a public symbolic process (although Garland's reflections have a rather idealized, historically unspecific character):

> The social tasks involved in punishment have been delegated to specialized agencies on the margins of social life, with the effect that they have become hidden ... What was once an open, ritualized dialogue between the offender and the community is now a much more oblique communication carried out in institutions which give little expression to the public voice. (Garland 1990: 186–7)

The private interest in policing and prisons

Common to most of the critical commentaries on the advance of private interest in the sphere of policing and punishment is the idea that there is a clear and principled distinction between the commercial and public interest. The straightforward recycling of this distinction does sometimes underestimate the significance of the changes that have occurred in modernist and Fordist societies, and the significance and scale of the 'penetration' of the private interest that has now occurred in market societies. Commentators who speak of the emergence of a 'correctional-commercial complex', almost as a kind of pressure group on the margins of what is assumed still be a centralized and still-powerful public sector, may be misunderstanding the scale of recent marketization.

We do also need to remember how progressive-liberal social commentators have sometimes underemphasized the contingent, limited character of the 'public sphere' in 'bourgeois' societies. That is to say that they have misunderstood the extent to which public law, public police and public systems of punishment were 'supernumerary' arrangements made by the propertied for the protection of their own persons and profit, rather than instruments constructed in practice for a universal public interest. Malcolm Feeley's history of transportation from England to the new colony of Virginia in the seventeenth and eighteenth centuries, for example, is a history of an essentially private initiative, resulting from what he calls 'the happy marriage' of commercial interest on the part of the profit-seeking merchants who arranged the shipping and the planters who purchased the human cargo being so transported (Feeley 1991). Craig Little has documented the logic that connects the development of private arrangements for the pursuit of horse thieves in Pennsylvania to the emergence of different forms of private policing and private security provision in the contemporary United States

(Little 1994). There is an important sense, that is, in which the forms of public policing which were to develop through the nineteenth century (and especially in the modernist twentieth century) emerged alongside, or subsumed, a set of well-established private and commercial processes.

The range of research undertaken by Clifford Shearing and Philip Stenning into the rapid emergence of new forms of private security policing in Canada and the United States, and the extensive resulting literature (Shearing and Stenning 1981, 1983, 1985a, 1985b; 1985c, 1987) was pioneering and important, not only for identifying and describing in close detail a development that was later researched in Britain (for example, by South (1988) and Johnston (1992)) and across the European Community (South 1994). In part as a result of the extensive interview and observational research they undertook into the perceptions, the increased use, and the different kinds of use of private security by corporate organizations in Canada in the early 1980s, Shearing and Stenning were able to argue that:

> what we are witnessing through the growth of private policing is not merely the reshuffling of responsibility for policing public order but *the emergence of privately defined orders*, policed by privately employed agents, that are in some cases inconsistent with, or even in conflict with the public order proclaimed by the state. (Shearing and Stenning 1987: 13)

So, for example, the private security policing organizations that developed in Canada to protect and defend newly built shopping malls were oriented in their routine practices, not to the arrest and process of people to be brought to a public trial in a criminal courtroom, but rather to the surveillance of public behaviour in the mall, and, in many instances, through the use of closed circuit television, to the screening of the entry of 'undesirable types' into these new consumer spaces. Private security forces developing around the new industrial and commercial mall developments on the perimeters of major Canadian conurbations were there for purposes of deterrence, and for purposes of strategic minimization of losses through thefts and raids, rather than as close allies of the public police in 'the war against crime'. Corporate executives interviewed by Shearing and Stenning spoke of their impatience with a State criminal justice system which might take some months to process a case (for example, of shoplifting) to court; given the development of all kinds of other alternatives (from CCTV and other forms of surveillance, on the one hand, to more effective and sometimes coercive training of employees in preventative techniques, on the other) any such public system was increasingly irrelevant to any rational business plan focused on minimization of commercial losses through theft. There is an important sense in which the efforts of these new forces in private security were directed not at the control of crime *per se*, and certainly not at the provision of some form of penal discipline (they often saw the imposition of penality as a costly irrelevance with which they actively did not want to be involved). Nor either, it should be added, were many of these private security forces very enthusiastic about any kind of close collaboration with a local public police force, who might prioritize the need to observe certain constitutional priorities (for example, on entry into private buildings or on the protection of the constitutional rights of suspected offenders). Something more significant is involved here than merely the introduction of additional forms of policing in particular localities. So also there is something other than a further expansion of Michel Foucault's vision of a linked configuration of 'archipelagos' of surveillance and discipline or Stan Cohen's all-seeing 'Punitive City'. There is, instead, a sense of the private interest 'breaking free' of the constraints of the State, and of obligations to the public institutions of the police, the courts and the justice system, in its own specific commercial interest, looking after itself. There is a powerful sense of the emergence of a new feudalism, in which, in effect, powerful private interests police the territory over which they have a commercial hegemony, whilst leaving huge tracts of residual territory ('the territories beyond the walls') under generalized surveillance but substantially unattended. Private police forces, of course, refuse most demands to exercise an oversight over spaces which are paying no fee, no matter how close these territories may be in a spatial, geographical or human sense. This limitation of responsibility is, of course, a defining feature of market society as a whole, in which, as the New Zealand example first elaborated, 'the user pays'.

In the light of the encouragement given to the development of private interest in the political life of many societies during the last years of the Fordist period, the marked increase in the numbers of people employed in private security – beginning, in the United States, in the early 1970s – has been no surprise (Shearing and Stenning 1981). It was absolutely no surprise either to those who understood the needs and demands of the developing business markets (involved in the marketing and storage of ever-increasing consumer products) when the numbers employed in the protection of private businesses expanded at great speed, such that by 1977, indeed, the numbers of people employed in security work in the United States exceeded the numbers employed in federal, state or city police (Shearing and Stenning 1981).

Twenty years on from this critical moment of change in the composition of the labour market in the United States, it is important to register some sense of the current size and scope of activity of the private market in policing and in penal provision.

1 The private prison industry

In his first exploration of the growth of 'crime control as industry', Nils Christie (1993) relied heavily, in his search for evidence on American developments, on *Corrections Today*, the official publication of the American Correctional Association. He was particularly impressed by the growth in the size, and the glossy and professional quality of this journal during the early 1990s, and also by the numbers of private corporations of different sizes offering a variety of services to prisons, from the production of stun-guns and leather restraints to the construction of whole prison buildings (in one instance guaranteeing completion within six months from signing of the contract) who were placing expensive advertisements in this magazine. In

July 1991, for example, Christie counted 269 advertisements in one issue of this magazine, each aiming for a distinct 'market-niche'.

One of the 'market leaders' in the private prison field in the USA, the Corrections Corporation of America (based in Nashville, Tennessee) had a net income in the first six months of 1997 of $23.6 million, and was responsible for 44,639 beds in fifty-nine facilities in the United States, Puerto Rico, Australia and the United Kingdom,[19] whilst the Wackenhut Corrections, founded in Texas in 1984, reported an overall revenue for 1996 of $137.8 million).[20] Other significant players in the international private prison market include Group 4 Securitas, owned by the millionaire Joergen Philip-Soerensen and registered in the Netherlands Antilles (claiming a worldwide 'turnover' in twenty-six different countries in 1992 of £467 million[21]) and Sodexho (a French company which has expanded out from its previous involvement in contract catering[22]). There are also large numbers of new companies and conglomerates in different countries (like UK Detention Services, a subsidiary formed of the design engineers John Mowlem plc, the construction company of Sir Robert McAlpine and the Corrections Corporation of America) which have been specifically created to try and obtain a slice of what is now estimated to a market worth $1 billion a year to private providers.[23]

Three specific points are important. One is to note the international character of the private prison business, and to see how this positions these corporations in a powerful position vis-à-vis individual national governments – for example, in collaborating with competitors to control the range of alternative penal products that such a national government might buy. There are distinct echoes of the more general 'globalization' of major capitalist activity that has been the focus of critical investigation, along different lines, by scholars of international political economy over the last twenty years (e.g. Wallerstein 1974).

Secondly, it is important to understand that for many of these corporations, their involvement in the management of prisons was just one aspect of a portfolio of commercial activities with different vertical or horizontal relationships to prisons as such. In this sense, these new players in the prison industry are quintessentially post-Fordist actors;[24] that is, they can move out from these activities to others, should there be a powerful commercial reason for so doing. The logic which informed the entry of Sodexho into the prison business (mass contract catering) was rather different to that which influenced the Wackenhut corporation (an organization which has specialized, since its formation, in a variety of 'penal products', from the provision of different types of detention to 'pre-employment screening' on individual job applicants, undertaken by the Wackenhut National Research Center at the behest of private business).[25]

Finally, it is important to register that the growth of influence, and the numbers of contracts won, has shown remarkable unevenness across different societies. In 1993, for example, it was estimated by Charles Thomas, a controversial academic criminologist-turned-consultant to the private prison business, based at the University of Florida, that only 1.5 per cent of the

1,350,000 people in prison in 4,000 penal institutions in the United States were in private institutions (worldwide the figure was about 20,698 adult prisoners). But commentators on the first-wave privatization of prisons in England and Wales (which began in 1989 with a target completion date of 1995, involving, at the time, six new private jails[26]) observed that about 10 per cent of the prison population would be in private institutions by 1995.[27]

There is no necessary or direct relationship between the unfolding of market society and the entrée of private industry into the management of the prison system. There are, in effect, market societies (France, Italy) in which political decisions have been taken to 'ring-fence' the justice system from the full-blown logic of commercial markets, and in which efficiency of the system is underwritten by other instruments. But even the most cursory reading of the corporate literature of the private prison industry in 1998 suggests that this industry sees itself to be a crucial point of what Walter Rostow once called the point of 'take-off' (Rostow 1953, 1963): that the industry, now firmly established in the United States, Britain, and many other major societies, is now in a position to move on to conquer other lucrative national markets. There is a vital sense in which the future shape of prison will be driven by the challenge of the market rather than by deliberations taking place, in familiar fashion, within the apparatus of State or indeed by penal reformers and/or concerned academics working with and through the State.[28] Prison entrepreneurs – involved in campaigns to persuade government and media of the superiority of their product – will no doubt engage in a variety of careful business strategies – limiting the size of the client populations (as has already happened in the UK), in the case of new-build prisons, and agreeing only to certain take-overs, in the case of buy-outs of existing public facilities. The publication in the British press of league-tables purporting to measure the different quality of prison buildings and management,[29] the quality of food,[30] the numbers of suicides (Howard League for Penal Reform 1993) and other individual measures of prison regimes, as well as the availability through reports from HM Inspectorate of Prisons of data on numbers of escapes from these institutions, in this sense constitute a body of information that is likely to inform strategic decision-making by private prison entrepreneurs.

2 Private policing

Conventional assessments of the development of private policing tend to focus on the growth in the number of people employed within this business. Figures are hard to come by in the major market societies, but Les Johnston has drawn on a number of studies in America to provide an overall map of developments in that country (Johnston 1992). The numbers of people employed in private sector policing in 1950 had been recorded at 282,000 (by comparison with the 199,000 public police officers), By 1970 – consequent on the huge investment in law enforcement at the end of the 1960s, there were roughly equal numbers employed in public and private policing. From 1970 onwards, however, there was a further and dramatic increase in the numbers of people employed in different forms of private policing, and one estimate suggested that by 1982 the numbers employed by the private sector (excluding Federal Government civil and military security workers) had come to exceed public police on a ratio of 2 : 1 (Hallcrest n.d., quoted in Johnston 1992: 79). Nigel South quotes a National Institute of Justice study of 1991 which recorded that:

> the private security industry has grown to where it now dwarfs public law enforcement: it employs two and a half times the personnel of public agencies and outspends them by 73% ... While public expenditures for law enforcement will reach $44 billion by the year 2000, they will be dwarfed by private security expenditures which will reach $104 billion. The average annual rate of growth in private security will be 8% or double that of public law enforcement. (NIJ 1991, quoted in South 1994: 221)

In Britain, figures for the total numbers of people employed in private policing were equally difficult to identify. Johnston suggests that the 'best estimates' in 1992 would vary between the 100,000 suggested by the Managerial Administrative Technical and Supervisory Association (MATSA) and the General Municipal, Boilermakers and Allied Union (GMB)) and the figure of 250,000 identified by Bruce George MP, a parliamentarian who has devoted considerable time and effort to the need for the regulation of the private security industry (Johnston 1992: 73). There is clearly no consensus on the boundaries of private policing (should the count include manufacturers of thief-locks for private cars? etc.). In 1992, there were some 125,000 police officers employed from public funds for England and Wales (Johnston 1992: 114). What is more important to understand, over and above the increase in the numbers of people employed in private policing and security, are the ever-expanding range of tasks that are being taken on by such private agencies. Johnston identifies the following activities: 'static guarding, mobile patrol, cash-in-transit, wage processing, undercover surveillance, guarding services, VIP protection, private investigation, risk management, specialized fraud investigation, consultative work related to industrial and domestic services, and so on' (1992: 94). He also points to the bifurcation of the private security industry between 'companies located at the respectable end of the market' (like Securicor, who have committed themselves never to engage in strike-breaking activity or other political activity) through to a range of smaller 'cowboy' companies, many employing staff at wages below any previous recognized statutory minimum and with minimalist or no systems for checking on the backgrounds of those so employed. Along with Nigel South, and other researchers in the field, Johnston also notes, with some bemusement, the complete absence of any national system of registration of private police or private security in Britain, by comparison with the relatively well-developed system of registration and oversight of professional standards in the United States.

My earlier discussion of the development of a new actuarial and managerialist penology in market societies and this brief examination of the growth of private systems of prisons and policing in such societies ought to be alerting us to two connected aspects of the dynamics of social control in market societies – on the one hand, the off-loading of responsibility being assumed by the State (and therefore by any authoritative agency) for shared public space and territory and, on the other, the increased reliance of those individuals and institutions well-placed in market society to insure their position through some form of 'private protection'. The increasing visibility of private security in commercial buildings and in industrial locations throughout market society (and, indeed, the penetration of private security systems, like identity card-operated entry systems and CCTV into public buildings like schools and hospitals, taking control of their own fortune) is one expression of this development. So also are the private police forces who, like the nightwatch-men of the medieval cities, deliver a sense of security to their fortress neighbourhoods.

The industry in private security and protection has been one of the fastest-growing industries in market societies, especially in the USA (where the successful marketing of a vast range of technologies to private households may, indeed, be responsible for the reduction in domestic burglaries which is so important an element in the overall reduction in reported crime in the 1980s and 1990s). *Pace* Karl Marx and Paul Hirst, and the classic argument that 'crime' has never played a critical role in capitalist development, it is important to note the scale of expansion of this new industry in privately marketed social control in market society and also to note the considerable product innovation taking place within this market sector – the development of building- and car-alarms, thief-locks for cars, new forms of perimeter lighting and laser surveillance for domestic and public buildings, new forms of identity card and ID-activated systems, devices for securing desk-top com-puters, closed circuit television systems, new police truncheons and new protective body garments, amongst many other products.

For all these developments, it is important to go beyond the surface description of such private initiatives, as did the discussion of industrial self-regulation in the last chapter, to identify a deeper logic. There are increasing numbers of self-contained islands of security and fortress neighbourhoods throughout most marketizing societies. But there are also vast stretches of human territory in most market societies which have been either identified for benign self-regulation (and thereby not directly controlled) or simply residualized – left unattended and without supervision – *not* under control, in a way that would have been unconscionable at the high point of modernist industrial society, dominated by a supervisory State.[31] This is one of the pressing issues to which I turn in the final chapter.

8

CRIME IN THE FUTURE(S) MARKET

We need men and women who tell us when state power is corrupted or
systematically misused, who cry out that something is rotten, and who
reiterate the regulative principles with which we might set things right.

Michael Walzer, 1983: 490

Unless we are prepared to make demands on one another, we can enjoy
only the most rudimentary kind of common life.

Christopher Lasch, 1995: 88

In the introduction to this long and therefore unfashionable book, I observed
that it would be unlikely to find its way into the Real Crimes section at
Waterstones. This is not only a question of its length, but also its orientation.
We live in a time in which the value-commitments of 'progressive', radical or
critical social commentators have been very significantly dis-orientated (at
one level, by the end of the Cold War and, at another, by the different
(liberatory as well as divisive) consequences of marketization). The globalization of markets, for example, does carry with it a liberating acquaintance
with a wider world, which was rarely available to the mass of citizens of
Fordist societies imprisoned within the restricted world and culture of the
local factory. The market liberals' attack on unaccountable bureaucracies
within the old Keynesian welfare state was overdue and, if anything, under-
stated.

But the emergence of a liberalized and liberating 'market society' has also
been accompanied, as commentators as far apart as Zygmunt Bauman,
Jürgen Habermas, Fredric Jameson, Christopher Lasch and John O'Neill
have all observed from different perspectives, by a strong reaction-formation
in the social science academy against all aspects of the kinds of 'materialist'
thought which were associated with the radical critique of high modern

Fordist capitalism in the late 1960s and early 1970s. Across a vast range of disciplines (from psychoanalysis and philosophy to neo-classical economics and forensic psychiatry, young and old scholars alike have returned to the exploration of the social world through the examination of 'the individual'.[1] The paradox of some of these individualistic theories is that they so often finish up undermining their own starting point – as, for example, those neo-classical economic commentators who have moved into the study of crime (as 'free choice') but who finish up describing a highly patterned (not so very 'individual') and allegedly measurable set of human responses to 'situations of opportunity' or labour market circumstances (Pyle 1983, 1989).

The direction and flavour of much contemporary social analysis is surely a reaction, in part, against the more wooden forms of Marxism which worked within a narrow and deterministic tradition, wanting to read off the inevitability of a historical logic from the identification of class interest and contradictions in the developments of the larger social and economic formation. But the effects of that strong reaction against 'materialism' in different fields are important to grasp. In the field of criminology, for example, the 'cutting edge' of theoretical advance is said, by some commentators, to lie with writers like Jack Katz, who wants us to travel on an analytical quest, after the example of Norman Mailer, to understand 'the moral and sensual attractions of doing evil' (Katz 1988). So we are presented in Katz's text with one-dimensional, naturalistic reportage, along with *ex post facto* opinionated interpretation, in which the primary analytical focus is on the 'motivations' claimed for themselves by individual rapists and murderers, and other miscreants (i.e. the actors' own accounts). Katz's strategy achieves no serious distance on these accounts – for example, in the way that David Matza (1964, 1969), in his pioneering analysis of the 'drift into deviance', was able to do. So instead Katz presents only a sophisticated version of the talk-show confessional, with quite the same ambiguity in terms of any claim to systematic explanation. At another extreme in the criminological literature, we are still presented with the agnostic position, spoken from privileged positions within pure theory, that seems to want us to believe that anything said at all about actually occurring crime, including even the murder of a two-year-old by two older children (the Jamie Bulger murder) ought to be understood just as a construction of an agitated 'crimino-legal complex' (A. Young 1996) – a kind of hyperactive 'moral panic'.

I have tried in this book to offer an analysis of 'contemporary crime' – in all its manifold representations and its real and material effects and presence – that focuses primarily on 'the market' – in the specific sense of wanting to argue that the transformations in economic life of the last two decades have produced a new social reality, with specific and analysable implications for the 'life-chances' and opportunities for individuals situated at different points within that new social reality. Following Raymond Williams, I have been concerned to be sensitive to the process whereby 'the market' has been transformed from being an 'emergent' set of political and social arguments (in opposition to the hegemonic reality of planned and ordered Fordist societies, in their various different forms) into being the hegemonic social form itself. With Anthony Giddens, I have recognized that the everyday reproduction of market-relationships involves the active participation and initiative of 'reflexive individuals', but in the long-established tradition of critical social enquiry, I have also wanted to recognize the ways in which 'market society', like the Fordist system which preceded it, may be experienced as an alien and disorienting social reality – as a set of social arrangements 'not of the actor's own making or choosing'. The fact that 'market society' (presented without the kinds of reservations articulated by Michael Harrington (1993), Alec Nove (1983) or other thinking commentators) is now so routinely and rhetorically advanced as the only way in which economic life can currently be organized gives it as a unchallengeable status as an apparently inescapable, immediate 'social fact'. It is within that framework – the given-ness of a life to be spent in market society – that I have tried to make sense of the ongoing and continuing struggles over the definition and prevalence of different kinds of crime, the prevalence and costs of these different forms of such crime, and the sets of anxieties and fears associated with it. Recognizing that these issues do not reduce straightforwardly – as well they might have done in Fordist circumstances – to issues simply of 'class, gender, ethnicity and age', I have tried, as has James Messerchmidt (1997), to attend to the unevenness of individuals' positions vis-à-vis different markets of 'opportunity' and 'threat' in 'market society'.

In this final chapter, I want to draw together my examination of 'crime in market society' around three concluding summary themes – (1) the reality of crime in market society, (2) the challenge of developing a sociological account of the character of everyday life and culture in market society, and, finally, (3) the public interest problem.

The 'Reality of Crime' in Market Society

The writing of this text has, of course, been significantly influenced by my earlier involvement, in the period of late Fordism, with the development of a 'critical criminology' (Taylor, Walton and Young 1973, 1975) – and by my more tangential involvement, at a defining moment of transition into market society in Britain, with the development of the particular variant of critical criminology known as 'left realism' (Lea and Young 1984; J. Young 1987).[2] The continuing legacy of that realist influence in this text are evident in two important respects. I have been concerned, first, 'to take crime seriously' – offering an analysis that is open and attentive to the realities of criminal victimization (from car-theft and burglary to fraudulent appropriation of personal pension funds) as well as to the considerable anxieties which the perceived prevalence of crime produces in so many different places, and in so many different moments, in everyday life within market society. Secondly, I share with left realism a commitment to a 'realist' (as distinct from an idealist) strategy with respect to the actual analysis of 'crime' (as both behaviour and mass-media representation).[3] That is to say, I have attempted, as Jock Young puts it:

to be true to the actual shape of the phenomenon and the forces which have brought it into being. Realism is not empiricism, it does not merely reflect the world of appearances ... Rather, it attempts to unpack the phenomenon, display its hidden relationships and pinpoint the dynamics which lie behind the apparent obviousness of a single criminal incident at a particular point in time. (J. Young 1987: 337)

The realist project – critical as it always was of the limitations of vision of purely administrative criminology, with its unprincipled swings between liberal pragmatism and outright 'correctionalism' – was still itself defined, and in some ways constrained, by a continuing analytic preoccupation with the (national) State. One of Jock Young's lasting contributions to the develop-ment of criminological ideas – the famous 'Square of Crime' (see figure 4) – insists on the analysis of any criminal incident in terms of the co-presence of four elements: the offender(s) (the actor(s)) and his or her victim(s); the 'informal control systems' surrounding the actor(s) and the incident; and the formal representatives of State social control, the police.

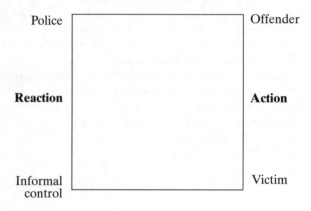

Figure 4 Jock Young's Square of Crime
Source: Young 1987: 340

The definition, and subsequent treatment, of a particular incident as 'crime', has to be analysed as an outcome on the unfolding of specific processes of 'action and reaction' in particular historical and geographical contexts.[4] The presence of the police within these processes is confirmation, above all, of the centrality within these processes of 'the State' – in the form, specifically, of its front-line troops of social control – the police – performing a vanguard role on behalf of the more extended infrastructure of the courts and the broader justice and penal system. There is an important sense, then, in which the presence of police in the process of production of crime becomes in itself the occasion for forms of criminological critique – of the police themselves (on the grounds, for example, of their declining rates of success in 'clearing-up' reported crime) or, alternatively, of the State itself (for its unenlightened and unimaginative strategies of crime-prevention, pursued, often without coordination, across different departments of state[5]). The realist project within criminology in Britain in the 1980s was in part to be understood, as I have argued elsewhere (Taylor 1992b), as the attempt to persuade a Labour Party, thrown into opposition by the right-populist electoral victory of Margaret Thatcher in 1979, of a more imaginative and comprehensive, but realist and populist, *national* project of social reform in the sphere of crime-control, mobilized through the national State.

The importance of 'the State' in the identification of crime (through law) and the apprehension and processes of behaviours so categorized (through the criminal justice system) is inescapable – though I noted in chapter 7 the ways in which new forms of private policing and surveillance, operative particularly in commercial settings, identify certain events as crime only in an accountancy sense, that is, as financial losses which may or may not have been managerially anticipated. The continuing intimate involvement of critical criminology only with the critique of the State and state social control (see e.g. Melossi 1990) threatens to displace attention from the 'etiological' link between crime and 'the market'.

Beginning with the treatment of 'the marketization of social relations' in chapter 1, I have also tried to offer an account which is attentive to the increasing presence and importance of 'the market' in the everyday life (or civil society) in the last years of the twentieth century. My argument is that 'the market' has a critical importance in the production of crime (both as a social practice and as a pattern of victimization) in different specific ways in different 'locales' within market society. The market can be critically implicated, for example, in those processes of 'differential association' occurring among young professionals employed in the City of London – encouraging a vast range of different frauds, knowingly but cavalierly pursued, in the name of 'flexible accumulation'. Many other forms of fraud – perhaps less cavalier in their execution – may have been encouraged in the impersonal world of financial exchange and trading made possible by the creation of a 24-hour system of stock exchanges around the world. Bodies of national law – for example, company law, financial services legislation, consumer law – created over the years within individual societies in the name of the protection of individual bank and insurance customers and clients, or pension-holders – may pale into insignificance in such an international market place, dominated as it is by an endless war of 'enterprising individuals' and corporations for financial position and return. The presence of the 'nation-state' may be substantially negated, indeed, by the continuing creation of 'offshore' financial havens as a shield for the 'entrepreneurial' company or for an individual account.[6] The status (and, indeed, 'the reality') of such frauds – and the actual victims of these frauds (as, for example, the 32,000 pensioners of the *Daily Mirror* newspaper in the United Kingdom) – may only be revealed when the transactions involved are shown later to have involved a reckless or fatal miscalculation, or, indeed, a use of 'other people's money' that is retrospectively revealed to have been illegal within that particular national State jurisdiction.

The examination, in chapter 5, of the range of different frauds attracting attention in the public media was intended as an exploration of parallels and differences in 'financial risk-taking and crime' occurring at different market-locations in market society. I did not intend to suggest that the behaviours of a person making a fraudulent return on personal income tax, a business-person engaged in the avoidance of Value Added Tax on domestic or international trades or an insurance salesperson engaged in a 'rebate selling' pyramid can or should all be thought of as engaging in 'flexible accumulation' *per se*: the levels of return from such activities may not merit such a description. But I did intend to suggest that the search for additional or alternative sources of revenue, or for ways of reducing costs, may be becoming a generic feature of market society for many different groups of actors at different levels of the social formation (i.e. in what I have identified as different market-positions within market society). I certainly wanted to display an in-principle interest, following Sykes and Matza (1957), in the 'techniques of neutralization' that accompany engagement in these different and flexible strategies of income generation. I do want to suggest that this new flexibilization of sources of income may necessitate a revision of very familiar, well-established models within sociology (especially the middle-level sociology of Robert Merton) which purport to explain conformity and deviance within 'modern society' against the assumed backdrop of an ordered Fordist market in personal advancement and accumulation dominated exclusively by one, unitary 'structure of legitimate opportunities'.

I have also been concerned to display the link between the growth of competitive 'market society', the production of new and heightened forms of social marginality – involving structures of disadvantage across a range of different markets of opportunity – and the development and consolidation of different local 'economies of crime'. This particular aspect of life in market society, especially in the large urban centres, is by some distance the most widely recognized in the public mind. But in the work of Enzo Mingione (1983) and other researchers attentive to the realities of life at different new market-positions in market society, these local economies of crime have for a long time been understood not necessarily as *accumulative* activity in the ordinary sense of self-interested acquisition on a grand scale – but nonetheless as material adaptations to the realities of particular local markets, integral to *subsistence and survival* within those locales. The ways in which such local economies of survival, when successful (for example, the cigarette smugglers of market Europe in the late 1990s), embark on a pattern of growth (which may involve 'hostile take-overs' by larger corporate enterprises) has a familiar ring to students of markets in all kinds of commodities.

A Sociology of Everyday Life and Culture in Market Society

The 'lost world' of Fordism – with its more or less orderly, more or less predictable everyday character – continues to exercise an enormous purchase on the common sense reasoning and people's 'cognitive maps of the world' in market society, especially in the ways they attempt to make sense of (or, more often, deplore) specific events,[7] everyday practices[8] or particular phenomena[9] within market society. The evidence points to a population of market society which acquiesces in 'the freedoms' of market society – the opportunities presented to 'enterprising' and dynamic individuals, which might not have been previously available within Fordism – but which cavils at the inevitable *commodification* of more and more realms of culture and civil society. I have also at various points in this text touched on a range of other issues that have been thrown up with the advancing marketization of social relations – for example, the continuing 'acceleration' of work and also the spread of low-wage occupations, in which the level of return is often such as to encourage, or require, taking on 'a second job'. Making sense of everyday life, especially working life, in market society clearly involves a substantial revision of Robert Merton's famous 'typology of individual adaptations' to 'modern (American) society', as first understood by him in the late 1930s (Merton 1938, 1957). The starting point for any such project of sociological revision, I want to suggest, should be a detailed understanding of the radical transformation that has occurred in the Fordist labour market and also in the cultures of the workplace. The 'culture of enterprise' associated with market society is a culture in which Merton's distinction between 'the conformist' and 'the innovator', in many specific locales, begins to collapse.[10] In many workplaces, 'innovation' is conformity. In some workplaces – where employment is temporary and contractual and where employees on contract are expected, entrepreneurially, to create their own subsequent employment – the question of what constitutes 'legitimate means' is particularly starkly posed. Table 15 presents a provisional diagrammatic representation of what we might call the legitimate and illegitimate markets in opportunity (for employment and/or financial resources) in market society, as the benchmark from which revision of the fate of Merton's 'individual adaptations' might proceed. In contrast to Merton's ideal-typical representations of different kinds of behavioural orientation, this table identifies the utility, and the projected present and future 'market value', in both legitimate and illegitimate labour markets of people performing particular kinds of market roles.

The objective of table 15 is to take seriously the arguments advanced throughout this text – in particular, the impact that the transformation of the Fordist society has had on local labour markets and on the long-established 'Fordist' assumption of 'a job for life', and to think through the restructuring of local labour markets that may be occurring in different localities. My argument has been that these local transformations of the labour market constitute the definitive local framework within which individuals in different market-positions 'drift into crime', initially, perhaps (as the 'rational choice' economists insist), as a consequence of particular situations of opportunity.

Table 15 is particularly concerned to highlight the new configurations of skills and attitude that are in demand in the newly emergent legitimate local labour markets (in small business enterprises, in service industries, or in the financial sector itself), and which therefore advantage or 'accredit' any young or middle-aged person seeking some form of post-Fordist employment. In this way, it also records the virtual collapse within most legitimate labour

Table 15 The markets in employment and other financial opportunity in market societies

	Legitimate market place	Illegitimate market place
'Entrepreneurs'	++	++
Managers (in flexible enterprises)	+	+
Managers (in inflexible, single-product industries)		−
Non-commercial service providers (local authority workers etc.)		−
Skilled workers (the labour aristocracy)	0	0
Experienced unskilled workers	−	+
Unskilled apprentices	− −	

++ Vanguard presence
+ Valuable supporting role
− Declining value
− − Severely declining value?
0 No presence

markets of the demand for unskilled workers (and certainly the demise of the idea of lifelong unskilled labour) as well as the general lack of opportunity within the new market societies for the development of skills over long periods of employment within particular crafts. In that sense, the concern is to register the specific transformation in life chances which 'the crisis of Fordism' has involved both for the 'reserve army of labour' and craftsmen.

Importantly, also, table 15 attempts to recognize the kinds of skills and attitudes that may be required of young or middle-aged people who grasp those illicit opportunities for gain which may be routinely thrown up in particular localities, and who then, under certain conditions, may be recruited into a more full-time pursuit of such illegitimate alternatives. Bourgois' study of Puerto Rican crack-dealers in the Barrio district in New York City is an account of a group of young uneducated and unskilled 'entrepreneurs' opening up new markets for crack cocaine in the area, but then developing experience and skill (and, Bourgois insists, some sense of self-respect) in the everyday management of a dangerous and difficult business, characterized by unpredictable swings of both supply and demand, and by very limited financial margins (Bourgois 1995). The little research we have about the fast-developing post-Fordist labour markets in other parts of the world – for example, in the 24-hour 'youth cultural consumption' economies in major North of England cities, involving employment in everything from fly-posting to barmanship – describes a world in which personal 'job security' and advancement requires a challenging range of skills, flexibility and personal courage (a new kind of street wisdom regarding survival in new market conditions). These are, of course, highly portable skills and attitude – the kinds of skills and attitudes which would advantage people in the different kinds of local illegitimate alternatives. As my discussion in chapter 4 was intended to suggest, the initial advancement of illegitimate over legitimate markets (such as recruitment of unemployed miners into cigarette smuggling in South-East England) is likely to be a very local phenomenon – a product of the relative lack of legitimate alternatives as well as of geographical location. But the activation of those skills, and the continued play of an entrepreneurial sensibility prioritizing survival and advancement in the new market societies, may then inform a more extensive sphere of 'illegitimate' but more gainful involvements. What may then be difficult, at the level of local market activity 'on the street' is to distinguish between legitimate and illegitimate providers of services or goods.[11]

THE PROBLEM OF THE PUBLIC INTEREST

The familiar 'progressive' response to the advance of private commercial interest during the Fordist period was usually to rehearse a set of familiar arguments emphasizing the moral or normative sovereignty of the 'public interest' (see e.g. S. Becker and MacPherson 1988; Stretton 1987; Wilkes and Shirley 1984). But the lively debate that occurred during the 1980s, for example, around Jürgen Habermas's attempts to theorize a foundational idea of the Public Sphere has been testimony to the problems associated with a purely rhetorical embrace of the idea of 'public interest'. Not least of the issues has been what kind of Public Interest is being referenced in societies whose male-dominated and monocultural public spheres have remained oblivious to equality of gender opportunity and to the advance of cultural pluralism. The advance of the market also clearly throws up the issue of how such a public sphere could be reconstituted to enable 'inclusion' in democratic dialogue and policy-making of the ever-increasing numbers of excluded and marginalized populations within 'market society'. One measure of the challenge presented here is the way in which nearly all initiatives in the public sphere of crime prevention in market societies are defined by their inclusion of all sections of the population, other than the excluded themselves.[12]

The two other inescapable challenges, however, derive from the implosion of the nation-state itself and the associated development of transnational institutions for governance of market activity.

Liberal governance and 'community crime prevention'

At the end of the 1990s, the field of professional criminology, and of popular talk about talk, reduces, with extraordinary predictability and lack of intellectual curiosity, into a practical discussion about some new idea about 'best practice' in the 'prevention of crime'. In Britain and most other market societies, the dominant refrain (the discourse) of all those who speak about this issue focuses on the shift towards 'a partnership approach' to such activities of prevention, where 'partnership' refers to the opening-out of publicly financed occupations (the police) or public authorities (local councils) to other agencies and interest groups, 'sharing ideas' about the progression of the practical local problem of reduction of crime and of fear.

The continuing development of these different 'community partnership schemes' in the field of crime prevention from the early 1980s onwards may be understood – as defenders of the existing public institutions will maintain – as a question of declining resources. It is certainly the case that State institutions, at both national and local level, in North America, in Britain and in some other European member-states, have suffered considerably in resources from the tax revolts of the middle class over this period. But it is also important to recognize, as did Christopher Lasch in his last book (Lasch 1995), that the declining role and declining political and cultural effectivity of public State institutions may also be evidence of what he calls a crisis in competence in such institutions, which often runs parallel with a deep crisis in the kinds of progressive ideas ('empowerment', 'tolerance' (in and of itself), 'participation' etc.) that informed the actions of many public institutions in the earlier post-war period. This crisis of competence has been identified by a number of commentators in other public service-providing institutions, from the local town hall through to schools and local transport systems, whether in the name of modernity *per se* or in the name of specifically 'free market' capabilities.

Nikolas Rose and Peter Miller have argued that we have been witness through the 1980s and 1990s to the rapid development of new sets of 'political powers beyond the State' – a vast range of agencies, institutions and ad-hoc partnerships which operate as resources of ideas and problem-solving capacities in market society (Rose and Miller 1992). Rose and Miller argue, in particular, that these new forms of 'liberal governance' are situated not at the level of 'the State' at local or national level, but rather within the set of interconnected networks that exist between public and private sector institutions in particular local regions, 'nations' or, indeed, 'international' spaces or territories. State institutions may play a role in these new 'technologies of governance' but their role may vary considerably from one field of activity to another. These governmental networks work with and through a specific set of discourses which elaborate an essentially actuarial and 'calculative' approach to the management of particular problems. This form of governance works 'at a distance' from the problems in question and from the established 'local authorities' (*sic*), though it may send in special task forces to deal with certain specific issues (for example, under-performing schools or police forces, or an environmental disaster). Above all, this form of 'liberal governance' wants always to investigate and record the effectivity of these measures through systems of evaluation and audit: statistical measures of performance of institutions or of individuals become the primary instruments for the scrutiny of 'government'. The development of these new forms of 'liberal governance' is seen by Rose and Miller as a defining feature of the transformation of power in all late capitalist societies – it is *not* seen by them to be linked specifically to the marketization of economic and social life. But this 'hollowing-out' of the pre-existing forms of the 'Keynesian welfare state' of the late Fordist period has profound implications – not least, in respect of the capacity of 'the town hall' (the seat of democratically elected local government) or, indeed, any other one institution or agency (like the police) to respond to 'the public will', however that might be expressed, rather than remaining faithful to the performative demands of the new regimes of governance.

Transnational markets and the public interest

The 'hollowing-out' of State institutions at national level runs in parallel to other processes directed at the creation of partnerships and networks *at a transnational level*. The marked shift towards 'free trade' within larger international markets has involved not just the finalization of the North American Free Trade Agreement between the United States, Canada and Mexico in 1992, but also the increasingly eager moves taking place within the fifteen-member European Union to further enlarge the size of its market place. The South-East Asian countries have been contemplating closer international partnership for some time: it remains to be seen whether this process will continue after the downturn of 1998. In the European Union, in particular, the pressure being placed on further enlargement and liberalization of markets accompanies the urgent moves taking place towards the consolidation and, indeed, the institutionalization in European law of new forms of transnational governance. This is most evident, as was mentioned in chapters 5 and 7, in the sphere of crime and policing, in the attempts that are being made to encourage the incorporation of the 'Schengen Acquis (or Accord)' as the so-called Third Pillar of the European Union. The Amsterdam Summit of June 1997 may have delayed the implementation of any such further international consolidation in law of policing and 'security' matters across Europe – and, in particular, the project of construction of Europol as a transnational European institution, complete with cross-border powers (for example, the right of pursuit); but *de facto* the international policing of the European market place will continue to develop very rapidly (den Boer 1997; Taylor 1998). The level of cooperation between European police forces, especially those units of police working in specialized areas (fraud, computer crime, money laundering etc.), merits the inclusion of the police as one of what the German political scientists Wolfgang Streeck and Philippe Schmitter identify as the new 'organized interests' of the European Single Market (Streeck and Schmitter 1991), and critical criminologists certainly need to be attentive to the crime-control priorities of this powerful international organized network, as well as to the ways in which international policing in a market society is linked, horizontally, with other transnational institutions of governance (the European Commission itself, the customs and immigration authorities, private police forces and security companies etc.) as well, vertically, as with the national institutions of policing in individual societies.[13] The role of these transnational institutions of police may be understood as a response to the two self-evidently international forms of criminality – 'the Mafia' or the international drug cartels. But the discussion of developments in respect of 'the private temptations' of market society in chapter 5 was intended to illuminate a range of criminalities (from cigarette smuggling to corruption within the European Union's own budgets) that have increasingly also to be understood in terms of their transnational as well as local presence (their 'glocality'). This was another way of indicating that the futures of 'crime' and of crime control in Europe are inextricably bound up with the future evolution of the 'single market' itself, and the consequences of this unfolding of the market logic (for example, the single currency) across that new and extended, marketized European territory.

This is a prospect that is likely to pose serious challenges for applied academic disciplines like criminology, with its continuing reluctance to deal in the broader political or cultural rationales for its work. The challenges of 'market-Europe', however, will in substance be identical with the challenges that have been posed by the unleashing of a 'liberal market' at the level of national states – in the crowded market place that a liberalized Europe may become, the question of identifying and defending, transnationally as well as the purely national level, some notion of a 'public interest' against an increasing variety of injuries from the liberal market itself, as well as from the increasing variety of crimes that will be associated with the advance of that liberal market, will be inescapable.

NOTES

Introduction

1 Close scrutiny of these shelves says something about the character of the market for books on Real Crime. The several hundred titles in this section are organized under subheadings – Crime Reference (half a shelf), Trials (one shelf), Crime Investigations (half a shelf), British Police (half a shelf), American Police (half a shelf), Punishment (half a shelf), British Gangs (half a shelf), Mafia and Organized Crime (two shelves), the Kennedy Assassination (half a shelf), Crime Cases (five shelves) and Serial Homicide (five shelves). There is also a small selection of 'criminal psychology' texts, primarily emanating from the United States. The punishment section focuses heavily on capital punishment, especially hanging (as for example in Rocky Stockman's *The Hangman's Diary*), and the crime section on particular Gothic examples (Richard Glyn Jones's *The Mammoth Book of Killer Women* (1993), whilst the serial killers section contains several competing titles on Jack the Ripper, the Yorkshire Ripper (Peter Sutcliffe) and the most recent case of Fred and Rosemary West. This is a body of literature which sustains its own set of very successful authors (e.g. David Yallop) as well as a body of fans, notably through the bi-monthly magazine (*Crimetime*) also on sale in the store.

2 An Americanized version of *Cracker*, also centred on a forensic psychiatrist called Fitz, was released on NBC television in 1997.

3 This renaissance of nineteenth-century biological positivism as a form of 'scientific explanation' of crime has run in parallel with a similar intellectual reappraisal of a more classically moralistic form of explanation of human action (as the product of a more or less effectively tutored or regulated individual 'free will'). In the USA one of the most prominent spokespeople for this classical orthodoxy has been Ernest van den Haag; in the UK its adherents have included Digby Anderson (1992), Christie Davies (1975), Patricia Morgan (1978), Melanie Phillips and Norman Dennis and George Erdos (1992). The tensions between these two different dimensions of analytical individualism are considerable, both in the intellectual field and in the struggles over policy-construction within Conservative and Republican governments (see Taylor 1987).

4   I exclude here a small number of advisory pieces published in the late 1970s, specifically identifying the social science academy in the United States with the rise of a new conservatism in that country, actively engaged in a subversion of the tenets of liberal-progressive penal policy in particular (Platt and Takagi 1977) and liberal social thought and policy in general (Gordon and Hunter 1977–8; Steinfels 1977). It is symptomatic of the general inertia of the liberal social science academy in the USA that one of the most insightful appraisals of the social impact of the first years of the Reagan administration should have come from a journalist, Thomas Byrne Edsall (1984), rather than from a tenured liberal social scientific academic.

5   Perhaps the most useful summary of the terminological debates over 'postmodernism' as a term is that provided by Mike Featherstone (1988).

6   In research recently undertaken in the North of England, one of the most common interpretations encountered of recent transformations – especially among men of the old working-class – was simply that there had been 'one ruddy long recession' (Taylor, Evans and Fraser 1996: ch. 3). Amongst other groups, especially women but also, sometimes resentfully, amongst men without work, the interpretation of recent economic change focused on the increasing number of women who had been able to find some kind of paid employment in the local labour force. The interpretation which seemed to be operative here of recent changes focused on the 'bloody-mindedness' of determined local women, more than it did on any structural reconfiguration of labour markets.

Chapter 1 Social Transitions of the Late Twentieth Century

1   In the 1980s and 1990s 'professional' criminology has been challenged by a different form of individualistic account, which has increasing purchase in the wider culture, namely the belief in the increasing prevalence of *evil*, amoral individuals (serial killers and child-murderers, children themselves possessed by 'evil' predispositions, 'villains' and many others). The response of official, administrative criminology to this other form of individualistic account has too often taken the form of avoidance of debate (see Sparks and Loader, 1993).

2   One of the best investigations of this truth in the sociological literature on class-divided Fordist Britain, with its associated rigid 'ordering' of class and gender relations and its structuring of narrow life-chances is the work of Paul Willis (1977, 1978).

3   Roger Cohen, 'Europe Weighs Four-day Week to Tackle Jobs Crisis', *Guardian*, 24 Nov. 1993.

4   Jonathan Steele, 'Militants Push Leaders to Work for the Jobless', *Guardian*, 13 Apr. 1995.

5   *Labour Market Trends*, June 1997 (London: United Kingdom Central Statistical Office), table 2.18.

6   Ibid.

7   *Employment Gazette*, Dec. 1994, table 2.8.

8   This particular doomsday scenario has now been somewhat modified, in the light of the American economy's capacity, notably via its explosive growth in part-time and short-term contract work, to reduce the overall official total of unemployment in that country: official rates of unemployment in the United States were measured at only 4.7 per cent in April 1997.

9 Department of Social Security, *Households below Average Income 1979–1991/2* (London: HMSO, 1994).

10 Will Hutton, 'Growing Inequality Means the Poor Keep Getting Poorer', *Guardian*, 10 Feb. 1995.

11 Department of Social Security, *Households below Average Income*.

12 Will Hutton, 'Crime, the Politician's Rich Reward', *Guardian*, 3 July 1992.

13 One of the strongest criticisms, constructed in the name of an orthodox Marxist perspective, of the movement towards greater social equality was that advanced by John Westergaard (Westergaard, 1965; Westergaard and Resler 1975), but even this critique did not anticipate that the egalitarian project of 'bourgeois capitalist' political parties could be put into reverse.

14 The financial crises which began to unfold, very quickly, in Singapore, Malaysia and Japan in 1997 and 1998 began to produce some re-analysis of these prognoses. So also, in the late 1990s, the capacity of the US economy to produce a decline in overall rates of unemployment (in the form of a large increase in short-term, contractual and part-time employment) – down to 4.7 per cent by the middle of 1997 – brought a shift in the economic debate elsewhere – for example, in the European Union. By 1998, there was a widespread perception that the Clinton Administration and the Blair Government were acting in concert to urge a universal adoption of flexible labour markets as the only conceivable national policy within global post-Fordist economies.

15 Baumgartner's close study of a suburban area in New York state suggests that any gathering of young people in the area was a source of considerable anxiety, usually resulting in calls to the police in excess of the numbers made to the police in troubled inner-city areas (Baumgartner 1988).

16 Will Hutton, 'High Risk Strategy', *Guardian*, 30 Oct. 1995.

17 This interpretation of the relation between a State police and popular communities will be challenged by that form of Marxism which reduces all exercises of State power to the play of capitalist interest (Scraton 1987), and certainly the police are often used to such a purpose (as in the miners' strike in Britain in 1983–4). But historical evidence from the eighteenth and nineteenth century illustrates the support of working-class movements and local communities for a local police presence, provided by the State (Donajgrodzki 1977; Ignatieff 1979) and also of the very contemporary, persistent demands by poor and dislocated communities for effective policing by the State.

18 This sense of the RCMP as a marker of Canadian difference in North America is the source of the Canadian television series *Due North*, successfully marketed in both the United States and Britain in the mid-1990s. The star of this series, Paul Gross (playing Fraser Sr), is presented as an unarmed young gentleman, whose display of traditional moral sensibilities is signified by the naming of his inseparable companion, a 'deaf' wolf, as 'Diefenbaker', Conservative Prime Minister of Canada from 1957 to 1963 (*Due North*, released by CBC/CTV/Alliance Communications Corporation 1994; Producer: Paul Haggis).

19 Rachel Nickell was a young mother, attacked and murdered 'in broad daylight' whilst pushing her toddler through Wimbledon Common, a heavily used London park, one lunchtime in December 1992. Two-year-old Jamie Bulger was abducted from a shopping mall in Bootle, Merseyside, in February 1993 and murdered by two eleven-year-old boys on a nearby railway line. Benji Stanley was a fourteen-year-old boy of West Indian background, living in Moss

Side, Manchester, who was shot down in November 1993 whilst waiting in a queue in a Jamaican Pattie fast-food store. Dennis Nilsen was found guilty, in 1983, of the murder of fifteen homosexual men, often as a result of extended sexual rituals. Fred and Rosemary West were charged, on separate occasions in 1994 and 1995 with the murders of a minimum of ten young women in their private home in Gloucester, again in the context of sexual 'excess'. Fred West committed suicide in prison on New Year's Day 1995 and Rosemary West was sentenced to life imprisonment in November 1995. The reportage of these individual cases, especially the Bulger murder, was accompanied by an agitated national debate characterized, in nearly every instance, by the belief that these crimes were without historical precedent. Each of these crimes also touched an important nerve in the moral constitution of English society – the safety of mothers, young children, the troubled issue of race, the suppressed issue of homosexuality, and the ever more intrusive issue of the well-being of the increasing number of young homeless people on the streets, in and out of 'care' in a society which wanted still to see itself as a caring social formation.

20   In 1997 the American media pronounced on the arrival of a new kind of serial killer, in which a 'chain' of victims was linked by the theft, in sequence, of the cars belonging to each victim. One of these was the fashion designer, Giovanni Versace.

21   In Europe, amongst the most severe anti-immigration measures were those passed in France in 1993, at the insistence of the Gaullist interior minister, Charles Pasqua. In 1995, some 45,000 people on visitors' visas in France were declared to be illegal immigrants and expelled, and Gaullist MPs were competing with the Front National in advancing proposals to deny immigrants all access to education and health services in France (*Guardian*, 17 Apr. 1995). In early 1996, attention also focused on the severe detention regimes and strict asylum and refugee policies which were now being adopted even in the 'liberal' Netherlands.

22   Throughout individual European societies at the end of the twentieth century, this feeling – that the economic resources have reached a new limit, requiring new limits on the numbers of people having a claim upon them – finds one of its clearest expressions in a variety of new measures taken to curtail the numbers of people who claim entry into these societies as refugees or asylum-seekers. This rationalization of processes of exclusion occurs at a time of increasing conflict and war in different parts of Europe, which is itself an expression of the same intensification of a politics of particularism.

23   Many other American writers have focused attention on these new urban no-go areas. Mike Davis speaks of these areas as a new form of 'bantustan', reservations for the new poor of a free market America (Davis 1990) and this line has been pursued in a series of powerful journalistic enquiries by Parenti (1993, 1994a, 1994b). Jay MacLeod's *Ain't No Makin' It* (1987), Mercer Sullivan's *Getting Paid* (1989) and Martín Sánchez Jankowski's *Islands in the Street* (1991) are the best examples of a new ethnographic tradition in American social enquiry, reporting on the conditions of life in these anxious and isolated 'low-income neighbourhoods' in three different American cities.

24   Not least of the crises of the 'ghetto culture' in the US is the particular crisis of masculinity itself, in which a racialized variant of the more generalized lumpen-proletarian form of socially disconnected and irresponsibly hedonistic masculinity has taken over, at least rhetorically, from the collectivism of slave culture, on the one hand, and proletarian solidarity, on the other. The crisis of

black masculinism in America, and its 'infantilist' use of violence, became an organizing feature of the political activity of both the Rev. Jesse Jackson and the Black Muslim leader Louis Farrakhan in the 1990s, and also informed the extraordinary Million Men March in Washington DC in the fall of 1995. It is also an organizing theme in the activity of the so-called Promise Keepers, a predominantly white and male Christian movement dedicated to the idea of a 'virtuous' and 'responsible' male (Thompson 1996).

25   These confrontations are usually not staged between equally matched sides, and can sometimes take the form, precisely, of a lynching. The most recent instance of this in Britain was the murder of the young Anglo-West Indian Stephen Lawrence by three young white assailants as he was standing at a bus stop in South London in April 1993. Other infamous instances of racial crime in Britain have included the New Cross fire of 1981, in which thirteen people were killed after the firebombing of a West Indian shebeen party (Carter and Coussins 1991).

26   Quoted in Keith 1995: 271.

27   There was evidence of a deep reluctance on the part of the Conservative administrations in power in Britain from 1979 to 1987 to confront any outbreak of racial violence by whites. In April 1996, the British Government refused to sign up to the European Community's *Horizon* anti-racism initiative; and in the following month, after the collapse of the prosecution of three young whites for the murder of the black teenager Stephen Lawrence, the chairman of the Commission for Racial Equality openly accused the Crown Prosecution Service of 'going soft' on hate crimes and of discrimination against its own black employees (*Observer*, 5 May 1996). In June 1997, the new Labour administration established an official inquiry into the prosecution process in the Lawrence case.

28   'Race Hate in Britain Condemned', *Observer*, 11 May 1997.

29   Alan Travis, 'More Race Attacks Reported to Police', *Guardian*, 12 Apr. 1996.

30   *Criminal Statistics, England and Wales, 1996*: (Cm. 3764) Para 5.12, p. 102.

31   For example, Morrison and O'Donnell's study of 214 people convicted of armed robbery in the Metropolitan Police District (Greater London) in 1990 uncovered only three females (Morrison and O'Donnell 1994: 41).

32   This exposé of a male violence unrecognized by a gender-neutral criminology was widespread in the 1970s in America, beginning with the work of Susan Griffin (1971) on the massive under-reportage of rape. This suppression of discussion of male violence by the criminological discipline in this period, and in earlier parts of the century, mirrors the lack of interest of police and the criminal justice system in such violence, especially in the domestic sphere, but it provides no excuse for social commentators at large. The routinized use of violence by working-class men controlling the private sphere of the household at the highpoint of mass manufacturing is well documented by Robert Roberts (1971) and Bernice Martin (1981), whilst the early novels of Pat Barker and others bring out a violent misogyny of the miner as head of household in the north-east of England, well known to the women of the area. In the USA the routine use of violence, including predatory sexual violence, by men in some parts of the black underclass in the Southern states is, of course, the subject of Alice Walker's *Color Purple*.

33 I discuss the therapeutic and rehabilitative 'criminology', psychiatric and social work literature of the early post-war period of social construction in Britain in more detail elsewhere (Taylor 1981: ch. 1).

34 This 'desertion' of liberal-left intellectuals (including some of President Kennedy's key advisers) in America to the New Right, and especially to its libertarian market fringe, was first noticed by Steinfels (1977), but then interrogated with great prescience in a review of the same book by Michael Walzer (1978).

35 It goes without saying that the right-wing populist reaction against the women's movement in the 1970s contained very few prescriptions with respect to the new responsibilities of men, even given the obvious changes occurring in the wider labour market and the necessity for change in the domestic division of labour. The new right's 'radicalism' in this sense was radical only in its intended reaction against the independence of women.

36 In Britain, for example, Michèle Barrett and Mary McIntosh's *The Anti-Social Family*, published in 1982, took up many of R. D. Laing's critiques of the family (as a prison-house of thwarted needs and desires) and added to it an analysis of the family as a patriarchal structure, with built-in and gendered inequalities of power (Barrett and McIntosh 1982). Barrett and McIntosh's final chapter, 'Strategies for Change', is devoted to some prescriptions about the domestic division of labour between adults, the rhetorical call 'Beware of Domesticity', some suggestions for reform about family law, and, finally, a charter of parents' rights. It says next to nothing, it must be remarked, about the socialization of children, the rights of children within a household or, indeed, about the private household as a haven, however imperfect, from the travails of the real world outside it, or, very curiously for Marxists of that period, from 'the mass culture' of consumer capitalism.

37 The debate around the 'problem' of parenting in the black family has been led, politically, by the Rev. Jesse Jackson, and documented sociologically by William Julius Wilson. In 1995 the issue was further dramatized by the Million Man March, led by the Black Muslim leader Louis Farrakhan and the Promise Keepers organization, committed to 'taking back their role in the family'; (see *Utne Reader*, 73 (Feb. 1996).

38 John Carvel 'Britain Tops European Table for Lone-Parent Families', *Guardian*, 2 Dec. 1993.

39 A good example of an essentially behaviourist account of the role of 'inadequate' or 'inconsistent' socialization of children in the production of crime and delinquency is to be found in the work of Gordon Trasler (1962). It was significant enough, for many critical commentators, that for Trasler 'consistent socialization' was found to be concentrated primarily in the middle class.

40 This representation of the division of labour in the family in the earlier post-war period would be challenged by writers like Norman Dennis in Britain, who have recently been engaged in a nostalgic evocation of the role of the Father in working-class families (Dennis and Erdos 1992). While not denying the importance of fathers in the informal and intimate aspects of socialization within the family, I am not convinced that the North-East miner, for all his other many qualities, is the best available model of parenting available, particularly for young girls or, for that matter, for young boys who want to escape the pit.

41 Foremost amongst a series of such instances was the murder of their parents committed by Erik and Lye Menendez in Beverly Hills, California, in 1989. The Menendez brothers were sentenced to life in March 1996.

42 In the early 1990s, for example, there was a quite widespread concern in Italy about the numbers of young men from affluent backgrounds in North Italy, especially in the Veneto region around Verona, who appeared to be attracted by the idea either of random murder ('for fun') or, alternatively, of their parents, in order, ostensibly, to speed the arrival of their inheritance (Ed Vulliamy, 'Killing for Fun', *Guardian*, 17 Jan. 1994). A particular concern, central to the subsequent clinical work of the 'juvenile criminologists' (Umberto Gatti, Giovanni Traverso), was the fact that these young people were in all respects typical, relatively well-educated, and certainly very economically secure products (the '*rampanti*') of the region in which the 'economic miracle' in Italy during the 1960s and 1970s had had most effect.

43 See e.g. Simon Tisdall, 'When Commonsense Collides with the Courts', *Guardian*, 5 Aug. 1993.

44 This support is in part nostalgic. There is no question that some of the pro-family rhetoric is straightforwardly reactionary in the sense that it yearns for a return to a period in which family life was dominated by 'the Law of the Father'. Some of the reaction to the activities of the Child Support Agency in Britain is underpinned by this kind of sentiment, and some of the pro-familial activism that feeds into the anti-abortion crusades in the United States must be so understood. But as Christopher Lasch (1993) suggests, another element in this nostalgia for other kinds of familial order may be a reaction to the unhappiness of existing family forms; in this sense it is in principle utopian.

Chapter 2 The Ninth Transition: The Rise of Market Society

1 See also the arguments advanced ten years later by the veteran American social democrat Michael Harrington, arguing for a 'socialism' organized around decentralized democratic enterprise, consumer choice and an efficient non-market sector (Harrington 1993: ch. 8).

2 It is worth noting how this same definition of the benefits of free enterprise has been transferred into free-market Russia during the 1990s, by reference to the smaller numbers of 'cowboy capitalists' who achieved millionaire status in a matter of months, during the initial privatization of resources of the old Soviet state.

3 In Britain, Stuart Hall's continuing and courageous essays challenged progressive opinion to confront the veracity of these claims from the free market camp, with what seems to have been real effect on the political thinking of New Labour, though rather less effect in the 'progressive' academy (Hall 1978, 1980, 1981, 1982).

Chapter 3 Young People, Crime and Fear in Market Societies

1 There are several important senses in which the 'crisis of the nation-state' does play into the lives of young people. Most obvious of all is the ever-increasing salience of the international (globalized) market place of consumption – a distant parameter in what Abram de Swaan (1995) has spoken of as the 'widening circles of identification'. The importance of international political communities or of the international elites, like the leaderships of the European Commission, may have been more obvious to young people whose first language was not English than it has been to young people in Britain as a whole: the acquisition of English (the lingua franca of international business

and politics) is one of the fastest growing industries of the new Europe and of Asia.

2   *International Herald Tribune*, 7–8 June 1997.

3   A York University study of families in north-east England in 1988, for example, concluded that about a third of these households were witness to 'an unrelieved struggle to manage with dreary diets and drab clothing' (Newell 1994).

4   In England and Wales, the level of malnutrition amongst children of school age is often linked to the abolition of free school meals in 1979 (the numbers of children eating school meals in England and Wales declined from 4.9 million in 1979 to 2.8 million in 1988).

5   In 1995, for example, a record number of children (28,500) were placed on children's protection registers in England and Wales, an increase of 15 per cent on 1993–4. (*Guardian*, 3 Feb. 1995).

6   See in particular Stein, Rees and Frost (1994), which focuses on the vast range of risks faced by young children and adolescents who 'run away' from home.

7   The notion of 'hot spots' of crime in the criminological literature derives from Lawrence Sherman's important detailed analysis of calls made to the police in Minneapolis in 1986. Over 50 per cent of these calls were made in respect of only 3 per cent of the full sample of possible addresses (Sherman et al. 1989). Young people's negotiation of urban space involves the development and use of a range of different mental maps with a distinctive set of 'hot spots' or 'symbolic locations', which may correspond only very unevenly to the places most feared by adults.

8   For the best account of young people's routine strategic adaptations to 'a night out on the town' in Britain in the 1990s, see the study of night-life in Newcastle upon Tyne by Bob Hollands (1995).

9   The Minister of Education in the last Conservative Government in Britain, Gillian Shephard, in 1990 initiated the idea of a behavioural contract, in which entry into a school would be conditional on a pledge of good behaviour by the child, countersigned by parents (*Guardian*, 30 July 1990). The Labour Opposition then responded by calling for the introduction of 'parental responsibility orders' in which parents of children deemed to be disruptive would be required to attend counselling sessions to help them cope with their children. Though these proposals have not been legislated in this form, the strategic aspects – namely that entry to schools is no longer automatic, but is a function of an exchange of commitments between contracting parties – is now part of the common sense of management in many secondary schools in Britain.

10 In Britain, the Education Act of 1993 gave school governors, head teachers and local authorities new powers to exclude children from school on a 'fixed-period' or permanent basis (Department for Education and Employment, *Exclusions from School*, Circular 10/94). In November 1996, the Department of Education and Employment announced that some 11,084 pupils had been 'permanently excluded' from school during 1994–5 (press release, 21 Nov. 1996). The Government minister was at pains to suggest that this represented only 'a tiny proportion' of the school population, but the broader significance of the 'exclusion mandate' (like the changes taking place in the management of difficult tenants in public housing estates) lies in the transformation of the disciplinary regimes governing the provision of 'public services' in market society and the unmistakeable shift towards exclusion.

11 In Britain, the call for a night-time curfew on young children was first enunciated by Jack Straw, then the Shadow Home Secretary, in a speech of 1 June 1996. The idea was referenced in terms of an experiment in Coventry to allow police to remove young people engaged in public drinking from the streets, but also in terms of the 'teen curfews' in place in some American cities, requiring under-18s to be off the streets at night (*Observer*, 2 June 1996). This speech was followed by a second intervention in September 1996, in which Mr Straw called for the streets of British cities 'to be reclaimed from aggressive begging of winos, addicts and squeegee merchants' (*Guardian*, Sept. 1996). The front bench of the Labour Opposition then became complicit in the conflation of public anxiety over aggressive beggars and other problems (for example, the issue of young men in groups, drinking) in a fundamentalist response derived from the propaganda then emanating from the New York Police Department; in an interview to the *Big Issue* magazine in January 1997, Mr Blair called for 'zero tolerance' towards 'people homeless on the street' as a contribution to 'making our streets safe for people' (*Big Issue*, 140 (6–12 Jan. 1997): 16–18).

12 It is entirely unclear how the difficulties involved in this transition can primarily be understood in terms of particular types of early childhood socialization.

13 These incidents are often summarized – certainly in Britain's Conservative press, but not only there – as expressions of the general prevalence of 'yobbishness'. In June 1997, for example, the *Sunday Telegraph* gave prominence to a report from the Association of Chief Police Officers which suggested that police forces in England and Wales were now being called to 'incidents of civil disorder' 'every 10 seconds'. The report also suggested that there had been over 3 million such incidents in the twelve months to March 1997, and that, in some areas, 'vandalism, drunkenness, assaults and other offences' by under-18-year-olds accounted for nearly a third of all offences reported in that area (*Sunday Telegraph*, 29 June 1997).

14 These 'systems of male socialization' would include certain formal aspects – the apprenticeship system which was so important a feature of Fordist work organization in Britain and North America in the mid-twentieth century (and which remains important in Germany today) – as well as informal aspects in the local working-class neighbourhood (as nurtured in public houses or, in family groups, at the football stadium etc). But, as Paul Willis's studies, cited earlier in this chapter, clearly demonstrate, the socialization of working-class young men for the world of work in Fordist societies would also begin early in secondary school, in the 'profane culture' of resistance and adaptation constructed by young men in preparation for a life of subordination (Willis 1978).

15 These new men's magazines increased their circulation from about 300,000 copies a month in 1993 to nearly a million in August 1996 (Martin Wroe, 'Ladmags Defy the Feminists', *Observer*, 11 Aug. 1996). This explosion in the lad-mag market occurred alongside the closure of the modern-day postfeminist *Everywoman* magazine, forced into liquidation in 1996.

16 These men's magazines, with their massive circulations, are very different cultural items from the literature consumed by men in earlier historical periods, and can be read in part as instructional guides for young men in adapting to the realities of changed conditions of life in market societies, whilst still accentuating a primordial version of masculinism.

17 Linda Grant, 'Under Pressure', *Guardian*, 11 Mar. 1996.

18 The violence of underclass men is a complicated issue, as Jack Katz's *Seductions of Crime* tries to explore (1988). From our perspective, Katz's preoccupation with 'sensual pleasure' – speaking of violent crime as being on a par with many other human sensory pleasures – fails to address the impact of this form of 'pleasure-seeking' on others, but also suppresses the connection, widely understood in psychoanalytical circles, between the nihilistic engagement of men in 'sensory' violence and their own subsequent (sometimes immediate) desire to resolve contradictions in their own lives (perhaps through their own deaths). This issue was first explored – in fairly conventional psychoanalytical terms by Donald West (1968) in his study of the frequency with which murderers subsequently committed suicide.

19 As discussed in ch. 4, the young men and boys living in these residual housing areas, in the absence of many viable alternatives, spend their time hanging around 'on the street' (to a greater extent, even, than cohorts of young men in earlier post-war periods, who might have ventured out more regularly to public parks, football playing fields or even the open country, and thereby extended their own symbolic and experiential world).

20 Local areas in many parts of the city of Salford, in Greater Manchester, are dominated by a long-established cultural prohibition, widespread amongst many local men, that 'one does not grass' to authority. The origins of this prohibition lie in the heyday of the Manchester Docks, where many local men were once employed as loaders or warehousemen, with a view to creating some leeway for workers engaged in pilfering from the ship and warehouse owners. In the 1990s, the prohibition has been reinterpreted to apply to anyone giving information to local police, whether in respect of domestic violence or more professional forms of crime (including the organization of protection rackets around local public houses).

21 This process is registered in *Friends*, the phenomenally popular television series, distributed worldwide by Warner Brothers (and routinely supported by advertising which, like the programme itself, knowingly targets this new cohort of young post-Fordist professionals, working in insecure jobs, conscious of their spending, but trying to maintain a certain style of life and humour).

22 Janet Watts, 'A Future in the Balance', *Guardian*, 27 June 1997.

23 The collapse of this regime of regulation is apparent in both Hollywood (*Reservoir Dogs, Silence of the Lambs, Grosse Pointe Blank*) and British cinema (*Shallow Grave*). In the case of Hollywood cinema, this has resulted in the decision by Dustin Hoffman to direct his energies and talents to other filmmaking opportunities.

24 The thesis that 'recreational drug use' was now a normal feature of adolescence in north-west England has been challenged by Shiner and Newcombe (1997), for its exaggerating the numbers of regular users and for trying to generalize from total responses to a large-scale survey to the 'meaning' of sporadic experimentation with drugs use by young people.

25 As Mugford and O'Malley have observed (from a critical perspective), this tendency to link drug-abuse and involvement in one analytical move to patterns of economic deprivation, through a structuralist sociology, is a feature of Elliott Currie's work in the United States, as well as that of Dorn and South in Britain. (Mugford and O'Malley 1991).

26 Luke Harding, 'Straw to Get Tough over Teenage Drinking Craze', *Guardian*, 17 May 1996.

27 Survey research by the University of Exeter's Health Education Unit, published in 1997, suggested that 3 per cent of boys aged 12–13 admitted to consuming 21 units of alcohol a week, and over 7 per cent of boys aged 14–17 (*Guardian*, 30 June 1997).

28 Alcohol Concern, *Alcopops – Research Findings* (April 1997).

29 Then, as now, the empirical objections which flowed from critics of the capitalist market, suggesting that this 'trickling down' of wealth from the rich elites to the pauperized masses was difficult to observe, would be countered by apologists for the dominant order by suggesting that further improvements in living standards were soon about to emerge. In the last years of the nineteenth century, consequent on the growth of Empire, this claim began to have popular purchase (Hobsbawm 1987).

30 In Canada, which in 1989 signed up to the North American Free Trade Treaty, a similar rapid expansion in vocational 'skills' education, responsive to changes in high-technology labour markets, has had a particularly immediate effect. In Canada's most populous province of Ontario, applications from school-leavers for places in community colleges, which have dedicated their programmes to this new post-Fordist economic reality within NAFTA, have recently exceeded the number of applications for places in universities.

Chapter 4 Crime in the City

1 There has been, however, a series of anxious reports in the press in England during the 1990s over 'new forms' of rural crime – anxieties focused, at the one extreme, on the drunken weekend behaviours of young professionals living in commuter villages in the Home Counties, to reported incidents – after the fashion of Peter Schaeffer's *Equus* – involving attacks on horses in farm stables.

2 As Lee Harvey (1970) has shown, there has been a degree of myth-making about the degree of unanimity over the method and theoretical perspective in the Chicago Department during the 1920s and 1930s.

3 For a more extended analysis of the axiate growth model and other definitive aspects of Chicago ecological theory, see Taylor, Walton and Young (1973): 110–14.

4 In Birmingham in the mid-1960s, they argued that the definitive 'housing classes' were '(1) the outright owner-occupiers (2) the council house tenants (3) the tenants of whole private housing (4) the lodging house proprietors and (5) the tenants of lodging-houses' (Rex and Moore, 1967: 36). Rex's later essay on the concept of the housing class (Rex 1973) was particularly concerned, on an analogy with some forms of Marxist theory, with the idea that particular class positions in the housing market might be associated with specific forms of consciousness, especially when thought in relation to the experience of being a West Indian or Asian immigrant confronting a public housing market dominated by representatives of the organized, white 'working class' of the host, colonial society.

5 In the same period, a parallel process of urban development was the steady emergence of cities on the western frontier, like Denver.

6 It is not even clear that many cities in the New World itself can effectively be understood in such terms. The applicability of the concentric zone model was examined in respect of Baltimore, Maryland, by Lander (1954) and rejected. None of the subsequent studies of urban forms or local cultures of New York,

San Francisco or Boston make use of Chicagoan analogies (For further discussion, see Bottoms 1994.) Understanding the built form of the major cities of Canada (Montreal, Toronto, Vancouver) or Australia (Brisbane, Melbourne, Sydney) is not much helped by the use of this model. But each of these cities contains a number of well-known, discrete and dispersed territories that are firmly identified in the cognitive map of the city used by local residents to identify the presence of sin, danger or, simply, the dangerous underclass.

7   Cf. for example, the street market that has now colonized the Moor in Sheffield, and required its pedestrianization. In the 1950s, this same street functioned as the central thoroughfare in that city for all public transport and private cars.

8   One of the best surviving examples of such a walled fortress town is Lucca, built up during the eleventh to fourteenth centuries on the basis of its silk trade, and enjoying complete independence until being subjugated by the neighbouring city of Pisa in 1314. Lucca's perimeter wall, with outlying rings of moats and earthworks, totalling over four kilometres, was continually consolidated for purposes of defence until the late sixteenth century, when it was transformed by the Bourbons into an artifact of the city's gardens. (Belford et al. 1990: 470–4).

9   Another effect of the 'Haussmannization' of Paris, widely understood at the time, was the way in which the creation of some dozen boulevards radiating out from the centre of Paris (like spokes on a wheel) contributed to the overall process of surveillance and social control of the urban population as whole, in easing quick entry by troops (and the gendarmerie) from the main thoroughfares into different areas and neighbourhoods.

10   The willingness and capacity of local police forces, as now organized, to intervene 'in the public interest' into particularly troubled local areas (in our own period, the multiply-deprived public housing estates of post-Fordist Europe) is a separate issue.

11   In Britain, the primary example of such a planned city, complete with a rational grid of highways and feeder roads, is Milton Keynes.

12   These accounts of the unseen violence of the patriarchal working-class household in the old industrial societies finds an echo in the spate of autobiographical novels on the gender order of the American South in the 1980s, most notably Alice Walker's *Color Purple*.

13   Further illustrations of women's strategic management of their husbands and other men in the household are to be found in Pat Barker's *Union Street* (1982) – based on the author's own experience, as a woman, of the mining villages of the north-east of England.

14   Throughout the 1970s and 1980s, there were increasing numbers of demands by young women in Canada for access to the facilities and minor leagues of Canadian ice hockey – campaigns which were given considerable purchase by the enactment of the Canadian Charter of Rights (see Gruneau and Whitson 1993: 168–73).

15   In Britain, throughout the early twentieth century, this point was usually underlined in women's discussions by reference to the routine absence of women's toilets in public places.

16   There has been a sudden emergence in the United States of a rather different literature of critical enquiry into the lived character of life in the typical American suburb – after the example of the cult movie, *Blue Velvet*, an exploration of the gap between 'appearances' and suppressed realities (see e.g.

Lefkowitz 1997). Some of the tensions in the private world of young people 'imprisoned' in the English suburb are explored in Richards (1994: ch. 8).

17 Martin Walker, 'Behind the Bars of Fortress Suburbia', *Observer*, 6 July 1997.

18 In his discussion of postmodern urban spaces in the United States, Peter Marcuse identifies five different varieties of walls or fortification – 'prison walls' (to prevent intrusive observation), (defensive) barricades, (aggressive) stockades, stucco walls (exuding status and wealth) and ramparts (signifying domination and power). He then argues that these different fortifications have an essentially ambivalent character that does not reduce in practice to these particular 'functions'. He is particularly interested in ways in which these fortifications introduced into particular sights (River Island, New York, or Harbour Point, Boston) work 'momentarily' as a kind of heritage or tourist gloss, concealing inequality (Marcuse 1995: passim).

19 The analogy between the gated communities of southern California and the fortress cities of Europe – especially their function in defending of the community against incursions and invasions from outsiders – was first suggested by a reading of T. Coraghessan Boyle's *The Tortilla Curtain*, a novelesque account of the nervous fortress community of Arroyo Blanco Estates, a fictitious suburban development south of Los Angeles (Coraghessan Boyle 1995).

20 One of the defining effects of the post-Fordist transformation on the character of cities is the radical modification of the role performed by the 'zone of transition' throughout the Fordist period, as a *temporary* port of call of a migrant population with more or less realistic aspirations to move on outwards to improved housing circumstances in the suburbs. Like the sink estate in the public market, these inner-city areas in the private market take on a role as an area of permanent occupation for their beleaguered residents, with few obvious or realistic routes available to alternative housing, except for determined individualists, looking at the possibility of a move into housing association property.

21 In Britain, in the late 1990s, this fascination with the underclass was evident, for example, in BBC Television's *Rab C. Nesbitt* but, much more morbidly, in the representations of problem families and disturbed, usually unemployed, young men in *Cracker* and other work of the Liverpool television playwright Jimmy McGovern. In the United States, the most famous televisual representation of a 'problem family' in the late 1980s and early 1990s was that provided in *Roseanne*.

22 As both David Harvey and Christopher Jencks have argued, the very idea of 'housing crisis' for many conservative-minded social commentators, especially in the United States, is equated with the emergence of public housing developments in the late 1950s and 1960s (Jencks 1984; D. Harvey 1994). In 1972, President Nixon celebrated the demolition of the modernist Pruit-Igoe housing project with the refrain that 'the housing crisis was over' (Harvey 1994: 361). For conservatives, the creation of such estates is now widely understood to produce unmanageable spaces which are beyond the capacity of public authority to maintain. The cycle of decline that inevitably emerges is evidence of the fact that essentially self-regarding human beings cannot effectively take ownership of shared or public facilities. This argument is a serious challenge for a purely liberal-humanist version of social housing, as an argument to provision within the private market. In the 1980s, the general argument about the unmanageability of vast stretches of public space found particular expression

in the development of theories of 'defensible space' (Newman 1972) – especially, the introduction of clear defining boundaries between public and private space on the perimeters of individual dwellings.

23 Philip Bassett, 'Jobless Analysis Highlights Splintering Labour Market', *Times*, 17 Sept. 1997.

24 See e.g. the special issue of *Newsweek* ('Are Cities Obsolete?'), 9 Sept. 1991.

25 'Police Fight "War" in French suburbs', *Guardian*, 31 Oct. 1995; 'Juppé Unveils his Plan to Save Blighted Suburbs', *Guardian*, 19 Jan. 1996.

26 'Negative equity' arose when houseowners found themselves actually making a loss in the housing market, in the specific sense of owing more on their mortgage than could be realized through the sale of the house. The negative equity crisis in England and Wales had its own negative effect on the labour market, in the sense of making it difficult for houseowners to move on into other areas of the country in furtherance of their employment and career prospects. For a period, unknown numbers of 'professional people' were forced into a weekend commuter existence between rented accommodation near their new employment and the houses they could not afford to sell.

27 Gardner and Sheppard's identification of the new malls as 'cathedrals' anticipates the developing preferences of the architects brought in by development companies to create such malls around a central nave, topped by a cupola, after the fashion of the *Duomo* in Florence (Gardner and Sheppard 1989).

28 On one estimate in 1990, there were a total of 25,000 shopping mall developments in the United States (*Guardian*, 26 Oct. 1990).

29 *Guardian*, 14 Sept. 1996.

30 Pressure from local authorities in Britain (representing the interests of existing town-centre business and employment) has generally been successful in limiting the numbers of mall developments granted planning permission by national Government. The last mall development given planning permission in the 1990s was the Trafford Centre in south Manchester, opening in the autumn of 1998.

31 The pioneering work on the idea of mental maps is that of Yi-Fu Tuan (1975), but there is a very creative use of them in the development of 'cultural geography' of cities by Peter Jackson (1989).

32 There is no limit in principle to the range of consumer products that could be marketed in these spaces: the Meadowhall Centre in Sheffield wants to include a casino in its plans for expansion.

33 We should, however, remember that these new urban spaces do contain many miles of highly controlled walkways, often demanding a particular, some would say postmodern, ability in the navigation of a new form of urban complexity.

34 Cf., for example, the level of maintenance and cleanliness of the New York subway and the Toronto and Montreal subways.

35 The conventional attribution in Britain of the term 'symbolic locations of crime' is to the report by Lord Justice Scarman into the Brixton riots in 1981 (Scarman 1982).

36 It does, of course, have to be said that the patterned character of crime was already very well understood in the early nineteenth century by enthusiasts for the newly developing techniques of statistical analysis – people like Adolphe Quetelet, André-Michel Guerry and Gabriel Tarde – whose interest in crime was alerted by the release by the Government of France of the first set of national criminal statistics, *La compte générale de l'administration de la justice*, in 1835.

37 We should, of course, confirm that we are not saying that our different respondents' use of space 'reduced', in some uniform or essential fashion, to the facts of gender, age, class or ethnicity.

38 In this interpretation of the relation of the hyper-ghetto and post-Fordist transformation, the Los Angeles riots of May 1992 (in which 55 people died and 600 buildings were burnt out or destroyed) are merely the first instance of what become an ongoing series of urban confrontations (cf. 'The Fire this Time', *Time* magazine, 11 May 1992). In the summers of 1996 and 1997, national and international press attention focused on levels of tensions and confrontation in St Petersburg, Florida, but informed commentators in the United States identify a vast number of potentially explosive instances of post-Fordist inequality and community implosion. There were also fears that the Los Angeles riots could easily be repeated, in a city in which little of the $6 million of government aid promised in 1992 had actually materialized (Christopher Reed, 'Unregenerated Los Angeles is Ready for the Fire Again', *Guardian*, 26 Apr. 1997).

39 Suicides among African-American males aged 15–24 (hitherto very much a minority activity amongst such men) rose by some 63 per cent between 1980 and 1993 (*Guardian*, 24 July 1996).

40 Sue-Ann Pressley, 'Homeless are Run out of Town', *Washington Post*, Jan. 1996.

41 This desire for distance in public space (being 'alongside' but not 'with' others making use of that space) is one of the themes informing Zygmunt Bauman's attempts to theorize different 'forms of togetherness' in what he sees to be a fragmented postmodern society (Bauman 1995: ch. 2).

42 For example, as late as 1989, an official rate of violent crime in the Western region of the USA of 754 offences per 100,000 inhabitants by comparison with 710 in the Northeast (including New York), 675 in Southern states and 528 in the Midwest (FBI, *Uniform Crime Rates*, 1989: 47, quoted in Siegel 1992: figure 4.1).

43 Dirk Johnson, 'Nice City's Nasty Distinction: Murders Soar in Minneapolis', *New York Times*, 30 June 1996.

44 Ian Katz, 'Dead End Streets', *Guardian*, 27 Aug. 1996.

Chapter 5 Fraudsters and Villains: The Private Temptations of Market Society

1 National Opinion Poll Survey, 1993, commissioned by HM Treasury and the London Stock Exchange.

2 Jeremy Hughes, press office, London Stock Exchange, private communication, 15 Jan. 1998.

3 Ibid.

4 The impact of technological change on job insecurity in particular occupations (bank tellers, supermarket cashiers, fast food providers) is an important research area in itself. Barclays Bank, for example, has reduced numbers of staff in the UK by 15 per cent in just five years. But in many regional post-Fordist labour markets, it is *only* highly insecure jobs that are on offer as alternatives to local hidden economies of crime (cf. the recent criminological literature on different localities in the United States: Bourgois (1995) on Harlem, New York City; Currie (1991) on 'Iron City' and 'Rivertown' in northern California; Jankowski (1991) on Boston, Los Angeles and New York;

MacLeod (1987) on an anonymous 'north-eastern city'; and Sullivan (1988) on Brooklyn).

5   The self-regulatory organizations created were the Investment Management Regulatory Organization (IMRO), the Life Assurance and Unit Trust Regulatory Organization (LAUTRO), the Personal Investment Authority (PIA) and the Securities and Futures Authority (SFA). These organizations were subjected to continuing critique by the Labour opposition in the British parliament during the early 1990s for their self-evident failure to identify and prevent a series of major financial frauds in the financial services fields (notably the 'Maxwell Pension Fund fraud' of 1991, the BCCI fraud of the same year and, finally and critically, the fatal frauds conducted within Barings financial house, revealed in 1995). In May 1998, the new British Government moved to establish a unified system for the oversight of financial services under the auspices of a reorganized and strengthened Securities and Investment Board.

6   In a chapter entitled 'Murderous Managers', Messerschmidt (1997) offers a fascinating account of the men in charge of the American space programme, and works outwards to a discussion of masculinism in the American engineering industry.

7   Michael Milken was the most famous example of these bright young professionals given an opportunity within the new global financial markets. He was offered employment by the highly reputed Wall Street brokerage of Drexel Burnham Lambert and rapidly promoted within it.

8   In June 1996, the Sumitoro Corporation of Japan reported it had lost some £1.6 billion as a result of fraudulent activity in the copper market by its trader Yasuo Hamanaka. The previous year, the Daiwabank of Japan had lost £680 million on transactions in US Treasury bonds, conducted by Toshihida Iguchi (Alex Brummer, 'Global Attack on Bank Fraud', *Guardian*, 31 Mar. 1997).

9   The latest example of such an inquiry by the Department of Trade and Industry in Britain was that undertaken into the Guinness take-over of Distillers in 1986. The report of this inquiry whose production was costed at £3.15 million – was published in November 1997, eleven years after the original event, and *inter alia* concluded that many of the extraordinary financial arrangements entered into by the core group orchestrating the take-over were international in character, involving investments (for example, by Ivan Boesky in the United States) which were beyond the purview of securities legislation in Britain and, in all likelihood, the United States itself.

10 There is a vast literature on the differential level and enforcement of legal and financial penalties on fraud (see e.g. Braithwaite, 1985; M. Clarke 1986; Levi 1987a: ch. 6; Snider 1982, 1987), which I do not have the space to explore here. Much of this literature tends to assume the existence, and potential capacity, of a unitary nation-state, working 'in partnership' with its criminal justice system and a system of financial regulation. This image or vision of the nation-state and its capacity to regulate contains a profoundly Fordist set of assumptions. This literature also probably over-rationalizes the actual capacity and sophistication of civil servants, accountants and police officers to make sense of the rapidity of change within the Post-Fordist market place.

11 Jonathan Freedland, 'Saint Michael', *Guardian*, 16 Nov. 1995.

12 A director of the Serious Fraud Office in Britain, Rosalind Wright, has argued, at the 1997 Cambridge Symposium on Economic Crime, for an end to the use of juries in fraud trials, and their replacement by a criminal tribunal staffed by professionals and judges. Her argument was almost entirely framed in terms of

the problem of the complexity of evidence that is often involved in such trials, along with the problems which confront the prosecuting agency if it tries (as the SFO did in the (unsuccessful) prosecution of Robert Maxwell's two sons in respect of the loss of the *Daily Mirror* pension fund) to simplify the evidence by presenting it in a series of discrete and separate 'sub-trials'. Ms Wright's arguments certainly make sense as a way of rectifying the SFO's uneven track record in respect of successful prosecutions, but it does have to be said that the domination of fraud trials in the future by professionals speaking in a private language might further undermine public trust and interest in such matters, and thereby undermine prospects for a democratically and publicly supported project to tackle the range and costs of major financial fraud.

13 Students of the long history of economic crime in Britain from the early days of industrialization to the late 1980s might begin with George Robb's excellent study of the prevalence and range of different forms of fraud in the period from 1845 to 1929 (Robb 1992), whilst beginning examination of subsequent developments in M. Clarke (1986) and Doig (1984) – in particular, Doig's excellent résumé of the career of John Poulson (the urban architect and developer based in Wakefield) between 1962 and his final trial in 1974 (1984: ch. 5). This book also contains a very valuable overview of patterns of minor fraud within local government circles in the 1960–80 period, reminding us of the importance of grasping the specificity of the forms of fraud in different historical moments.

14 I am very much aware that it would also be possible to draw up a map of the social locatedness of the different kinds of *victims* of financial crime (from victims of pension fraud scams to victims of price-fixing arrangements by private providers of domestic house or motor car insurance).

15 'New Figures Show Fraud is Still a Serious Problem', Press release, UK Benefits Agency, 31 July 1997.

16 David Brindle and David Hencke, 'Row over Bogus Disabled as Claims of 17 pc Benefit Fraud are Disputed', *Guardian*, 15 Jan. 1998.

17 Another important opportunity provided corporations operating in different countries is that of 'inter-jurisdictional allocation' of assets and liabilities, to maximize tax advantages in these different jurisdictions (Bird and Bream 1986). This strategy continues to confound advisers of national government revenue departments striving to obtain a just contribution to domestic exchequers.

18 Not least of these strategies was the diversion of spending that might otherwise have been subject to VAT onto the new National Lottery (Inland Revenue 1997: 10).

19 The advent of electronic trading, in part via the Internet, in 1997 threatens to replace the traditional trading floors of the Stock Exchanges of London, New York and Tokyo.

20 In 1996, the UK's National Criminal Intelligence Service handled over 14,000 individual reports of 'insider trading', nearly all involving very large sums of money. The NCIS reported, however, that requests for assistance from individual police forces in the UK were frequently assigned low priority, and also that coordinated action against insider trading was one of many matters which was being delayed by the failure of the European Commission, Parliament and elected political leadership to agree a mandate, under a new 'Third Pillar' of the European Union, to coordinate EUROPOL and other activity against financial crime (*Observer Business*, 31 Mar. 1996). (For a helpful précis of the struggle over the Third Pillar, see den Boer 1997.)

21 The prevalence of actually occurring inside-trades is almost impossible to ascertain on existing knowledge. Despite a number of initiatives taken in the early 1990s within Stock Exchanges to oversee the exchange of 'sensitive' commercial information (recording of telephone conversations, creation of 'Chinese walls' systems to limit access to information etc.) the Serious Fraud Office was reporting in 1996 that insider trading was 'as prevalent as ever'. The SFO had successfully prosecuted 213 out of 388 cases between 1988 and 1996, but there was still a widespread view, internationally, that London was 'soft on insider trading' (Lisa Buckingham, 'City Fails to Get Fraud Taped', *Guardian*, 2 Oct. 1996).

22 A report by KPMG Peat Marwick released in 1991 suggested that very large numbers of the cases of companies going into receivership in the first year of the new decade showed evidence of fraudulent representation of accounts and other manipulations (*Yorkshire Post*, 9 July 1991).

23 Referencing the involvement of 'respectable' people (or of people from 'respectable' occupations) in crime is to point to a long tradition of so-called exposé criminology, interested in uncovering the range and the severity of the social cost of white-collar crime (see e.g. Geis and Meier 1977; Geis and Stodtland 1980; Box 1983: ch. 2; Croall 1992). I will deal later with the scale of VAT fraud by businesspeople, especially those involved with cross-border transit, and also with some aspects of fraud committed by national and local government officials. There are also studies outlining serious and persistent fraud in a variety of 'respectable' professional occupations during the earlier Fordist period – for example, by physicians and other health professionals in a variety of billing 'scams' in the United States (Pontell et al. 1982) and in Canada (P. Wilson et al. 1986) by lawyers involved with national legal aid schemes, and by a variety of other professions, including, of course, the police themselves. Many of these occupations (like those involved in the health service in Britain) have been subject to fundamental reorganization around market principles in recent years (in the case of the local doctor's surgery, into 'fund-holders' within the service, operating within an internal market). It would be a subject of a separate research project to investigate the extent to which the coexistence of this market competition, independent fund-holding and generalized pressure for resources, as well as pressure on individual incomes, is more or less conducive to different forms of white-collar crime within the various professions, and to compare the scale of such expropriation from clients and patients with other processes taking place within entirely private health care delivery.

24 Roland Rudd, 'Mortgage Fraud Costs Taxpayers £3 billion a Year', *Independent on Sunday*, 24 Feb. 1991.

25 Ayres and Braithwaite (1992) have argued that the self-regulatory agencies launched in most developed capitalist societies during the years of market liberalization during the 1980s should not be interpreted as forms of deregulation, but rather as the 're-regulation' of the new regimes of delivery of financial services (see also Braithwaite and Ayres 1991). Certainly the scale and cost of the regulatory systems introduced should not be underestimated. In May 1992, for example, the financial services sector in the United Kingdom was estimated to be employing over 1,000 people as compliance officers and spending over £100 million a year on supervisory legislation (Bill Jamieson, 'The Price We Pay for Moral Hazard', *Sunday Telegraph*, 24 May 1992).

26 The problem of insurance fraud by agents and salespeople was already well known in countries, like Canada, with a differently regulated insurance environment. James Fleming's study of the insurance industry in Ontario is a valuable résumé of the range of tactics employed by insurance agents, in a competitive market environment, to sell insurance (for example, on a 'rebate' basis, against future income) to clients who cannot currently afford it (Fleming 1986). In this instance, the agent buys the insurance on behalf of the client, and then charges the client a premium above the level of inflation or interest. Fleming also provides an account of the practice of 'pyramid' selling (where agents secretly club together to buy a mass of policies, in order to earn the commission from the company on a previously agreed share of return). Some of these practices, and others, have been reported in Britain during the 1990s, but the specificity and range of insurance agent frauds in Britain and in the European Union at large are in need of close research.

27 Jeremy Hughes, press office, the London Stock Exchange (private communication).

28 Lisa Vaughan, 'Credit Card Fraud Costs Barclays £25 million', *Independent*, 1 Mar. 1991.

29 Adam Raphael, 'Credit Card Fraud: Little Interest from the Banks', *Observer*, 28 Apr. 1991.

30 Neasa McErlean, 'Card Sharps Prompt New Identity Crisis', *Observer*, 21 July 1996.

31 James Meikie, 'CD and Cassette Pirates "Skim off" £3 billion a Year', *Guardian*, 19 Sept. 1997.

32 Larry Elliott, 'UK Gangs Take £300 million Market in Brand Fakes', *Guardian*, 12 Jan. 1998.

33 The editing of Edwin Sutherland's original manuscript was demanded by the publisher, Dryden Press. Dryden's legal counsel had advised this publishing company that it might be liable to damages on the grounds that the book indicted a large number of well-known companies in the United States as 'criminal'. After much soul-searching and discussion, Sutherland acceded to Dryden's request and the censored version of *White Collar Crime* remained in print for more than thirty years (Geis and Goff 1983: x–xi). Only in 1983 were Gilbert Geis and Colin Goff able to arrange for the publication, by Yale University Press, of 'the uncut version' in which the various corporations, and some individuals, who had been accused by Sutherland of different forms of white-collar crime – which in this text Sutherland explained to be serious in its costs and effects – were named.

34 Sutherland's belief in the possibility of a regulated and less criminogenic capitalism was identified by one critic in the 1970s as *ideological*, in the specific (traditionally Marxist) sense that it advanced a misleading account (or implicit analysis) of the essential character of American capitalism. The vision of a free market society which was threatened by the *external* threat from white-collar crime rested on a conception of an 'imaginary social order', a just capitalist society, open to all (with several million shareholders), engaging in market competition in an essentially civilized and orderly fashion (Pearce 1973, 1976). For this commentator, and for others (D. Gordon 1980), this separation out of 'crime' from 'capitalism' was an ideological deceit.

35 Perhaps the most dramatic example of the offshore bank haven in the 1980s was the Cayman Islands where, according to Blum, there had been only two banks in 1964. By 1987, the islands were home to 360 branches of foreign banks

and ran postal addresses (box numbers) for over 8,000 registered companies. By 1987, the islands also had 'more telex machines *per capita* than any other country in the world' (Blum 1984: 22). Other offshore banking havens serving the United States in the late 1980s included Panama and the Dutch Antilles. The concept of an 'offshore haven' does not necessarily involve small islands off the coast of larger tax jurisdictions, though the Isle of Man, Guernsey and Jersey have become increasingly important banking havens off the shores of the United Kingdom (as well as France and Spain) during the 1990s. The most significant 'offshore havens' for the European Union at large (precisely because they are outside the jurisdiction of the EU) are Andorra, Liechtenstein, Gibraltar, and, most importantly of all, Switzerland. In 1995, the European Union finally acceded, amidst great controversy, to a proposal to designate Trieste as 'an international financial and insurance services centre' embracing a whole series of tax breaks and concessions – with a view to the stimulation of trade with Central and Eastern Europe (John Hooper, 'No Sanctuary in Tax Havens', *Guardian*, 18 Aug. 1997). The future role of Trieste, as an entrepôt between Eastern Europe and the West, and a key locale in the enlargement of the EU, will bear close observation by European criminologists as much as by other observers.

36   The increasing commerce of transnational licit business with local market enterprise of uncertain origins is most obvious in Russia and the old Soviet republics, but the issue is in no sense confined to that region of the world.

37   The importance of bribes in the international arms industry was underlined in the United Kingdom by revelations in 1994 regarding the activities of a civil servant in the Ministry of Defence, Gordon Foley, who was eventually found guilty of receiving a minimum of £1.5 million of personal bribes from British, German and Italian arms companies. Future analysis of the routine, close relationships between the civil service and arms companies should focus on the key role played by the 'middlemen' (entrepreneurs positioning themselves to act as negotiators of all such deals). The commissions earned in this way by Mr Mark Thatcher in the early 1990s are estimated to have amounted on individual deals to some £12 million (Peter Koenig, 'Middle Men', *Observer*, 16 Oct. 1994). These business deals may not have involved what students of economic crime would identify as fraud (in that they may not involve infraction of any identifiable body of criminal law). But this then raises, in rather stark and unmistakable a fashion, the relationship between forms of fast-moving 'realistic' business practice in the new global market, and the idea of a criminology of human rights (as distinct from a criminology interested only in the spheres of strict illegality).

38   One of the annual publications of the British Government, routinely released to little public response, is the *Report of the Committee of Public Accounts into Fraud and Irregularities at Defence Establishments*. The average amount of fraud revealed in such reports during the 1990s has been in the order of £1 million a year.

39   The $750 million contract for the building of the Turkwel Gorge dam in Kenya, for example, was awarded to a French company in 1986 without competitive bidding. Subsequent inquiries by a delegate of the European Commission suggested that the costs of the turbines and other key infrastructural elements of this dam cost twice the amount they should have in a competitive bidding situation (Nicholas Moss, 'Who Bribes Wins', *European*, 11–17 Dec. 1997).

40 Mark Atkinson and Dan Atkinson, 'The Bung Bang', *Guardian*, 13 Dec. 1997.

41 Not the least of the analytical considerations involved in this reappraisal of Sutherland is his assumption that there was a clear consensus in the dominant culture of the United States in the 1940s as to the proper and respectable conduct of business practice (his argument is that departure from these practices was learnt in particular and specific inter-actional contingencies – through 'differential association' – *against* the overall prescriptions of the dominant culture). A really important issue in the febrile post-Fordist world of the late 1990s is what kind of business practices are now dominant and acceptable. The developing interest in the margins of the business world in ideas of 'ethical business' may be a symptom of a larger problem.

42 McIntosh's analysis of the forms of professional and organized crime in Fordist Britain can be understood as a much more systematic representation of the relationship between these forms of crime and local labour markets, neighbourhood cultures and family relationships, as confirmed in various classic journalistic investigations (Borrell and Cashinella 1975; Campbell 1996).

43 This feature of the British criminal underworld in the post-Fordist period has been the subject of some inventive reinterpretation in recent years, as commentators conjure up a nostalgic image, for example, of the Kray brothers' activities in Bethnal Green and the broader East End of London as an exercise in social civics. Similar processes of romantic re-representation have also been evident in some discussions of the activities of the heads of the drug-cartels of Medellin and Cali in Colombia.

44 For example, the smuggling of uncensored Danish pornography into Britain in the 1970s was initiated by local criminal entrepreneurs in Britain, in response to local demand for what was then a scarce product on the British market, rather than being the result of any internationally active criminal syndicate or even of any criminal organization headquartered near the point of production of the desired market product in Denmark.

45 The 'Welfare to Work' programmes introduced by the British Government in June 1997 outline four labour market options for unemployed young people (aged 16 to 21). In order to continue being entitled to payment of the State benefit (the Job Seekers' Allowance), young people must participate in six months' employment in the private sector (employment which would be subsidized by the Government to the level of £60 per week (or £75 in the case of young people who have been unemployed for over a year); six months' voluntary work 'in the community', six months on an environmental task force, or they must return into full-time education (in a community college). Some 250,000 young people were identified as being subject to this new regime of work-related benefits. The spread of different types of 'welfare-to-work' programmes in North America and Europe ought to be the subject of a separate study. The 'welfare-to-work' programme introduced by the newly elected Government of France in August 1997, for example, is far less coercive, and far more financially generous, than the British equivalent. The Ministry of Labour, headed by Mme Martine Aubry, announced that it would be creating twenty-two new employment categories, notably in community service, which would all be subject to Government subsidy, with further support being invited from local councils, charities and business associations. Some 350,000 new positions were envisaged, all paid at the national minimum wage of £700 a month.

46 I pay homage here to the late Ken Pryce, a young sociologist of Anglo-Caribbean background, who met his death attempting to follow up his work on inner-city life in Bristol (Pryce 1979) by following in the steps of Charlie Nicholl in *The Fruit Palace* (1986) and exploring the character of the international drug business in British Guyana and the surrounding region.

Chapter 6 Lethal Markets: The Legal and Illegal Economies in Firearms

1 From the perspective I want to argue in this chapter – on the relationship between 'risk' and everyday life in free market society, the gun is not the only – or indeed the essential – lethal instrument. The use of knives in personal assaults often attracts considerable attention in media reports (especially when the knives are used during intrusions into schools, as they were in two major incidents in Britain in 1995 and 1996), and especially when the knife is accorded more extraordinary definition – for example, as 'a machete'.

2 In the United States, of course, the scale of firearms ownership (on some estimates, equivalent to one firearm per household) is less easily ignored, in this sense, and the size and significance of the 'legitimate' firearms trade (i.e. of the *market* in firearms) more widely understood.

3 These knives were the subject of a sustained moral panic in Britain in 1995, resulting in the passage of the Dangerous Weapons Act in 1996, prohibiting the sale of a range of different kinds of knives to 'under-age consumers'.

4 It has rarely been more clearly put than in the introduction contributed by Brig. Gen. J. B. Sweet (Ret.) to the National Rifle Association's *The Book of Rifles*: 'The ability to shoot a rifle is an American tradition. Our country was established and its boundaries expanded westward by men with rifles in their hands. The rifle gave the settlers protection against marauding Indians and other foes, and was an important means of securing food for the pioneer family' (Smith and Smith 1948: i).

5 The Colt 45 was a development from the prototype revolver invented by the American Samuel Colt in 1835, thus producing the first handguns capable of shooting five shots in one loading. The Colt 45 (.45 calibre) as such was not developed until 1873 but it became the standard sidearm of the US Cavalry until 1890, and was copied by British and American arms manufacturers (Rosa and May 1976: 49).

6 The Winchester first emerged in 1866, but the specific type that is claimed as 'the Gun that won the West', the Winchester '73, was not available until 1873. Specialist historians claim that Custer's Last Stand, at Little Big Horn in 1876, would have been even more prolonged had more Winchesters been available, instead of the 'defective Springfield carbine which jammed and overheated' (Rosa and May 1976: 73).

7 The roll-call for such incidents during the 1980s and 1990s would include the murder of twenty-one people in a McDonald's restaurant in San Ysidro, California (July 1983), the murder of six people and the wounding of eight others in a law office in San Francisco, by Gian Ferri, a local mortgage broker, wielding a 9 mm Uzi machine-gun and a .45 calibre semi-automatic pistol (July 1984); and a total of three massacres in 1989: in May, in a supermarket in Palm Bay, Florida, when six people died; in September, when Patrick Purdy killed six elementary school children and wounded twenty-nine others in Stockton, California; and, in the same month, the killing by Joseph Wesbecker, using an

AK-47 assault rifle, of seven people, with fifteen others wounded in a printing plant in Louisville, Kentucky. In August 1991, an unemployed seaman, George Hennard, killed twenty-two people in a crowded restaurant in Killen, Texas, and in August 1993 a further four people were killed, and eight wounded, in an attack by a 22-year-old young man, again in a restaurant, in Fayetteville, North Carolina. In October 1991, meeting the day after the Palm Bay massacre, the US House of Representatives voted 247–177 against a measure that would have banned thirteen assault weapons. In the early 1990s, however, opinion polls in America suggested that about 40 per cent of Americans would support a ban on private ownership of handguns (about half the proportion of the British population interviewed by national newspapers in 1996; Kleck 1991: 9). Some 25 per cent of Americans opposed any systems of firearms registration *per se.*

8   Formed in 1871 by two senior army officers in New York State as a club for people who were interested in improving their marksmanship, the National Rifle Association has subsequently grown and changed complexion, campaigning very publicly against each and every attempt to control the private ownership of firearms. It is now headquartered in Virginia, close to the corridors of power in Washington, DC, and has increased its membership from 1 million in the mid-1970s to some 3.3 million in the mid-1990s (Spitzer 1995).

9   This is one reason, amongst others, why so little attention has been paid in American debates to the seminal work of Arthur Kellerman and his associates into the widespread but different dangers associated with firearms ownership in the domestic sphere in America (accidents, suicides, use of firearms in domestic violence etc.). One of Kellerman's recent controlled studies also shows that 'homes where guns are kept are almost three times more likely to be the scene of a homicide than comparable homes without guns, even after the independent effects of victim-age, sex, race, neighbourhood, previous family violence, anyone using drugs, and any other history of previous arrests were taken into consideration' (Kellerman 1994, summarizing Kellerman et al. 1993).

10 See e.g. the special issue of the *Tennessee Law Review* (spring 1995) dedicated to the Standard Model.

11 For an extended critique of the Standard Model argument (especially with respect to the idea of the people as 'a standing army') see Gary Wills 'The Right to Bear Arms', *New York Review of Books*, 21 Sept. 1995: 62–73.

12 There are actually many different examples of civic provision by public authorities in the United States (from the National Parks themselves to the network of superb museums provided in many cities and towns) – but it is instructive as to how infrequently these public amenities and enhancements of local quality of life are attributed to 'the State', at either local or national level.

13 The 51-day siege of the Branch Davidian Cult's compound in Waco, Texas, by the officers of the Bureau of Alcohol, Firearms and Tobacco was ended on 19 April 1993, with the loss of seventy lives.

14 Though the Brady Bill makes the sale of handguns to juveniles illegal, there is widespread evidence of thriving networks in troubled areas of American cities of 'straw purchasers' – adults who will buy firearms in the local dealership for others at a fee.

15   One such survey in Virginia in 1995 revealed that 18 per cent of all adult inmates, and 24 per cent of all juveniles, had had possession of a stolen firearm (Zawitz 1996: 3).

16   The massacre at Dunblane, Scotland, in March 1996 involved the shooting-down of sixteen infants and their teacher in the gymnasium of their school. The murderer, who finally turned one of his four guns on himself, was Thomas Hamilton, a fully-licensed firearms owner.

17   The rapid passage of the 1921 Firearms Act has also been interpreted by some commentators as involving a fear of revolution by armed sections of the British working class. There is very little evidence for this kind of syndicalist nostalgia: the firearms in use on the street in 1919–20 were not characteristically held by the leading cadres of the British Communist Party, so much as they were carried, in case of trouble, by young men who were likely to encounter trouble.

18   The 1988 Firearms (Amendment) Act was a consequence of the massacre of sixteen people, and the wounding of eleven others, by Michael Ryan, a 27-year-old gun collector, in the small town of Hungerford, Berkshire, on 19 August 1987. The central provision was to extend the class of prohibited weapons to include pump-action rifles and shotguns and smooth-bore revolvers (both of which had been used by Ryan), and also rocket launchers and mortars, explosive shells, bombs, and rockets. In an official pamphlet released at the time, the Home Office explained that it was not moving to prohibit private ownership of handguns, or their retention at home, on the grounds that 'the great majority of firearms and shotgun certificate holders are responsible individuals who pose no threat to public safety' (Home Office, *The Control of Firearms in Britain*, 60/89 (February 1989).

19   The 'Rattening Outrages' in Sheffield in 1866 were the nearest exception, involving as they did the placing of gunpowder down the chimneys of saw- and steel-grinders who refused to join the union (hence, 'blacklegs'). Earlier instances of popular agitation or labour organizing had, of course, met with violent response, but with authority making use of its preferred weaponry, the sabre (perhaps the best example being the Peterloo Massacre of 1819 in Manchester, when eleven handloom-weavers were killed and several hundred injured, as a result of a charge by the part-time militia, the Manchester Yeomanry).

20   One expression of this was the statement by the Metropolitan Commissioner of Police, Sir Paul Condon, on taking up his post in 1993, to the effect that 'a creeping process' was in progress which would result in police officers in Britain carrying arms as a routine matter *within ten years* (*Independent on Sunday*, 20 June 1993).

21   The journalist Peter Beaumont reported in some detail in 1993 on the prevalence of combat gear, the vocabulary of violence and particular guns' 'celebrity status' in a range of gun clubs he visited in the South of England ('Dressed to Kill – Just for Thrills', *Observer*, 12 Sept. 1993).

22   The reported circulation of gun magazines in Britain in March 1996 was as follows: *Sporting Gun*, 31,600 monthly; *Target Gun*, 28,000; *Gun Mart*, 27,500; *Shooting Gazette*, 25,000; *Guns and Shooting*, 22,500; *Air Gunner*, 22,500 and *Guns Review*, 20,000. Publishers of the UK gun magazines claim that these magazines are read by people wanting to use guns 'for sport', where the American magazines are organized significantly around the 'self-protection market'.

23 The abolition of border controls did not happen in 1992, and the Schengen project now looks to be significantly threatened by France's withdrawal in 1995 from the Schengen Agreement.

24 In August 1993, the Metropolitan Police uncovered a shipment of seventeen smuggled firearms, which included three Israeli Uzi machine guns. Much larger consignments were intercepted during 1994, 1995 and 1996, including one consignment of over 40 machine guns intercepted in 1996 at Teesport docks.

25 The combined global total of arms sales was reported by the Stockholm International Peace Research Institute as having declined by 2 per cent in 1994, following on from a decline of 6 per cent the previous year (Sköns and Gill, 1996: 411). More recent reports suggest that there has been a significant recovery in the small-arms market.

26 The killings at the University of Montreal were not the first of such events in Canada in the 1980s: in May 1983, three people were killed and thirteen others wounded in the main building of the Province of Quebec's National Assembly by M. Dennis Lortie. The killings committed by Marc Lepine six years later acted as confirmation in the imagination of Canadians that the problem of lethal firearms in Canada extended beyond an individual incident.

27 In August 1987, twenty-four people were shot, and six killed, by a lone but heavily armed gunman, in Clifton Hill, a residential area north of Melbourne city centre.

28 In August 1991, 33-year-old Wade Frankum, a part-time cab-driver, killed seven people in Sydney, using a Chinese 7.62 mm self-loading assault rifle.

29 In the Australian case, the overall importance of the dramatic incidents, especially the massacres, in influencing public opinion is clear. The actual number (and rate) of firearms deaths in Australia had declined quite significantly in the ten years to 1993 – from an overall total of 93 fatal assaults in 1983 (0.60 per 100,000) to 64 (0.36) in 1993 – as had, also, the number of accidents involving firearms and the number of suicides involving firearms (Mukherjee and Dagger 1995).

30 Other measures in the Australian gun control legislation of 1996 include a ban on domestic violence offenders holding a gun licence for five years; a ban on all private sales of guns between citizens; a banning of all semi-automatic and pump action shotguns (except for farmers who can prove they have a vermin problem that exceeds the capacity of a bolt-action rifle or shotgun). Target shooting with semi-automatics was banned.

31 I have in mind the success of the Snowdrop Petition (formed by parents from Dunblane primary school) and the Gun Control Network in Britain in persuading the new Government to promote legislation in the Firearms (Amendment) Act of 1997, as revised in 1998, for a complete ban on the ownership of handguns by private individuals.

Chapter 7 The Market in Social Control

1 US Department of Justice, Bureau of Statistics (The Sentencing Project, 1997).

2 US Department of Justice, *Americans Behind Bars: U.S. and International Use of Incarceration 1995* Washington DC: The Sentencing Project 1997 (www.sproject.com/press-12.htm).

3 US Department of Justice, *Facts about Prisons and Prisoners* Washington DC: The Sentencing Project, 1997.

4   *NACRO Criminal Justice Digest*, 94 (Oct. 1997), 2, 9.

5   In the United States, there was often an explicit reference in this radical prison literature to the role played by the prison in the deterrent control of the subordinate black population within 'White America'. This approach was often following up the writings produced in prison by George Jackson, the 'Soledad Brother' as well as Malcolm X, the leader of the Black Muslims (Jackson 1970). The tradition of identifying the US prison's specific role in racial repression has a lineage going back to the work of Du Bois.

6   In ch. 10 of *Punishment and Social Structure*, Rusche and Kirchheimer present some selected evidence as to the marked increase in the use of the fine by the courts in different European countries during the period from 1880 to the early 1930s, and also point to the ways in which some jurisdictions in the 1930s began to allow for the payment of fines by instalment, in order to avoid crowding prisons with fine-defaulters.

7   This version of 'rehabilitation' in prison settings was particularly marked during periods of expansion in the provision of formal education, including, as in the 1960s in Britain, Canada and other societies, of education delivered in prison to higher and further education level.

8   These two 'functions' were subsequently identified by Jankovic (1977) as the 'severity' and 'utility' hypotheses implicit within the Rusche–Kirchheimer text. Jankovic then proceeded to operationalize these hypotheses against the unemployment and imprisonment rates in the United States for the period 1926 to 1974. The 'utility hypothesis' was not supported, but there was significant statistical support for there being a 'direct' relationship between unemployment rate and imprisonment rates, 'independent of changes in criminal activity' (Jankovic 1977: 28).

9   There are different ways of 'reading Rusche', not least (as I argue later) in respect of the interest shown in *Punishment and Social Structure* in the specific role that penal policy can play in the reconstruction and authoritative (not to say repressive) affirmation of ideas of conforming citizenship in particular societies at particular times (e.g. Fascist Germany in the 1930s). There is no doubt this theme would have informed the manuscript which Rusche had written, in his native German, on the evolution of Nazi penal policy – a manuscript which is thought to have been lost at sea in 1940 when the boat carrying Rusche and others, in process of evacuation from wartime Britain as an alien, was sunk by a U-boat (Melossi 1980).

10   It is not clear here whether Garland is wanting to argue a kind of Weberian argument, that the creation of the penal estate is the creation of a public bureaucracy with an inherent tendency to grow and expand; if so, this is open to the objection that many a manager of prison with a personal commitment to rehabilitation and reform has wanted to try and limit the expansion of the prison population.

11   The evidence is that chs 9–13 were written by Kirchheimer, in exile (with many other members of the Frankfurt Institute for Social Research) in New York.

12   Commentators on the sociology of punishment like David Garland (1990) and Adrian Howe (1994) pay attention to the claims that can be made for Emile Durkheim, especially in terms of his essay 'Two Laws of Penal Evolution' as the pioneering figure in the development of a specifically sociological account of the relation between the social formation and penality. Durkheim wanted to argue that the development from 'mechanical solidarity' to 'organic solidarity' would be accompanied by the replacement of 'repressive (penal) law' by

restitutive (civil) law. He also anticipated that increased social complexity would mean that individualistic conceptions of crime (crimes against the person) would increasingly replace collective concepts (like blasphemy or sacrilege). Attempts to identify supporting evidence for such general logics have not been conclusive (Spitzer 1975), and commentators have generally rejected the teleological notion of 'moral evolution', not least in the light of the lessons of twentieth-century history.

13 The Sentencing Project Briefing Sheet (1997), Washington DC: Department of Justice.

14 The best-known example of such an intervention was Ken Kesey's *One Flew over the Cuckoo's Nest* (Kesey 1962), later achieving even greater fame as a movie starring Jack Nicholson.

15 The familiar popular refrains seem to involve a subversion of the ideas of Norbert Elias, a notion that the 'civilizing process' has gone into reverse – coupled with some version of the Kelling and Wilson thesis – i.e. that there is no longer anyone looking after public spaces and delimiting the boundaries of interpersonal behaviour.

16 This emphasis on the 'reconstitution' of modernist industrial society, and of all the key organizations and associations, is central to other post-Foucauldian approaches, especially within the postmodern frame of reference. Stuart Henry and Dragan Milanovic have published an impressive outline of such an enterprise, committed to the analysis of individual acts of crime as being the result of meaningful action, constructed in and through the larger frames of culture and society (Henry and Milanovic 1996). I share that commitment, whilst wanting to situate the condition and character of this culture and set of social relations against the history of its political economy.

17 In theorizing, in the same essay, that 'capital that is not legal property is a contradiction that sets very definite limits to its function as capital', Hirst wanted to downplay the role of 'illegal' or 'illicit' enterprise in the development of capitalist markets – a perspective I have already questioned so far as contemporary market society is concerned in ch. 6. Jachcel (1977) develops a powerful argument for the critical role of piracy in the development of mercantile capitalism.

18 It is also clear, however, that Charles Logan would not recognize the description of punishment's public and educative purposes as outlined by Garland and Sparks. Nils Christie has understood how Logan's consequentialist arguments for the privatization of prisons run in parallel with a radically libertarian version of the idea of a contract between strong individuals and a very minimalist State, as found in the work of Robert Nozick (1974). The idea of rights in this approach are individual rather than 'public-collective' (Christie 1993: 101), and more firmly lodged in the political culture of the United States, according to Christie, than to 'Europe'.

19 Corrections Corporation of America, Letter to Shareholders, 24 July 1997 (http//www.streetlink.com/cxc).

20 http//www.wackenhut.com/wcc-org.htm.

21 Nick Cohen, 'Much Profit in a Prison', *Independent on Sunday*, 5 Sept. 1993.

22 Alan Travis, 'Howard Speeds Change to Private Jails', *Guardian*, 3 Sept. 1993.

23 The growth of the private prison business (and other aspects of its practices, including its capacity to hit its targets in respect of cost-cutting) is monitored

continually by the UK-based Prison Reform Trust's monthly prison privatization reports (on the internet at http//www.penlex.org.uk/propre14.html).

24   There is increasing interest amongst international political economists in the
variety of different types of post-Fordist capitalist economies, especially in
regard to different means of production and different chains of distribution (cf.
Harvey and Quilley 1997).

25   Samples of the Pre-employment Screening Reports which can be prepared for
private employers by the Wackenhut National Research Center are available
on the internet at http//www.wnrc/com/sample.html.

26   In the event, financial constraints on the Conservative Government restricted
the number of new private jails built in England and Wales in this period to
four: Blakenhurst (May 1993), Buckley Hall (December 1994), Doncaster
(June 1994) and Wolds (April 1992). In June 1997, the new Home Secretary in
Britain, Mr Jack Straw, announced that for operational and financial reasons
'he had no alternative' but to proceed with the previous administration's plans
for two further private prisons – an 800-place category B institution at Salford
in Greater Manchester and a young offender institution to be built near
Bristol.

27   Mr Adam Sampson, Deputy Director of the Prison Reform Trust in Britain,
noted how 'overnight we have become leaders in penal capitalism' (quoted in
Nick Cohen, 'Much Profit in a Prison', *Independent on Sunday*, 5 Sept. 1993).

28   Considerable anxiety has been provoked in many of these familiar penal
reform circles by the increasing influence played by supporters of prison
privatization in national and international conferences on the prison. The role
of Professor Charles Thomas's Private Prisons Project, based at the University
of Florida, in the advance of private prisons (for example, at an industry-
sponsored conference at the Australian Institute of Criminology in July 1997)
has been a subject of widespread concern.

29   The Prison Reform Trust *The Good Jail Guide*, *Guardian*, 14 Sept. 1994.

30   Duncan Campbell, 'The Food in Prison was Seen as Part of the Punishment',
Guardian, 24 Aug. 1993.

31   One of the intriguing ironies in the receipt, within professional criminology, of
the famous 'Broken Windows' article by the two conservative scholars, James
Q. Wilson and George Kelling, is the refusal to theorize the broader origins of
the emergence of such untended and unsupervised spaces in American cities as
an expression of the underdevelopment of a *universal* sense of civic responsibility in American cities, i.e. a sense of local city council having responsibility
pro bono publico for the maintenance and custodianship of public space, very
broadly defined. This kind of commitment is *not*, it hardly needs to be said, a
mark of contemporary conservative thinking in America.

Chapter 8 Crime in the Future(s) Market

1   The exception to this generalization in the social sciences and cultural studies
is the mushrooming literature in postmodern theory. My own account, in chs 1
and 2, of the 'nine crises at the end of the twentieth century' involves a sense of
deep crisis in the culture of modern societies, but I have been concerned in the
body of this text to be open to the ways in which this crisis is, in part, an
expression of the 'commodification' of culture involved in the wholesale
marketization of Fordist society (for example, its public broadcasting media).
Postmodern analysis does not in itself yield what we could call a compre-

hensive sociology of everyday life in market society, so much as it offers more or less insightful appraisal of the various texts thrown up as commodities in the entertainment, advertising and other consumer market places.

2 For my own statement of position in the first years of the transition in Britain, see Taylor (1981), and for a further outline of some questions raised about the realist project as it had developed in the 1980s, see Taylor (1992).

3 I do not here deny the ways in which the 'fear of crime' has taken on a life of its own (i.e. almost as a 'free-floating' signifier) in contemporary mass media representation – a routinely available resource of easily available stories by journalists trading in the everyday anxiety of life in market society (Kidd-Hewitt and Osborne 1995; McRobbie and Thornton 1995). There may be some advantage, indeed, in thinking of the 'crimino-legal' complex described by Alison Young (1996) as being a particular kind of supplier of product in a particular kind of 'market' – that is, 'consumption market' driven by an unconscious need for confirmation of a felt condition of anxiety.

4 Another aspect of the Square of Crime analytical strategy, of course, is that it provides the grounds on which other theoretical or empirical work within criminology can be indicted for its 'partiality'.

5 This kind of critique of State initiative was evident, for example, in the report completed by M. Gilbert Bonnemaison into youth crime and disorder on residualized housing estates in France in the early 1980s. The outcome of the Bonnemaison Report was the launch of coordinated and multifaceted programmes directed at reversing 'social exclusion' on a number of connected fronts (labour market, housing, leisure and play spaces). However well coordinated these initiatives may have been, they clearly did not 'solve' the problem of unemployment, in particular, as the outbreak of disorder in the *banlieux* during the 1990s confirms. The struggle over unemployment in France in the late 1990s now presents itself as a continuing struggle between Statist and market conceptions and strategies for employment-protection and job-creation in a global market place.

6 The issue of the *European* newspaper for 19–25 Jan. 1998, for example, contains advertisements for over 25 offshore companies, including one company offering ready-made facilities in the Bahamas, British Virgin Islands, Belize, the Cayman Islands, Delaware, Nevis, Panama, Isle of Man, Ireland, Liberia, Mauritius, Hong Kong, Seychelles, Turks and Caicos Islands, and Western Samoa. This company, the Overseas Company Registration Agents Ltd. operates its own offices in Luxembourg, Liechtenstein, Finland, Sweden, Lithuania, Hungary, Poland, Greece, Cyprus, Madeira, Mauritius, Seychelles, Singapore, Hong Kong, the People's Republic of China and the United States, advising locally interested parties on the establishment of shell companies 'in the world's low-tax areas'.

7 For example, the fraudulent theft from the *Daily Mirror* pensioners by Robert Maxwell.

8 For example, as was evident in the extraordinarily hypocritical response of citizens of market society in the aftermath of the death of Princess Diana to the activities of the 'paparazzi' working to feed the world's press, in its unceasing search for 'newsproduct'.

9 For example, the salaries which the chairmen of the newly privatized utility companies in Britain quickly awarded themselves in the early 1990s. So also is

there some significant popular ambivalence with respect to the transfer payments and salaries paid to super-star footballers in the marketized British football, and to equivalent sports-stars in North America.

10 I want to note here how the conflict between 'conformity' and 'innovation' in many specific labour market locales has been problematized even further by the accelerating introduction of computer technology, and the gulf that has opened up between senior staff without knowledge and skill in the use of such technology and a junior staff which has. It is beyond the scope of this text to examine this particular form of market-conflict, though I do want to reference the idea that this conflict within the legitimate market place has an intriguing parallel in illegitimate local markets, where young apprentices in local craft-criminal organizations often exhibit far greater knowledge about the capacity of individual computer hardware than do the front-line troops of the local police forces themselves. The uneven development of computer knowledge in the flexible markets of local crime, and the relatively inflexible labour markets of policing and other parts of the public sector in market society, is an important research area in its own right.

11 This obfuscation of the clear distinction between 'legitimate' and 'illegitimate' business activity in market society is also apparent, of course, as discussed in ch. 5, in the sphere of financial services, insurance and banking.

12 One notable exception to this generalization is La Fondation d'Entreprise pour la Citoyenneté – the organization created in Paris in 1994 by the current Chief of Security of the Paris Metro, Gérard d'Andrea – which has succeeded in involving young men in the most residualized of estates in crime-prevention and community safety schemes based around the stations of the Metro system.

13 I have argued elsewhere (Taylor 1997b) that we can think of this reorganization of policing and related European institutions on an analogy with Jürgen Habermas's application of Claus Offe's structural models of the State in order to understand the three levels, or arenas, of political communication in a 'communication society' (Habermas 1989). In this perspective, the police forces of Europe may be thought of as second-order 'elites' operating between the first elites of 'Europe' (the Commission, major transnational 'organized' interests) and 'third-order' 'elites' (individual nation-states, individual local authorities, and other bodies that may claim to represent the interests of a local population within the EU).

BIBLIOGRAPHY

Åkerström, Malin (1994) *Crooks and Squares: Lifestyles of Thieves and Addicts in Comparison to Conventional People* New Brunswick, NJ: Transaction Books

Albert, Michael (1993) *Capitalism versus Capitalism: How America's Obsession with Individual Achievement and Short Term Profit has Led it to Collapse* Boston: IWEW

Alcohol Concern (1997) *Measures for Measures: A Framework for Alcohol Policy* London: Alcohol Concern

Amin, Ash (ed.) (1994) *Post-Fordism: A Reader* Oxford: Blackwell Publishers

Anderson, Benedict (1983) *Imagined Communities: Reflections on the Origin and Spread of Nationalism* London: Verso

Anderson, Digby (ed.) (1992) *The Loss of Virtue: Moral Confusion and Social Disorder in Britain and America* London: Social Affairs Unit

Anderson, Simon; Kinsey, Richard, Loader, Ian and Smith, Connie (1994) *Cautionary Tales: Young People, Crime and Policing in Edinburgh* Aldershot: Edinburgh

Appadurai, Arjun (1996) *Modernity at Large* Minneapolis: University of Minnesota Press

Arantes, Antonio (1996) 'The War of Places: symbolic boundaries and liminalities in urban space' *Theory, Culture and Society* 13(4): 81–92

Arlacchi, Pino (1986) *Mafia Business: The Mafia Ethic and the Spirit of Capitalism* London: Verso

Aronowitz, Alexis (1994) 'A Comparative Study of Hate Crime: legislative, judicial and social responses in Germany and the United States' *European Journal on Criminal Policy and Research* 2(3): 39–64

Aronowitz, Stanley (1973) *False Promises: The Shaping of American Working-class Consciousness* New York: McGraw-Hill

Aronowitz, Stanley and Difazio, William (1994) *The Jobless Future: Sci-Tech and the Dogma of Work* Minneapolis: University of Minnesota Press

Audit Commission (1996) *Misspent Youth: Young People and Crime* London: Audit Commission

Auld, John; Dorn, Nicholas and South, Nigel (1986) 'Irregular Work, Irregular Pleasures: Heroin in the 1980s' in Roger Matthews and Jock Young (eds) *Confronting Crime* London: Sage

Austin, James and Cohen, Robyn (1996) *Why are Crime Rates Declining? An NCCD Briefing Report* San Francisco: National Council on Crime and Delinquency

Ayres, Richard and Braithwaite, John (1992) *Responsive Regulation: Transcending the Deregulation Debate* Oxford: Oxford University Press

Baldwin, James (1963) *The Fire Next Time* London: Michael Joseph

Barker, Pat (1982) *Union Street* London: Virago

Barrett, Michèle (1980) *Women's Oppression Today* London: Verso

Barrett, Michèle and McIntosh, Mary (1982) *The Anti-Social Family* London: Verso

Barry, Norman (1987) 'Understanding the Market' in M. Loney et al. (eds) *The State or the Market: Politics and Welfare in Contemporary Britain* London: Sage/Open University

Barthes, Roland (1973) 'Myth Today' in *Mythologies* London: Paladin

Bates, Inge and Riseborough, George (eds) *Youth and Inequality* Buckingham: Open University Press

Bateson, Gregory; Jackson, D., Haley, J. and Weakland, J. (1956) 'Toward a Theory of Schizophrenia' *Behavioral Science* 1: 251

Baudrillard, Jean (1988) *America* London: Verso

Baudrillard, Jean (1991) *La Guerre du Golfe n'a pas eu lieu* Paris: Galilée (translated 1995 as *The Gulf War Did Not Happen* Sydney: Power Institute)

Bauman, Zygmunt (1987) 'Fighting the Wrong Shadow' *New Statesman* 25 September: 20–2

Bauman, Zygmunt (1988) 'Britain's Exit from Politics' *New Statesman* 29 July: 34–8

Bauman, Zygmunt (1993) *Postmodern Ethics* Oxford: Basil Blackwell

Bauman, Zygmunt (1995) *Life in Fragments: Essays in Postmodern Morality* Oxford: Blackwell Publishers

Bauman, Zygmunt (1996) 'The Moth Seeks Out the Lamp' *New Statesman* 1 November: 21–2

Baumgartner, M. P. (1988) *The Moral Order of a Suburb* New York: Oxford University Press

Beauvoir, Simone de (1974) *The Second Sex* Harmondsworth: Penguin

Beck, Ulrich (1992) *Risk Society: Towards a New Modernity* London: Sage

Becker, Gary S. (1968) 'Crime and Punishment: an economic approach' *Journal of Political Economy* 76: 169–217

Becker, Howard S. (1963) *Outsiders: Studies in the Sociology of Deviance* Glencoe: Free Press

Becker, Saul and MacPherson, Stewart (1988) *Public Issues, Private Pain* London: Insight Books

Belford, Ros; Dunford, Martin, Woolfrey, Celia and Ellingham, Mark (1990) *Italy: The Rough Guide* London: Rough Guides

Bell, Daniel (1976) *The Cultural Contradictions of Capitalism* New York: Basic Books

Bird, R. M. J. and Bream, D. J. S. (1986) 'The Interjurisdictional Allocation of Income and the Unitary Taxation Debate' *Canadian Tax Journal* 34(6): 1377–416

Bjorgo, Tore and Witte, Rob (1993) *Racist Violence in Europe* London: Macmillan

Blanchflower, David and Freeman, Richard (1997) 'Creating Jobs for Youth' *New Economy* 4(2): 68–73

Block, Fred; Cloward, Richard, Ehrenreich, Barbara and Piven, Frances (1987) *The Mean Season: The Attack on the Welfare State* New York: Pantheon Books

Blum, Richard (1984) *Offshore Haven Banks, Trusts and Companies: The Business of Crime in the Euromarket* New York: Praeger

Borrell, Clive and Cashinella, Brian (1975) *Crime in Britain Today* London: Routledge and Kegan Paul

Bottoms, Anthony E. (1994) 'Environmental Criminology' in Mike Maguire, Rod Morgan and Robert Reiner (eds) *The Oxford Handbook of Criminology* Oxford: Clarendon Press

Bottoms, Anthony E. and Wiles, Paul (1986) 'Housing Tenure and Residential Crime Careers in Britain' in A. J. Reiss and M. Tonry (eds) *Crime and Justice: A Review of Research*, vol. 8. *Communities and Crime* Chicago: University of Chicago Press

Bottoms, Anthony E. and Wiles, Paul (1992) 'Explanations of Crime and Place' in D. J. Evans, N. R. Fyfe and D. T. Herbert (eds) *Crime, Policing and Place: Essays in Environmental Criminology* London: Routledge

Bottoms, Anthony E. and Wiles, Paul (1995) 'Crime and Insecurity in the City' in C. Fijnaut, J. Goethals, T. Peters and L.Walgrave (eds) *Changes in Society, Crime and Criminal Justice in Europe*, vol. 2 The Hague: Kluwer

Bottoms, Anthony E. and Wiles, Paul (1997) 'Environmental Criminology' in Mike Maguire, Rod Morgan and Robert Reiner (eds) *The Oxford Handbook of Criminology* (2nd edn) Oxford: Clarendon Press

Bottoms, Anthony E. and Wiles, Paul (1998) 'Crime and Housing Policy: a framework for crime prevention analysis' in T. Hope and M. Shaw (eds) *Communities and Crime Reduction* London: HMSO

Bourgois, Philippe (1995) *In Search of Respect: Selling Crack in El Barrio* Cambridge: Cambridge University Press

Box, Steven (1971) *Deviance, Reality and Society* London/New York: Holt, Rinehart and Winston

Box, Steven (1983) *Power, Crime and Mystification* London: Tavistock

Box, Steven and Hale, Chris (1982) 'Economic Crisis and the Rising Prisoner Population in England and Wales' *Crime and Social Justice* 17: 20–35

Box, Steven and Hale, Chris (1985) 'Unemployment, Imprisonment and Prison Overcrowding' *Contemporary Crises* 9: 209–28

Bowlby, John (1946) *Forty-four Juvenile Thieves: Their Character and Home Life* London: Baillière, Tindall and Cox

Braithwaite, John (1985) *To Punish or to Persuade* Albany, NY: State University of New York Press

Braithwaite, John (1993) 'Shame and Modernity' *British Journal of Criminology* 33(1): 1–18

Braithwaite, John and Ayres, Richard (1991) 'Transcending the Regulation versus Deregulation Debate'. Paper presented to the Second Liverpool Conference on Fraud, Corruption and Business Crime (April)

Bramley, Glen (1994) 'An Affordability Crisis in British Housing: dimensions, causes and policy impact' *Housing Studies* 9(1): 103–24

Brenner, M. Harvey (1971) *Time Series Analysis of Relationships between Selected Economic and Social Indicators*, vol. 1 (Text and Appendices) Washington, DC: US Government Printing Office

Brenner, M. Harvey (1977) 'Health Care Costs and Benefits of Economic Policy' *International Journal of Health Services* 7: 581–623

Brenner, M. Harvey (1978) 'Impact of Economic Indicators on Crime Indices' in *Unemployment and Crime* (Hearing before the Sub-committee on the Judiciary, House of Representatives, 59th Congress, first and second sessions, serial no. 47: 20–54)

Bright, Jon (1997) *Turning the Tide: Crime, Community and Prevention* London: Demos Paper No. 27

Brinkley, Ian (1997) 'Underworked and Underpaid' *Soundings* 6 (Summer): 161–71

Bronfenbrenner, Urie (1976) 'Is Early Intervention Effective?' in A. M. Clarke and A. D. B. Clarke (eds) *Early Experience: Myth and Evidence* London: Open Books

Bunyan, Tony (1991) 'Towards an Authoritarian European State' *Race and Class* 32(3): 19–27

Burgess, Ernest (1925) 'The Growth of the City' in R. E. Park, E. W. Burgess and R. D. Mackenzie (eds) *The City* Chicago: University of Chicago Press

Butler, Tim and Michael Rustin (eds) (1997) *Rising in the East? The Regeneration of East London* London: Lawrence and Wishart

Butts, Jeffrey A. (1996) *Offenders in Juvenile Courts* 1993 Washington, DC: US Department of Justice (Office of Juvenile Justice and Delinquency Prevention Juvenile Justice Bulletin, July)

Calhoun, Craig (ed.) (1994) *Social Theory and the Politics of Identity* Oxford: Blackwell Publishers

Campbell, Beatrix (1993) *Goliath: Britain's Dangerous Places* London: Methuen

Campbell, Duncan (1991) *That was Business: This is Personal* London: Mandarin

Cantor, David V. and Alison, Laurence J. (eds) (1997) *Criminal Detection and the Psychology of Crime* Aldershot: Dartmouth

Carlen, Pat (1996) *Jigsaw: A Political Criminology of Youth Homelessness* Buckingham: Open University Press

Carrigan, Tim; Connell R. W. and Lee, John (1985) 'Towards a New Sociology of Masculinity' *Theory and Society* 14: 551–604

Carson, W. G. (1982) *The Other Price of Britain's Oil: Safety and Control in the North Sea* London: Martin Robertson

Carter, Harold (1983) *An Introduction to Urban Historical Geography* London: Edward Arnold

Carter, Trevor and Coussins, Jean (1991) 'Back to School? The police, the education system and the black community' in Ellis Cashmore and Eugene McLaughlin (eds) *Out of Order? Policing Black People* London: Routledge

Center for Research on Criminal Justice (1975) *The Velvet Fist and the Iron Glove: An analysis of the U.S. Police* Berkeley, Calif.: Center for Research on Criminal Justice

Chambliss, William (1964) 'A Sociological Analysis of the Law of Vagrancy' *Social Problems* 12(1): 67–77

Chambliss, William (1978) *On the Take: From Petty Crooks to Presidents* Bloomington, Ind.: Indiana University Press

Chaney, David (1995) 'Authenticity and Suburbia' in Sallie Westwood and John Williams (eds) *Imagining Cities: Scripts, Signs, Memories* London: Routledge

Christie, Nils (1993) *Crime Control as Industry: Towards Gulags, Western Style?* London and New York: Routledge

Christopherson, Susan (1994) 'The Fortress City: Privatized Spaces, Consumer Citizenship' in Amin (ed.) (1994)

Ciacci, Margherita (1975) 'Psychiatric Control: A Report on the Italian situation' in H. Bianchi, M. Simondi and I. Taylor (eds) *Deviance and Control in Europe* London: John Wiley

Ciale, Justin and Leroux, Jean-Pierre (1983) 'Armed Robbery in Ottawa: a descriptive study for prevention' University of Ottawa, Department of Criminology

Clarke, Allan (1982) 'Television Police Series and Law and Order' in Open University Popular Culture course (U203) *Politics, Ideology and Popular Culture 2 Unit 22*: 35–58 Milton Keynes: Open University Press

Clarke, John (1980) 'Social-democratic Delinquents and Fabian Families' in National Deviancy Conference (ed.) *Permissiveness and Control: The Fate of the Sixties Legislation* London: Macmillan

Clarke, Michael (ed.) (1983) *Corruption* London: Frances Pinter

Clarke, Michael (1986) *Regulating the City* Milton Keynes: Open University Press

Cloward, Richard and Ohlin, Lloyd (1960) *Delinquency and Opportunity: A Theory of Delinquent Gangs* New York: Free Press

Cohen, Albert K. (1955) *Delinquent Boys: The Culture of the Gang* Chicago: Free Press

Cohen, Albert K.(1965) 'The Sociology of the Deviant Act: anomie theory and beyond' *American Sociological Review* 30(1): 5–14

Cohen, Lawrence and Felson, Marcus (1979) 'Social Change and Crime Rate Trends: a routine activity approach' *American Sociological Review* 44: 588–608

Cohen, Phil (1984) 'Against the New Vocationalism' in Inge Bates et al. (eds) *Schooling for the Dole* London: Macmillan

Cohen, Phil (1990) 'Teaching Enterprise Culture: individualism, vocationalism and the New Right' in Ian Taylor (ed.) *The Social Effects of Free Market Policies: An International Text* Hemel Hempstead: Harvester Wheatsheaf

Cohen, Phil (1997) *Rethinking the Youth Question: Education, Labour and Cultural Studies* London: Macmillan

Cohen, Stanley (1972) *Folk Devils and Moral Panics: The Creation of the Mods and Rockers* London: MacGibbon and Kee (second edition published 1987 by Basil Blackwell)

Cohen, Stanley (1979a) 'Community Control: a new utopia' *New Society* (15 March): 609–11

Cohen, Stanley (1979b) 'The Punitive City: notes on the dispersal of social control' *Contemporary Crises* 3: 339–63

Coffield, Frank; Borrill, Carol and Marshall, Sarah (1986) *Growing Up at the Margins: Young Adults in the North East* Milton Keynes: Open University Press

Colvin, M. (1981) 'The Contradictions of Control: prisons in class society' *The Insurgent Sociologist* 10(4): 33–45

Commission on Social Justice (1994) *Social Justice: Strategies for National Renewal* London: Vintage

Common, Jack (1938) *The Freedom of the Streets* London: Secker and Warburg (reprinted by People's Publications in association with The Common Trust, Newcastle upon Tyne 1988)

Connell, R. W. (1987) *Gender and Power: Society, the Person and Sexual Politics* Cambridge: Polity Press

Connell, R. W. (1995) *Masculinities* Cambridge: Polity Press

Cook, Dee (1989) *Rich Law, Poor Law: Different Responses to Tax and Supplementary Benefit Fraud* Milton Keynes: Open University Press

Cook, Dee (1991) 'Dual Standards: the regulation of tax and social security fraud'. Paper presented to the Second Liverpool Conference on Fraud, Corruption and Benefit Crime (April)

Cook, P. J. (1986) 'The Demand and Supply of Criminal Opportunities' in M. Tonry and N. Morriss (eds) *Crime and Justice: An Annual Review of Research VII* Chicago: University of Chicago Press

Cooke, Philip (1988) 'Modernity, Postmodernity and the City' *Theory, Culture and Society* 5(2–3): 475–92

Cooper, Mark (1989) 'Welcome to L.A.' *Sunday Correspondent* (1 October): 33–8

Coraghessan Boyle, T. (1995) *The Tortilla Curtain* London: Bloomsbury

Cornish, Derek and Clarke, Ron (1986) *The Reasoning Criminal: Rational Choice Perspectives on Offending* New York: Springer-Verlag

Courtenay, Gill and McAleese, Ian (1994) *Cohort 4: Young People 17–18 Years Old in 1990, Report on Sweep 2* Sheffield: Employment Department (ED Research Series, Youth Cohort Report No. 27)

Crace, John (1994) *Cracker: The Truth behind the Fiction* London: Granada/Boxtree

Craine, Steve (1997)'The 'Black Magic Roundabout': cyclical transitions, social exclusion and alternative careers' in Robert MacDonald (ed.) *Youth, the 'Underclass' and Social Exclusion* London: Routledge

Croall, Hazel (1992) *White-collar Crime* Buckingham: Open University Press

Currie, Elliott (1990) 'Heavy with Human Tears: free market policy, inequality and social provision in the United States' in Ian Taylor (ed.) *The Social Effects of Free Market Policies* Hemel Hempstead: Harvester Wheatsheaf

Currie, Elliott (1991) *Dope and Trouble* New York: Pantheon

Currie, Elliott (1993a) *Reckoning: Drugs, Cities and the American Future* New York: Hill and Wang

Currie, Elliott (1993b) 'Towards a Policy on Drugs' *Dissent* (Winter): 65–71

Currie, Elliott (1995) 'The End of Work: public and private livelihood in post-employment capitalism' in Stephen Edgell, Sandra Walklate and Gareth Williams *Debating the Future of the Public Sphere: Transforming the Public and Private Domains in Free Market Societies* Aldershot: Avebury

Curry, G. David; Ball, Richard A. and Decker, Scott H. (1996) 'Estimating the National Scope of Gang Crime from Law Enforcement Data' *National Institute of Justice Research in Brief* (August) Washington DC: US Department of Justice.

Customs and Excise (UK) (1997) *Annual Report 1996–7* Cm. 3776

Dahrendorf, Ralf (1985) *Law and Order* London: Stevens (for the Hamlyn Trust)

Darwin, Charles (1871) *The Descent of Man* London: John Murray

Davies, Christie (1975) *Permissive Britain* London: Pitman

Davies, Nick (1994) 'The Dark Heart of Britain' *Guardian* (27, 29, 30, 31 August, 1 September)

Davis, Mike (1986) *Prisoners of the American Dream: Politics and Economy in the History of the Working Class in America* London: Verso

Davis, Mike (1990) *City of Quartz: Imagining the Future in Los Angeles* London: Verso

Deacon, Alan; Vincent, Jill and Walker, Robert (1995) 'Whose Choice, Hostels or Homes? Policies for single homeless people' *Housing Studies* 10(3): 345

Dean, Malcolm (1997) 'Haunted by the Spirits' *Guardian* (21 March)

Debord, Guy (1967) *La Société du Spectacle* (Society of the Spectacle) Paris: Buchet-Chastel (Detroit: Black and Red) Republished by Zone Books, New York (1994)

Defert, Daniel (1991) ' "Popular Life" and Insurance Technology' in G. Burchell, C. Gordon and P. Miller (eds) *The Foucault Effect: Studies in Governmentality* London: Harvester-Wheatsheaf

Della Porta, Donatella (1997) 'The Vicious Circles of Corruption in Italy' in Donatella Della Porta and Yves Mény (eds) *Democracy and Corruption in Europe* London: Pinter

den Boer, Monica (1997) 'Step by Step Progress: an update on the free movement of persons and internal security' *Eipascope* (European Institute of Public Administration) 2: 8–11

Dennis, Norman (1993) *Rising Crime and the Dismembered Family: How Conformist Intellectuals have Campaigned against Common Sense* London: Institute for Economic Affairs

Dennis, Norman and Erdos, George (1992) *Families without Fatherhood* London: IEA Health and Welfare Unit

Department of Social Security (1993) *Households below Average Income: A Statistical Analysis 1979–1990/1* London: HMSO

De Swaan, Abram (1995) 'Widening Circles of Social Identification: Emotional Circles in Sociogenetic Perspective' *Theory, Culture and Society* 12(2): 25–39

Ditton, Jason (1977) *Part-time Crime: An Ethnography of Fiddling and Pilferage* London: Macmillan

Dixon, V. (1976) 'World Views and Research Methodology' in L. King, V. Dixon and W. Nobles (eds) *African Philosophy: Assumptions and Paradigms for Research on Black Persons* Los Angeles: Fanon Centre

Dobash, Rebecca and Dobash, Russell (1979) *Violence against Wives: a Case against Patriarchy* New York: Free Press

Dobrée, Bonamy (ed.) (1966) *Thomas De Quincey* New York: Schocken

Doig, Alan (1984) *Corruption and Misconduct in Contemporary British Politics* Harmondsworth: Penguin

Donajgrodzki, A. P. (1977) ' "Social Police" and the Bureaucratic Elite: a vision of order in the age of reform' in A. P. Donajgrodski (ed.) *Social Control in Nineteenth Century Britain* London: Croom Helm

Donald, James (1992) 'Metropolis: the city as text' in Robert Bocock and Kenneth Thompson (eds) *Social and Cultural Forms of Modernity* Cambridge: Polity Press in association with the Open University

Donzelot, Jacques (1979) *The Policing of Families* New York: Pantheon

Dorn, Nicholas and South, Nigel (1983) *Of Males and Markets: A Critical Review of 'Youth Culture' Theory* London: Middlesex Polytechnic, Centre for Occupational and Community Research, Research Paper 1

Dostoevsky, Fyodor (1865–6) *Crime and Punishment* Published in English by Penguin Books and by Oxford University Press 1995.

Duchen, C. (1986) *Feminism in France* London: Routledge

Durkheim, Emile (1973) 'Two Laws of Penal Evolution' *Economy and Society* 2: 285–308

Dyos, H. J. and Wolff M. (eds) (1973) *The Victorian City: Images and Realities* London: Routledge

Edsall, Thomas Byrne (1984) *The New Politics of Inequality* New York: W. W. Norton

Ehrenreich, Barbara (1989) *Fear of Falling: The Inner Life of the Middle Class* New York: Pantheon

Emms, Peter (1990) *Social Housing: A European Dilemma?* Bristol: School of Advanced Urban Studies

Engels, Friedrich (1885) *The Condition of the Working Class in England in 1844* London: Penguin 1987

Ericson, Richard V. and Haggerty, Kevin D. (1997) *Policing the Risk Society* Toronto and Buffalo: University of Toronto Press

Esping-Anderson, G. (1990) *The Three Worlds of Welfare Capitalism* Cambridge: Polity Press

Etzioni, Amitai (1993) *The Spirit of Community: the Reinvention of American Society* New York: Touchstone

European Parliament (1997) *Report of the Committee of Enquiry into the Community Transit System* (Rapporteur: E. Kellett-Bowman) (http://www.europarl.eu.int.dg7)

Ewald, François (1991) 'Insurance and Risk' in G. Burchell, C. Gordon and P. Miller (eds) *The Foucault Effect: Studies in Governmentality* London: Harvester-Wheatsheaf

Falcone, Giovanni (1992) *Men of Honour: The Truth about the Mafia* London: Fourth Estate

Farrington, David (1992) 'Criminal Career Research: Lessons for Crime Prevention' *Studies in Crime and Crime Prevention* 1(1): 7–34

Featherstone, Mike (1988) 'In Pursuit of the Postmodern: an introduction' *Theory, Culture and Society* 5 (2–3): 195–216

Feeley, Malcolm and Simon, Jonathan (1992) 'The New Penology: notes on the emerging strategy of corrections and its implications' *Criminology* 30(4): 449–74

Felson, Marcus (1994) *Crime and Everyday Life* Thousand Oaks, Calif.: Pine Forge Press

Finestone, Harold (1957) 'Cats, Kicks and Colour' *Social Problems* 5: 3–13

Fingerhut, L. A. and Kleinman, J. C. (1989) *Firearms Mortality among Children and Youth* Advanced Data from Vital and Health Statistics, National Centre for Health Statistics No. 178

Fitch, Robert (1994) 'New York's Road to Ruin' *New Left Review* 207: 17–48

Fleming, James (1986) *Merchants of Fear: An Investigation of Canada's Insurance Industry* Toronto: Penguin

Fordham, Peta (1965) *The Robbers' Tale: The True Story of the Great Train Robbery* London: Hodder and Stoughton

Forrest, Ray and Murie, Alan (1988) *Selling the Welfare State: The Privatisation of Public Housing* London: Routledge

Forrest, Ray and Murie, Alan (1994) 'Home Ownership in Recession' *Housing Studies* 9(1): 55–74

Foster, Janet (1990) *Villains: Crime and the Community in the Inner City* London: Routledge

Foster, Janet (1993) 'Island Homes for Island People: competition, conflict and racism in the battle over public housing on the Isle of Dogs'. Paper presented to Annual Conference of the British Sociological Association

Foucault, Michel (1967) *Madness and Civilisation: A History of Insanity in the Age of Reason* London: Tavistock (first published in French as *Histoire de la folie* Paris 1961)

Foucault, Michel (1973) *The Birth of the Clinic* London: Tavistock (first published in French as *Naissance de la clinique* Paris: Presses Universitaires de France 1963)

Foucault, Michel (1977) *Discipline and Punish: The Birth of the Prison* New York: Pantheon (first published in French as *Surveiller et punir: naissance de la prison* Paris: Gallimard 1975)

Foucault, Michel (1980) *The History of Sexuality, vol. 1: An Introduction* New York: Vintage (first published in French as *La Volonté de savoir* Paris: Gallimard 1976)

Francis, Diane (1988) *Contrepreneurs* Toronto: Macmillan of Canada

Fraser, Derek (1973) *The Evolution of the Welfare State* London: Macmillan

Frazier, E. Franklin (1965) *Black Bourgeoisie* New York: Free Press

Friedenberg, Edgar (1959) *The Vanishing Adolescent: Coming of Age in America* Boston: Beacon Press

Fyvel, T. R. (1961) *The Insecure Offenders: Rebellious Youth and the Welfare State* Harmondsworth: Penguin

Galbraith, John Kenneth (1992) *The Culture of Contentment* New York: Houghton Mifflin (Harmondsworth: Penguin)

Gambetta, Diego (1993) *The Sicilian Mafia: The Business of Private Protection* Cambridge, Mass.: Harvard University Press

Gamble, Andrew (1979) 'The Free Market and the Strong State' in R. Miliband and J. Savile (eds) *The Socialist Register 1979* London: Merlin Press

Gardner, Carl and Sheppard, Julie (1989) *Consuming Passion: The Rise of Retail Culture* London: Unwin Hyman

Garland, David (1990) *Punishment and Modern Society: A Study in Social Theory* Oxford: Clarendon Press

Garofalo, Raffaele (1914) *Criminology* Boston: Little, Brown

Garreau, Joel (1991) *Edge City: Life on the New Frontier* New York: Doubleday

Geis, Gilbert and Goff, Charles (eds) (1983) *White-Collar Crime: The Uncut Version* New Haven: Yale University Press

Geis, Gilbert and Meier, Robert F. (eds) (1977) *White Collar Crime* New York: Free Press

Geis, Gilbert and Stodtland, E. (eds) (1980) *White Collar Crime: Theory and Research* Beverly Hills, Calif.: Sage

Gellner, Ernest (1995) 'Nationalism: real or imaginary?' *Prospect* 3 (December): 18–21

Gershuny, J. I. (1977) *After Industrial Society* London: Macmillan

Gershuny, J. I. (1979) 'The Informal Economy: its role in industrial society' *Futures* 11(1): 103–14

Gershuny, J. I. (1983) *Social Innovation and the Division of Labour* Oxford: Oxford University Press

Giddens, Anthony (1990) *The Consequences of Modernity* Cambridge: Polity Press

Giddens, Anthony (1991) *Modernity and Self-identity: Self and Society in the Late Modern Age* Cambridge: Polity Press

Gilinsky, Yakov (1998) 'The Market and Crime in Russia' in Vincenzo Ruggiero, Nigel South and Ian Taylor (eds) *The New European Criminology: Crime and Social Order in Europe* London: Routledge

Gilligan, Carol (1982) *In a Different Voice* Cambridge, Mass.: Harvard University Press

Gillis, John (1974) *Youth in History* New York: Academic Press

Glueck, S. and Glueck, E. T. (1950) *Unraveling Juvenile Delinquency* Cambridge, Mass.: Harvard University Press

Goffman, Erving (1961) *Asylums: Essays on the Social Situation of Mental Patients and Other Inmates* New York: Doubleday

Goffman, Erving (1963) *Stigma: Notes on the Management of Spoiled Identity* Englewood Cliffs, NJ: Prentice-Hall

Goode, Erich (1994) 'Round up the Usual Suspects' *American Sociologist* 25(4): 90–104

Goodman, Paul (1956) *Growing Up Absurd* New York: Vintage Books

Gordon, David (1980) 'Capitalism, Class and Crime in America' in R. Andreano and J. Siegfied (eds) *The Economics of Crime* New York: John Wiley

Gordon, Linda and Allen Hunter (1977–8) 'Sex, Family and the New Right' *Radical America* 11(6): 8.25

Gottfredson, M. and Hirshi, T. (1990) *A General Theory of Crime* Stanford, Calif.: Stanford University Press

Gough, Ian (1979) *The Political Economy of the Welfare State* London: Macmillan

Graham, Peggotty and Clarke, John (1996) 'Dangerous Places: Crime and the City' in John Muncie and Eugene McLaughlin (eds) *The Problem of Crime* London: Sage/ The Open University

Graham, Stephen and Marvin, Simon (1996) *Telecommunications and the City: Electronic Spaces, Urban Places* London; Routledge

Greenberg, David (1977) 'The Dynamics of Oscillatory Punishment Processes' *Journal of Criminal Law and Criminology* 68(4): 643–51

Grieder, William (1997) *One World, Ready or Not: The Manic Logic of Global Capitalism* New York: Allen Lane

Griffin, Christine (1993) *Representations of Youth: The Study of Youth and Adolescence in Britain and America* Cambridge: Polity Press

Griffin, Susan (1971) 'Rape: the all-American crime' *Ramparts* (September): 26–35

Grossberg, Larry (1994) *We Gotta Get out of this Place* London: Routledge

Gruneau, Richard and Whitson, David (1993) *Hockey Night in Canada: Sport, Identities and Cultural Politics* Toronto: Garamond Press

Gurney, Craig (1995) ' "Oh, *We* Wouldn't Live in a Council House": contested meanings of home and housing tenure'. Paper presented to the British Sociological Association Annual Conference 'Contested Cities: Social Process and Spatial Forms', University of Leicester

Gusfield, Joseph (1963) *Symbolic Crusade: Status Politics and the American Temperance Movement* Urbana: University of Illinois Press

Habermas, Jürgen (1989) 'The New Obscurity: the crisis of the welfare state and the exhaustion of utopian energies' in Sherry Weber Nicholson (ed.) *The New Conservatism: Cultural Criticism and the Historians' Debate* Cambridge: Polity Press

Habermas, Jürgen (1992) *The Structural Transformation of the Public Sphere: An Enquiry into a Category of Bourgeois* Society Cambridge, Mass.: MIT Press

Hagan, John and McCarthy, Bill (1997) *Mean Streets: Youth Crime and Homelessness* Cambridge: Cambridge University Press

Hagan, John and Peterson, Ruth D. (eds) (1995) *Crime and Inequality* Stanford, Calif.: Stanford University Press

Hall, Steve (1997) 'Visceral Cultures and Criminal Practices' *Theoretical Criminology* 1(4): 453–78

Hall, Stuart (1978) 'The Great Moving Right Show' *Marxism Today* (December) reprinted in Stuart Hall, *The Hard Road to Renewal: Thatcherism and the Crisis of the Left* London: Verso

Hall, Stuart (1980) 'Popular-Democratic vs. Authoritarian Populism: two ways of "taking democracy seriously" ' in *Marxism and Democracy* London: Lawrence and Wishart, reprinted in Hall (1988)

Hall, Stuart (1981) 'The Little Caesars of Social Democracy' *Marxism Today*, reprinted in Hall (1988)

Hall, Stuart (1982) 'The Battle for Socialist ideas in the 1980s' in R. Miliband and J. Savile (eds) *The Socialist Register 1982* London: Merlin Press, reprinted in Hall (1998)

Hall, Stuart and Jacques, Martin (1990) *New Times: The Changing Face of Politics in the 1990s* London: Lawrence and Wishart

Hall, Stuart and Jefferson, Tony (eds) (1976) *Resistance through Rituals* London: Hutchinson

Hall, Stuart; Clarke, John, Critcher, Chas, Jefferson, Tony and Clarke, John (1978) *Policing the Crisis: Mugging, the State and Law and Order* London: Macmillan

Hallett, Graham (ed.) *The New Housing Shortage: Housing Affordability in Europe and the USA* London and New York: Routledge

Handelman, Stephen (1994) *Comrade Criminal: The Theft of the Second Russian Revolution* London: Michael Joseph

Harding, Sandra (ed.) (1987) *Feminism and Methodology* Milton Keynes: Open University Press

Harding, Sandra (1991) *Whose Science? Whose Knowledge? Thinking from Women's Experience* Milton Keynes: Open University Press

Harloe, Michael (1995) *The People's Home: Social Rented Housing in Europe and America* Oxford: Blackwell Publishers

Harrington, Michael (1962) *The Other America: Poverty in the United States* London: Macmillan

Harrington, Michael (1993) *Socialism: Past and Future* London: Pluto Press

Harriss, Thomas (1988) *The Silence of the Lambs* New York: St Martins Press

Harvey, David (1973) *Social Justice and the City* London: Edward Arnold

Harvey, David (1989) *The Condition of Post-Modernity* Oxford: Oxford University Press

Harvey, David (1994) 'Flexible Accumulation through Urbanization: reflections on "Postmodernism" in the American City' in Amin (1994)

Harvey, Lee (1987) *Myths of the Chicago School of Sociology* Aldershot: Avebury

Harvey, Mark and Quilley, Stephen (1997) 'Varieties of Capitalism: Embeddedness and the "Logic" of the Market' Paper presented to the joint CIC/Geography Seminar *Cultures of Innovation* University of Manchester, June (unpublished draft)

Hay, Douglas (1975) 'Property, Authority and the Criminal Law' in D. Hay, P. Linebaugh and E. P. Thompson (eds) *Albion's Fatal Tree: Crime and Society in Eighteenth-Century England* London: Allen Lane

Hebdige, Dick (1979) *Subculture: The Meaning of Style* London: Methuen

Hebdige, Dick (1988a) *Hiding in the Light: On Images and Things* London: Comedia/Routledge

Hebdige, Dick (1988b) 'A Tale of Two Cities' *News Statesman and Society* (30 September): 30–2

Heelas, Paul and Morris, Paul (1992) *The Values of the Enterprise Culture* London: Routledge

Henry, Stuart (1978) *The Hidden Economy: The Context and Control of Borderline Crime* London: Martin Robertson

Henry, Stuart and Milovanovic, Dragan (1996) *Constitutive Criminology: Beyond Postmodernism* London: Sage

Hess, Henner (1970) *Mafia and Mafiosi* Lexington Books

Hibbert, Christopher (1963) *The Roots of Evil* Harmondsworth: Penguin

Hirst, Paul Q. (1972) 'Marx and Engels on Law, Crime and Morality' *Economy and Society* 1(1): 28–56, reprinted in I. Taylor, P. Walton and J. Young (eds) *Critical Criminology* London: Routledge and Kegan Paul 1975

Hirst, Paul Q. and Thompson, Grahame (1996) *Globalization in Question: The International Economy and the Possibility of Governance* Cambridge: Polity Press

Hobbs, Dick (1988) *Doing the Business: Entrepreneurs, Detectives and the Working Class in the East End of London* Oxford: Clarendon Press

Hobbs, Dick (1995) *Bad Business* Oxford: Oxford University Press

Hobbs, Dick (1997a) 'Professional Crime, Change, Continuity and the Enduring Myth of the Underworld' *Sociology* 31(11): 57–72

Hobbs, Dick (1997b) 'Criminal Collaboration: youth gangs, subcultures, professional criminals and organized crime' in Mike Maguire, Rod Morgan and Robert Reiner (eds) *The Oxford Handbook of Criminology* (2nd edn) Oxford: Clarendon Press

Hobbs, Dick and Dunningham, Colin (1998) 'Global Organized Crime: context and pretext' in Vincenzo Ruggiero, Nigel South and Ian Taylor (eds) *The New European Criminology: Crime and Social Order in Europe* London: Routledge

Hobsbawm, Eric J. (1987) *The Age of Empire: 1875–1914* London: Weidenfeld and Nicholson

Hobsbawm, Eric J. (1994) *Age of Extremes: The Short Twentieth Century 1914–1991* London: Michael Joseph

Hochschild, Arlie (1990) *The Second Shift: Working Parents and the Revolution at Home* London: Piatkus

Hofer, Hans von, Sarnecki, Jerzy and Henrik Tham (1996) 'Ethnic Minorities and Crime: an international perspective'. Unpublished MS, University of Stockholm, Department of Criminology

Hohenberg, Paul M. and Hollen Lees, Lynn (1985) *The Making of Urban Europe 1000–1950* Cambridge, Mass.: Harvard University Press

Hollands, Robert (1995) *Friday Night, Saturday Night: Youth Cultural Identification in the Post-industrial City* Newcastle upon Tyne: Department of Social Policy, University of Newcastle

Holtermann, Sally (1995) *All our Futures: The Impact of Public Expenditure and Fiscal Policies on Britain's Children and Young People* London: Barnardo's

Home Office (1989) *The Control of Firearms in Britain* Circular 60/89 London: Home Office

Hope, Timothy and Foster, Janet (1992) 'Conflicting Forces: Changing the Dynamics of Crime and Community on a "Problem" Estate' *British Journal of Criminology* 32(4): 488–504

Horrabin, Winifred (1935) *Is Women's Place in the Home?* London: Socialist League

Howard League for Penal Reform (1993) *Dying Inside: Suicides in Prison* London: Howard League for Penal Reform

Howe, Adrian (1994) *Punish and Critique: Towards a Feminist Analysis of Penality* London: Routledge

Hunt, Alan (1997) 'Moral Regulation and Making-up the New Person' *Theoretical Criminology* 1(3): 275–302

Hunter, Teresa (1997) 'City Policeman Who Needs a Human Face' *Guardian* (Money section) 24 May: 4–5

Hutton, Will (1995) *The State We're In* London: Michael Joseph

Ianni, Francis A. and Ianni, Elizabeth Reuss (1972) *A Family Business: Kinship and Control in Organised Crime* London: Routledge and Kegan Paul

Inland Revenue (UK) (1997) *Annual Report of the Board of the Inland Revenue 1996–7*

Ignatieff, Michael (1978) *A Just Measure of Pain: The Penitentiary in the Industrial Revolution 1750–1850* London: Macmillan

Ignatieff, Michael (1979) 'Police and People: the birth of Mr Peel's "blue locusts"' *New Society* (30 August): 443–5

Ignatieff, Michael (1994) *Blood and Belonging: Journeys into the New Nationalism* London: Verso

Jachcel, Edward (1977) 'Illegality and the Development of Capitalism', PhD thesis, University of Sheffield

Jackson, George (1970) *Soledad Brother: The Prison Letters of George Jackson* Harmondsworth: Penguin

Jackson, Peter (1989) *Maps of Meaning: An Introduction to Cultural Geography* London: Unwin Hyman

Jacobs, Jane (1969) *The Economy of Cities* New York: Random House

Jacques, Martin (1995) 'The Asian Century' *Demos* 6: 6–8

James, Oliver (1995) *Juvenile Violence in a Winner–Loser Culture: Socio-economic and Familial Origins of the Rise of Violence against the Person* London: Free Association Books

Jameson, Fredric (1984) 'Post-modernism, or the Cultural Logic of Late Capitalism' *New Left Review* 146 (July–August): 53–93

Jameson, Fredric (1991) *Post-modernism or the Cultural Logic of Late Capitalism* London: Verso

Jamieson, Ruth (1998a) 'Towards a Criminology of War in Europe' in Vincenzo Ruggiero, Nigel South and Ian Taylor (eds) *The New European Criminology: Crime and Social Order in Europe* London: Routledge

Jamieson, Ruth (1998b) 'Contested Jurisdictions, Border Communities and Cross-Border Crime: the case of Akwesasne' in Emilio Viano (ed.) *Global Organised Crime and International Security*

Jamieson, Ruth; South, Nigel and Taylor, Ian (1997) *Economic Liberalisation and Cross-Border Crime: The North American Free Trade Area and Cross-Border Crime. Salford Working Papers in Sociology* 21, reprinted in *International Journal of Sociology of Law* 21(2) (June 1998) and 21(3) (September 1998)

Jankovic, I. (1977) 'Labour Market and Imprisonment' *Crime and Social Justice* 8: 17–31

Jankowski, Martín Sánchez (1991) *Islands in the Street: Gangs and American Urban Society* Berkeley: University of California Press

Jefferson, Tony and Carlen, Pat (eds) *Masculinities, Social Relations and Crime* (special issue of *British Journal of Criminology* 36(3))

Jencks, Charles (1984) *The Language of Post-modern Architecture* London: Architectural Press

Jessop, Bob (1994) 'Post-Fordism and the State' in Amin (ed.) (1994)

Johnston, Les (1992) *The Rebirth of Private Policing* London: Routledge

Jordan, Bill (1982) *Mass Unemployment and the Future of Britain* Oxford: Basil Blackwell

Judt, Tony (1995) 'Turbo-Charged Capitalism and its Consequences' *London Review of Books* (2 November): 6–8

Judt, Tony (1996) 'Europe: the grand illusion' *New York Review of Books* 42(12) (11 July): 6–9

Katz, Jack (1988) *The Seductions of Crime: Moral and Sensual Attractions in Doing Evil* New York: Basic Books

Keane, Jonathan (1997) 'Ecstasy in the Unhappy Society' *Soundings* 6 (Summer): 127–39

Keat, Russell and Abercrombie. Nick (1991) *Enterprise Culture* London: Routledge

Keith, Michael (1995) *Race, Riots and Policing: Lore and Disorder in a Multi-Racist Society* London: UCL Press

Keith, Michael and Pile, Steven (1994) 'The Politics of Place' in M. Keith and S. Pile (eds) *Place and the Politics of Identity* London: Routledge

Keith, Michael and Rogers, Alistair (eds) (1991) *Hollow Promises: Rhetoric and Reality in the Inner City* London: Mansell

Kellerman, Arthur (1994) Editorial, *Western Journal of Medicine* 161(6): 614–15

Kellerman, Arthur; Rivara F. P., Rushworth N. et al. 'Firearms Ownership as a Risk Factor for Homicide in the Home' *New England Journal of Medicine* 329: 1084–91

Kelley, David (1985) 'Stalking the Criminal Mind' *Harper's Magazine* 271(1623) (August): 53–9

Kelling, George and Coles, Catherine (1996) *Fixing Broken Windows: Restoring Order and Reducing Crime in our Communities* New York: Free Press

Kemp, Tom (1990) *The Climax of Capitalism: The US Economy in the Twentieth Century* London: Longman

Kennett, Lee and Anderson, James LaVerne (1975) *The Gun in America: The Origins of a National Dilemma* Westport, Conn.: Greenwood Press

Kenniston, Kenneth (1960) *The Uncommitted: Alienated Youth in American Society* New York: Harcourt Brace Jovanovitch

Kesey, Ken (1962) *One Flew over the Cuckoo's Nest* New York: Signet Books

Kidd-Hewitt, David and Osborne, Richard (1995) *Crime and the Media: The Post-Modern Spectacle* London: Pluto Press

Killias, Martin (1989) 'Criminality amongst Second-generation Immigrants. in Europe: a review of the evidence' *Criminal Justice Review* 14: 13–42

Kinsey, Richard; Lea, John and Young, Jock *Losing the Fight against Crime* Oxford: Basil Blackwell

Kittrie, Nicholas N. (1971) *The Right to be Different: Deviance and Enforced Therapy* Baltimore: Penguin

Kleck, Gary (1991) *Point Blank: Guns and Violence in America* New York: Aldine de Gruyter

Korn, Arthur (1953) *History Builds the Town* London: Lund Humphries

Koser, Khalid and Lutz, Helma (eds) (1998) *The New Migration in Europe: Social Constructions and Social Realities* London: Macmillan

Kroker, Arthur and Cook, David (1986) *The Postmodern Scene: Excremental Culture and Hyper-Aesthetics* Montreal: New World Perspectives

Kroker, Arthur (1989) *The Panic Encyclopedia* Montreal: New World Perspectives

Krugman, Paul (1990) *The Age of Diminished Expectations: U.S. Economic Policy in the 1990s* Cambridge, Mass.: MIT Press

Kumar, Krishnan (1975) 'Holding the Middle Ground: The BBC, the public and the professional broadcaster' *Sociology* 9(3), reprinted in J. Curran, M. Gurevitch and Woollacott (eds) *Mass Communication and Society* London: Edward Arnold 1977

Kurtz, Lester R. (1984) *Evaluating Chicago Sociology: A Guide to the Literature* Chicago: University of Chicago Press

Kuttner, Robert (1997) *Everything for Sale: The Virtues and Limits of Markets* New York: Alfred A. Knopf

Laing, R. D. and Esterson, David (1964) *Sanity, Madness and the Family* London: Tavistock

Lander, Bertram (1954) *Towards an Understanding of Juvenile Delinquency* New York: Columbia University Press

Langan, Mary (1996) 'Hidden and Respectable: Crime and the Market' in John Muncie and Eugene McLaughlin (eds) *The Problem of Crime* London: Sage, in association with the Open University

Lasch, Christopher (1977) *Haven in a Heartless World: The Family Beseiged* New York: W. W. Norton

Lasch, Christopher (1991) *The True and Only Heaven: Progress and its Critics* New York: W. W. Norton

Lasch, Christopher (1995) *The Revolt of the Elites and the Betrayal of Democracy* New York: W. W. Norton

Lash, Scott and Urry, John (1987) *The End of Organized Capitalism* Cambridge: Polity Press

Lash, Scott and Urry, John (1994) *Economies of Signs and Space* London: Sage

Lawless, Paul; Martin, Ron and Hardy, Sally (1998) *Unemployment and Social Exclusion: Landscapes of Labour Inequality* London and Philadelphia: Jessica Kingsley Publishers for the Regional Studies Association

Lea, John and Young, Jock (1984) *What is to be Done about Law and Order?* Harmondsworth: Penguin

Lefebvre, Henri (1991) *The Production of Space* Oxford: Oxford University Press

Lefkowicz, Bernard (1997) *Our Guys: The Glen Ridge Rape and the Secret Life of the Perfect Suburb* Berkeley: University of California Press

Lemert, Edwin (1967) *Human Deviance, Social Problems and Social Control* Englewood Cliffs: Prentice-Hall

Lerman, Paul (1975) *Community Treatment and Social Control: A Critical Treatment of Juvenile Correctional Policy* Chicago: University of Chicago Press

Letkemann, Peter (1973) *Crime as Work* Englewood Cliffs, NJ: Prentice-Hall

Levi, Michael (1987a) *Regulating Fraud: White Collar Crime and the Criminal Process* London: Tavistock

Levi, Michael (1987b) 'Does the Punishment Fit?' *Times Higher Educational Supplement* (6 November)

Leyton, Elliott (1989) *Hunting Humans* Harmondsworth: Penguin

Lerman, Paul (1975) *Community Treatment and Social Control* Chicago: University of Chicago Press

Little, Craig (1994) 'Private Crime Control: from 19th century horse companies to contemporary contract security' Canberra: Research School of Social Sciences, Australian National University (Administration, Compliance and Governability Program Working Paper No. 20)

Lloyd, John (1998) 'Mafia Capitalism: the warning from Russia' *Prospect* 26 (January): 34–9

Loader, Ian (1997a) 'Thinking Normatively about Private Security' *Journal of Law and Society* 24(3): 377–94

Loader, Ian (1997b) 'Private Security and the Demand for Protection in Contemporary Britain' *Policing and Society* 7: 143–62

Logan, Charles (1990) *Private Prisons: Cons and Pros* New York: Oxford University Press

Logan, John R. and Molotch, Harvey (1987) *Urban Fortunes: The Political Economy of Place* Berkeley: University of California Press

Luttwak, Edward (1995) 'Turbo-charged Capitalism and its Consequences' *London Review of Books* (2 November): 6–7

Lyotard, Jean-François (1984) *The Post-Modern Condition: A Report on Knowledge* Manchester: Manchester University Press

McCrae, Susan (1987) *Young and Jobless: The Social and Personal Consequences of Long-term Youth Unemployment* London: Policy Studies Institute

MacFarlane, Alan (1987) *The Culture of Capitalism* Cambridge: Cambridge University Press

McGuigan, Jim (1992) *Cultural Populism* London: Routledge

McIntosh, Mary (1971) 'Changes in the Organisation of Thieving' in Stanley Cohen (ed.) *Images of Deviance* Harmondsworth: Penguin

McIntosh, Mary (1975) *The Organisation of Crime* London: Macmillan

Mack, John (1964) 'Full-time Miscreants, Delinquent Neighbourhoods and Criminal Networks' *British Journal of Sociology* 15: 38–53

Mack, John (1975) *The Crime Industry* Farnborough: Saxon House

McLaren, Peter (1995) 'Gangsta Pedagogy and Ghettoethnicity: the hip-hop nation as counterpublic sphere' *Socialist Review* 95(2): 9–55.

MacLeod, Jay (1987) *Ain't No Makin' It: Aspirations and Attainment in a Low-income Neighbourhood* Boulder, Colo.: Westview Press (revised edn 1995)

McMurtry, John (1995) 'The Social Immune System and the Cancer Stage of Capitalism' *Social Justice* 22(4): 1–25

McRobbie, Angela (1980) 'Settling Accounts with Subculture: a feminist critique' *Screen Education* 39 (Spring), reprinted in A. McRobbie *Feminism and Youth Subculture: From Jackie to Just Seventeen* London: Macmillan 1991

McRobbie, Angela (1994) *Post-Modernism and Popular Culture* London: Routledge

McRobbie, Angela, with Jenny Garber (1975) 'Girls and Subcultures' *Working Papers in Cultural Studies* 7/8, reprinted in Stuart Hall and Tony Jefferson (eds) *Resistance through Rituals* London: Hutchinson 1978

McRobbie, Angela and Thornton, Sarah I. (1995) 'Rethinking "Moral Panic" for Multi-Mediated Social Worlds' *British Journal of Sociology* 46(4): 559–74

Maddison, Angus (1991) *Dynamic Forces in Capitalist Development* Oxford: Oxford University Press

Madrick, Jeff (1995) 'The End of Affluence' *New York Review of Books* (21 September): 13–17

Maffesoli, Michel (1995) *The Time of the Tribes* London: Sage

Magaziner, Ira and Reich, Robert (1982) *Minding America's Business: The Decline and Rise of the American Economy* New York: Harcourt Brace

Mannheim, Hermann (1965) *Comparative Criminology* London: Routledge and Kegan Paul

Manning, Peter K. (1977) *Police Work: The Social Organisation of Police Work* Cambridge, Mass.: MIT Press

Marcuse, Herbert (1964) *One-Dimensional Man* Boston: Basic Books (London: Sphere 1968)

Marcuse, Peter (1995) 'Not Chaos, but Walls: postmodernism and the partitioned city' in Sophie Watson and Katherine Gibson (eds) *Postmodern Cities and Spaces* Oxford: Blackwell Publishers

Mars, Gerald (1974) 'Dock Pilferage' in P. Rock and M. McIntosh (eds) *Deviance and Control* London: Macmillan

Mars, Gerald (1982) *Cheats at Work: An Anthology of Workplace Crime* London: George Allen and Unwin

Martin, Bernice (1981) *A Sociology of Contemporary Cultural Change* Oxford: Basil Blackwell

Marx, Karl (1969) *Theories of Surplus Value* Moscow: Foreign Languages Publishing House

Massey, Doreen (1994) *Space, Place and Gender* Cambridge: Polity Press

Massey, Doreen and Meegan, Richard (1982) *The Anatomy of Job Loss: The How, Why and Where of Employment Decline* London: Methuen

Mattera, Philip (1985) *Off the Books* London: Pluto Press

Matza, David (1961) 'Subterranean Traditions of Youth' *Annals of the American Academy of Political and Social Science* 338: 102–18

Matza, David (1964) *Delinquency and Drift* New York: John Wiley

Matza, David (1969) *Becoming Deviant* New York: Prentice-Hall

Maxfield, M. G. (1987) 'Explaining Fear of Crime: evidence from the 1984 British Crime Survey' London: Home Office (Research Study No. 78)

Mayhew, Henry (1861) *London Labour and London Poor* London: Griffin, Bohn and Co.

Measham, Fiona; Newcombe, Russell and Parker, Howard (1994) 'The Normalization of Recreational Drug Use among Young People in North-West England' *British Journal of Sociology* (Summer): 287–312

Melossi, Dario (1978) Review of Rusche and Kirchheimer *Punishment and Social Structure in Crime and Social Justice* 9: 73–85

Melossi, Dario (1980) 'Georg Rusche: a biographical essay' *Crime and Social Justice* 14: 51–64

Melossi, Dario (1985) 'Punishment and Social Action: changing vocabularies of motive within a political business cycle' *Current Perspectives in Social Theory* 6: 169–97

Melossi, Dario (1990) *The State of Social Control: a sociological study of the concepts of state and social control in the making of democracy* Cambridge: Polity Press

Melossi, Dario and Pavarini, Massimo (1981) *The Prison and the Factory* London: Macmillan (originally published in Italian as *Carcere e Fabbrica* Bologna: Il Mulino 1977)

Merrifield, Andy and Swyngedouw, Erik (eds) (1996) *The Urbanization of Injustice* London: Lawrence and Wishart

Merton, Robert (1938) 'Social Structure and Anomie' *American Sociological Review* 3: 672–82

Merton, Robert K (1957) *Social Theory and Social Structure* New York: Free Press

Merton, Robert K. and Nisbet, Robert (eds) (1966) *Contemporary Social Problems* New York: Harcourt, Brace and World

Messerschmidt, James (1986) *Capitalism, Patriarchy and Crime: Towards a Socialist-feminist Criminology* Totowa, NJ: Rowman and Littlefield

Messerschmidt, James (1993) *Masculinities and Crime* Lanham, Md.: Rowman and Littlefield

Messerschmidt, James (1997) *Crime as Structured Action: Gender, Race, Class and Crime in the Making* Thousand Oaks, Calif.: Sage

Miles, Jack (1992) 'The Struggle for the Bottom Rung: Blacks vs. Browns' *Atlantic Monthly* (October): 41–68

Miller, Walter B. (1958) 'Lower–Class Culture as a Generating Milieu of Gang Delinquency' *Journal of Social Issues 15*: 5–19 (Reprinted in M. Wolfgang, L. Savitz and N. Johnston (eds) *The Sociology of Crime and Delinquency* New York: John Wiley 1962)

Mingione, Enzo (1983) 'Informalization, Restructuring and the Survival Strategies of the Working Class' *International Journal of Urban and Regional Research* 4(1): 1–20

Mingione, Enzo (1994) 'Life Strategies and Social Economies in the Postfordist Age' *International Journal of Urban and Regional Research* 18(1): 24–45

Mirrlees-Black, C. and Aye Maung, N. (1994) *Fear of Crime: Findings from the 1992 British Crime Survey* London: Home Office (Research and Statistics Department)

Montaldo, Jean (1993) *Mitterand and the Forty Thieves* Paris: Albin Michel

Morgan, Patricia (1978) *Delinquent Fantasies* London: Maurice Temple Smith

Morrison, Shona and O'Donnell, Ian (1994) *Armed Robbery: A Study in London* University of Oxford, Centre for Criminological Research, Occasional Paper No. 15

Mort, Jo-Ann (1997) 'Sweated Shopping' *Guardian* (8 September)

Mukherjee, S. and Dagger D.(1995) *Crime in Australia: The First National Outlook Symposium on Crime in Australia Data Handbook* Canberra: Institute of Criminology

Muncie, John (1984) *'The Trouble with Kids Today': Youth and Crime in Post-war Britain* London: Hutchinson

Murdock, Graham and McCron, Robin (1979) 'The Television-and-Violence Panic' *Screen Education* 36 (Autumn): 51–68

Murray, Charles (1990) *The Emerging British Underclass* London: Institute for Economic Affairs

Murray, Charles (1994) *Underclass: The Crisis Deepens* (with commentaries by Pete Alcock, Miriam David, Melanie Phillips and Sue Slipman) London: Institute for Economic Affairs

Myers, Gustavus (1909) *The History of the Great American Fortunes* Chicago: C. H. Kerr

National Playing Fields Association (1996) *Playing Fields at Risk* London/Edinburgh: NPFA

Naylor, R. T. (1987) *Hot Money and the Politics of Debt* Toronto: McLelland and Stewart

Naylor, R. T. (1994–5) 'Loose Cannons: covert commerce and underground finance in the modern arms black market' *Crime, Law and Social Change* 22(1): 1–57

Naylor, R. T. (1995–6) 'From Underworld to Underground' *Crime, Law and Social Change* 24(2): 79–150

Nelken, David (1997) 'White-Collar Crime' in Mike Maguire, Rod Morgan and Robert Reiner (eds) *The Oxford Handbook of Criminology* (2nd edn) Oxford: Clarendon Press

Newburn, Tim and Stanko, Elizabeth A. (1994) *Just Boys Doing Business: Men, Masculinities and Crime* London: Routledge

Newman, Oscar (1972) *Defensible Space: People and Design in the Violent City* London: Architectural Press

New York City Police Department (1995) *The Year of Change: Re-engineering the New York City Police Department* New York: NYPD and Office of the Mayor of the City of New York

Nicholl, Charlie (1986) *The Fruit Palace* New York: St Martin's Press

Nozick, R. (1974) *Anarchy, State and Utopia* Oxford: Basil Blackwell

Nove, Alec (1983) *The Economics of Feasible Socialism* London: Allen and Unwin

Nuttall, Jeff (1970) *Bomb Culture* London: Paladin

O'Connor, James (1973) *The Fiscal Crisis of the State* New York: St James Press

O'Malley, Pat (1992) 'Risk, Power and Crime Prevention' *Economy and Society* 21(3): 252–75

O'Malley, Pat and Mugford, Stephen (1994) 'Crime, Excitement and Modernity' in Gregg Barak (ed.) *Varieties of Criminology: Readings from a Dynamic Discipline* Westport, Conn.: Praeger

O'Neill, John (1968) 'Public and Private Space' reprinted in D. Ioan Davies and Kathleen Herman (eds) *Social Space: Canadian Perspectives* Toronto: New Press 1971

Oppenheimer, Peter (1970) 'Muddling through: the economy 1951–1964' in V. Bognanor and R. Skidelsky (eds) *The Age of Affluence* London: Macmillan

Pahl, Ray (1984a) *Divisions of Labour* Oxford: Basil Blackwell

Pahl, Ray (1984b) 'The Restructuring of Capital, the Local Political Economy and Household Work Strategies' in D. Gregory and J. Urry (eds) *Social Relations and Spatial Structures* London: Macmillan

Pain, Rachel H. (1995) 'Local Contexts and Fear of Crime: elderly people in north east England' *Northern Economic Review*

Pallister, Minnie (1929) *Socialism for Women* London: Independent Labour Party

Paoli, Letizia (1995) 'The Banco Ambrosiano Case: an investigation into the underestimation of the relations between organised and economic crime' *Crime, Law and Social Change* 23(4): 345–65

Paoli, Letizia (1998) 'The Pentiti's Contribution to the Conceptualization of the Mafia Phenomenon' in Vincenzo Ruggiero, Nigel South and Ian Taylor (eds) *The New European Criminology: Crime and Social Order in Europe* London: Routledge

Parenti, Christian (1993) 'Weed and Seed: the fortress culture' *Crossroads* (September): 17–18

Parenti, Christian (1994a) 'Urban Militarism' *Z Magazine* (June): 47–52

Parenti, Christian (1994b) 'Sidewalk Mercenaries vs. the Homeless' *Z Magazine* (November): 18–21

Park, Alison (1994) *Cohort 4: Young People 18–19 Years Old in 1991, Report on Sweep 3* Sheffield: Employment Department (Ed. Research Series, Youth Cohort Report No. 29)

Park, Robert (1967) *The City* Chicago: University of Chicago Press

Parker, Howard (1996) 'Young Adult Offenders, Alcohol and Criminological Cul-de-Sacs' *British Journal of Criminology* 36(2): 282–98

Parker, Howard and Bottomley, Tim (1996) 'Crack Cocaine and Drugs-Crime Careers' *Research Findings No. 34* (Home Office Research and Statistics Directorate) London: Home Office

Pasquino, Pasquale (1980) 'Criminology: the birth of a special savoir' *Ideology and Consciousness* 7: 17–32

Pearce, Frank (1973) 'Crime, Corporations and the American Social Order' in Ian Taylor and Laurie Taylor (eds) *Politics and Deviance* London: Penguin

Pearce, Frank (1976) *Crimes of the Powerful* London: Pluto Press

Pearce, Frank and Tombs, Steve (1992) 'Realism and Corporate Crime' in R. Matthews and J. Young (eds) *Issues in Realist Criminology* London: Sage

Pearson, Geoffrey (1983) *Hooligan: The History of Respectable Fears* London: Macmillan

Peck, Jamie and Tickell, Adam (1994) 'Searching for a New Institutional Fix: the *after*-Fordist crisis and the global–local disorder' in Amin (ed.) (1994)

Pfohl, Steven (1992) *Death at the Parasite Cafe: Social Science (Fictions) and the Postmodern* New York: St Martin's Press

Pfohl, Steven (1994) *Images of Deviance and Social Control: A Sociological History* New York: McGraw-Hill (2nd edn)

Piore, Michael and Sabel, Charles (1984) *The Second Industrial Divide: Possibilities for Prosperity* New York: Basic Books

Pirenne, Henri (1925) *Medieval Cities* Princeton, NJ: Princeton University Press

Platt, Anthony (1969) *The Child Savers* Chicago: University of Chicago Press

Platt, Tony and Takagi, Paul (1977) 'Intellectuals for Law and Order: a critique of the "New Realists"' *Crime and Social Justice* 8 (Fall–Winter): 1–16

Polanyi, Karl (1944) *The Great Transformation* Boston: Beacon Books

Pontell, H. M.; Jesilow, P. D. and Geis G. (1982) 'Policing Physicians: practitioners fraud and abuse in a government medical program' *Social Problems* 30(1): 117–25

Power, Anne (1995) *Hovels to High Rise: State Housing in Europe since 1850* London: Routledge

Power, Anne (1997a) *Estates on the Edge: The Social Consequences of Mass Housing in Northern Europe* York: Joseph Rowntree Trust and London: Macmillan

Power, Anne (1997b) 'Raising the Floor' *Prospect* 23 (October): 14–15

Power, Anne and Tunstall, Rebecca (1997) *Dangerous Disturbances: Riots and Violent Disturbances in Thirteen Areas of Britain 1991–1992* York: Rowntree Foundation

Priemus, Hugo; Kleinman, Mark, MacLennan, Duncan and Turner, Bengt (1994) 'Maastricht Treaty: consequences for national housing policies' *Housing Studies* 9(2): 163–82

Pryce, Ken (1979) *Endless Pressure: A Study of West Indian Life-styles in Bristol* Harmondsworth: Penguin

Putnam, Robert (1996) 'Who Killed Civic America?' *Prospect* 6 (March): 66–72

Pyle, Derek (1983) *The Economics of Crime and Punishment* London: Macmillan

Pyle, Derek (1989) *Crime in Britain* London: Social Market Foundation Discussion Paper

Pyle, Derek (1993) *Crime in Britain* London: Social Market Forum Discussion Paper (May)

Quinney, Richard (1970) *Crime and Justice in Society* Boston: Little, Brown

Quinney, Richard (1970) *The Problem of Crime* New York: Dodd, Mead

Quinney, Richard (1973) *Critique of Legal Order: Crime Control in Capitalist Society* Boston: Little, Brown

Quinney, Richard (ed.) (1974) *Criminal Justice in America: A Critical Understanding* Boston: Little, Brown

Ramsay, Malcolm and Percy, Andrew (1996) 'Drug Use Declared: Results of the 1994 British Crime Survey' *Research Findings No. 33* (Home Office Research and Statistics Directorate) London: Home Office (June)

Rawlinson, Patricia (1998) 'Russian Organised Crime: moving beyond ideology' in Vincenzo Ruggiero, Nigel South and Ian Taylor (eds) *The New European Criminology: Crime and Social Order in Europe* London: Routledge

Reich, Robert (1991) *The Work of Nations: Preparing Ourselves for Twenty-first Century Capitalism* New York: Knopf

Rex, John (1973) 'The Concept of Housing Class and the Sociology of Race Relations' in *Race, Colonialism and the City* London: Routledge

Rex, John and Moore, Robert (1967) *Race, Community and Conflict: A Study in Sparkbrook* London: Routledge and Kegan Paul

Richards, Barry (1994) *Disciplines of Delight: The Psychoanalysis of Popular Culture* London: Free Association Books

Robb, George (1992) *White-collar Crime in Modern England: Financial Fraud and Business Morality 1845–1929* Cambridge: Cambridge University Press

Roberts, Ken (1968) 'The Entry into Employment: an approach towards a general theory' *Sociological Review* 16: 165–84

Roberts, Ken (1975) 'The Developmental Theory of Occupational Choice: a critique and an alternative' in G. Esland et al. (eds) *People and Work* Edinburgh: Holme McDougall

Roberts, Ken (1995) *Youth and Employment in Modern Britain* Oxford: Oxford University Press

Roberts, Robert (1971) *The Classic Slum: Salford Life in the First Quarter of the Century* Manchester: University of Manchester Press

Robertson, Roland (1995) 'Glocalization: time–space and homogeneity–heterogeneity' in Mike Featherstone, Scott Lash and Roland Robertson (eds) *Global Modernities* London: Sage (in association with *Theory, Culture and Society*)

Rosa, Joseph G. and May, Robert (1976) *An Illustrated History of Guns and Small Arms* Secaucus, NJ: Castle Books

Rose, Nikolas (1992) 'Governing the Enterprising Self' in Heelas and Morris (eds) (1992)

Rose, Nikolas and Miller, Peter (1992) 'Political Power beyond the State: problematics of government' *British Journal of Sociology* 43(2): 173–205

Rostow, W. W. (1953) *The Process of Economic Growth* Oxford: Clarendon Press

Rostow, W. W. (1963) *The Economics of Take-off into Sustained Growth* London: Macmillan

Rothman, B. (1987) *Signifying Nothing: The Semiotics of Zero* London: Macmillan

Rothman, David (1971) *The Discovery of the Asylum* Boston: Little, Brown

Rothman, David (1980) *Conscience and Convenience: The Asylum and its Alternatives in Progressive America* Boston: Little, Brown

Rowntree Foundation (1994) *Children Living in Re-ordered Families* (Social Policy Research Findings No. 25) York: Joseph Rowntree Foundation

Ruggiero, Vincenzo (1996) *Organized and Corporate Crime in Europe: Offers that Can't be Refused* Aldershot: Dartmouth

Ruggiero, Vincenzo and South, Nigel (1997) 'The Late-Modern City as a Bazaar: drug markets, illegal enterprise and the "barricades" ' *British Journal of Sociology* 48(1): 54–70

Rusche, Georg (1933) 'Arbeitsmarkt und Strafvollzug' Research proposal to the Frankfurt Institute for Social Research, published in *Zeitschrift für Sozialforschung* 2 (993): 63–78 (published in English as 'Labour Market and Penal Sanction: thoughts on the sociology of criminal justice' (trans. Gerda Dinwiddie) *Crime and Social Justice* 10 (1978): 2–8)

Rusche, Georg and Kirchheimer, Otto (1939) *Punishment and Social Structure* New York: Russell and Russell (Republished by Columbia University Press 1967)

Rustin, Michael (1994) 'Incomplete Modernity: Ulrich Beck's *Risk Society*' *Radical Philosophy* 67 (Summer): 3–12

Rutter, Michael and Smith, David (eds) (1995) *Psycho-social Disorders in Young People: Time Trends and their Causes* Chichester: John Wiley

Sahlin, Ingrid (1995) 'Strategies for Exclusion from Social Housing' *Housing Studies* 10(3): 381

Samuel, Raphael (1960) ' "Bastard Capitalism" ' in E. P. Thompson (ed.) *Out of Apathy* London: New Left Books/Stevens and Sons

Santino, U. (1988) 'The Financial Mafia: the illegal accumulation of wealth and the financial industry complex' *Contemporary Crises* 12(3): 203–44

Saraga, Esther (1996) 'Dangerous Places: the family as a site of crime' in John Muncie and Eugene McLaughlin (eds) *The Problem of Crime* London: Sage/The Open University

Sassen, Saskia (1994) *Cities in a World Economy* Thousand Oaks, Calif.: Pine Forge Press

Scarman, Lord Justice (1982) *The Scarman Report* Harmondsworth: Penguin

Schihor, David (1995) *Punishment for Profit: Private Prisons/Public Concerns* Thousand Oaks, Calif.: Sage

Schorr, Alvin L. (ed.) (1974) *Children and Decent People* New York: Basic Books

Schur, Edwin (1965) *Crimes without Victims: Deviant Behaviour and Public Policy: Abortion, Homosexuality, Drug Addiction* Englewood Cliffs, NJ: Prentice-Hall

Schur, Edwin (1971) *Labeling Deviant Behavior: Its Sociological Implications* New York: Random House

Schur, Edwin (1980) *The Politics of Deviance: Stigma Contests and the Uses of Power* Englewood Cliffs, NJ: Spectrum

Schwartz, Tony (1989) 'Acceleration Syndrome' *Utne Reader* 31 (Jan.–Feb.): 36–41

Schwendinger, Herman and Schwendinger, Julia (1976) 'Marginal Youth and Social Policy' *Social Problems* 24(2): 184–91

Scraton, Phil (ed.) (1987) *Law, Order and the Authoritarian State* Milton Keynes: Open University Press

Scull, Andrew T. (1977) *Decarceration: Community Treatment and the Deviant – a Radical View* Englewood Cliffs, NJ: Spectrum

Seabrook, Jeremy (1978) *What Went Wrong? Working People and the Ideals of the Labour Movement* London: Gollancz

Seabrook, Jeremy (1985) 'Beveridge's Five Evils Return' *New Society* (28 February): 320–2

Sennett, Richard (1970) *The Uses of Disorder: Personal Identity and City Life* Harmondsworth: Penguin

Sennett, Richard (1990) *The Conscience of the Eye* London: Faber and Faber

Sennett, Richard (1994) *Flesh and Stone* London: Faber and Faber

Sennett, Richard and Cobb, Richard (1972) *The Hidden Injuries of Class* New York: Vintage

Shaw, Clifford and Mackay, Henry (1942) *Juvenile Delinquency and Urban Areas* Chicago: University of Chicago Press

Shearing, Clifford and Stenning, Philip (1981) 'Private Security: its growth and implications' in M. Tonry and N. Morris (eds) *Crime and Justice: An Annual Volume of Research*, vol. 3 Chicago: University of Chicago Press

Shearing, Clifford and Stenning, Philip (1983) 'Private Security: implications for social control' *Social Problems* 30: 493–505

Shearing, Clifford and Stenning, Philip (1985a) 'Police Perceptions of Private Security' *Canadian Police College Journal* 9(2)

Shearing, Clifford and Stenning, Philip (1985b) 'Public Perceptions of Private Security' *Canadian Police College Journal* 9(3): 225–53

Shearing, Clifford and Stenning, Philip (1985c) 'Corporate Perceptions of Private Security' *Canadian Police College Journal* 9(4): 367–90

Shearing, Clifford and Stenning, Philip (1985d) 'From the Panopticon to Disney World: the development of discipline' in A. Doob and A. Greenspan (eds) *Perspectives in Criminal Law* Toronto: Canada Law Book Co. (Extracted in J. Muncie, E. McLaughlin and M. Langan (eds) *Criminological Perspectives* London: Sage 1996)

Shearing, Clifford and Stenning, Philip (eds) (1987) *Private Policing* Newbury Park: Sage (Sage Criminal Justice Annuals 23)

Sherman, Lawrence; Gartin, Patrick R. and Buerger, Michael E. (1989) 'Hot Spots of Predatory Crime: Routine Activities and the Criminology of Place' *Criminology* 27(1): 27–55

Shevsky, E. and Bell, W. (1955) *Social Area Analysis* Stanford, Calif.: Stanford University Press

Shields, Rob (1989) 'Social Spatialization and the Built Environment: the West Edmonton Mall' *Society and Space* 7(1)

Shiner, Michael and Tim Newburn (1997) 'Definitely, Maybe Not? The Normalisation of Recreational Drug Use among Young People' *Sociology* 31(3): 511–30

Shirley, Ian (1990) 'New Zealand: the advance of the new right' in Ian Taylor (ed.) *The Social Effects of Free Market Policies* London: Harvester-Wheatsheaf

Sibley, David (1995) *Geographies of Exclusion: Society and Difference in the West* London: Routledge

Silver, Allan (1967) 'The Demand for Order in Civil Society' in David Bordua (ed.) *The Police: Six Sociological Essays* New York: Wiley

Sim, Joe (1987) 'Working for the Clampdown: Prisons and Politics in England and Wales' in Phil Scraton (ed.) *Law, Order and the Authoritarian State* Milton Keynes: Open University Press

Sim, Joe; Scraton, Phil and Gordon, Paul (1987) 'Crime, the State and Critical Analysis' in Phil Scraton (ed.) *Law, Order and the Authoritarian State* Milton Keynes: Open University Press

Simon, Jonathan (1987) 'The Emergence of a Risk Society: insurance, law and the state' *Socialist Review* 17: 60–89

Simon, Jonathan (1988) 'The Ideological Effects of Actuarial Practices' *Law and Society Review* 22(4): 771–800

Sinclair, Upton (1900) *The Jungle* New York: Doubleday Page (republished by Robert Bentley, Cambridge 1974)

Sinfield, Adrian (1981) *What Unemployment Means* Oxford: Martin Robertson

Skogan, Wesley G. (1990) *Disorder and Decline: Crime and the Spiral of Decay in American Neighborhoods* New York: Free Press

Sköns, Elisabeth and Bates, Gill (1996) 'Arms Production' in *Sipri Handbook 1996* Stockholm: Stockholm International Peace Research Institute/Oxford University Press

Smart, Carol (1990) 'Feminist Approaches to Criminology or Postmodern Woman meets Atavistic Man' in Lorraine Gelsthorpe and Allison Morris (eds) *Feminist Perspectives in Criminology* Milton Keynes: Open University Press

Smigel, Erwin O. (ed.) *Handbook on the Study of Social Problems* Chicago: Rand McNally

Smith, Dennis (1988) *The Chicago School: A Liberal Critique of Capitalism* London: Macmillan

Smith, Dusky Lee (1966) 'Robert King Merton: from middle range to middle road' *Catalyst* 2 (Summer): 11–40

Smith, Gavin (1994) 'Towards an Ethnography of Idiosyncratic Forms of Livelihood' *International Journal of Urban and Regional Research* 18(1): 71–87

Smith, W. H. B. and Smith, Joseph E. (1948) *The Book of Rifles* Harrisburg, Pa.: The Stackpole Company

Snider, Laureen (1982) 'Traditional and Corporate Theft: a comparison of sanctions' in P. Wickham and T. Dailey (eds) *White-Collar Crime and Economic Crime* Lexington, Mass.: Lexington Books

Snider, Laureen (1987) 'Towards a Political Economy of Reform, Regulation and Corporate Crime' *Law and Policy* 9(1): 37–68

South, Nigel (1988) *Policing for Profit* London: Routledge

South, Nigel (1994) 'Privatizing Policing in the European Market: Some Issues for Theory, Policy and Research' *European Sociological Review* 10(3): 219–31

Sparks, Richard (1994) 'Can Prisons be Legitimate?' *British Journal of Criminology* 34: 14–28

Sparks, Richard (1995) 'Are Prisons Part of the Public Sphere? Privatization and the problem of legitimacy' in Stephen Edgell, Sandra Walklate and Gareth Williams (eds) *Debating the Future of the Public Sphere* Aldershot: Avebury

Sparks, Richard (1996) 'Prison Histories: reform, repression and rehabilitation' in Eugene McLaughlin and John Muncie (eds) *Controlling Crime* London: Sage for the Open University

Sparks, Richard and Loader, Ian (1993) 'Ask the Experts' *Times Higher Educational Supplement* (9 April): 16

Spitzer, Robert J. *The Politics of Gun Control* Chatham, NJ: Chatham House Publishers

Spitzer, Steven (1975) 'Towards a Marxist Theory of Deviance' *Social Problems* 22(5): 638–51

Spitzer, Steven (1983) 'The Rationalization of Crime Control in Capitalist Society' in Stanley Cohen and Andrew Scull (eds) *Social Control and the State* Oxford: Martin Robertson

Stallybrass, Peter and White, Alison (1986) *The Politics and Poetics of Transgression* Ithaca, NY: Cornell University Press

Stanko, Elizabeth (1985) *Intimate Intrusions* London: Unwin Hyman

Stanko, Elizabeth (1990) *Everyday Violence: How Men and Women Experience Sexual and Physical Danger* London: Pandora

Stanley, Chris (1992a) 'Cultural Contradictions in the Legitimation of Market Practice: paradox in the regulation of the City' in Leslie Budd and Sam Whimster (eds) *Global Finance and Urban Living: A Study in Metropolitan Change* London: Routledge

Stanley, Chris (1992b) ' "Serious Money": legitimation of deviancy in the finance markets' *International Journal of the Sociology of Law* 20: 43–60

Stanley, Chris (1993) 'Urban Narratives of Dissent: hacking– wrecking–raving' *Working Papers in Law and Popular Culture* Manchester Metropolitan University: Institute for Law and Popular Culture, Working Papers Ser. 2, No. 1

Stanley, Chris (1994) 'Speculators: Culture, Economy and the Legitimation of Deviance' *Crime, Law and Social Change* 21: 229–51

Stanley, Chris (1995) 'Teenage Kicks: urban narratives of dissent not deviance' *Crime, Law and Social Change* 22: 91–119

Stanley, Chris (1997) *Urban Excess and the Law: Capital, Culture and Desire* London: Cavendish

Stedman-Jones, Gareth (1971) *Outcast London: A Study in the Relationship between Classes in Victorian Society* Oxford: Oxford University Press

Stein, Mike; Rees, Gwyther and Frost, Nick (1994) *Running – the Risk: Young People on the Streets of Britain Today* London: Children's Society

Steinfels, Peter (1977) *The Neo-Conservatives: The Men who are Changing America's Politics* New York: Simon and Schuster

Stenson, Kevin and Watt, Paul (1995) 'Young People, Public Space and Sovereignty' Paper presented to the Annual Conference of the British Sociological Association, University of Leicester (April)

Stevenson, John and Cook, Chris (1977) *The Slump: Society and Politics during the Depression* London: Jonathan Cape

Stewart, Walter (1982) *The Canadian Banks: Towers of Gold, Feet of Clay* Toronto: Totem Books

Storper, Michael (1994) 'The Transition to Flexible Specialisation in the US Film Industry: external economies, the division of labour and the crossing of industrial divides' in Amin (ed.) (1994)

Stratton, Jon (1996) 'Serial Killing and the Transformation of the Social' *Theory, Culture and Society* 13(1): 77–98

Streeck, Wolfgang and Schmitter, Philippe (1991) 'From National Corporatism to Transnational Pluralism: organized interests in the Single European Market' *Politics and Society* 19: 133–64

Stretton, Hugh (1987) *Political Essays* Melbourne: Georgian House

Sullivan, Mercer (1988) *Getting Paid: Youth, Crime and Work in the Inner City* Ithaca, NY: Cornell University Press

Sumner, Maggie and Parker, Howard (1995) *Low in Alcohol: A Review of International Research into Alcohol's Role in Crime Causation* London: Portman Group

Sutcliffe, Anthony (ed.) (1984) *Metropolis 1890–1940* London: Mansell

Sutherland, Edwin H. (1940) 'White-Collar Criminality' *American Sociological Review* 5: 1–12

Sutherland, Edwin H. (1949) *White-Collar Crime* New York: Holt, Rinehart and Winston

Sutherland, Edwin H. and Cressey, Donald R. (1966) *Principles of Criminology* Philadelphia: Lippinott

Sykes, G. M. and Matza, David (1957) 'Techniques of Neutralization: a theory of delinquency' *American Sociological Review* 22 (December): 664–70 (reprinted in M. Wolfgang, L. Savitz and N. Johnston (eds) *The Sociology of Crime and Delinquency* London: John Wiley 1962)

Talahay, Michael; Farrands, Chris and Tooze, Roger (1997) *Technology, Culture and Competiveness* London: Routledge

Taylor, Ian (1981) *Law and Order: Arguments for Socialism* London: Macmillan

Taylor, Ian (1987) 'Law and Order, Moral Order: the changing rhetorics of the Thatcher Government' in Ralph Miliband, Leo Panitch and John Saville (eds) *The Socialist Register 1987* London: Merlin Press

Taylor, Ian (1989) 'Money-Laundering and the Free Market Economy'. Unpublished report to Research Division, Ministry of the Solicitor-General, Canada

Taylor, Ian (1992a) 'The International Drug Trade and Money-Laundering: Border Controls and Other Issues' *European Sociological Review* 8(2): 181–93

Taylor, Ian (1992b) 'Left Realist Criminology and the Free Market Experiment in Britain' in Jock Young and Roger Matthews (eds) *Rethinking Criminology: The Realist Debate* London: Sage

Taylor, Ian (1994) 'Crime and the Market Society' in *What Price a Safe Society?* Fabian Pamphlet No. 562

Taylor, Ian (1995a) 'Private Homes and Public Others: an analysis of talk about crime in suburban South Manchester in the mid-1990s' *British Journal of Criminology* 35(2): 263–85

Taylor, Ian (1995b) 'Critical Criminology and the Free Market: theoretical and practical issues in everyday social life and everyday crime' in Lesley Noaks, Michael Levi and Mike Maguire (eds) *Contemporary Issues in Criminology* Cardiff: University of Wales Press

Taylor, Ian (1996) 'Fear of Crime, Urban Fortunes and Suburban Social Movements: some reflections from Manchester' *Sociology* 30(2): 317–37

Taylor, Ian (1997a) 'Threats to Europe: a criminological analysis'. Paper presented to Annual Conference of the Dutch Society of Criminology (June), forthcoming in Grat van de Heuvel (ed.)

Taylor, Ian (1997b) ' "Virtual Frontiers": current resolutions to the problem of European Union border control'. Paper presented to the International Conference

'Migrations, Interactions and Conflicts in the Making of a European Democracy' Regione Emilia Romagna/Università di Bologna, Comune di Bologna (December)

Taylor, Ian (1998) 'Le "Community Service Order" en Angleterre: exposé et critique' in Phillipe Mary (ed.) *Travail d'intérêt générale et médiation pénale* Brussels: Université Libre de Bruxelles, Ecole de Criminologie

Taylor, Ian and Jamieson, Ruth (1983) 'Young People's Responses to the Job Crisis in Canada: a framework for theoretical work and empirical analysis'. Unpublished MS (Ottawa; Statistics Canada)

Taylor, Ian and Jamieson, Ruth (1997) ' "Proper Little Mesters": nostalgia and protest masculinity in de-industrialised Sheffield' in Sallie Westwood and John Williams (eds) *Imagining Cities: Scripts, Signs, Memory* London: Routledge

Taylor, Ian and Jamieson, Ruth (1998) 'Fear of Crime and Fear of Falling: English Anxieties approaching the millenium' *Archives Européenes de Sociologie* 39(1): 149–75

Taylor, Ian and Walklate, Sandra (1994) *Crime Audit 1994: An Audit of Crime in the City of Salford* (2 vols) Salford: Salford City Council: Chief Executive's Department

Taylor, Ian; Walton, Paul and Young, Jock (1973) *The New Criminology: For a Social Theory of Deviance* London: Routledge and Kegan Paul

Taylor, Ian; Walton, Paul and Young, Jock (1975) *Critical Criminology* London: Routledge and Kegan Paul

Taylor, Ian; Evans, Karen and Fraser, Penny (1996) *A Tale of Two Cities: Global Change, Local Feeling and Everyday Life in the North of England – A Study in Manchester and Sheffield* London: Routledge (International Library of Sociology)

Taylor, Laurie (1984) *In the Underworld* Oxford: Basil Blackwell

Thompson, Keith (1996) 'The Virtuous Male' *Utne Reader 73* (Jan.–Feb.): 68

Thornton, Sarah (1995) *Club Cultures: Music, Media and Subcultural Capital* Cambridge: Polity Press

Thrasher, Frederic (1927) *The Gang* Chicago: University of Chicago Press

Thrift, Nigel and Leyshon, Andrew (1994) 'In the Wake of Money: the City of London and the accumulation of money' in Leslie Budd and Sam Whimster (eds) *Global Finance and Urban Living* London: Routledge

Tickell, Adam (1996) 'Taking the Initiative: Leeds' financial centre' in Graham Haughton and Colin C. Williams (eds) *Corporate City? Partnership, Participation and Partition in Urban Development in Leeds* Aldershot: Avebury

Toynbee, Arnold (1970) *Cities on the Move* New York: Oxford University Press

Trasler, Gordon (1962) *The Explanation of Criminality* London: Routledge

Tremblay, Michel (1986) 'Designing Crime: the short life expectancy and the workings of a recent wave of credit card bank frauds' *British Journal of Criminology* 26: 234–53

Tuan, Yi-Fu (1975) 'Images and Mental Maps' *Annals of the Association of American Geographers* 65(2): 205–13

Turner, Bryan and Rojek, Chris (eds) (1993) *Forget Baudrillard?* London: Routledge

Turner, Louis and Hodges, Michael (1992) *Global Stake-Out: The Challenge for Business and Government* London: Century Business

Turner, M. A. and Reed, V. (1990) *Housing America: Learning from the Past, Planning for the Future* Washington, DC: Urban Institute

Turner, Ralph (1960) 'Sponsored and Contest Mobility and the School System' *American Sociological Review* 25(5), reprinted in A. H. Halsey, J. Floud and C. A. Anderson (eds) *Education, Economy and Society* London: Collier Macmillan (New York: Free Press) 1961

Turner, Victor (1967) *The Forest of Symbols* Ithaca, NY: Cornell University Press

Turner, Victor (1969) *The Ritual Process* Harmondsworth: Penguin

Turner, Victor (1982) *From Ritual to Theatre* New York: Performing Arts Journal Publications

Tyrrell, R. E.(1977) *The Future that doesn't Work: Social Democracy's Failures in Britain* New York: Doubleday

Tyson, Laura d'Andrea (1992) *Who's Bashing Whom: Trade Conflict in High Technology Industries* New York: Institute for International Economics

Ulbrich, Rudi and Wullkopf, Uwe (1993) 'Housing Affordability in the Federal Republic of Germany' in Graham Hallett (ed.) *The New Housing Shortage: Housing Affordability in Europe and the USA* London: Routledge

Urry, John (1981) 'Localities, Regions and Social Class' *International Journal of Urban and Regional Research* 5: 455–74

Utting, David; Bright, John and Henricson, Clem (1993) *Crime and the Family: Improving Child-rearing and Preventing Delinquency* London: Family Policy Studies Centre, Occasional Paper No. 16

van Duyne, Petrus (1993a) 'Implications of Cross-Border Crime Risks in a Borderless Europe' *Crime, Law and Social Change* 20(2): 99–112

van Duyne, Petrus (1993b) 'Organized Crime Markets in a Turbulent Europe' *European Journal on Criminal Policy and Research* 3: 10–31

van Duyne, Petrus (1996) 'The Phantom and Threat of Organized Crime' *Crime, Law and Social Change* 21(4): 241–77

van Duyne, Petrus (1996–7) 'Organized Crime, Corruption and Power' *Crime, Law and Social Change* 26(3) 201–38

van Duyne, Petrus and Block, Alan (1994–5) 'Organized Cross-Atlantic Crime' *Crime, Law and Social Change* 22(2): 127–47

Varese, Federico (1995) 'Is Sicily the Future of Russia? Private protection and the rise of the Russian Mafia' *European Journal of Sociology/Archives Européennes de Sociologie* 35(2): 224–58

Varnava, Tracey (1995) 'Fear of Crime: a new perspective'. Paper presented to the British Criminology Conference, University of Loughborough

Vergara, Camilo José (1995) *The New American Ghetto* New Brunswick, NJ: Rutgers University Press

Vidich, Arthur J. (1991) 'Baudrillard's *America*: Lost in the Ultimate Simulacrum' *Theory, Culture and Society* 8(2): 135–44

Wacquant, Loïc (1994) 'The New Urban Color Line: the state and the fate of the ghetto in Postfordist America' in Craig Calhoun (ed.) *Social Theory and the Politics of Identity* Oxford: Blackwell Publishers

Wacquant, Loïc (1996) 'Red Belt, Black Belt: racial division, class inequality and the state in the French urban periphery and the American ghetto' in Enzo Mingione (ed.) *Urban Poverty and the Underclass* Oxford: Blackwell Publishers

Walden, Keith (1982) *Visions of Order: The Canadian Mounties in Symbol and Myth* Toronto: Butterworths

Walklate, Sandra (1995) *Gender and Crime: An Introduction* London: Prentice-Hall/Harvester-Wheatsheaf

Walkowitz, Judith (1992) *City of Dreadful Delight: Narratives of Sexual Danger in Late-Victorian London* London: Virago

Wallace, Claire (1987) 'Between the Family and the State: Young People in Transition' in Michael White (ed.) (1987) *The Social World of the Young Unemployed* London: Policy Studies Institute

Wallerstein, Immanuel (1974) *The Modern World-System: Capitalist Agriculture and the Origins of the European World-Economy* New York: Academic Press

Wallerstein, Immanuel (1980) *The Modern World-System*, vol. 2: *Mercantilism and the Consolidation of the European World-Economy* New York: Academic Press

Wallerstein, Immanuel (1989) *The Modern World-System*, vol. 3: *The Second Era of Great Expansion of the Capitalist World-Economy* San Diego, Calif.: Academic Press

Walzer, Michael (1979) 'Nervous Liberals' *New York Review of Books* (11 October): 6–9

Walzer, Michael (1983) 'The Politics of Michel Foucault' *Dissent* 30(4): 481–90

Walzer, Michael (1991) 'The Idea of Civil Society: a path to social reconstruction' *Dissent* 38(2): 293–304

Walzer, Michael (1992) 'The New Tribalism: a difficult problem' *Dissent* 39(2): 164–71

Walzer, Michael (1993) 'Exclusion, Inclusion and the Democratic State' *Dissent* 40(4): 55–64

Weber, Max (1921) *The City* (first published in *Archiv für Sozialwissenschaften und Sozialpolitik*, vol. 47) New York: Free Press 1958

Weiner, Martin (1981) *English Culture and the Decline of the Industrial Spirit* Cambridge: Cambridge University Press

Weiner, Martin (1993) 'Market Culture, Reckless Passion and the Victorian Reconstruction of Punishment' in T. L. Haskell and R. F. Teichgraeber III (eds) *The Culture of the Market* Cambridge: Cambridge University Press

West, Donald J. (1965) *Murder Followed by Suicide* London: Heinemann

Westergaard, John H. (1965) 'The Withering Away of Class: a contemporary myth' in P. Anderson (ed.) *Towards Socialism* London: Fontana

Westergaard, John and Resler, Henrietta (1975) *Class in a Capitalist Society* London: Heinemann

White, Michael (ed.) (1987) *The Social World of the Young Unemployed* London: Policy Studies Institute

White, Michael and McCrae, Susan (1989) *Young Adults and Long Term Unemployment* London: Policy Studies Institute

Whyte, William H. (1956) *The Organization Man* New York: Simon and Schuster (Harmondsworth: Penguin 1958)

Wikström, Per-Olof (1992) 'Context-specific Trends in Homicide in Stockholm 1951–1987' *Studies in Crime and Crime Prevention* 1(1): 88–105

Wilkes, Chris and Shirley, Ian (1984) *In the Public Interest: Health, Work and Housing in New Zealand* Auckland: Benton Ross

Wilkins, Leslie (1960) *Delinquent Generations?* (Home Office Studies in the Causes of Delinquency and the Treatment of Offenders No. 3) London: HMSO

Wilkinson, Helen and Mulgan, Geoff (1995) *Freedom's Children: Work, Relationships and Politics for 18–34 Year Olds in Britain Today* London: Demos

Williams, P. and Dickinson, J. (1993) 'Fear of Crime: Read All about It? The relationship between newspaper crime reporting and the fear of crime' *British Journal of Criminology* 33(1): 33–56

Williams, Raymond (1974) *Television: Technology and Cultural Form* London: Chatto and Windus

Williams, Raymond (1983) *Towards 2000* London: Chatto and Windus

Willis, Paul (1977) *Learning to Labour: How Working-Class Kids get Working-Class Jobs* Aldershot: Gower

Willis, Paul (1978) *Profane Culture* London: Routledge and Kegan Paul

Willis, Paul (1984) 'Youth Unemployment' (three-part series) *New Society* 30 March, 5 April, 12 April

Wills, Gary (1995) 'The Right to Bear Arms' *New York Review of Books* (21 September): 62–73

Wilson, James Q. (1975) *Thinking about Crime* New York: Basic Books

Wilson, James Q. and Herrnstein, Richard (1985) *Crime and Human Nature* New York: Simon and Schuster

Wilson, James Q. and Kelling, George (1982) 'The Police and Neighbourhood Safety' *The Atlantic* (March): 29–38

Wilson, Paul R.; Lincoln, Robyn and Chappell, Duncan (1986) 'Physician Fraud and Abuse in Canada: a preliminary examination' *Canadian Journal of Criminology* 28(2): 129–46

Wilson, Roger (1963) *Difficult Housing Estates* London: Tavistock

Wilson, William Julius (1987) *The Truly Disadvantaged: The Inner City, the Underclass and Public Policy* Chicago: University of Chicago Press

Wilson, William Julius (1996) *When Work Disappears: The World of the New Urban Poor* New York: Knopf

Wolfe, Tom (1987) *The Bonfire of the Vanities* London: Picador

Wright, Patrick (1985) *On Living in an Old Country: The National Past in Contemporary Britain* London: Verso

Wright Mills, C. (1943) 'The Professional Ideology of Social Pathologists' *American Journal of Sociology* 49(2), repr. in C. Wright Mills (ed.), *Power, Politics and People: The Collected Essays of C. Wright Mills* (ed. I. L. Horowitz) New York: Oxford University Press

Wright Mills, C. (1958) *The Causes of World War Three* London: Secker and Warburg 1959

Yablonsky, Lewis (1959) 'The Delinquent Gang as a Near-group' *Social Problems* 7 (Fall): 109–17

Yochelson, Samuel and Samenow, Stanton (1976) *The Criminal Personality* Northvale NJ: J. Aronson

Young, Alison (1996) *Imagining Crime* London: Sage

Young, Jock (1975) 'Working–Class Criminology' in Ian Taylor, Paul Walton and Jock Young (eds) *Critical Criminology* London: Routledge

Young, Jock (1987) 'The Tasks Facing a Realist Criminology' *Contemporary Crises* 11(4): 337–56

Young, Jock (1998) 'From Inclusive to Exclusive Societies' in V. Ruggiero, N. South and I. Taylor (eds) *The New European Criminology: Crime and Social Order in Europe* London: Routledge

Young, Jock and Lea, John (1984) *What is to be done about Law and Order?* Harmondsworth: Penguin

Zaretsky, Eli (1976) *Capitalism, the Family and Personal Life* London: Pluto Press (New York: Harper and Row)

Zawitz, Marianne (1995) 'Firearm Injury from Crime' *Bureau of Justice Statistics Selected Findings* (April) NCJ–160093 Washington, DC: US Department of Justice

Zawitz, Marianne (1996) 'Guns Used in Crime' *Bureau of Justice Statistics Selected Findings* (July) NCJ–148201 Washington, DC: US Department of Justice

Zukin, Sharon (1989) *Loft Living: Culture and Capital in Urban Change* New Brunswick, NJ: Rutgers University Press
Zukin, Sharon (1995) *The Cultures of Cities* Oxford: Blackwell Publishers

Author Index

Subject and Place Index